Religion in American History

Edited by

Amanda Porterfield
and John Corrigan

WILEY-BLACKWELL

A John Wiley & Sons, Ltd., Publication

This edition first published 2010

© 2010 Blackwell Publishing Ltd except for editorial material and organization © 2010 Amanda Porterfield and John Corrigan

Blackwell Publishing was acquired by John Wiley & Sons in February 2007. Blackwell's publishing program has been merged with Wiley's global Scientific, Technical, and Medical business to form Wiley-Blackwell.

Registered Office
John Wiley & Sons Ltd, The Atrium, Southern Gate, Chichester, West Sussex, PO19 8SQ, United Kingdom

Editorial Offices
350 Main Street, Malden, MA 02148-5020, USA
9600 Garsington Road, Oxford, OX4 2DQ, UK
The Atrium, Southern Gate, Chichester, West Sussex, PO19 8SQ, UK

For details of our global editorial offices, for customer services, and for information about how to apply for permission to reuse the copyright material in this book please see our website at www.wiley.com/wiley-blackwell.

The right of Amanda Porterfield and John Corrigan to be identified as the author of this work has been asserted in accordance with the Copyright, Designs and Patents Act 1988.

Library of Congress Cataloging-in-Publication Data

Religion in American history / [edited by] Amanda Porterfield and John Corrigan.
    p. cm.
    Includes bibliographical references and index.
    ISBN 978-1-4051-6137-4 (hardcover : alk. paper) – ISBN 978-1-4051-6138-1 (pbk. : alk. paper)
1. United States–Religion. 2. United States–Church history. I. Porterfield, Amanda, 1947–
II. Corrigan, John, 1952-
    BL2525.R4653 2009
    200.973–dc22
                                                                        2009001950

A catalogue record for this book is available from the British Library.

Set in 10/13pt Galliard by SPi Publisher Services, Pondicherry, India
Printed and bound in Singapore by Fabulous Printers Pte Ltd

1   2010

Religion in American History

Fashion in American History

Contents

Figures

How to Use This Book

Think of this book as a kaleidoscope, with four sections, each divided into four parts. The book can be opened and read as it is, following each section in chronological order, or turned to follow one topic, and then another, across chronological periods. The book will reward readers who take the time to read it in both ways. It will also reward those who play with the structure and read it in their own ways.

Like the colorful shapes in a kaleidoscope, many of the events and people described appear repeatedly, in different contexts and relationships to one another. This kaleidoscopic approach reflects the interplay of religious traditions in American history, and purposively avoids a mono-narrative in order to reveal multiple patterns and perspectives. The book's divisions into sections and topics provide an organizational framework that readers can use to study religion's significant role in American history. The short introductory section to each chapter situates that chapter in the context of others and broaches themes that are of particular importance in the chapter.

Notes on Contributors

Candy Gunther Brown is an Associate Professor of Religious Studies at Indiana University at Bloomington.

John Corrigan is the Lucius Moody Bristol Distinguished Professor of Religion and Professor of History at Florida State University.

Heather D. Curtis is an Assistant Professor of Religion at Tufts University.

Martha L. Finch is an Associate Professor of Religion at Southwest Missouri State University

Robert Fuller is a Caterpillar Professor of Religion at Bradley University.

Tracy Neal Leavelle is an Associate Professor of History at Creighton University.

Charles H. Lippy is the LeRoy A. Martin Distinguished Professor of Religious Studies at the University of Tennessee at Chattanooga.

Katherine Lofton is an Assistant Professor of Religious Studies and American Studies at Yale University.

Stephen Marini is the Elisabeth Luce Moore Professor of Religion at Wellesley College.

Kenneth P. Minkema teaches American Religious History at Yale University.

Mark A. Noll is the Francis A. McAnaney Professor of History at the University of Notre Dame.

Amanda Porterfield is the Robert A. Spivey Professor of Religion at Florida State University.

Sarah Rivett is an Assistant Professor of English at Princeton University.

Jon Sensbach is Professor of History at the University of Florida.

Christopher White is an Assistant Professor of Religion at Vassar College.

Peter W. Williams is the Distinguished Professor of Comparative Religion and American Studies at Miami University.

Introduction

Amanda Porterfield and John Corrigan

Alligators in Paradise, Palm Trees in Hell

The Robert Sayer map of 1786 shown on the cover depicts "America, north and south" in relation to the Caribbean islands, western Africa, and western Europe. In other words, it draws the Atlantic world. It identifies that world in text within an ornamental cartouche in the bottom right corner of the map. The art of that cartouche informs as much as the text. A map, as a commercial artifact, often represented through ornamentation the products of the region it depicted. In addition to the usual figures of Neptune and a cherub, a cartouche could include images of fish, game, lumber, crafted commodities, a cornucopia of fruit and grains, and other goods, as well as images of prospective trading partners, depending on how much the printer wished to advertise reasons to travel to the place. Information about the cartographer and about nations with interests in the area also could be included. In the case of the Sayer map, the cartouche identifies the recently formed "United States of America" as well as the "several European possessions." This information is framed by a most interesting circle of images: an alligator sitting on a rock, an Indian headdress and wampum belt, layers of waterfalls, a dense sampling of exotic trees, twisting vines and flowering plants, the material ruins of a civilization, and a beaver. No human figures are present. The beaver, of course, was hunted for its fur, which was the crucial component of the felt hats that were so popular in Europe well into the nineteenth century. The Indian artifacts likewise were meant to identify the possibilities for commercial exchange with natives. But would an alligator attract people to America? Would a ruined civilization entice? Would the absence of people appeal? Would snake-like vines draw interest? Would a place thick with jungle-grade vegetation prove an incentive to commercial investment? Thomas Pownall's competing map, also printed in 1786,[1] included a cartouche decorated with drawings of handsome Native Americans at peace with nature, thriving in a rich material culture, smiling as they sat peaceably petting a sleepy cougar. Why was the Sayer map different and what was its message?

The Sayer map represents a conception of North America that was common in the sixteenth and seventeenth centuries and that remained in residue in the eighteenth and nineteenth centuries. For the earliest European explorers and colonists, America was an enchanted land. Explorers expected to discover the Garden of Eden in the Americas. The Fountain of Youth was thought to be hidden in the New World jungles. Cities of gold, wonderful places, were rumored to exist in the continent's interior. Amazing animals, breathtaking natural beauty, waterfalls framed in palm trees and blooming vines, and such an abundance of game and fish as to astound and bewilder, all of these were enchantments. But there were alligators in paradise, and the most sought-after treasures – gold, youth, innocence – after all lay concealed somewhere in a seemingly endless wilderness that was as terrifying and deadly as it was beautiful. Religion provided a set of categories by which the European experience of the Americas could be organized. Religion supplied myths to explain the history of the Americas and to imagine the region's glorious Christian future. Religion also furnished explorers and colonists with understandings of their suffering as they crossed swamps, contracted malaria, died of starvation, fought with Native Americans, or were eaten by alligators. The New World, then, for all of its beauties, was also an enchantment of horrors, of terror and tragedy. It could appear, as New Englander William Bradford wrote, as a "dungheap," or worse: for the Spanish missionary Bartoloméo las Casas, the European slaughter of Native Americans was an eyes-wide-open journey into hell. The magic of America – from its alligators in paradise to its palm trees in hell – was powerful. It undergirded a European imaginary of the New World as a place where anything was possible and everything was dangerous. It informed exploration and fostered the development of trade. Most importantly, it framed the planting of European religions and the adaptation of those religions, over time, to the changes that came with the ever more complex encounters between Euroamericans, Indians, and persons from Africa, as well as among Euroamericans themselves as all became Americans.

Thinking Historically about Religion

Europeans discovered the Americas at a turning point in European history. European encounters with the lands, resources, and inhabitants of the Americas contributed significantly to the processes of modernization and empire building getting underway in Europe. These encounters shaped American history even more. Only by seeing how European dreams and conflicts played out in the Americas, and how religion contributed to those dreams and conflicts, can the history of the Americas be understood.

Religion has always been a major force in the Americas. Archeological evidence indicates that, prior to the age of discovery, religious ceremony played a significant role in human life in the Americas, especially in death rites and in the governance of chiefdoms. Religion played a no less significant role in Europe prior to the age of discovery; written records show that Christianity, the dominant religion of medieval Europe, focused people's attention on life after death, and that it promoted charity, compassion, deference to ruling elites, and participation in their wars. At the beginning of the modern era, religious thinking and behavior were an integral part of the historic changes occurring in Europe. The religious reformations and counter-reformations rocking Europe during the sixteenth century stimulated the growth of modern technologies associated with printing, and religious aspirations impelled the growth of European empires, leading to conflict between empires and new forms of global enterprise. Religion was ever-present in the European competition for wealth and power, and in the discovery, depiction, and colonization of the Americas.

In the North American regions with which this book is primarily concerned, Spanish, French, English, Dutch, and Russian empires vied for control of land, resources, and native peoples. Spain took the lead in colonization during the sixteenth century, establishing a command center in Mexico City with outposts in Florida, the Caribbean, the Gulf of Mexico, New Mexico and California. France established influence along the St. Lawrence Seaway, the Mississippi River, the Gulf of Mexico and the Caribbean. With small colonies along the Atlantic coast and in the Caribbean, Britain's presence in North America was relatively weak until the second half of the eighteenth century, when wars in Europe and in the Americas strengthened Britain's hold in North America. The American Revolution broke that hold but strong cultural ties to Britain persisted. The Revolution and the Louisiana Purchase of 1803 launched a new English-speaking empire, independent of Britain in government but strongly influenced by British legal and religious traditions.

Despite conflict over slavery and state's rights that led to Civil War in the 1860s, the new American Empire grew in size and strength in the nineteenth century with the annexation of Florida and Texas, the industrialization of labor and development of a national economy, and the immigration of millions of new settlers. The religious beliefs and behaviors of these newcomers increased religious diversity in the United States even as those immigrant traditions changed in response to new opportunities and challenges, including the necessity of coexistence with Anglo-Protestants who dominated political and economic life, and often expressed fear and disdain for foreigners. Meanwhile, Native Americans struggled to survive and to preserve elements of religious identity that had characterized their ancestors prior to the arrival of Christian missionaries. Spanish and French influences also persisted, especially in the borderlands of the Southwest, where Spanish-speaking and Latino religiosity often prevailed and in New Orleans, where Afro-Caribbean religions preserved elements of French Catholicism.

Throughout the history of the United States, religion has contributed both to centrifugal forces of diversity, fragmentation, and factionalism and to centripetal forces of union and cultural homogeneity. As an agent of diversity, religion preserved ethnic traditions, inspired countless forms of charity, education, and social activism, and brought an esthetic complexity to American life that stimulated the arts and enriched many lives. Religious diversity also contributed to the fragmentation and factionalism of American life, promoting boundaries between groups, and stimulating misunderstanding and hatred. Along with this fragmentation and factionalism, religion also operated as an agent of national unity and cultural homogenization. Religion contributed to overarching conceptions of nationhood and to patriotic devotion to the ideals of liberty, equality, and justice that people have often believed America to represent. While disputes raged over the meaning and practical application of those ideals with respect to a variety of issues, such as slavery and racial segregation, marriage and women's roles and rights, labor unions, affirmative action, abortion, and gun control, those disagreements only amplified moral claims about the meaning of American ideals. These moral claims largely derived from religious idealism about America and its historic role in the world.

In addition to religion's role in an overarching, patriotic commitment to American ideals, religion also contributed to underlying forces of cultural homogenization that have been at least as powerful as patriotism. Consumerism and secularity are powerful underlying forces that have gained ground over the course of several centuries, shaping American behavior and thinking, and working to make Americans increasingly alike. The gradual meshing of religion with consumerism and secularity contributed to the processes of cultural unification, even as particular forms of religious expression differentiated Americans.

Religious diversity in the United States has encouraged religious competition, religious exchange, and strategies for marketing and branding religion that have made religion increasingly a matter of consumer choice. As this consumerizing process has evolved, the contents of religion have become less otherworldly and more tied to behaviors and thinking associated with the secular work of business, sports, entertainment, and healthcare. As a result of its fusion with consumerism and secularity, religion in the United States today is often less concerned with some of the things that used to preoccupy religious people more, such as life after death and the transcendent nature of God.

Since the eighteenth century, more than a few philosophers and social scientists have predicted that religion would die out as secularity advanced, and while declines in religious belief among Europeans seemed to bear this prediction out, by the end of the twentieth century it was clear that theories about the incompatibility of religion and secularity were wrong, especially when applied to the United States. Consumerism and secularity seem to have fueled rather than inhibited the proliferation of religious options and the saturation of secular society with religion and religious choice. Religion has not disappeared in the process of infiltrating many forms of industry, recreation, and media technology. Indeed, religious people often lead the way in developing industry, recreation, and media. Through their doings religion has become more fluid, interchangeable, and accessible, not only for Americans but for people around the world affected by globalization and the exportation of American culture.

New immigrants from Eastern and Southern Europe and from Asia and Africa have also contributed to the vitality of American religious life today, to the religious choices available to Americans, and to the religious freedom and eclecticism of American society. Escalating interest in the practical benefits of religion, and declining interest in systematic theologies that focus on the otherworldly nature and will of God have made religion part of the fabric of American society.

Tracking religion's fusion with consumerism and secularity implies that the meaning of the term "religion" has changed over time, and that to look for some common denominator may be to miss religion and its effects in particular times and places. Rather than imposing an abstract definition of religion for the study of religion in American history, this book invites readers to think about religion as an historical phenomenon continually subject to new meaning and interpretation. In exploring what people have meant by religion over the course of American history, this book focuses on the place of religious behavior and thinking within larger forces of social and intellectual change.

Historical Periods and Themes: Overview

This book is organized both by chronological period and by theme. This means that there are two optimal ways of reading this book. One way is to select a theme and to follow it through the four chronological periods of American religious history. The other way is to focus on each period, one at a time but consecutively, reading across the four themes that organize the religious history of each period before advancing to the next. For persons who prefer to undertake the study of American religious history through the exploration of specific topics – community, for example, or religious practice – this book offers an opportunity to directly track developments in those areas from the time of first contacts between Europeans and Native Americans up to the present day. Readers whose preference is for a chronological view can follow the thread of development of religious history as it is organized in each period under four headings, and then see how that history develops in the next period under those same headings.

Four periods of American religious history are distinguished herein. We begin with *Part I: Exploration and Encounter (1492–1692)*, which focuses on religion in America from the time of the arrival of Columbus to the Salem witchcraft trials. In this part of the book, we have placed particular emphasis on the ways in which engagements between Europeans and Native Americans led both parties to religious adaptation and innovation. The colonial setting, and especially the relationship between Europeans as colonizers and Indians as a dominated people, profoundly shaped the development of religion in America during this period. The colonial mentality, forged in dramatic and complex relationships with natives, was reinforced in subsequent racial contexts – and especially with regard to a growing African American population. That mentality has survived to some degree in religious thinking about power, destiny, purity, war, and global mission up to the present day. The early colonial period of United States history was equally characterized by a dynamism that came from the exchanges and associations among the many different migrant European groups. Encounters between Protestants and Catholics, Jews and Christians, sectarian groups and larger, well-established churches, as well as confrontations between like-minded religionists of different nationalities, all contributed to the lively and sometimes violent history of religion during this period. Although religious institutions developed steadily – meetinghouses and churches were built, people went to church, ministries were organized and funded, and so forth – religious life remained deeply entrenched in a rich bed of popular beliefs and practices that flourished alongside official religion. The witchcraft episode at Salem in 1692 demonstrated just how important popular ideas about the invisible world and its inhabitants were to late seventeenth-century Americans. It also marked the end of a period characterized by the transplantation of European religions to North America and the beginning of a period of accelerated experimentation with and refinement of religion within a coalescing Atlantic world.

In *Part II: The Atlantic World (1692–1803)*, we turn to a consideration not only of the movement from colonial empires to nationhood, but to the ways in which religion in America developed distinctive features even as it absorbed influences from Europe, Africa, the Caribbean, and South America. Most of the defining features of an American religious landscape of the period – the Great Awakening, the founding of the California missions, the rise of rational religion and deism, the integration of African and Afro-Caribbean influences, the coalescence of regional differences – came about through contact with persons, ideas, and traditions from the larger Atlantic world. Even as the European colonies and territories in North America pulled more closely together, they fed more hungrily on cultural raw materials that were in circulation in the Atlantic. Accordingly, at the same time that the eastern seaboard colonies were fashioning a rudimentary collective identity and banding together to resist English rule, they were borrowing freely from models of religious culture in England and elsewhere. Religious agendas and the conflicts that arose from them in other parts of the Atlantic world thus were played out, in some measure, in North America as well. The religious differences that conditioned relations among Spain, France, and England – and that shaped conflicts within each of those nations as well – framed confrontations between religions in America. The process of blending traditions that took place at an accelerated rate in the West Indies translated, especially, to the American South, including to the Louisiana territory, which was not yet under the flag of the United States. During this period, the emergence of a political order that decoupled church and state was a recognizably American innovation, however. So also was the American experiment of joining religious feeling to the practice of virtue, a complicated enterprise that set the terms initially for a distinctive understanding of republican virtue, and prepared the way for a subsequent century of lively religious debates and inventions.

After the purchase of the vast Louisiana Territory during Thomas Jefferson's presidency, the nation turned its attention decisively westward. Westward migration had been increasing in the late eighteenth century, but in the years after 1803, the imagination of the nation by degrees came to be as much sparked by the Pacific as the Atlantic. The religious history narrated in *Part III: American Empire (1803–1898)* is a history of both expansion and consolidation. Churches took on more and more of an official look, especially in the larger urban areas: funding was secure, ministers were educated, doctrine was defined – sometimes in painstaking detail – and communities were bonded in approved collective practice and a shared sense of the comportment of religious values with the nation's political life. The movement westward, however, challenged all that was thought safe and secure in the older communities. An amazing efflorescence of new religious ideas and ways of living, appearing seemingly overnight and with a force that was irresistible to many, characterized the period as much as the settling-in of more traditional religious orientations. Shakers, Mormons, Millerites, Campbellites, Spiritualists, Christian Scientists, religious communities such as Oneida and the Amana societies, the Ghost Dance, New Thought, Unitarianism, the growth of black denominations and black congregations and the migration of black religious practice to white churches, all of these dynamic and powerful changes came during the period of American Empire. The Civil War also defined this period. It prompted thinking about difference, about virtue and morality, and about the religious meanings of both nationhood and violence. The mass immigration of Jews and Catholics towards the end of the period also led to reflection on those themes, and while, for some, religious differences still led to violent encounters, for others, such as those who organized the World's Parliament of Religions in Chicago in 1893, there was hope for an American future of religious diversity.

In 1898, America went to war with Spain, a Catholic country. Many in the Protestant majority worried that American Catholics would take the Spanish side, but that did not happen, and anxieties about Catholic patriotism, while not disappearing, began to slowly recede. *Part IV: Global Reach (1898–Present)* addresses the movement of America onto an international stage, and the religious developments, both domestic and as part of American global influence, that were a part of that process. During this period, religion took stumbling steps in coming to terms with what was called the "modern." Science and religion found themselves at loggerheads in the Scopes "monkey" trial in Dayton, Tennessee, fundamentalist Christianity arose in force in reaction to a perceived sense of the erosion of tradition, religious bigotry resurfaced in a massive reconstituted Ku Klux Klan – and all of this took place in the first quarter of the twentieth century. While some religious groups launched ambitious mission campaigns to the far corners of the globe, others sought ever more energetically to shape the political order of the nation, and to foster conformity in religious and social practice. This was also a period of remarkable innovation, however. Americans crossed many conceptual boundaries in their thinking about what religion itself was, and all kinds of so-called "alternative" altars were built: Asian religions, healing and nature religions, ethical humanism, and New Age movements. The lives of people who belonged to more traditional congregations changed as well during the twentieth century, through two World Wars, dazzling science, rights movements, and many other ways. Many Catholics stopped praying in Latin, some Jews came to terms with the notion of women rabbis, and a few African American groups incorporated ideas and practices borrowed from non-Christian religions.

There are four themes that organize the history of religion in the United States: politics, cosmology, community, and practice. We begin with religion and politics, and in doing so we call attention at the outset to a specific kind of collective life, one that is conditioned by religious ideas but constructed just as much out of incentives arising from historical accidents and the social contingencies of everyday life. The chapters on politics in this book pay particular attention to the formal organization of authority in office and law, and describe the ways in which that government of local communities as well as the nation as a whole shapes and is shaped by religion. In the study of American religious history, the separation of church and state under the Constitution and the complex of pathways Americans have taken toward realizing that ideal are particularly important for appreciating why politics is central to American religious history. American notions of national religious destiny, and the campaigns that have been undertaken under the banner of that belief, are historical realities that make a focus on politics crucial to exploration of the nation's religious past.

The chapters on cosmology describe the ways religious groups thought about the world, including, among other things, good and evil, the past and future, the human and the divine, and the visible and invisible worlds. Cosmology – strictly speaking, a network of explanatory ideas about the cosmos and one's place in it – provides ideological grounding for religious thinking about the self and about collective identity. It frames reflection on what virtue is, how to live an ethical life, the kinds of social and political orders that are best suited to foster that life, what nature is, and what death is.

Religious community can be of many sorts. Communities can be old or new, small or large, defined by clearly marked and well-policed boundaries, or ambiguous and fluid. Communities are organized under the head of some authority or authorities, and appeal to religious tradition to enforce standards on their members and to defend the community against ideological challenges. Religious communities are never static. Most are constantly changing as social forces and events challenge them to adapt, as for example, with regard to gender roles, ethnic identification, and views of sexuality. Sometimes communities choose not to adapt, a decision that has led to violent confrontation, where they might prevail, or might be destroyed.

Religious practice includes all of the activities of devotion in which religious persons engage. Praying, dancing, healing, singing, working, and reading are obvious forms of practice, but religious practice can also include dress, thinking, dieting, viewing art, taking trips, organizing for a social cause, jogging, and reciting the Pledge of Allegiance. Because religious practices embody religious belief and carry out the implications of belief for behavior and the organization of relationships among people, study of these practices is essential for understanding religious life.

Religion, as mentioned above, is complex and fluid, and poorly captured by any abstract definition. In organizing this book with reference to four themes, we are proposing neither that we have completely encompassed religion nor do we believe that these four themes identify entirely distinct aspects of religion. All of these themes are interlocked. There is overlap among all of them. Attentive readers will recognize those overlaps, and is doing so will be positioned to appreciate how multifaceted religion is, and how, in American history, it has evidenced both concordances and contradictions. In other words, this book offers an open-ended story of religion in American history. It invites readers to think about the openings between the narratives given in each of these chapters. In veering away from a traditionally-conceived "grand narrative," it offers readers opportunities to reorganize some of the pieces of the story, or recalibrate some of the emphases, through critical reflection on the ways that each of the chapters stands in relation to the others. Religion is a complex and dynamic phenomenon. So also should be our reading about it.

Note

1 Thomas Pownall, *A New Map of North America, with the West India Islands* (London: Robert Sayer, 1786). See the David Rumsey map collection: http://www.davidrumsey. com/maps2473.html.

I
Exploration and Encounter
(1492–1692)

1

Politics

Amanda Porterfield

In September of 1679 in the historically Dutch town of Albany, Mohawk headmen representing the Iroquois confederacy met with William Kendall from the colonial government of Virginia at the invitation of Sir Edmund Andros, the British Governor of New York who had served as a diplomat to the Carib Indians in the Leeward Islands. Andros wanted the Iroquois to step up their efforts to control Indian violence in Virginia. After accepting presents of wampum, cloth, rum, tobacco, and bread, the unnamed Mohawk diplomat acknowledged Kendall's arduous journey, promised the Iroquois would do their part to keep their Covenant Chain with the British "clear and clean," and exhorted the British to do the same, punctuating each point of his speech with a gift of wampum, a belt made of shells or glass beads strung together, some with symbols of agreement embedded as part of the design.[1] This meeting illustrates a common political situation in North America during the sixteenth and seventeenth centuries; representatives of different groups establishing alliances with each other in a turbulent sea of competing interests.

Religion mediated politics in seventeenth-century Albany and in many other situations in North America prior to 1700. Although not always acknowledged or made explicit, religion served as a medium of political expression in two overlapping senses of the term – religion provided both means of decision making and the interpretive environment in which decision making occurred. The means that negotiators employed in decision making – gifts of wampum and invocations of a Covenant Chain – were symbolic forms of communication derived from religious belief and practice. The social and intellectual environments in which decision making took place were also profoundly shaped by religious belief and practice. For the Iroquois, gifts of wampum were symbols of political agreement that derived from kinship practices associated with spiritual power. For the British, the Covenant Chain was the metaphorical name for their political alliance with the Iroquois that derived from legal concepts of contractual agreement and also from religious practices of submission to authority associated with God's sovereignty and with the covenant agreement that British Christians believed God offered believers. For both Iroquois and British, then, beliefs and behaviors associated with spiritual realities played an important role in the environment of the Albany meeting and in the means the actors used in forging political agreement.

In North America before 1700, religious beliefs and practices shaped the ways people went about confirming relationships and dealing with enemies, and the expectations they brought to encounters with strangers. For both indigenes and colonists, religion figured importantly in the construction of group identity, in the formation of individual behavior, and in the determination of rank and social order. Religion provided norms of conduct, self-discipline, and social interaction that, while always subject to improvisation, served as guides for behavior and conceptualization. At the meeting in Albany in 1679, and in many other instances where people in North America came together for political purposes, religion mediated decision making and led to political outcomes that affected both individual lives and the balance of power among groups.[2]

This chapter considers two different regions in North America where relationships between Native Americans and Europeans that had been developing for decades came to a head in the 1670s. Focusing first on the eastern woodlands where Native groups adapted to increasing European, especially British, influence and then in the southwest where Native groups accepted, and also resisted, Spanish control, the chapter shows how religion functioned among both Indians and colonists as a means of arriving at and authorizing decisions about group behavior. It also shows how religion and politics in two regions of North America changed over the course of two centuries. In both the eastern woodlands and in the southwest, indigenes with religions based on kinship and colonists with religions based on submission to authority developed new forms of religious expression and formed new political alliances.

In the eastern woodlands at the end of Metacom's (King Philip's) War in 1676, representatives of the British Empire and the Iroquois Confederacy formalized a political alliance that enabled the British government to secure and extend its authority in North America. With British sanction, the Iroquois took responsibility for pacifying other Indian groups, and the meeting in Albany in 1679 was a reaffirmation and continuation of that arrangement. The alliance between the British Empire and Iroquois chiefs strengthened the latter, and was an important component of a larger British strategy for establishing political order and expanding commerce in her American colonies.[3] In essence, the British made use of the power of Iroquois kinship to establish British authority.

British victory in 1676 over the French and their allied Indian forces in northern and western New England enabled British settlers to secure their new homeland and expand commerce in the Connecticut River Valley. Regaining control of New York from the Dutch in 1674 also facilitated the expansion of British influence and enabled closer cultural alliances between New York and New England. In all the port towns along the eastern coast, rivers and British islands off North America, expanding commercial networks supported the growth of a politically powerful merchant class allied with Britain, and dominated by English religious beliefs and codes of conduct. In the southern colonies, especially Virginia, British authority in government, commerce, and social behavior increased as a result of the establishment of a class of wealthy planters who emulated upper-class British behavior and supported a parish system of Anglican ritual and moral governance.

Working against this extension of British influence, French explorers, soldiers, and missionaries developed ties with Native groups around the Great Lakes and rivers of

North America to expedite the fur trade. French *couriers de bois* lived among Natives and sired children who inhabited a middle ground between the cultures of their Native forbearers and that of French traders. Agents of France sought ports and passageways throughout the Caribbean and Gulf of Mexico, and around the Great Lakes and rivers of the eastern woodlands. Meanwhile, Spanish agents harried both the French and the British in the Caribbean and along the Gulf Coast, and competed for ports and waterways. In their quest for riches and converts, agents of the Spanish crown built forts and missionary outposts in Florida, Alabama, Louisiana, New Mexico, and California, and presided over villages of subjugated Indians who worked for colonial overlords and paid tribute to them. In all these situations, Native American life changed dramatically. Trade with Europeans transformed material cultures and economic practices and also diminished natural resources. New forms of disease eroded village populations, and conflicts over land forced Native survivors to abandon villages and hunting territories. Competition for trade goods and natural resources exacerbated conflicts among Native peoples but also led to new alliances forged for defense against European settlers.[4]

Religious beliefs and practices figured importantly in these transformations. In politics, religion provided the symbolic means – such as wampum and the Covenant Chain in the eastern woodlands, and dances and crosses in the southwest – with which people forged alliances and established plans of action. In addition to providing such symbolic expressions of decisions taken, religious beliefs and practices shaped the patterns of thought and behavior out of which those decisions emerged. In both the eastern woodland and the southwestern regions of North America, indigenous religions based on kinship coexisted, vied with, and capitulated to the power of colonial religions based on submission to authority.

Religion and Politics in the Eastern Woodlands

Prior to 1700, new centers of political influence emerged in North America while others receded or were recast. In the eastern woodlands at the end of the seventeenth century, the bargaining power of numerous Indian groups declined precipitously as British influence increased. Outbreaks of violence against Indians occurred often, sometimes in retaliation for Indian attacks against British settlers, sometimes out of sheer hatred or greed for Indian land. In 1676, in western Massachusetts and Connecticut (Figure 1.1), colonial militias squelched an uprising of Algonquian tribes and hunted down the Wampanoag leader Metacom (called King Philip by the English), jubilantly chopping off his head and one famously scarred hand, and then quartering his body. The body parts became trophies of victory against Indian enemies; Metacom's killer, an Indian allied with the colonial militia, received the head and hand as a prize, and subsequently "got many a penny" showing them off.[5] Almost simultaneously in Virginia, an upwelling hatred of Indians, and growing demand for Indian land, led to another outburst of violence. Poor entrepreneurs, servants, and slaves, losing out in the ruthless competition for tobacco land and slaves, followed the revolutionary Nathaniel Bacon in demanding rights and venting their rage on Susquehanna Indians and neighboring Algonquian tribes.[6]

While Algonquian Indians in New England and Virginia lost ground as a result of Metacom's War of 1675–76 and Bacon's Rebellion of 1676, the Iroquois confederacy

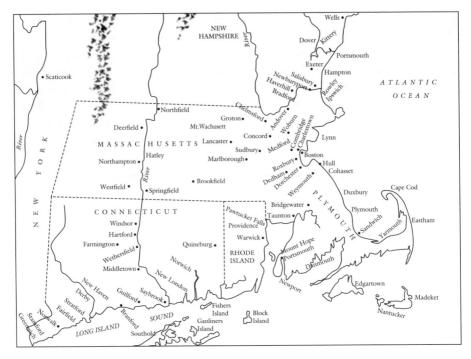

Figure 1.1   New England in 1675, at the outbreak of King Philip's War.

gained in strength and international status. Headquartered in upper New York and along the St. Lawrence Seaway, Iroquois tribes replenished their populations through adoption of refugees and captives, and Iroquois headmen played increasingly important roles as diplomats allied in one way or another with British, French, Dutch, and various Native groups. British agents strengthened their ties with the Iroquois in 1676 as a result of negotiations between the British Governor Edmund Andros and the much-admired sachem of the Iroquois Confederacy, Daniel Garacontié, a Christian and chief of the Onondaga Bear clan. When Garacontié committed to the Covenant Chain, Andros looked to the Iroquois to keep Algonquian tribes pacified. Meanwhile, the Iroquois chiefs expanded their political and military influence throughout the eastern woodlands, and their engagement in British trade.

The Iroquois managed their negotiations with the British according to traditional rites of diplomacy. At the meeting in Albany in 1679, when the unnamed Mohawk diplomat presented the Virginia emissary William Kendall with several belts or strings of wampum, he engaged the Englishman in an Iroquois rite. Gifts of wampum represented compensation for ills suffered, or points of agreement forged. As material embodiments of a highly personal and relational understanding of events, they reaffirmed existing relationships or established new ones.

Much of the treaty protocol that agents of Britain (and later, the United States) adopted in formal negotiations with other Native groups derived from diplomatic practices originally employed by the Iroquois. Iroquois diplomatic ritual derived, in turn, from the condolence ceremony associated with the founding of the Iroquois League in the sixteenth century, and from periodic reenactments of that ceremony occasioned by the death of one of the League's 49 chiefs. According to accounts of the condolence ceremony dating from the mid-nineteenth century, chiefs representing the Iroquois nations – Mohawk, Oneida, Onondaga, Cayuga, Seneca (and later, the Tuscarawas) – assembled at the death of a chief to condole his kin people. The ceremony attended to the mourner, pictured as an individual with eyes blinded, ears stopped, and throat choked with grief. In a ritual process with numerous steps punctuated by gifts of wampum, the clear-eyed condolers took pity on the stricken mourner, restored his sight, hearing, and speech, and then turned to welcome a new chief to replace the deceased in the confederacy's council of chiefs.

Iroquois informants in the nineteenth century linked the condolence ceremony to the founding of the confederacy by the god Dekanawidah and his spokesperson and disciple Hiawatha. By all accounts, blood feuding was rampant among the warring Iroquois tribes prior to the arrival of Dekanawidah who, with Hiawatha's help, convinced those tribes to stop fighting. This political transformation involved a reaffirmation of the importance of ancient matrilineal clans, named after Bear, Wolf, Turtle and other ancestral spirits, which extended across tribal boundaries. Chiefs representing each of these clans within each of the confederated tribes convened for ritual expressions of condolence that affirmed the power of these intertribal lineages to bind the confederacy together. Thus the political power of the confederacy derived from ritual practices that called for public catharsis of grief and reaffirmation of kinship ties. The political power of the confederacy also derived from individual leaders whose clan status, reputation, intelligence, oratorical skill, and personal presence manifested *orenda*, the Iroquois term for power, often interpreted as a spiritual force flowing through persons, including non-human beings conceptualized as persons, such as the sun.[7]

Although Europeans could also conceptualize political power as a spiritual force, their investment in kinship was not so all-encompassing as that of the Iroquois. For agents of the British crown, as for agents of other European states and American colonial governments, power had a kin-transcendent aspect that was foreign to the Iroquois and other Native groups until they learned about it from Europeans. In contrast to the Iroquois League's expansive network of kinship ties that brought different family groups together in a ritual that dramatized the grief survivors felt when the network was torn, the religiously authorized political power of the British crown was imperial, operating in the minds of its representatives as an authority on high with sovereign claims that transcended kinship. While both British and Iroquois admired spiritual power in individuals, the British understood that power to ultimately derive from the transcendent governing authority of God, and they performed rites of supplication to God and feared his wrath. The Iroquois were certainly not immune to fear, but fear of such transcendent authority was not engrained.

In their face-to-face societies, relationships among Iroquois people were essentially familial. Newcomers who exerted political influence received familial names and often become adopted members of established clans. Relationships with non-human beings also operated in the context of kinship, with human beings impersonating ancestral spirits through dances and other forms of religious dramatization that presupposed a symbiosis between the needs, demands, and identities of the spirits and those of their human descendants and living representatives.

If participation in the British system required deference to transcendent, sovereign authority that overshadowed kinship and limited people's freedom and autonomy, the advantages of identifying with such an elevated, centralized power were nevertheless significant. The crowned head of the British Empire was not only a royal personage with an exalted bloodline and elite host of royal relations and attendants, but was also the defender of British law. That law, compiled over centuries, provided rules and procedures for maintaining a system of social order, regulating industry and commerce, commanding armed forces, and protecting people and property in the monarch's realm. British law also empowered certain individuals; the Magna Carta, first issued by King John in 1215, allowed some rights and liberties to British free men.

Both the British monarchy and British law drew support from their religious associations. Solemn ceremonies and official documents asserted that God stood behind both; thus in the Magna Carta, John was king of England "*by the grace of God.*" The rights guaranteed to English free men also descended from God. Belief in a transcendent God who was both king and lawgiver supported the British political system, framing people's deference to authority within a cosmology that encompassed heaven and earth, stretched back in time to the creation of the world, and anticipated Christ's triumphal return. British leaders strengthened their own political authority by promoting reverence for the God who presided over this cosmos. In many cases, fear of God figured in the self-conceptions of rulers as servants of God.

British religion and politics changed dramatically during the sixteenth and seventeenth centuries, and evolved together to a considerable extent, with religion operating as a medium for new forms of political expression, and as a nursery for modern conceptions of government, individual liberty, political deference, and social control. While sharp differences and an array of opinion existed on these matters, the momentum of change with respect to increasing emphasis on the importance of individual conscience in both religion and government affected many British colonists.

Protestant commitments to a direct relationship between each believer and God mediated this increasing emphasis on individual conscience, as did Protestant practices of devotional reading, relentless sermonizing, and commitment to household government and piety. While Catholics also participated in these modernizing trends, Catholic belief in the Church's power to mediate grace limited the authority of individual conscience, as did devotional practices that involved supplication to saints in heaven. Protestant life did not necessarily lead to individual autonomy – conformity to biblical rule and submission to the authority of fathers restrained that – but freedom from the Church's control over judgment, forgiveness, and salvation made individual autonomy possible.

Early modern religious disputes over individual conscience occurred as part of the formation of nation states and often represented political differences about how society should be organized and individuals should be governed. A prince's alliance with, or independence from, the Church of Rome determined the official state religion and animosity between Catholic and Protestant churches provided fodder for numerous wars. However diverse and uncontrollable popular religiosity may have been in their realms, European monarchs in the sixteenth and seventeenth centuries linked their wills with the will of God and expected their people to fall in behind. But while the Catholic monarchs of Spain and France could rely on the Church's power over individual souls to help expand their realms and enforce their policies, British heads of state had a national church with weaker authority over people's eternal destinies. The diminished authority of the Church of England and the correspondingly larger opportunities for individual authority contributed to a proliferation of new religious groups in Britain, and to pleas for religious toleration. In this turbulent situation, Britain's colonies in North America offered a haven (or dumping ground) for religious groups whose beliefs differed from those of the monarch. English Catholics in Maryland, Puritans in New England, and Quakers in Pennsylvania all had charters from the King that allowed provisions for self-government these groups could not have enjoyed in England.

In the seventeenth century, English radicals on both sides of the Atlantic pushed the linkage between individual conscience and transcendent authority in ways that made religion appear to operate through a force of its own in visions, claims to supernatural revelation, and radical practices that bore only a condescending relation to government, as in the case of mystics who sought union with Christ and disregarded perceptions that their religious beliefs were a threat to the state. The New England Puritan Anne Hutchinson was one such mystic. She believed that she was sealed to Christ by the Holy Spirit, and that God spoke to her by "an immediate voice" much as he had spoken to the Old Testament prophet Abraham. Confident that God authorized her to speak her conscience even in defiance of political and ecclesiastical power, she was banished from the Massachusetts Bay Colony in 1638 as a threat to civil order.[8]

Against the challenge of Anne Hutchinson, Puritan leaders in New England worked hard to align church and state, and to construct the realms of religion and politics in concert with each other. These reformers conceptualized God's will in terms of government, beginning with self-government, and moving out from there to family government, church government, and state government. They sought systematic deference to divine authority in all aspects of life. Thus Anne Hutchinson's chief political opponent, Massachusetts Governor John Winthrop, attempted to establish a Christian commonwealth in New England in which he and others would "walk humbly with our God" and "be knit together in this work as one man." That enterprise required people to accept stations in life assigned to them by God, defer to superiors without resentment, and treat inferiors with civil condescension. Winthrop argued that Hutchinson had violated this hierarchical arrangement and, in particular, the fifth commandment – "thou shalt honor thy father" – and ought to be banished. She was. She had presumed to criticize men in official positions of authority instead of submitting to them as should an obedient daughter, or an obedient wife.[9]

Winthrop's view of the relationship between religion and politics reflected a belief long held by Christian theologians that people owed obedience to their earthly rulers because the power of rulers derived from God. The French Protestant reformer John Calvin put this belief most succinctly: resisting early rulers was to "revile God himself."[10] For Winthrop as for Calvin, political authority existed within a larger, religious system of government seated in God, the King of kings and ultimate authority over all. At the same time, however, as an Englishman proud of his individual rights, Winthrop believed that good government was based on the assent of the governed, or as he stated in 1637, "No common weale can be founded but by free consent."[11]

Winthrop's political understanding of the compatibility between free consent and the necessity of obedience paralleled his religious understanding of salvation in Christ. Similar to the freedom in Christ attained through submission to his authority, liberty in civil life, Winthrop explained in 1645, "is maintained and exercised in a way of subjection to authority." In politics as in religion, he believed, there were two kinds of liberty, one inevitably running to anarchy and immorality, the other instituted by God for moral law and civil order. The latter, morally positive liberty involved free assent "to that only which is good, just, and honest." The free election of magistrates preserved the liberties of the voters without undermining obedience to magistrates once they were elected.[12] Similarly, action undertaken in the spirit of Christ allowed for the exercise of human liberty in conformity with divine rule.

The dissenting minister Roger Williams challenged Winthrop's view that New England Puritans should establish theocratic governments modeled on ancient Israel. Williams argued that Christ had inaugurated a new era in God's relationship with mankind; God no longer entered covenants with nations, as he had in Old Testament times. With Christ's incarnation in individual human form and his atonement for the sins of God's elect everywhere, God's people were no longer a nation, but dispersed through all nations, and often hidden from the world. Consequently, Williams believed, no government had authority to exercise religious oversight. He accused the government of Massachusetts of acting against Christ in enforcing church attendance, demanding religious oaths, and requiring other forms of religious obligation. Banished from Massachusetts in 1636 as a threat to civil order, Williams became the founding president of Rhode Island, where he established religious freedom and a secular state.

Although some New England leaders thought Roger Williams was crazy – William Hubbard called him "divinely mad" in 1680[13] – their efforts to uphold the religious authority of the state ultimately failed. Increasingly strong claims for the authority of individual conscience eroded both the power of the British monarchy and the interdependence of church and state that theocrats like John Winthrop wanted to preserve. When the British monarchy was restored to power in 1660, Charles II recognized Parliament as a governing authority apart from his own authority as King of England and head of the Church of England. Parliament attained co-equal status with the monarchy in 1688 and passed the Act of Toleration the following year, protecting religious dissidents from persecution and limiting the government's ability to use religion to extend its authority. The Act of Toleration dismayed religious leaders in New England who felt their efforts to establish a model of Christian government based on mutual consent had been betrayed, and echoes of their commitment to a national covenant with God can still be heard today. But Protestant investment in individual conscience had worked to undermine weakened linkages between church and state they wanted to uphold.

In Britain's middle Atlantic colonies where colonial populations were more ethnically and religiously diverse, religious leaders welcomed the Act of Toleration. In New York and New Jersey, Reformed churches supported by Dutch settlers and their descendants grew alongside Anglican, Congregational, Presbyterian, Lutheran, Quaker, Mennonite, Catholic, and Jewish institutions. Pennsylvania's Quaker founder, William Penn, contributed to the debates in England leading to passage of the Act of Toleration and established his colony as a haven (and center of commerce) for people from a variety of different religious and ethnic backgrounds (Figure 1.2). With a land grant from Charles II in payment of debts the Stuart monarchy owed his father, Penn based the government of his colony on Quaker principles of pacifism and religious freedom. With its diverse population, enthusiasm for business, and broad streets laid out in orderly squares, Pennsylvania's City of Brotherly Love (Philadelphia) soon became colonial America's most cosmopolitan city.

Figure 1.2 *William Penn's treaty with the Indians when he founded the province of Pennsylvania in North America, 1681.* Painting by Benjamin West.

In the southern colonies of Virginia, Carolina, and Georgia, the colonial population was almost as ethnically homogeneous as that of New England prior to 1700, but religious leaders were much weaker, and much less successful in establishing control over society than in New England. In an effort to impose order in the 1610s, Virginia's governor Thomas Dale established a draconian code of "Articles, Lawes, and Orders – Divine, Politique, and Martiall" that included death sentences for some forms of theft. The colonial population of Virginia was aggressive and unruly, and sharply divided between land owners and poor laborers. Rituals conducted by a growing number of Anglican churches contributed to the social status of colonial elites and to the acceptance of political policies based on ownership of land and slaves.

Slavery was not always a permanent condition in the early colonial period but in many cases a form of servitude from which one could be freed, at least in principle. British law governed the political existence of slaves and other servants in British North America. In contrast to their treatment of Native Americans, though, the British never approached Africans in America as members of other nations whose allegiance or submission could be negotiated through diplomacy. In addition to this political dependence on British law, Africans in America were removed from kin-based tribal groups that, in Africa, had figured importantly in the formation of individual behavior and decision making, in the determination of rank and social order, and in religious constructions of group identity.

Uprooted from tribal societies where ancestral religious practices mediated political decision making, Africans on the American side of the Atlantic prior to 1700 improvised new forms of religious belief and practice that combined elements of different traditions centered on individual specialists whose skills of healing and augury gave them political influence as well as spiritual authority. A small number of Africans converted to English Christianity prior to 1700. The African American embrace of Christianity as a religion that promised freedom lay in the future.[14]

Small populations of free blacks existed in most of the British colonies before 1700, and colonists acquired bonded servants from a variety of different ethnic backgrounds, including African tribes raided by slave traders. While many Africans were forced into hard labor harvesting sugar cane in the Barbados or tobacco in Virginia, others became domestic servants and skilled laborers whose freedom, in a few cases, was purchased or bestowed. Still others escaped, in some cases joining or living near Indian tribes, in other cases migrating to urban centers. The vast majority of Africans in the British colonies before 1700 suffered horribly under British colonialism. A tiny minority eked out a living in colonial society with legal rights to individual freedom.

Although Native Americans had greater political independence, and often retained the religious beliefs and practices of tribal communities, British colonialism had disastrous effects, especially on Algonquian groups at odds with the Iroquois in the eastern woodlands. British efforts to develop resources in North America fostered dependencies that led to the decline or extinction of many Indian tribes, despite political and religious efforts of Native resistance. Still, Britain did recognize Indian rights, and some Native Americans, especially the Iroquois, benefited at least temporarily from trade with British colonists and alliances with British government. The influence of Iroquois diplomatic ritual on treaty making in North America is evidence not only of Iroquois power but also of British investment in religious and political principles of mutual consent. In this respect, British engagement with Native Americans was not as authoritarian as Spanish dealings with Indians in Florida and New Mexico. In contrast to the British, Spanish dealings with Native Americans prior to 1700 reflected a totalistic approach to the imposition of Christian authority.

Religion and Politics in the Southwest

Spanish exploration in the Americas began at the end of seven centuries of Christian effort to reclaim Spain from Islamic rulers, and Spanish discoveries in the New World built on the momentum of crusades against Islam. In January, 1492, six months before setting sail for America, Christopher Columbus watched the final act of the Christian *reconquista* of Spain in Granada, the last Islamic stronghold in Spain, as Ferdinand and Isabella accepted the surrender of Muhammad XII, Abu Abd Allah Bobadilla. Spanish perceptions of Islam carried over into perceptions of Native cultures in the Americas. The renowned *conquistador* of Mexico, Hernán Cortés, referred to Meso-American temples as mosques. His heritage as the son and grandson of minor noblemen who fought in the *reconquista* of Spain laid the groundwork for his fusion of military and religious fervor in the conquest of Mexico, which in turn established the basic strategy behind the northern *entradas*, the Spanish expeditions from Mexico City into North America.[15]

Cortés approached Mexico with total conquest in mind. In 1519, he and his men rode across country to the lake-encircled city of Tenochtitlán, the ritual center of the Aztec Empire, smashing "idols," planting crosses, and fighting along the way. Once across the causeway and into the city, Cortés came face to face with the Nahuatl ruler

Montezuma II. The Spaniard dismounted and attempted to embrace the chief, but Montezuma's men held Cortés off. Undeterred, the *conquistador* transferred a string of pearls and glass from his neck to Montezuma's. The chief gave two necklaces strung with gold shrimp in return and placed a royal house at Spanish disposal. After more displays of respect from Montezuma over the course of several days, which the Spanish interpreted as capitulation, Cortés imprisoned the Nahuatl chief and claimed dominion over all the lands and people of Mexico in the name of the Spanish king and Holy Roman Emperor, Carlos V. Montezuma's imprisonment sparked an uprising against the invaders, who managed to escape back across the causeway at night. Two years and thousands of dead indigenes later, Cortés and his men marched back to Tenochtitlán as victors. In Madrid, Carlos V welcomed the gold and silver that flowed into his coffers from Mexico and heard complaints that Cortés had been excessively brutal in carrying out the conquest.[16]

From their stronghold in Mexico City, Spanish soldiers and entrepreneurs embarked on *entradas* in search of more wealth. Lured by rumors of gold, silver, and emeralds, Francisco Vásquez de Coronado led an expedition north from Mexico City into the Rio Grande Valley in 1540. In the mountains and deserts along the way, Coronado lost many of the hundreds of Spanish soldiers and Mexican Indians, and many of the thousands of horses, cows, and sheep he started out with. Out of supplies, the company survived two difficult winters by commandeering food, blankets, shelter, and firewood from the Tiwa pueblos. In the warmer months, Coronado traveled from one pueblo to another in the Rio Grande Valley, hunting for stores of precious metals without success. His diminished and impoverished company returned to Mexico City in 1542.

As memories of the difficulties of that trip faded, Spanish dreams of gold in North America revived. In 1598, Don Juan de Oñate crossed the Rio Grande with about 140 men and claimed New Mexico for King Phillip II. Marching from one pueblo to another, Oñate and his men sometimes found all the people gone. In other pueblos, people acquiesced to the presence of the Spaniards, who demanded supplies and loyalty oaths, and performed military displays, including reenactments of Spanish victories over the Moors.[17]

Christianity played a central role in the establishment of Spanish rule in the Americas, and it operated in a more straightforwardly repressive way than in British America, where colonists were less dependent on Native labor, and less committed to Native conversions. The Spaniards linked their right to authority over Native Americans to papal bulls issued in 1493 and 1494 by the Spanish Pope Alexander VI. These edicts granted dominion to Ferdinand and Isabella and their successors over undiscovered lands on the western route to Asia, with the proviso that Spanish monarchs accept responsibility for the conversion of Native inhabitants. In some cases, the *conquistadors* announced their authority to these inhabitants in formal declarations. In addition to planting crosses to assert their Christian dominion over geographical space, Cortés and other Spanish explorers read aloud the *Requirimiento*, a legal document written in 1512 summarizing the history of the world beginning with Adam and Eve and proclaiming papal and Spanish right to jurisdiction over Indian souls and land.[18]

By contrast, British colonists operated free of such official edicts. In addition to being an officially Protestant nation that had severed ties with the Roman Catholic Church in 1534, Britain also lagged in time behind Spain in establishing colonies in

North America. As relative latecomers to American colonization, the British had the benefit of lessons taken from the inefficiencies and unsavory brutalities of Spanish *conquistadors*. But while the British government was moving in the direction of religious toleration and also in the direction of treating with Native groups as sovereign entities, British settlers in North America could be as brutal as any Spaniard in their encounters with Indians. Colonial British rule was more *laissez-faire*, with many British settlers becoming outright Indian haters, eager to simply run the savages off and take their land. Spaniards, on the other hand, made more concerted efforts to pacify, convert, and manage Indians under authoritarian rule.[19]

Few if any Spaniards questioned the right of Spain to subjugate Native Americans, but vigorous debates did take place in sixteenth- and seventeenth-century Spain about how harshly Natives should be treated, and whether or not they should be enslaved. These debates reflected conflicting ideas about the natural innocence or depraved character of Native Americans, and about whether Christianity allowed for the preservation of some aspects of Native tradition or required its complete uprooting. In practice, Spaniards in New Mexico treated settled communities of farmers in pueblo towns as vassals. They also condoned the enslavement of nomadic Indians who harassed Christian pueblos and *encomiendas*, the labor camps that colonial governors awarded to Spanish entrepreneurs.

Spanish laws governing the treatment of natives dwelt increasingly on the necessity of religious conversion, which had the effect, in New Mexico, of enhancing the political and religious power of missionary priests. After the conquest of Mexico, and the equally brutal conquest of Peru, Carlos V enacted New Laws to improve the treatment of Indians. In 1573, Phillip II extended these laws by condemning extreme violence against indigenes and making the establishment of missions for their conversion a requirement of further conquests in the King's name. Franciscan friars gained the most from these policies. Authorized by the Pope to celebrate the sacraments that saved people's souls from hell, dozens of these men settled in the pueblos of the Rio Grande Valley, where they took up the work of baptizing, catechizing, and supervising Indian behavior. They assumed control of much of the Indian labor in these pueblos and also supervised Natives in many of the *encomiendas*. In addition to managing supplies of labor and tribute to the provincial government, they benefited personally from the labor of the Indians who fed, clothed, housed, and served them.[20]

The concentration of religious and political power in the hands of Franciscan friars contributed to tensions within the Spanish population as well as to Indian resistance. The friars faced challenges to their authority from diocesan priests and bishops whose authority was directly tied to the colonial government, as Franciscan authority was not. Citing the friars' vows of poverty and commitment to missionary work, bishops sought to move them off the *encomiendas* once the initial work of conversion was done.[21]

A larger struggle for power between missionary friars and the provincial government of New Mexico took place that undermined the provincial government and contributed to the conflicts that engulfed the region in the seventeenth century. The governors of New Mexico depended on people's respect for their official appointments as upholders of the King's law and distributors of *encomiendas*. Given the six months travel time from the provincial capital of Santa Fe to Mexico City, not to mention the distance to Madrid, this respect proved difficult to maintain. The friars used their ability to excommunicate and withhold communion with increasing frequency.

Governors and their agents retaliated, criticizing the friars' morality and questioning their power over people's lives. This conflict between secular and religious authority came to a head in 1660, when Governor López de Mendizábal investigated numerous charges of sexual abuse by friars and arrested Fray Luis Martínez for "having committed the execrable crime of forcing a woman, cutting her throat, and burying her in an office, or cell, in the *convento* of Los Taos."[22]

In a further move to undercut Franciscan influence, Governor Mendizábal agreed to a request from the Indians of the Tesuque pueblo for permission to resume their traditional dances. The ban on traditional dancing had been essential to the Franciscan campaign against pagan worship and the ban's removal at Tesuque sparked a revival of religious dancing in other pueblos as well. Although the Governor represented the dances at Tesuque as harmless athletic events, they were really emboldened displays of traditional values and communal solidarity. The revitalization of dancing among the Tewa and other pueblos of the Rio Grande Valley generated momentum for the revolution against Spanish rule that erupted in 1680.[23]

Similar to the Iroquois condolence ceremony, which articulated kinship lineages drawing people from several tribes together in political enterprise, ritual dancing in the Tewa pueblos drew people of different subgroups within communities together in cooperative activity. Performed at specific times in seasonal rotation, Tewa dances inaugurated specific forms of labor such as planting, harvesting, and hunting. Dancers impersonated the ancestral spirits believed to inhabit the Tewa world and its elemental forces.[24] In the revitalization of religious dancing that preceded the Pueblo Revolt of 1680, the deities came out in the open, reaffirming communal solidarity and articulating elaborate subgroup linkages and pathways of community leadership.

The Pueblo Revolt of 1680 was not the first pueblo uprising against Spaniards. In 1598, the people of Acoma pueblo defeated Juan de Zaldívar and his company of 31 men, who had run out of food on the way join Zaldívar's uncle, Juan de Oñate, in his quest for a South Sea. With their pueblo situated on top of a stone mesa 360 feet high, the Acoma villagers enjoyed a strategic advantage. After being lured to the summit and into the village, thirteen Spaniards died in an attack, including Zaldívar; the others jumped off the mesa top, with a few landing on sand dunes living to tell the tale. Oñate took his revenge the next year, hauling two cannons by ropes up the mesa to the village, where he and his men killed an estimated 800 Indians and took another 500 as prisoners. Although no Spaniard died in that battle, Oñate ordered a foot cut off of each male prisoner over the age of 25 and distributed the amputees among his soldiers for 20 years of servitude each.[25]

Several more pueblos rebelled against Spanish authority between Oñate's revenge at Acoma in 1599 and the widespread pueblo revolt of 1680. Given the harsh treatment the Spanish routinely meted out and the stresses that pueblo people faced even without those overlords, some of the uprisings may have been attempts to avoid starvation as much as efforts to reclaim freedom. Even before the first Spanish soldiers arrived, maintaining agricultural villages in the arid land of the North American southwest required careful management of resources and successful strategies of community organization. Between efforts to husband precious agricultural stores through periods of drought and efforts to withstand raids from nomadic Apache, Navaho, and Comanche peoples, pueblo survival depended on effective political management grounded in religious ritual.

Germs emanating from Europeans passed along the trade routes that crisscrossed North America and into Meso-America, weakening pueblo populations even before the Spanish entered North America. But hard-won practices of social organization enabled the existence of more than 100 pueblos in the American southwest at the time of the expedition led by Cortés in 1519.[26] Four centuries earlier, a much grander cultural system had existed in the San Juan Valley to the north, where ancestors of both the western Hopi and eastern Rio Grande Valley pueblos lived. Called Anasazi by the Navajo, these ancestors participated in a vast cultural system, at the heart of which stood the spectacular trade, distribution, and ritual center of Chaco Canyon. Chaco culture collapsed in the twelfth century as a result of drought, deforestation, and loss of faith in the Chaco elites, and this collapse sent refugees to upland areas and cliff dwellings such as Mesa Verde. For reasons still obscure, the Anasazi abandoned Mesa Verde and other upland towns in the fourteenth century, immigrating (or fleeing) to the Rio Grande Valley and to Hopi and other pueblos further west.

The abandonment of Mesa Verde coincided with the arrival of a religious cult from Meso-America that involved new dances for bringing rain and enhancing fertility, and some Anasazi may have left the cliff dwellings for the pueblos further south to participate in the new religion. The deities represented in these dances developed differently in different pueblos. The Hopi called them kachinas. The Tewa "counterpart" to the Hopi kachinas, according to anthropologist Alfonso Ortiz, were the "Dry Food Who Never Did Become," a constellation of deities that included "all of the deities recognized by the Tewa, who were present before the emergence" of Tewa ancestors from a previous, underground world.[27]

The kachina-type religion adopted in many pueblos in the Rio Grande Valley was an effective way of absorbing refugees after the collapse of Anasazi society and the abandonment of cliff dwellings. Kachina rites offered new ways of combining disparate kinship groups within a single village through the means of religious societies dedicated to particular deities. Each of those religious societies had responsibility for staging particular events in the ritual calendar, and for leading activities associated with the production of food at particular times of the year.[28] In ways analogous to the Iroquois confederacy's achievement of political cooperation among warring tribes through condolence rituals centering on kinship, pueblo people created political cooperation within and among villages through the dances and divisions of labor associated with particular dances and deities. For pueblo peoples as for the Iroquois, religious practice mediated political organization and decision making.

Lifting the ban against open dancing galvanized community spirit in the pueblos. The deities forced out of public spaces by the Spanish friars returned, reasserting their power in the life of the people.[29] But as the deities returned, they were also transformed, influenced by Catholic images of the spirit world promoted by Franciscans and also by the new political context in which pueblo people found themselves. With people from different pueblos confronting a common invader more technologically advanced than anything their ancestors had ever seen, the meaning of the dances must have changed. Along with the reanimation of community strength through rituals associated with rain and fertility, the open expression of this strength offered a medium for new political expression, and a social context in which political deliberations across pueblos could take place.

In August, 1680, news of a coordinated pueblo plan to attack all the Spaniards in the region reached Governor Don Antonio de Otermín. When Otermín captured two youths sent by Tewa elders to the elders at other pueblos with knotted strips of deerskin representing the number of days before the rebellion should begin, he demanded of them, "what reason or motive they had for rebelling and losing respect for God and obedience to his majesty."[30] Otermín's terminology showed no understanding of the religious and political culture of pueblo peoples. Instead, it reflected his understanding of a relationship between religion and politics based not on kinship but obedience to transcendent authority.

Despite the leak in news about the revolt that gave Otermín some advance warning, the organized pan-pueblo uprising against Spanish overlords in the Rio Grande Valley succeeded, forcing the Spanish to abandon the region and return to Mexico. When the Spanish surrendered, the pueblo leaders simply allowed them to depart, and the southwest remained free of Spanish rule for a decade. When Spanish soldiers, missionaries, and entrepreneurs returned in 1690, the people of the pueblos were starved, exhausted, and willing to accommodate the return of Spanish authority. After 1690, Catholicism became increasingly entrenched in the southwest and also extended into California, where Catholic commitment to the linkage between political and religious control coalesced in an extensive system of missions in which priests forced Natives to surrender their autonomy and many of their ways of life.

In the southwest, the Tewa and other pueblos expanded the organization of their communities to protect the integrity of the old kachina-type societies while at the same time accommodating their communities to the structures of Spanish authority. Called *Towa é* by the Tewa, a new class of people arose within pueblo communities as buffer groups protecting traditional religious life and controlling assimilation to Spanish culture. Distinct both from pueblo people without any status in the kachina-type societies and from the Made People who led those societies, the *Towa é* developed as a managerial group responsible for stabilizing the political existence of the Tewa and for managing the Tewa people's double life as participants in Spanish Catholicism and civic organization on one hand and preservers of indigenous religious rites and kinship ties on the other.[31] Because of this persistence of pueblo religious life over centuries, pueblo communities to this day are the oldest continually inhabited towns in North America.

Like the Iroquois of the eastern woodlands, pueblo groups in the southwest conducted religious life through symbols and rites of kinship that involved representation of non-human forces and allowed for the absorption of new peoples and customs. For Europeans who moved into North America and encountered native peoples in the sixteenth and seventeenth centuries, religion involved a different element of submission to transcendent authority that brought kinship and family life under the aegis of a heavenly kingdom. In both cases, religion mediated politics, providing symbols and rites for use in collective decision making as well as imaginative frameworks for experiencing the world.

Notes

1   Richter (2001), pp. 130–133, quotation from p. 132.
2   This chapter takes a very basic and inclusive definition of politics borrowed from ethnohistorian Lynne Sebastian:

By *political* I mean things having to do with the structure of decision making. By *socio-political* I mean ... the social and economic relationships that arise as a consequence of a particular political structure. In this latter category I would include status differentiation, relations of production, etc., as well as the specific relationships of power and obligation that constitute the political realm. (Sebastian, 1992, p. 8)

3   Saunders Webb (1995).
4   White (1991); Daniels and Kennedy (2002); Bannon (1974; orig. 1970).
5   Thomas Church, *Entertaining Passages Related to Philip's War* (1716) quoted in Richter, *Facing East*, p. 92.
6   Morgan (2005; orig. 1975), pp. 250–270.
7   Wallace (1958), pp. 118–130; Wallace (1972; orig. 1969), pp. 94–98; Morgan (1901; orig. 1851); Hale (1895), pp. 45–65; Shimony (1961).

   Iroquois power (*orenda*) has been described as a spiritual force. Like other Native peoples, the Iroquois understood the exercise of power as flow and exchange of spiritual force among persons, both human and non-human. Forceful human beings could capture and enthrall others; they could also protect or favor others and expect to receive fealty or favors in return. Whether compassionate or ruthless, power was interpersonal. Even when ruthless, as in the case of the Huron chief who took a Seneca warrior captive in 1637 to assuage his grief over the recent killing of a nephew, power flowed through personal interchange. Bantering with his captors after being stoned, cut, and burned, the Seneca showed stoicism, courage, and defiance. His slow death by fire, as his captors finally forced him to break into screams, was a form of spiritual combat, and the distribution and feasting upon his body parts constituted the sharing and absorption of his spiritual power ("Relation of Father LeJeune, 1637," recounted in Wallace, *Death and Rebirth*, pp. 104–107).

8   Hall (1990; orig. 1968), quotation from p. 337.
9   Winthrop's reading of the Fifth Commandment also encompassed respect for the King's authority. Prior to the outbreak of civil war in England, the beheading of Charles I in 1649, and the establishment of a Puritan government under Oliver Cromwell, most Puritans accepted the King's authority as a matter of fact, and used deferential language to invoke it. Winthrop's respect for "the King's Majesty" coincided with his belief in God as the transcendent authority over all creation who invested earthly rulers with power to uphold law and justice. This respect for the King's Majesty is evident in Winthrop's description of a petition sent to the King and his council in 1633 by three disgruntled men who had experienced Puritan government in New England first hand. The petition claimed that the Puritan leaders in Massachusetts had rebelled against the King by establishing an independent government, and by setting up independent churches with preachers hostile to the Church of England and its bishops. All three signers of the petition had been punished in Massachusetts – Sir Christopher Gardiner for bigamy, Thomas Morton for bestiality, and Philip Ratcliffe for "most foul, scandalous invectives" against Puritan institutions. When the contents of the petition became known, Puritans in London rushed to the defense of the Massachusetts government, challenging the accusers and their "misdemeanors." Writing in his journal after the furor had died down, Winthrop acknowledged the King's authority and God's employment of it: "it pleased the Lord our gracious God and protector so to work with the lords and after with the King's Majesty that he said he would have them severely punished who did abuse his governor and the plantation" (Dunn and Yeandle, 1996, pp. 38 and 54).
10 John Calvin, *The Institutes of the Christian Religion*, Book IV, section 20.7, published as *Calvin: Institutes of the Christian Religion*, ed. John T. McNeill (1960), quotation from vol. 2, p. 1492.
11 John Winthrop, "A Defence of an Order of Court Made in the Year 1637," in Miller and Johnson, Vol. I, rev. edn (1963; orig. 1938), quotation from p. 200.

12 *Journal of John Winthrop*, quotations from pp. 282–283. Winthrop explained his view of the relationship between "the authority of the magistrates and the liberty of the people" in 1645, after being tried for impeachment in a dispute over the extent of his authority, as Lt. Governor of Massachusetts, to make decisions about local government in the town of Higham.
13 Quoted in Miller (1970), p. 31.
14 Raboteau (1978), pp. 3–92; Frey and Wood (1998).
15 Elliott (2006), pp. 19–20; TePaske (2002), pp. 29–41.
16 Elliott, *Empires of the Atlantic World*, pp. 3–5.
17 Knaut (1995), pp. 20–35.
18 Elliott, *Empires of the Atlantic World*, p. 11.
19 Elliott, *Empires of the Atlantic World*, p. 24; Drinnon (1980); Slotkin (1973).
20 Knaut, *The Pueblo Revolt*, p. 24.
21 Stafford Poole, "Iberian Catholicism Comes to the Americas," in Lippy et al. (1992), pp. 3–50.
22 Knaut, *The Pueblo Revolt*, p. 108.
23 Ibid., pp. 88–117.
24 Ortiz (1969), pp. 79–119.
25 Knaut, *The Pueblo Revolt*, pp. 36–46.
26 For a population estimate, see John (1975), p. 87.
27 Ortiz, *Tewa World*, quotations from p. 18.
28 Stuart (2000); Hegmon (2000); Sebastian, *The Chaco Anasazi*.
29 Gutiérrez (1991).
30 Knaut, *The Pueblo Revolt*, quotation from p. 4.
31 Ortiz, *Tewa World*, pp. 61ff.

References

Bannon, John Francis (1974 orig. 1970) *The Spanish Borderlands Frontier, 1513–1821*, Albuquerque, NM: University of New Mexico Press.

Calvin, John (1960) *The Institutes of the Christian Religion*, book IV, section 20.7, published as *Calvin: Institutes of the Christian Religion*, ed. John T. McNeill, Louisville: Westminster John Knox Press.

Daniels, Christine and Kennedy, Michael V. (eds.) (2002) *Negotiated Empires: Centers and Peripheries in the Americas, 1500–1820*, New York: Routledge.

Drinnon, Richard (1980) *Facing West: The Metaphysics of Indian-Hating and Empire Building*, New York: New American Library.

Dunn, Richard S. and Yeandle, Laetitia (eds.) (1996) *The Journal of John Winthrop 1630–1649*, Cambridge, MA: Harvard University Press.

Elliott, J.H. (2006) *Empires of the Atlantic World: Britain and Spain in America, 1492–1830*, New Haven, CT: Yale University Press.

Frey, Sylvia R. and Wood, Betty (1998) *Come Shouting to Zion: African American Protestantism in the American South and British Caribbean to 1830*, Chapel Hill, NC: University of North Carolina Press.

Gutiérrez, Ramón A. (1991) *When Jesus Came, the Corn Mothers Went Away: Marriage, Sexuality, and Power in New Mexico, 1500–1846*, Stanford, CA: Stanford University Press.

Hale, Horatio (1895) "An Iroquois Condoling Council," *Proceedings and Transactions of the Royal Society of Canada*, Ser. 2, I, pp. 45–65.

Hall, David D. (ed.) (1990, orig. 1968) "The Examination of Mrs. Anne Hutchinson at the Court at Newtown," *The Antinomian Controversy 1636–1638*, 2nd edn, Durham, NC: Duke University Press.

Hegmon, Michelle (ed.) (2000) *The Archeology of Regional Interaction: Religion, Warfare, and Exchange Across the American Southwest and Beyond*, Boulder, CO: University of Colorado Press.

John, Elizabeth A.H. (1975) *Storms Brewed in Other Men's Worlds: The Confrontation of Indians, Spanish, and French in the Southwest, 1540–1795*, College Station, TX: Texas A & M University Press.

Knaut, Andrew L. (1995) *The Pueblo Revolt of 1680: Conquest and Resistance in Seventeenth-Century New Mexico*, Norman, OK: University of Oklahoma Press.

Miller, Perry (1970) *Roger Williams: His Contribution to the American Tradition*, New York: Atheneum.

Morgan, Edmund S. (2005; orig. 1975) *American Slavery, American Freedom: The Ordeal of Colonial Virginia*, New York: W. W. Norton.

Morgan, Lewis Henry (1901; orig. 1851) *League of the Ho-D-No-Sau-Nee or Iroquois*, New York: Dodd, Mead & Co.

Ortiz, Alfonso (1969) *The Tewa World: Space, Time, Being, and Becoming in a Pueblo Society*, Chicago: University of Chicago Press.

Poole, Stafford (1992) "Iberian Catholicism Comes to the Americas," in Charles H. Lippy, Robert Choquette, and Stafford Poole, *Christianity Comes to the Americas*, New York: Paragon House, pp. 3–50.

Raboteau, Albert J. (1978) *Slave Religion: The "Invisible Institution" in the Antebellum South*, New York: Oxford University Press.

Richter, Daniel K. (2001) *Facing East from Indian Country: A Native History of Early America*, Cambridge, MA: Harvard University Press.

Sebastian, Lynne (1992) *The Chaco Anasazi: Sociopolitical Evolution in the Prehistoric Southwest*, New York: Cambridge University Press.

Shimony, Annemarie A. (1961) *Conservatism Among the Iroquois at the Six Nations Reserve*, New Haven, CT: Yale University Publications in Anthropology, No. 65.

Slotkin, Richard (1973) *Regeneration through Violence: The Mythology of the American Frontier, 1600–1860*, Middletown, CT: Wesleyan University Press.

Stuart, David E. (2000) *Anasazi America*, Albuquerque, NM: University of New Mexico Press.

TePaske, John Jay (2002) "Integral to Empire: The Vital Peripheries of Colonial Spanish America," in *Negotiated Empires: Centers and Peripheries in the Americas, 1500–1820*, New York: Routledge, pp. 29–41.

Wallace, Anthony F.C. (1958) "The Dekanawidah Myth Analyzed as the Record of a Revitalization Movement," *Ethnohistory*, V: 118–130.

Wallace, Anthony F.C. (1972; orig. 1969) *The Death and Rebirth of the Seneca*, New York: Vintage Books, pp. 94–98.

Webb, Stephen Saunders (1995; orig. 1984) *1676: The End of American Independence*, Syracuse, NY: Syracuse University Press.

White, Richard (1991) *The Middle Ground: Indians, Empires, and Republics in the Great Lakes Region, 1650–1815*, New York: Cambridge University Press.

Winthrop, John (1963; orig. 1938) "A Defence of an Order of Court Made in the Year 1637," in Perry Miller and Thomas H. Johnson (eds.) *The Puritans: A Sourcebook of Their Writings*, vol. I, rev. edn, New York: Harper & Row.

2

Cosmology

John Corrigan

Humans construct religious cosmologies as ways of acknowledging the interweaving of lived realities with imagination. Religious cosmologies are, in the strictest sense, ideological systems, ways of representing in ideas what we perceive about the world. Such representation can take the form of dramatic performances – singing, dancing, costuming, role-playing – but for the most part is accomplished through religious exploitation of language. Religious cultures tell stories about the creation of the world, about the inhabitants of the world, about good and evil, the visible and invisible, about time, space, and identity. A religious cosmology is in some respects a map of the world in which important locations and boundaries are marked through religious emphasis. In the religious cosmology of Islam, Mecca looms very large on such a mental map, while in Catholicism, Rome stands out, and for Buddhists, Bodhgaya, the site of the Buddha's enlightenment in northern India. By the same token, a religious group marks out on the mental map various truths that are to believed, whether it be the Trinity, or the uncleanness of pork, or the tricky cosmic importance of the coyote. A religious cosmology even maps what is invisible: the spirit world visited by a shaman, the soul that vivifies a person, or hell. Religious cosmologies are extensive, detailed, generally consistent in their arrangement of ideas but sometimes contradictory, and dynamic. Cosmologies can change as other aspects of culture change. To speak of religious cosmology is to enlarge upon what we ordinarily identify as the substance of theologies, but to stress the manufacture of human conceptualizations of order through cultural play.

Space, Time and Identity

In 1805, when the Seneca chief Red Jacket (Sagoyewatha) defended his religion to a group of New England Christians, he grounded his defense in a claim about the religious importance of place, explaining, in referring to the land inhabited by the Senecas before the arrival of Europeans:

> The Great Spirit had made it for the use of Indians. He had created the buffalo, the deer, and other animals for food. He made the bear and the beaver, and their skins served us

for clothing. He had scattered them over the country, and taught us how to take them. He had caused the earth to produce corn for bread. All this he had done for his red children because he loved them. (Drake 1843: 283–284)

Other Native American groups who encountered Europeans over the previous two hundred or so years likewise conceptualized themselves in relation to their inhabiting of space. Those "spaces" – in themselves without much intrinsic importance – were made "places" as Native American communities draped them with meanings, enriching location with layers of significance and purpose drawn from their reflection on the experiences of their everyday lives. Indigenous cosmologies, like all cosmologies, linked those spatial interpretations – space made place as it was imbued with meaning – with other ideas that together filled out the whole, the grand vision of cosmology.

Native Americans created place through narrating stories about the creation of the world, the living things that populate it, and the heavenly bodies that move across its skies. These cosmogonies, or stories of creation, sometimes were like those told by Christian and Jewish colonists, in that they described how divine power made the cosmos *ex nihilo*, that is, "out of nothing." A creator such as the Cherokee Someone Powerful could accomplish such a feat, as could the Yakima Great Chief Above, the Yuma Kokomaht the Creator, and the Cheyenne Great Medicine, whose work of cosmos-creating in fact is described is terms that might sound familiar to persons acquainted with the Old Testament account:

In the beginning, the Great Medicine created the Earth, and the waters upon the earth, and the sun, moon, and stars. Then he made a beautiful country to spring up in the far north … In this beautiful country the Great Medicine put animals, birds, fish, and insects of all kinds. Then he created human beings to live with the other creatures.(Erdoes and Ortiz 1984: 111)

In some cases, the creator was identified as female, as in the case of the Hopi goddesses Haruing Wahti (one of the east and the other of the west) who molded people from clay and taught them language. The central figure in the Apache story of Gomoidema Pokoma-Kiaka is a maiden whose daughter, conceived in relations with the sun and water, in turn conceived the Son of God. The availability of pre-existent raw materials with which a god could create the cosmos was common in Native American cosmogonies, so that it would seem that describing such cosmogonies as creation *ex nihilo* is inappropriate. But, as we shall see, that qualification is somewhat softened by the idea of time redolent in such cosmogonies. Time in monotheistic world religions moves in a straightforward linear fashion. That is not usually the case with Indian narratives. So, when Earth Diver – a common animal figure in North American Indian stories of creation – dived to the bottom of the sea to bring up a clump of land on which the human world would live, that performance was understood, in the curved time of Indian cosmology, both as a pure act of creation and a rearrangement of what already existed.

Stories of creation enrich the experience of space to make it place. That means that features of the landscape – topography, hydrology, vegetation, and so forth – are incorporated into cosmogonic myths. So also is the history of the people. A Sioux story of creation conjured Unktehi, a monster who flooded the land of the Sioux ancestors, the Black Hills. It literally embedded the history of the people in the place they inhabited.

The water swept over the hill. Waves tumbled the rocks and pinnacles, smashing them down on the people. Everyone was killed, and all the blood jelled, making one big pool. The blood turned to pipestone and created the pipestone quarry, the grave of those ancient ones. That's why the pipe made of red rock, is so sacred to us. Its red bowl is the flesh and blood of our ancestors, its stem is the backbone of those people long dead, the smoke rising from it is their breath. (Erdoes and Ortiz 1984: 94)

The story concludes with a description of the punishment of Unktehi by the Grandfather Spirit, who was turned to stone and whose back "forms a long, high ridge," and whose movement in the earth could still be felt, as the storyteller observed: "It scared me when I was on that ridge, for I felt Unktehi. She was moving beneath me, wanting to topple me" (Erdoes and Ortiz 1984: 94). The experience of landscape for Native Americans whose cosmology was shaped by such narratives was one of profound coordination of spatial location with cultural meaning.

The interrelatedness of people to the landscape also was reinforced in stories about the beginnings of things. A Jicarilla Apache myth explained that, "In the beginning the earth was covered with water, and all living things were below in the underworld. The people could talk, the animals could talk, the trees could talk" (Erdoes and Ortiz 1984: 83). In talking together, these living things were able to collaborate to solve the problem of their subterranean predicament, and to build mounds that enabled them to climb into the world above. In this "Emergence Cosmogony" (people climbing out of a hole in the earth's crust), local wildlife such as coyotes, rattlesnakes, aquatic creatures, and birds who are associated with humans before creation remained linked to them as all parties shared a place of habitation.

The Spanish who encountered American indigenous peoples in a multitude of exploratory and colonial enterprises also believed in an enchanted world. Spanish thinking about place – like the thinking of most European Christians – was steeped in Old Testament myths about the earthly paradise, the Garden of Eden, and Spanish explorers were keen to discover it. Christopher Columbus, author of numerous chronicles bearing on his explorations, also produced a theological work, *The Book of Prophecies*, in which the Garden of Eden appeared prominently. With an imagination fired by Pierre d'Ailly's *Imago Mundy*, which speculated on the location of paradise near the Canary Islands, and ingrained with cultural predilections to believe in an earthly place where Adam and Eve once lived in peaceful bliss, Columbus was enchanted by what he saw. Impressed with the beauty of the New World, its abundant game, remarkable rivers, and – sometimes – its handsome and seemingly innocent human inhabitants, Columbus ventured in his letters that he was close to discovering paradise itself (Figure 2.1). Of his third voyage, which brought his ships to the Orinoco River, he wrote to his patrons King Ferdinand and Queen Isabella:

There are great indications of the earthly paradise, for the situation agrees with the opinion of those holy and wise theologians, and also the signs are very much in accord with this idea, for I have never read or heard of so great a quantity of fresh water coming into and near the salt. And the very mild climate also supports this view. (Scalfi 1999: 68)

Other Spanish explorers were drawn into launching expeditions to locate other magical places. Juan Ponce de León, the governor of Puerto Rico, was said to have discovered Florida in 1513 while in the process of searching for a magical fountain that

Figure 2.1 A tale of religion, place, and power, Theodor deBry's *Columbus Landing in the Indies* pictured Europeans claiming place with a cross alongside a regal Columbus receiving gifts brought by indigenes.

restored health and sexual potency. Spanish writers familiar with a literary tradition about a Fountain of Youth embellished and popularized the story of de León's pilgrimage and served it to an embracing readership. In the southwest borderlands, Spanish adventurers sought another magical place, the mythical Seven Cities of Gold. The Spanish Viceroy Antonio de Mendoza organized expeditions to locate the cities in the 1530s and 1540s, and he and others explored extensively on the northern edges of New Spain – up through New Mexico and into the Great Plains – before giving up the quest. Álvar Núñez Cabeza de Vaca left a richer legacy derived from his own explorations, however. Cabeza de Vaca was a member of an ill-fated expedition exploring the shores of the Gulf of Mexico in the late 1520s. Washed up on what is now the coast of Texas during a hurricane, Cabeza de Vaca spent the next four years living with Native Americans as he traveled westward in fits and starts, until remarkably he met up with Spanish countrymen in 1536 in what is now northern Mexico. His account of his travels, which became popular reading in Spain, narrated his amazing experiences among native peoples, and especially his elevation to godlike status as a healer. He reported how he and his few surviving shipmates – called by Indians "children of the sun" – were presented with extraordinary gifts, including, in one place six hundred deer hearts, and in another, a remarkable native inclination seemingly to adopt the Christianity of the Spaniards:

> Throughout these lands those who were at war with one another made peace to come to greet us and give us all they owned. In this way we left the whole country in peace. We told them in sign language which they understood that in heaven there was a man whom we called God, who had created heaven and earth, and that we worshipped him and considered him our Lord and did everything that he commanded. We said that all good things came from his hand and that if they did the same, things would go very well for them. We found that they were so well disposed for it that, if we could have communicated perfectly in a common language, we could have converted them all to Christianity. We tried to communicate these things to them the best we could. From then on at sunrise, with a great shout they would stretch their hands towards heaven and run them over their entire bodies. (Cabeza de Vaca 1993: 90)

Tales such as those told by Cabeza de Vaca added to the mystery and allure of the New World. They exoticized the Americas for Europeans. Such tales also, however, reflected deeply-imbedded religious beliefs about space and place. The Spanish Christian cosmology imbued place with profound and complicated meanings, and, especially, associated place with power. The occupation of the Americas accordingly was not merely a commercial undertaking, but a religious one, one that was expected to lead to an increased share of Spanish power over the world, on the model of what humans were thought to have had in Eden.

English colonists, in their own reflections on life in the New World, also gauged their closeness to Eden, and they clothed their accounts of their colonial lives in prose overflowing with wonder. The sea captain Arthur Barlow, sent by Sir Walter Raleigh in 1584 to explore the eastern coast on North America, reported his encounter of the inhabitants of what is now Virginia as follows:

> We were entertained with all love and kindness and with as much bounty (after their manner) as they could possibly devise. We found the people most gentle, loving, and faithful, void of all guile and treason and such as lived after the manner of the golden age. The earth bringeth forth all things in abundance as in the first creation, without toil or labour. The people only care to defend themselves from the cold in their short winter and to feed themselves with such meat as the soil affordeth. Their meat is very well sodden, and they make broth very sweet and savoury … A more kind and loving people there cannot be found in the world. (David 1981: 450–451)

Michael Drayton's *Ode to the Virginian Voyage* (1606) struck a similar note: "Britons, you stay too long;/Quickly aboard bestow you,/And with a merry gale/Swell your stretch'd sail,/With vows as strong/As the winds that blow you! /…And cheerfully at sea/Success you still entice/To get the pearl and gold,/And ours to hold/Virginia,/Earth's only paradise!" (Hebel and Hudson 1941: 296–297). Such language, often found in English writing about the New World, represented a willingness to see a world of wonders, to envision life redolent with miracle and portent.

The Puritans who landed in Massachusetts Bay in 1630 brought with them an understanding of what their lives in that new place were meant to be. They identified New England as a place that God had set aside for them for their practice and defense of a Christianity purified of theological corruptions that had plagued Christianity for centuries. John Winthrop, the leader of that group of migrants, speechified aboard the *Arbella*, prior to the arrival in North America, that just as God had led the Jews safely to the Promised Land of Israel, so he would lead the band of English Christians to their own Promised Land. He said:

> We shall find that the God of Israel is among us, when ten of us shall be able to resist a thousand of our enemies; when He shall make us a praise and glory that men shall say of succeeding plantations, "may the Lord make it like that of New England." For we must consider that we shall be as a city upon a hill. The eyes of all people are upon us. (Winthrop 1630: 46)

The idea of America as a place where the Christian faithful would practice their religion without persecution and unregulated by government was interwoven with a sense of awe and marvel about the place. Like the Spanish and other explorers, English colonists were overwhelmed by the spectacle of America and in fact sometimes were terrified by it. For Puritans, New England was an amazing place, a magical wilderness, an "enchanted universe" richly textured with meaningful signs and extraordinary occurrences. New England was a place where the hand of God was always active in ordering life. It was a place of providence, as seventeenth-century Ipswich resident John Dane observed in reflecting on his lost pig. Dane and the pig became separated when Dane, his family being without food, had gone hunting. Dane took the missing pig as a sign and, thinking about its meaning, began to return home. On the way, a flock of geese flew overhead, he shot and killed one, and he arrived home certain that God had intervened in his life, mercifully providing for his family. America, for English Christians and especially for Puritans, was a place in which the supernatural was interwoven with the everyday. It was a place of enormous power, to be embraced, and also to be feared. Accordingly, alongside the positive expressions of wonder, Puritans, especially, worried about the "howling wilderness" of the New World, with its unknown dangers and lurking threats.

French explorers and colonists were less likely than their English or Spanish counterparts to view North America as a place embodying either the bounty or the innocence of the Garden of Eden. The fur trade, although profitable, was seasonal and organized largely as free agent enterprise. For that reason, and because the semi-feudal system installed by the French was not geared to rapid and steady colonial development, fur trading was not a strong platform for the construction and enlargement of governmental and social institutions in the St. Lawrence valley and beyond. Montreal and Quebec eventually grew from trading settlements into colonial towns by the mid-eighteenth century. But French presence in the St. Lawrence, Great Lakes, and Louisiana – the last comprising a large territory acquired by the United States in 1803 – remained diffuse and unstable in comparison to the developing British colonies. In 1566, the number of settlers in all of New France was only slightly more than 3000. French colonists and missionaries did not arrive with an embedded ideal of the New World as Eden, and they only sparingly appealed to it in the years that followed.

French missionaries, like their colleagues in New Spain and the British colonies, sometimes held contradictory ideas about the space they shared with Native Americans, but the theological tone of the Jesuits in New France was distinguished by a comparative reluctance to view North America as pristine and pure. Pierre Biard, writing about his experiences as the overseer of the French Jesuit mission in Acadia, compared that place to France in terms unflattering to North America:

> *A Garden of delight lies before him, behind him a solitary wilderness.* For verily all this region, though capable of the same prosperity as ours, nevertheless through Satan's malevolence, which reigns there, is only a horrible wilderness, scarcely less miserable on account of the scarcity of bodily comforts than for that which renders man absolutely miserable, the complete lack of the ornaments and riches of the soul; Whence such an unequal division of happiness and of misfortune? of garden and of wilderness? of Heaven and of Hell? (Thwaites, *JR*: 3.14.32–33)

French missionaries nevertheless sometimes ventured the opinion that through dedicated labor and ongoing spiritual regeneration of the Indians – and the colonists – New France could become a Christian land that reflected some of the glory of paradise. The key lay in waging constant moral warfare against Satan. So Father LeJeune, interpreting the Old Testament story of Adam and Eve in Eden to be a lesson in working hard and persevering, wrote:

> New France will some day be a terrestrial Paradise if our Lord continues to bestow upon it his blessings, both material and spiritual. But, meanwhile, its first inhabitants must do to it what Adam was commanded to do in that one which he lost by his own fault. God had placed him there to fertilize it by his own work and to preserve it by his vigilance, and not to stay there and do nothing. (Thwaites, *JR*: 9.26.188)

By the 1670s, it even became possible for one writer to glimpse in the experience of a converted Indian a sign of how the black robes had by their labors nudged the world of North America toward heaven:

> Moreover, when these poor Iroquois have once broken the bonds that kept them attached do their own country, and have come to us, they find great peace of mind and God grants them much inward consolation. One of them told me, some days after his arrival, that, on comparing the quiet life that he led here with the manner of living of the Iroquois with whom he had been, it seemed to Him that Hell had been changed into a little Paradise. (Thwaites, *JR*: 67.130.71)

Indian conversions in New France generally did not "take" for very long. Moreover, the religious lives of traders and other French colonists were overwhelmingly oriented towards duplicating a European experience in North America. In such a setting, Christians' reflections on the meanings of place were not as profound or detailed as in the English and Spanish spheres. There was not the same romantic embrace of the new land as an enchanted realm, an echo of Eden.

Time, like space, is a crucial component of religious cosmology. Space exists in time, and, just as religious communities construct distinctive ideas about space, so also do they invest in particular notions of time. For the peoples who inhabited North America prior to European contact, time was cyclical. In such a system, time does not move in a linear fashion from a beginning to an end, but rather, the ends of things are followed by beginnings. As we have seen, Native American cosmogonies, such as the Earth Diver or the Emergence stories, were chronologically complex, linking the creation of the world and its population by humans and animals with pre-existent underground or underwater worlds. In such accounts, the beginning of the world as we know it came on the heels of the end of another world. In Hopi and Navaho traditions, among others, various worlds were described as having been created and then, in time, replaced by new worlds, as people and other living things crawled or climbed from a world that was ending into the next one. The current world, for the Hopi, is the Fourth World, a place that came into being because of corruptions that took place in previous worlds. Navahos live in the Fifth World. For these groups and other Native American communities, time was a process of decay and renewal, a "natural" movement of creation in cycles. Contacts with Europeans, and especially meetings between missionaries and Indians, were complicated by the fact that those two parties conceived of time in different ways. When Christians spoke of the judgment of God that would take place at end of the world, the translation to a Native American scheme of time was difficult if not impossible. By the same token, Indian attempts to speak about the history of their connectedness to land – how that space existed in time – posed equivalent problems. Even more formidable were problems involving specifically religious ideas such as original sin (guilt passed from Adam and Eve to all of humanity), redemption, and purgatory. More than a few Natives reacted to Christian belief with surprise and skepticism.

The Spanish willingness to be enchanted by place, exemplified by their entertaining the possibility of discovering Eden and the Fountain of Youth, extended to their thinking about time. The religious culture of Spain in the sixteenth century was in flux, as the Spanish defenders of the Catholic faith responded to the challenges posed by the Protestant Reformation. That effort, which gave rise to crucial aspects of Catholic renewal sometimes referred to as the Counter-Reformation, included the production of various apocalypses, or accounts of visions of the end of the world. Typical were the visionary Franciscan writings in the sixteenth century, which profoundly shaped Spanish theological reflection about time and especially about the future of Christianity, and Spain herself. Apocalyptic literature in Spain not only revealed a vision of the end of the world, but was prophetic in its anticipation of the extension of the reign of Charles I of Spain (also known as the Holy Roman Emperor Charles V) over all peoples – Charles as the universal monarch. The creation of such literature as well as its circulation among readers of various sorts represented the Spanish investment in a notion of linear time, of time coming to an end, after which all chronological distinctions would be melted into the eternal. That sense of time, which had shaped the development of Christianity over 1500 years, informed Spain's self-understanding with respect to her territorial claims in the New World, as well as her desire to expand her empire. Spain looked forward to the culmination of her ambitions in a global kingdom, to an "end of time" in which she would rule as the undisputed power; she looked forward to the concluding of competitions among nations for land and power, in which she emerged as the victor. This sense of "imperial time," which was informed by Christian ideas about the end of the world and particularly by apocalyptic reasoning, provided, together with Spanish thinking about space, a foundation for Spanish identity as her presence in the Americas was enlarged. Franciscan missionaries, steeped in an apocalyptic tradition that was associated with the twelfth-century abbot Joachim of Fiore, believed specifically that their own mission to the Americas was the beginning of a "Third Age" in which the souls of the world would be gathered into the Catholic Church.

In the British colonies, and especially in New England, people likewise were thoughtful about the judgment of God. John Winthrop had expressed such a concern to his shipmates, and several generations of ministers continued to warn their congregations that they should "redeem the time," that is, fearing God, make the most of their opportunities to live a disciplined, godly life. Such a life included churchgoing, prayer and meditation, reading the Bible, learning about Christian truths from a minister, practicing virtue, refraining from labor on Sunday, and so forth. In New England in the latter part of the seventeenth century, ministerial concern about New Englanders' slippage in following such a course prompted pastors to cultivate a form of preaching specifically aimed at scolding persons for their drift from the Christian traditions of the founders of the colony. A genre of sermon called the jeremiad – which took its name from admonishments delivered by the Old Testament prophet Jeremiah to the people of Israel – increasingly took hold in the pulpits of Congregational churches. Ministers reminded their audiences of the commitment of their parents to Christian virtue, and urged them to remain steadfast in their own faith. At a time when society was changing rapidly in New England and a generation that had been born and raised in the small towns (the interconnected "holy commonwealths" of Puritan origin) was coming to its own terms with life in America, many worried that the religious legacy of the earliest European settlers was endangered. The jeremiads preached to stem the tide of perceived defection from that original religious vision were all about time: would the people force God's hand, cause God to punish them by revoking entirely his blessing for their community, and thus doom them and their religious experiment in America? The clock was ticking, and if people did not return to their spiritual roots, to an earlier, purer religion, an apocalyptic day of reckoning would ensue. Further south along the Atlantic seaboard, there was less anxiety about the spiritual life of the rising generation. But some in the south nevertheless from the early seventeenth century deployed the jeremiad as a form of criticism of local colonial culture (a practice that continued well into the eighteenth century). Captain John Smith's *Map of Virginia* (1612), for example, took his countrymen to task for their physical and spiritual laziness.

The colonial world of New France was organized with an eye to linear time, but neither the Jesuit missionaries there nor government officials were invested in a notion of "imperial time," nor did they preach the jeremiad in response to concerns about corruption of community religious life. Like much else in New France, and especially in the St. Lawrence/Great Lakes region, clerical reflection on the meaning of the place had to do with personal events rather than progress made in organizing and sustaining collectives comprised of Indians and French. Partly, this was because missions in New France were often little more than enhanced trading posts, quite different from the grand missions design of the Franciscans, where inculcation in Spanish Catholic culture, undertaken in a built environment resembling Spanish towns, was considered essential to the work of conversion. In New France, communities came and went, and even in cases where settlements could be sustained through the seasonal activity of trading and the warfare that frequently all but erased them, the clergy could not count on the conversions of the Native Americans who lived in such places to endure, even if the clergy remained actively involved in proselytizing them. Additionally, the territory of New France was enormous given the number of clergy, soldiers, government officials, and French traders who inhabited it and sought to conform the emergent colonial culture of New France to European standards and expectations. Accordingly, in such an unstable and unpredictable environment, there was little inclination either to imagine a time of collective perfection or to preach a jeremiad about impending punishment from God (an earthquake, drought, or other disaster) for a community's infidelity to a grand vision. Clergy instead were inclined to think about their own futures, and especially about the possibility of persecution and martyrdom, and the peer adulation or heavenly bliss that could follow from that. Personal apocalypses, in a sense, substituted for collective ones in New France. The shortfall of stability in Christian religious communities left indigenes freer to incorporate Christian elements into their cosmologies.

Identity in early colonial North America was forged through interactions of societies and it was grounded in ideas about the space and time in which people lived. Puritans believed that they were a chosen people brought by God to a promised land at just the moment in time when the prospects for a renewed Christianity in England were dim and the likelihood of a flowering of "purified" Christianity in America was good. They looked forward to the dawning of an age of exceptional religious vitality and achievement, and in fact, by the mid-eighteenth century, in the midst of a series of religious revivals, they believed that just such a remarkable renewal had begun, and that America truly was the Promised Land.

Spanish self-understanding, increasingly gilded as the movement of gold and silver and other valuable commodities from New Spain to Iberia developed on a massive scale, developed alongside hope in the promise of Spanish domination of the world (a vision that suffered a setback with the English victory over the Armada in 1588). That hope was enriched by Spanish wonder about the Americas – their habit of romanticizing and exoticizing much of what they encountered, so that exploration, even when it did not find Eden or the Seven Cities, or gold itself, led to settlement that nevertheless was understood as an enchanted enterprise. So, in the eighteenth century, a Franciscan writing about his experience at a borderlands mission could exult that upon his entry into a pueblo,

> What was most amazing and a cause of great joy was that they came out in a procession, led by a Cross that was adorned with their richest decorations … and sang with such harmony and recall that they seemed like long-time Christians. This was an amazing act for a people who had never had a priest in their land. (Pérez de Ribas 1999: 208)

For the French, religious identity remained poised on the border between a sense of collective belonging and a view of the self as an agent somewhat apart from the prospects or achievements of the group.

Native American engagement of European colonists took place as a profound clash of understandings about place and about time. Indian life was intimately informed by a sense of connectedness to the land, and by an experience of time that framed transactions between persons in cycles of reciprocity or graduated steps. Indians might give a gift to a European and then take it back, only to give it again, and yet again, before, perhaps, permanently bestowing it on the other party, a behavior that Europeans found difficult to understand. Had they been aware of Native ways of figuring time – as cyclical and repeating, characterized by endings and beginnings in ongoing series – they might have understood better. Native American cosmology shaped identity as tied to place but yet in flux because of the expectation that temporal cycles remade place alongside time. Native Americans' reflection on the future could include a sense of ultimacy – an afterlife, or a time when earthly life, having been tested, was perfected. Nevertheless, just as Indians' identity as a part of a coherent ecology defined by place, people, flora, and fauna conflicted with imperial and religiously aggressive European ideas of ownership of space, so also did Indians' sense of time complicate communication with European colonists. Negotiation of differences in such cases was difficult and sometimes degenerated into violence.

The Divine and the Human

Interactions between people and the divine formed the core of religious life and as such were carefully articulated in religious cosmologies. Contact with deities or holy figures, which was structured by ritual or in some cases happened in more spontaneous and open-ended fashion, took place within a framework of ideas about the nature of the divine, the capabilities of people, supernatural power, and the boundaries that distinguish gods from humans. Native American understandings of all of these things were constructed, preserved, and transmitted in oral culture. Things divine and human were detailed and explained in stories about events that involved people, deities, spirits, animals, other living things, the land, and heavenly bodies. Sometimes these stories were told in way that brought listeners directly and purposefully to certain kinds of conclusions. So, for example, in a Yakima creation story, the original inhabitants of the world quarreled so much that Mother Earth caused an earthquake to bury many of them under rocks shaken from the mountains. The story, like many others, ended with a clearly stated lesson:

> We did not know all this by ourselves; we were told it by our fathers and grandfathers, who learned it from their fathers and grandfathers. No one knows when the Great Chief above will overturn the mountains. But we do know this: the spirits will return only to the remains of the people in life who kept the beliefs of their grandfathers. (Erdoes and Ortiz 1984: 118)

More commonly in Native American oral culture, the presentation of truths about the relationship between gods and people was accomplished through the illustration of those truths in examples, rather than through systematic examination of specific points of belief about the nature of those relationships. Consequently, a full understanding of how the divine and human were interrelated was possible only through familiarity with many stories, and the cultivation of a habit of thought that fostered integration of the action of events, the motivations of the actors, and the lessons learned. Such integration was complicated by but also advanced by the fact that cosmological thinking was imbedded in storytelling. Language that was utilized to fashion mental images of people and gods and spirits doing important things in the past was a fluid, multivalent language that invited thinking in metaphor and analogy. In other words, the language of storytelling invited thinking across stories and blending parts of stories into larger understandings of how the universe was ordered. Skill was required so that the meanings of individual stories and symbols were not lost. But oral culture offered opportunity for creatively engaging received truths about the cosmos, and as a dynamic, flexible system made possible incorporation of new truths as they were discovered.

Some of the new truths that Indians discovered were about Christianity. Catholic and Protestant missionaries sought to catechize Indians and, learning indigenous languages, they translated Christian doctrines into words they believed would convey to their potential converts the core ideology of Christianity. One reason that conversions were so difficult and so short-lived was because such truths were presented as "religion" rather than as part of broad and interwoven sets of ideas – represented in stories – about all of life. Native American lives, like the lives that many people led in various early modern cultures, were shot through with religion; the world was thoroughly enchanted. That is, religious power was everywhere present and active, across the entire spectrum of experience. Unlike the Europeans who came to the Americas, however, Indians took little interest in distinguishing from the rest of life a formal area of experience that was "religious." Of course, Christians and Jews believed that their lives ought always to be driven by religion and that faith and devotion should inform every thought and deed. But in Europe, religion was recognized as a distinct component of life, separated out to some extent from other components such as government or commerce, and sometimes existing in conflict with other spheres of life. For Native Americans, the experience of religion was holistic. All of life unfolded under the umbrella of a religious cosmology. The notion that "religion" was a specific area of life made no sense in Native American cosmologies. Accordingly, Native American ideas about deity and religious power generally differed in important ways from European ideas. Missionaries who sought to convert Indians by explaining that divine power was located above all in God had trouble making inroads among people who, when they referred to "God," were likely to be denoting a kind of diffuse religious power or a spiritual connectedness among all things – Wakan (Sioux), Manitou (Algonquian), Orenda (Iroquois) – rather than a single almighty spirit.

In an enchanted world, where supernatural power animated and determined everything, the signs of that power were everywhere: in rainbows, earthquakes, the song of a bird, the rattle of a snake's tail, the wind, the faces of people. The divine revealed itself in all of creation, and for Native Americans, that revelation was profound, constant, and consequential. The world was full of signs and portents. Indians' understandings of relations between gods and people were guided by what those signs conveyed. Some signs could be obvious but others were best interpreted by persons whose experience and skill gave them an edge. Such persons generally were recognized on the basis of their charisma rather than because they had ascended by study and age to a specific status or office within the community.

For French and Spanish Catholics, things human and divine were explained in overwhelming detail in theological treatises that had been written in many languages and preserved in the libraries that formed the center of literate culture. Catholic thinking had unfolded for centuries in argumentative and outrightly polemical literature. The actual books that contained the substance of those arguments enjoyed the status of icons in the sixteenth and seventeenth centuries. The Bible, the writings of early Church Fathers, the new theologies of medieval thinkers, and the most recent works that challenged the upstart Protestant churches were revered as one might venerate the bones of a saint. Cosmology, for Catholics, was explained in writings, and those writings taken together with the Bible had an authority that surpassed any other.

The primary theological references through which Catholics in the colonial Americas comprehended the relationship of the human to the divine were the stories of the fall of humanity, the subsequent redemptive sacrifice of Jesus Christ, and the end of the world. For all of the writing and debate on these themes over centuries, however, Catholics still approached them as truths only partially understood. They were intuited, as it were, rather than grasped in a fully intellectual and systematic fashion. They were, in the language of catechism, "mysteries," and Catholics (and some Protestants) deployed that term not merely as a habit of prose, but because it reflected their religious experience as they lived it day to day. Jesus's atonement for humanity's sin was a mystery, and so also was the schedule for the arrival of the Last Judgment, at which time the faithful would be gathered into heaven. How could this have been communicated to potential converts? Their thinking shaped by such an intellectually complex and emotionally-charged investment in their religion and their mission, Jesuit missionaries, in their accounts of the proselytization of New France, typically interwove descriptions of their successes preaching for conversions with language about the incomprehensibility of the divine plan for salvation. Moreover, they came to believe that those whom they converted made the same investment: belief went hand in hand with unknowing for Indians as well. As one report observed in 1637, a Huron, Tsiouendsaentaha, took to worshipping

> sometimes in the fields, and (what pleased us more) in the presence of the Savages, he himself asking, of his own accord, to pray to God. One day, when Father Garnier showed him a Crucifix, he took it in his own hands, and began to preach in the presence of those of his cabin, upon the mystery of our redemption. (Thwaites, *JR*: 14.29.88)

When Jesuits preached, they understood their own work to be the cultivation of Indian understanding about a God whose activities ultimately were incomprehensible. In the mission field, the phrase "mystery of redemption" was more than just a stock theological term. Its meaning was ironically enriched, so that it identified the reality of missionary inability to explain as much as it designated a point of faith.

Some missionaries believed that they were not the first to have undertaken such difficult labor among Native Americans. Marc Lescarbot, in his account in 1610, cited Jesus's words proclaimed in the Gospel of Mark, "This Gospel of the kingdom, shall be preached in the whole world, for a testimony to all nations, and then shall the consummation come," and then reported that he had heard a story that the "mysteries of our redemption" had been preached to "the Brazilians" in the distant past (Thwaites, *JR*: 1.1.58). Such legends about Christian missionaries in the Americas centuries earlier were widespread. Indeed, among both Catholics and Protestants, the idea that Indians were somehow linked to European Christians through some sort of shared background exercised increasingly powerful influence over European thinking about encounter. The Spanish, especially, embraced the idea that Native Americans were descended from the Ten Lost Tribes of Israel that had been scattered throughout the world early in the history of the Jews. Missionaries who took Indians as descendants of Jews accordingly found it particularly important, urgent, and somehow cosmically predestined that Indians should be brought into the Church through the efforts of Catholic missionaries in the New World. Indians were, in the language of missionizing, "prepared" by God for conversion because of their Jewish background. The Spanish bishop Bartolomeo de Las Casas (1484–1566), who became an advocate for Indians and a sharp critic of Spanish atrocities, changed his thinking several times about Native American genealogy, but at one point was convinced that the Indians, as distant Jews, were primed to receive the Christian gospel, and that with their conversion would come the completion of God's plan for salvation, and the glorious end of time. He argued that the conversion of the Indians would precipitate the final stage in the redemption of humanity, the dawn of the messianic era, and he claimed to be able to prove from the Bible that Native Americans were in fact descended from the Ten Lost Tribes (Kingsborough 1831–1848: 7).

Against this background of encounter, the religious lives of the Spanish and the French in the Americas took on specific features with regard to thinking about the supernatural and the human. In certain respects the same was true for the English, the Dutch who settled New Netherland (f. 1614) and the settlers in New Sweden (f. 1638) along the Delaware River. Interaction with native peoples was a crucible for the colonial cosmologies. Jesuits and Franciscans and European lay immigrants throughout the Americas, in conceptualizing Indians as radically other but paradoxically similar (that is, as distant Jews and perhaps as former Christians), brought to the forefront certain emphases in their definitions of themselves. Where domination and the often ruthless exercise of power structured relations between colonizer and colonized, Christians built a sense of their world through observing indigenes, circumscribing and defining indigenous cultures as savage and corrupt, and then characterizing themselves in relation to those people as holy, pure, and moral. That process in turn shaped colonists' thinking about divine power, and about their relationship to that power. In the Americas, Christians embraced even more fervently a self-understanding that identified them as a people called out by God from all of the rest of the population of the Earth and protected and fostered in their purity and separateness by the hand of divine providence. Moreover, Christians in a colonial environment were inclined to imagine themselves as even more separate, and pure, than they did in Europe. In their thinking about their relationship to the divine, they pictured themselves as especially close to God, especially favored. As they conceptually opened the space between themselves and indigenes – that is, as they saw deeper and more profound differences – they felt themselves pull closer to God. Consequently, in turn, they conceptually positioned themselves even further from the colonized people.

In such a setting, the achievement of gaining converts from among Native Americans came to be valued as an extraordinary triumph, and a testament as much to the high spiritual status and skill of the human agent of conversion as well as the amazing power of God. Many Christian missionaries, and especially those in New France, by the late seventeenth century sought postings in the Americas for the opportunity to suffer and die as martyrs because of the superior value of their prospective martyrdom in the colonial environment there. The colonization of North America, which from first contacts was rooted for Christians in a sense of religious entitlement, of having been awarded the land by God, likewise became a mission in itself. The land increased in cosmic value, the relationship of colonists to God became more precious and intimate, and the enterprise of subduing Satan wherever he might be found imbedded in the traditions of indigenes became more urgent. At the same time, however, some colonists, and especially those who sought the conversion of Native Americans, wanted to believe that Indians somehow were their kindred, remotely but concretely connected to them by both genealogy and religious background. Accordingly, when conflicts emerged between colonists and

Indians, the former took the latter as traitors to that shared background, and responded in extreme, often violent fashion. Indians were conceptualized in those instances not as others or as kin, but as traitors and apostates. Because religions historically have taken apostasy – a betrayal of the faith – as the worst and most dangerous kind of religious offense, and its practitioners the most worthy of erasure through any possible means, encounters between Euroamericans and Native Americans included many occasions of violent, even genocidal, religiously-driven violence against Indians.

The English-speaking Protestants who settled the seaboard, and especially those in New England, carried with them from Europe their own specific concerns about living up to the standards placed upon them by God. As a self-identified chosen people, Puritans were preoccupied with maintaining purity within their communities. That project was largely structured by a Puritan sense of being in covenant with God. Religious New Englanders considered themselves the recipients of a special commission from God, one that promised protection and support for the colonial enterprise. In exchange for that support, they promised ongoing commitment to a form of Christianity that had been "purified" of Roman Catholic ideas and practices that they considered corruptions of the Christian faith preached by Jesus's disciples. Early New Englanders also believed themselves to be related to God through a personal covenant with him. They pledged their devotion and God responded with saving grace. Although initially the terms of that relationship outlined a process in which God was not required – could not be forced by human activity – to provide grace that reformed persons and oriented them to the doing of good, over time the terms changed. In the 1630s, New Englanders were expected to publicly demonstrate how their souls had turned to God through careful self-examination and contrition for sin, and how consequently they had experienced a religious conversion. Conversion was understood as a remaking of persons in such a way as to set them on the path to "sanctification," that is, a life of godly virtue and steadfastness in faith. In such fashion, communities of "saints" (regenerate persons who held full membership in their local church) were created and maintained in the seventeenth-century towns. Subsequent generations were less inclined to experience conversions, however, and as a result religious leaders adjusted the notion of covenant so as to be able to include among the society of saints those who were striving for conversion but had not yet achieved it. Predicated on the belief that ongoing exposure to the "means of grace," which included Bible-reading, churchgoing, and prayer, would, eventually, lead to conversion, the so-called "Halfway Covenant" allowing baptism to children whose parents were not full church member emerged in the 1660s as a response to changes in colonial life. That change in thinking about the relationship of the individual to God understandably went hand in hand with alterations in thinking about the relationship of the community to God. As standards for church membership were relaxed, anxieties about the religious integrity of communities rose, fueling the preaching of jeremiads and provoking persons to deeper reflection on the invisible world that existed alongside the visible world.

The Invisible World

Native Americans had little interest in heavens and hells where humans were rewarded or punished for the ways in which they had lived their lives. Although Native American religions differed in important ways from one community to another, in general, the emphasis was on living as part of a collective and on remaining linked to that collective after death, and oftentimes, through reemergence into life. European notions of the salvation of the individual as individual made little sense to Indians who questioned the integrity and spiritual status of persons who sought to set themselves apart from the community in any way. Indian cosmology nevertheless was constructed with a keen interest in the invisible world, understood as the underworld, which was a place different from the current world, and as a dimension of existence intertwined with everyday life, where powerful forces and personalities operated undetected by the senses – until they were disclosed in profound moments of revelation.

The underworld, which was invisible but considered truly a place, where persons lived much as they lived in this world, appeared in stories as the place of the dead, where ancestors carried on in eating, hunting, weaving, laughing, drawing, and all of the other activities that made up everyday life. The underworld was a place even the living might visit. A Serrano (California) story about a wife who died and who brought her husband with her to the underworld tells of the happy reunion between her and her parents and brothers and sisters who previously had died. The husband, having not yet died, had trouble adjusting to the communal life there, being unable to eat the food as it was prepared for consumption by dead people, and experiencing difficulty seeing during the daylight hours. When he demonstrated his skill in hunting, however, he was accepted by the people of the land of the dead, and plans were made for his eventual complete integration into the community after he died (Erdoes and Ortiz 1984: 438–439).

The spirits and ghosts and demons who lived unseen alongside people in this world were the more important inhabitants of the invisible world in terms of their influence over the affairs of people. The spirits of ancestors often were present within a community, and Indians customarily appealed to them for guidance given in signs. Ghosts could be playful or dangerous, or both. Ghosts could hunt and fish and enjoy themselves in much the same way that people did, but they could also use their distinctive powers to confound or hurt people. Demons posed a more serious and constant threat to the community. They could steal the soul of a person and take it away with them into the invisible world, necessitating a trip by a shaman into the invisible world to retrieve the soul. Demons killed livestock, caused the rain to stop falling, brought about earthquakes and fires and disease, and caused trouble between persons in the community, inciting them to hatreds and jealousies. Demons could possess persons, driving them to violence against others or themselves, and, especially, were involved in making persons ill. Communities frequently interpreted wrinkles or tears in the social fabric as the work of demons, and launched witch hunting campaigns to flush out and exorcise possessed persons or to identify and destroy individuals who traded with demons. Demons were everywhere – in the air, in the water, in trees and plants and animals, inside human bodies – and awareness of the trouble that they caused was passed along in terrifying stories from generation to generation. Accordingly, the precautionary regimens taken to protect against them, and the sense of urgency in fighting them, were inculcated and maintained as a priority of community life, a necessity for survival.

Catholics in New France and New Spain likewise believed in an invisible world populated by all kinds of living things, from saints and angels, to demons, ghosts and other entities. Catholic cosmology included places such as heaven and hell, purgatory (where those who had died in sin were purified in suffering before they were allowed to enter heaven) and limbo, a place for unbaptized infants whose entry to heaven was assured, but delayed until the end of the world. Missionaries had difficulty explaining to Native Americans much of Catholic thinking about those places, and Protestants as well as Catholics had trouble conveying concepts like heaven and hell and their linkage to sin, atonement, redemption and other theological doctrines. Informing the richly detailed Christian belief in an invisible world was Christian suspicion of earthly existence. Catholicism, for all of its art and ritual that appealed to the senses, was deeply suspicious of the body and at times of earthly life in general as a distraction from human cultivation of love of God. Sexual lust was feared above all, but anxiety about enjoying the pleasures that came to one through any sensuous activity was paradoxically a central feature of Catholic devotion. Protestants, for their part, and especially those who settled New England, built meeting houses without stained glass, decoration (paintings, statuary, elaborate wood carvings), organs, or seat cushions for the hard, straight-backed pews. They wore plain dress and claimed to speak in plain language and cultivated in their pulpits what they referred to as "plain style," a way of preaching that avoided sonorous or ornamented prose (but which nevertheless sometimes drifted into highly sensual rhetoric when the subject was the relationship of the individual to God). For both Catholics and Protestants, the tortures of hell and the delights of heaven could be made to seem more real and more meaningful than the experience of embodied human life in the world. Ghosts, and especially demons, could appear as more important than the realities of one's neighbors or even one's own family. When demons or devils entered an embodied creature, whether it be a human or animal, and turned it to evil, Christians who believed such a thing possible approached the phenomenon as hyper-real. They took it as something of such great cosmic significance that it caused all other experience, whether of the everyday, visible world or the ordinarily unseen invisible world, to pale in comparison.

Crucial encounters between European colonists and Native Americans, as well as relations among colonists or among Native Americans, often were played out in fear of witchcraft. Among Southwest Indians such as Hopi, Zuni, and other pueblos, a witch could be a person born with two hearts, a good one and an evil one, where the evil one over time had come to dominate and destroy the good one. Or, as was the case more commonly in Indian cultures, a witch could be a person who had been entered by a demon and controlled by that demon, as a zombie-like instrument or otherwise enslaved body. Children, as persons who had not yet been initiated into the secrets and privileges of adulthood, as well as outsiders, were prone to accusations of witchcraft. Executions (sometimes mass executions) of witches in Native American communities are evidenced as far back as the precontact Anasazi cultures of the tenth to fourteenth century in the Colorado Plateau (Darling 1998: 732–735). French missionaries in the St. Lawrence frequently reported Native American campaigns against witches and their invisible allies, undertaken within indigenous communities or against enemies, both Indian and European. More frequently, they reported Indian attempts to heal illness through witchcraft, adding that Indians believed that "sorcery" had to be used to fight illness that had been caused by witchcraft in the first place. Some Jesuits approached the topic of witchcraft uncertain of whether it was as present or as powerful as Native American informants claimed, one missionary to the Huron writing that he was not so sure whether "there really are Sorcerers in this country,—I mean, men who cause death by witchcraft" (Thwaites, *JR*: 33.46.216–217). Others took Native American reports of the practice of witchcraft much more seriously. Father François du Peron, writing in 1639, drew upon his own knowledge of witchcraft in Christian places to describe the widespread appearance of it in Indian communities and its deployment against the French, observing that "the devil was unchained here as well as in France. There was only deviltry and masquerading at that time through-out the Huron country; two or three of our Christians were debauched therein, and many others, who were inclined to baptism, have become cold." According to the Jesuit, "all their actions are dictated to them directly by the devil, who speaks to them, now in the form of a crow or some similar bird, now in the form of a flame or a ghost." Detailing the means by which the Indians sought to cure their sick through witchcraft, he concluded by reporting on the existence of orders of demonic clergy among the Indians: "The devil has his religious; those who serve him must be deprived of all their possessions, they must abstain from women, they must obey perfectly all that the devil suggests to them. The sorcerer of this village came to see us on the 26th of March, and told us all these things" (Thwaites, *JR*: 15.31.176).

Indeed, among Christians as well, certain kinds of disease or physical abnormalities were thought to be associated with witchcraft. When Anne Hutchinson, who was in trouble with authorities in Massachusetts for her unorthodox religious views and her public airing of them, delivered a stillborn child in 1638, John Winthrop declared it a "monstrous birth." The grossly deformed thing – represented in legend as having a tail and horns – was taken as a sign of her coupling with the devil and proof of her witchcraft. Further south on the Atlantic seaboard, in Virginia, colonists likewise were from the outset wary of the power of evil in that place and its capability to cause them physical harm and ruin their fledgling plantation. William Crashaw, writing about Virginia, asserted in 1613 that "Satan visibly and palpably raignes there, more than any other known place in the world," and in doing so echoed what Hernando Cortés had declared a century earlier about the native peoples of North America who "work in the service of the Devil" (Crashaw 1613: 25). Witchcraft fears among English colonists in Virginia reached a tipping point in 1656 with the whipping and banish-ment of William Harding, and continued to shape colonists' experience of the land, Native Americans, and fellow colonists through the colonial period, most famously in the case of Grace Sherwood, a Virginia widow convicted and imprisoned for witch-craft in 1706. Her crimes including causing the death of livestock, destroying crops, and conjuring storms. The invisible world intruded most tragically into the lives of English colonists in 1692, when the residents of Salem began accusing their neigh-bors of witchcraft. It was not the first witchcraft hysteria to have seized New England, but it was the most far-reaching and dramatic. When the dust finally settled in 1693, over 160 persons had been accused, 19 convicted witches had been executed by hang-ing, another 5 had died in prison, and 1 had been tortured to death. Dozens of persons, under interrogation, admitted to making covenants with the Devil, and 47 persons in total confessed to witchcraft of some sort. All who confessed were spared execution. Of those executed, all insisted on their innocence. The majority of those executed, 14 were women. The frenzied hunting of witches in Salem bespeaks colonists' pro-found investment in ideas about the invisible world and its various denizens. The crisis at Salem, moreover, illustrates how cosmological ideas about place, time, contact

Figure 2.2 Cotton Mather, in *The Wonders of the Invisible World* (1693), reported on "remarkable curiosities" in New England just as the witch trials in Salem came to an end.

with the divine, and trust in the reality of demons, ghosts and devils were interrelated in an overall scheme of Euroamerican self-understanding. The place was enchanted in both good and bad ways – devils lurked even where God's providence simultaneously protected and nourished the lives of individuals and the growth of Christian communities. New Englanders took a religious view of time, believing that God had a plan for them in time, as chosen people on a path to glory, yet they fretted that they were not redeeming the time they had been given to maximum effect, not playing their proper role in the advance towards the Christian millennium foretold in scripture. Oftentimes, colonists blamed Indians for what they imagined as their failures to live with God, to fight the Devil, and to live virtuously in the place and time they had been given. Sometimes, they blamed each other, rooting out from among themselves those whom they believed were corrupted by false doctrine, pride, lusts, priestcraft, materialism, and other evils. In succeeding centuries, Americans would continue to campaign violently against both sets of enemies, the campaigns against one set of enemies reciprocally shaping thinking about the other.

The clash of cosmologies that took place between Native Americans and colonists, while often hardening each side to the other and leading to entrenched ideological positions, also prompted some to question the validity of their own traditions. This was especially true for Native Americans, whose communities were decimated by disease and violence, and who glimpsed in European-brokered Christianities materials that could be useful for remaking their conceptual worlds. Christian colonists for their part also became more skeptical. In the wake of the Salem witch trials, an influential minority of New Englanders spoke out against extreme forms of supernaturalism, criticizing not only the ideas of those who fanned the witchcraft fears, but the authority of those who presided over the inquisition (Figure 2.2).

From the year of contact, 1492, through the Salem witch trials, American Indians and colonists alike lived out their lives in a world characterized by wonders and signs, hidden powers and lurking evils, enchanted places and holy time. The cosmologies of Native Americans and Euroamericans equipped them with the means to interpret and order their lives in a fashion that sometimes led to stability and prosperity, and sometimes led to volatile relations with others that could result in violence, such as that which took place at Salem, or in Connecticut, where in 1637 a New England militia burned alive the inhabitants of an entire Pequot Indian village. America proved in the two centuries after 1492 to be something other than the Eden that Columbus had foreseen. The cosmologies of Native Americans and those who came from across the Atlantic – including, by 1619, enslaved Africans – nevertheless retained much of their explanatory power and remained foundations for the organization of everyday life and the encounters between different communities.

References and Further Reading

Cabeza de Vaca, A. (1993) *The Account: Álvar Núñez Cabeza de Vaca's Relación*, trans. Martin A. Favata and José B. Fernández, Houston, TX: Arte Público Press.

Cortés, Hernando (1928) *Five Letters 1519–1529*, trans., J. Bayard Morris, London: George Routledge and Sons.

Crashaw, William (1613) "The Epistle Dedicatory" to Alexander Whitaker, *Good News From Virginia* (London), in W. F. Craven (ed.) (1976) *Early Accounts of Life in Colonial Virginia 1609–1613*, Delmar, NY: Scholars Facsimiles and Reprints.

Darling, J. Andrew (1998) "Mass Inhumation and the Execution of Witches in the American Southwest," *American Anthropologist*, 100: 732–752.

David, Richard (1981) *Hakluyt's Voyages*, London: Chatto and Windus.

Drake, Daniel (1843) *Lives of Celebrated American Indians*, Boston: Bradbury, Soden & Co.

Erdoes, Richard and Ortiz, Alfonso (1984) *American Indian Myths and Legends*, New York: Pantheon.

Hall, David D. (1990) *Worlds of Wonder, Days of Judgment: Popular Religious Belief in Early New England*, Cambridge, MA: Harvard University Press.

Hebel, J. William and Hudson, Hoyt H. (eds.) (1941) *Poetry of the English Renaissance 1509–1660*, New York: F. S. Crofts & Co.

Kingsborough, Edward K. (1831–1848).*Antiquities of Mexico*, vol. 6, London: R. Havell and Colnaghi, Son, and Co.

Pérez de Ribas, Andrés (1999).*History of the Triumphs of our Holy Faith Amongst the Most Barbarous and Fierce Peoples of the New World*, trans. Daniel T. Reff, Maureen Ahern, and Richard K. Danford, Tucson, AZ: University of Arizona Press.

Scalfi, Alessandro (1999) "Mapping Eden," in Denis E. Cosgrove (ed.) *Mappings*, London: Reaktion.

Thwaites, Reuben Gold (ed.) (1898–1901) *The Jesuit Relations and Allied Documents 1610–1671*, Cleveland, OH: Burrows Brothers.

Winship, Michael P. (1996) *Seers of God: Puritan Providentialism in the Restoration and Early Enlightenment*, Baltimore, MD: Johns Hopkins University Press.

Winthrop, John (1630) *A Modell of Christian Charity* (1630) in *Collections of the Massachusetts, Historical Society*, 3rd series, 7 (1838).

3

Community

Sarah Rivett

From the fall of Constantinople in 1453 to the Protestant Reformation of 1517 to the Restoration of Charles II in 1660, Western Christianity underwent a series of radical transformations. Seizing control of the Holy Land, the Ottoman Empire unleashed knowledge from ancient texts, making the reinterpretation of religious truths possible for disparate theologians and religious leaders for centuries to follow. Perhaps the most famous example of this, the Protestant Reformation contested religious authority in unprecedented ways, prompting a fragmentation of ecclesiastical power that led to the proliferation of theologies and sects designed to promote a particular religious vision. Throughout the sixteenth century, the Reformation ideals of *sola scriptura* and *sola fides* fueled a variety of sectarian visions, united only through their collective indictment of Catholicism. While these transformations took place throughout Europe, England initiated a new plan for state intervention in religious affairs through Queen Elizabeth's settlement of 1559, which mandated conformity with the Church of England. While facilitating a temporary resolution, authority soon splintered further as Puritans and other radical Protestant sects, refusing to conform to the laws of church and state, left England in search of new lands and communities where they could practice their faith free from fear of persecution.

To study the emergence of new communities requires a willingness to think about how various component parts of religion are intertwined and embodied in the social realities. Religious community does not exist apart from religious ideas, or religious practice, or the world of politics. Religious community is in fact organized on the basis of religious ideas, it forms a crucial framework for religious practice, and it stands as the most important manifestation of religion in connection with law, government, and nation. By focusing on community, by allowing an emphasis on the collective to lead our investigation into religion, we create opportunities to glimpse the ways in which religious self-understanding is formed and to analyze the factors relevant to its development. In scrutinizing community we are able more fully to understand collective identity, and to appreciate the sometimes fragile nature of identity – its changeableness and variability. We especially position ourselves to comprehend the exchanges and negotiations that take place in encounters between different religious communities.

Throughout Europe and the New World, new communities anchored the theologies and practices that took place from 1492 to the Restoration of Charles II in 1660. This chapter traces this process, while also proposing that religious communities also facilitated the transformation of Christianity in ways more subtle and nuanced than the familiar, big historical markers through which we view the emergence of modern Christianity. As both an inwardly-directed spiritual practice and a metaphor of encounter, conversion provides a framework of analysis through which to view these transformations across disparate communities. Plotting historical time offers one framework for understanding these transformations, yet the geographic dispersal throughout the Atlantic World provides another. Plans for utopian religious communities were inspired by the fictional work of such Renaissance authors as Thomas More as well as by the millennial promotional perspective offered in John Cotton's *God's Promise to His Plantation* (1630). Sermons, travel narratives, novellas, and letters promised the possibility of setting up new societies in New Worlds, while also envisioning these societies as partaking in an errand into the wilderness that would inaugurate the second coming of Christ. As a consequence of these powerful representations, historically unprecedented migratory patterns and permanent settlements appeared throughout the New World. Subjected to persecution or determined to fulfill a religious ideal in a less encumbered setting, religious people moved across the Atlantic Ocean in pursuit of the life that they believed to be dictated by their faith. Upon arriving in a new place, whether it was Geneva, the colonies of the eastern seaboard of North America, or Mexico City, spiritual seekers had to form new communities in order to implement their religious ideas in practice and facilitate the social organization of settlement. Viewed from the perspective of a spatial trajectory of geographical movement and population dispersal, the transformation of Christianity adds a crucial dimension to our more traditional understanding of history as proceeding according to linear time and unfolding a sequence of events that played a causal role in shaping modern forms of Protestantism and Catholicism.

Communities in Comparison

The formation of New World communities across both American continents offers an important point of contrast between the Anglo-Protestant and Iberian-Catholic paradigm, as John H. Elliot has recently explained. In Latin and South America, the Spanish maintained distinctly ordered cities, built on the remains of Aztec, Incan, and Mayan civilizations. Philip II issued an ordinance in 1573, stipulating that New World towns should consist of a "plaza mayor, bordered by a church and civic buildings, and a regular pattern of streets on the grid-iron plan."[1] By contrast, there was little regularity to the English communities established in seventeenth-century North America. English promotional tracts represented the land as ripe, plentiful, and uninhabited in contrast to the complexity of indigenous civilization recorded by the Spanish. New communities soon sprinkled the eastern seaboard of North America, plotting the settlement of the Anglo-American World. New England communities emerged in contradistinction to the urban regularity of Spanish towns as they sought a corporate identity that was based upon a homogenous configuration of elect members who had mutual understanding of an authentic connection to God. Accordingly, Puritans,

Pilgrims, Quakers, and Anglicans forged close-knit communities built around the individualized notion of *sola fides* and *sola scriptura* as this model of faith proliferated out from the individual to a sense of collective responsibility, corporate identity, and eschatological fulfillment.

In the Anglo context, there were no clear road maps for how to establish these New World communities. Laws, social structures, and customs were imported from England but without the proximity of the state and its various supporting institutions. Additionally, the Puritans and Pilgrims migrated with the intention of contesting state power; they believed in a Calvinist-based religion that espoused a separation of church and state but that also privileged the spiritual authority of the individual to such a degree as to leave no clear signposts about how the disparate individuals practicing these faiths should form communities. Finally, the settings for English communities in the New World were not the plentiful wilderness imagined in promotional tracts but rather the often "howling wilderness" depicted in Mary Rowlandson's captivity narrative, inhabited by indigenous people with civilizations, social structures, and religious practices of their own that either had to be removed for the purposes of European occupation or negotiated and incorporated into the settlers' plans.

Native American populations soon became a measure of the success of European religious communities as missionaries framed their endeavor as a culminating phase within the cycle of the New World errand. Over the course of the seventeenth century, the Praying Towns of New England, the Jesuit missionary communities in the Great Lakes region, and the pueblos of New Mexico, all became communal sites of a dynamic interaction between European Christianity and indigenous religions. These spaces of intimate colonial encounter reveal the blending of different worlds. Far from the hegemonic imposition of Christianity upon a passive and subjugated population, missionary communities display complex syncretic blends of religious practice where missionaries both looked to native populations for certain kinds of Christian truth and native populations correspondingly adapted Christianity to their own purposes.

Christian-Iroquois communities in Canada's Great Lakes region, the Franciscan settlements in New Mexican pueblos, the Praying Town system set up for Northeastern Algonquians, and even the conversion symbolized through John Rolfe's marriage to Pocahontas in Jamestown, provide compelling comparative case studies for the central argument of this chapter: as Christianity took hold across the remote edges of empire – the farthest reaches of the Anglo, Franco, and Spanish worlds – it transformed through a complex series of colonial encounters. Missionaries, converts, and other groups traveled to the New World on a spiritual quest. The Native populations that they encountered occasionally supplied them with what they were looking for – affirmation of their own deeply held religious convictions and faith-based certainty of God's design. But even while affirming the Europeans' own preconditioned belief, native populations taught missionaries and settlers something else. Encounters at the edges of empire redefined spiritual epistemologies and religious practices, reshaping Christianity into new forms that then reentered a pattern of Atlantic circulation where news from the New World traveled back to Europe, back to the central axis of power controlling each Atlantic empire, to represent Christian truth in an entirely new light.

Our archival access to these missionary communities is fragmented and elusive. Written records, if they exist at all, are ideologically skewed by the colonial power authoring them. Reconstructing the cultural interactions that took place within these communities is challenging work, often requiring a cross-disciplinary analytical frame as we read the documents with an anthropological focus on the complexities of human interaction or a literary critical attention to the representational power of the written word. Yet such attentive analysis is crucial to mapping the complex ways that New World settlement transformed Christianity. Historical change is much more difficult to discern on a local level in communities scattered across a vast geographical expanse than it is as articulated through such sweeping historical markers as the Protestant Reformation or the Act of Toleration that followed from Charles II's restoration to the throne. Yet this local communal context is integral to understanding how the New World facilitated the transformation of Christianity into the modern evangelical forms and millennial-nationalist paradigms that are still with us today.

Spanish and French Communities

Before exploring in comparative detail the core issue of community – which we will investigate with respect to the religious lives of English colonists and Native Americans – some perspective is warranted. French and Spanish religious enterprises in the New World had much in common with English. All were missions-oriented and linked religious ideas and legal government to the organization and maintenance of community. All also juggled commercial initiative with the embrace of moral tradition and were engaged in an ongoing project of adapting and refining religiously-grounded visions of community with the experience of collective life in an unfamiliar place and among indigenous strangers. English, French, and Spanish colonialism, however, differed in conceptualizing the boundaries of community. That is, each relied upon different conceptions of how the boundaries of community were to be drawn, and how diligently those boundaries needed to be policed. Moreover, each defined community in distinctive ways, and especially with regard to what was expected of persons in their performances of membership in the collective.

The Spanish built mission villages. They built them in strings across deserts, mountains, swamps, and flatlands. As we have seen, there were clearly articulated blueprint specifications for such towns. Part of the reason for the careful oversight of place construction among the Spanish was efficiency of operation. Well-designed places, in the Spanish experience, were conducive to the organization of community on an everyday public level. They streamlined commercial practice, and they effectively staged the enactment of all of the rituals that signaled the locations of power and, in so doing, reinforced imperial authority. Mission villages made place more familiar to the Spanish military, clergy, and colonists, and as such fostered a familiar style of religious community. The religious mission of Spanish colonialism also was advanced through the representation of public life in the built environment of the town. For the Spanish, and especially for the Franciscans who labored in Mexico and the borderlands, the process of conversion was understood to begin with the civilizing of American natives. That is, the model of regeneration, of making Christians out of Indians, began with the reformation of behavior. The padres sought to turn Indians into Spaniards, at least in as much as Indians could be persuaded to adopt Spanish customs regarding sex and marriage, dress, protocols of commercial exchange, recognition of and deference to social superiors, and so forth. Through reformation of the behavior of persons would come the renewal of the soul. The Spanish, with some exceptions, worked from the outside in. It was expected that when a prospective convert had advanced far enough along in the mastery of Christian behavior, the heart would turn fully to God in conversion.

With conversion as the goal of all missionizing, it therefore was crucial that community be engineered to provide a maximally supportive setting for Christian (that is, Spanish Catholic) behavior. Everyday life was rich with opportunities for Indians to take behavioral steps toward conversion. The rhythms of community life, marked by the tolling of the mission bell, included time for work, family, public recreation, and religious observance. Community rested on the trust that the modeling of Christian behavior was the best way to teach it. Each day by design brought multiple occasions for contact between models and aspirants, as all assembled within the church, gathered in the public square, worked together in orchards and fields, or met in groups to be catechized. Community in Spanish missions consequently was both conceived and practiced as intensely social and practical. The boundaries of community, like the walls of the mission compound, were easily recognizable. But within those walls, alongside the converted, were persons striving to fully belong (as well as some who never would fully belong, as the Spanish discovered in the Pueblo Revolt of 1680). Religious community, then, while experienced as an encompassing reality, was to some extent also an imagined future. For the Spanish, to "live" community meant to participate on a daily basis in a society rigged for constant social interaction, but that also was incompletely formed. Community, as concrete and clearly defined as it was, was nevertheless a work in progress, and for all involved, it remained so during the entire history of the Spanish missions in America. In the twenty-first century, the profound intertwining of everyday life with Catholicism, and the attention paid to proper behavior among pious Hispanic Catholics represent part of the legacy of the earliest Spanish Catholic communities.

The French Jesuits and other clergy who sought the conversion of Indians in the St. Lawrence, Great Lakes, Mississippi Valley, and Gulf coast traveled great distances by water to reach Indian villages. Once there, they remained for a relatively short while before traveling to a new place. The French did not build strings of missions. There was nowhere in New France an achievement approaching the string of the 54 Spanish missions stretching west across the Florida panhandle from St. Augustine (f. 1565), or the mission road in California, along El Camino Real from San Diego (f. 1769) to north of San Francisco (f. 1776). Jesuits in New France conceptualized missionizing as expeditionary rather than as occupational. French Jesuits made repeated forays into Indian territories, but for the most part did not endeavor to occupy the land by explicitly carving out a space for the construction of a permanent French Catholic culture. This was partly because the territory explored by France was so vast, and human resources so scarce. It was also because the commercial project of the French, which was overwhelmingly the fur trade, unfolded as a matter of individual enterprise and mobile activity, and so did not rely upon the settled community life of towns for its success (except to require a port for export). The French founded cities: Montreal (f. 1642) and Quebec (f. 1608) most importantly, and also settlements that eventually grew into Detroit, New Orleans, Biloxi, Mobile, and Erie, among others. French activity nevertheless was predominantly focused on small villages and mission hamlets, some of which disappeared and then reappeared several times over, sometimes under different names.[2]

The Jesuit mission to Native Americans was driven by the belief that preaching could reach immediately into the hearts of natives and convert them to Christianity. Jesuit efforts to convert Indians accordingly required knowledge of native languages in order to succeed. Jesuits, while valuing moral behavior and endeavoring to instill an understanding of Christian virtue in their target population of Indians, did not organize their work with an eye to changing behavior first, as did the Spanish. French missionaries approached their work armed with Christian doctrine. They believed that upon hearing the truths of Christianity, Indians would come to know the Christian God. They would be converted by the grace of God through their grasp of religious truth. Jesuits worked from the inside out. Having turned the souls of persons to the divine, they could trust that God would lead those persons to reform their behavior. Jesuits provided models for that behavior, but in the small villages they visited they did not install programs for the ongoing inculturation of French Catholic ways of life in the Indian population. Religious community outside of Montreal and Quebec therefore was ambiguous. There was a fluidity and indeterminacy to community in the French territories, and because of that conversions often did not last long. Community was idealized rather than actualized, and discipline for the enforcement of religious standards for community identity was lax.

In contrast to the situation in the mission field, the lives of French colonists in Quebec and Montreal were fairly well defined. Religious infrastructure in the form of a college, a hospital, a seminary, and a convent school was set in place in Quebec in the 1630s. In terms of the migration of religion from Europe, there were a few Huguenots in the first decades of French settlement in North America, but for most of the period New France was exclusively Roman Catholic. Community was unitary, not diverse, in Quebec and there was very little give and take there between Catholicism and Indian religions. That kind of exchange took place further westward and southward, and shaped both Catholic and Indian sensibilities through the nineteenth century.

England's Errand into the New World

Over the course of the seventeenth century, new religious communities emerged throughout Europe as well as the North American coast as a direct consequence of the political changes that ensued from the Stuart reclamation of the throne in James I's rise to power. What Karen Kupperman has recently termed the "Jamestown Project" developed only a few years after James I became King of England. Unlike the Plymouth and Massachusetts Bay Colonies to follow, Jamestown was not a settlement established exclusively on religious principles. Rather, the project fueled mercantile and political interests in opening trade routes to expand the economic and territorial domain of the English nation. Nonetheless, Kupperman explains that the Jamestown project also came on the brink of a millennial climate of world-historical drama that fueled the proliferation of religious communities throughout the Anglo world: "For all European Christians, America was central to the divine cosmic drama they believed was entering its final stages as the events foretold in the Book of Revelation played out."[3] Jamestown is thus as foundational, from Kupperman's perspective, to the establishment of America as a sacred space of national and millennial promise as the commensurate myths that have long been attached to parallel communities in New England.

As recorded in the annals of John Smith's *History of Virginia* (1624), a framework of providential design mediated the various encounters between Smith and Powhatan, between English custom and the Paspahegh tribe of the Chesapeake Algonquians. Smith defines his own plantation project in contrast to the black legend of the Spaniards' failure, read as a direct consequence of God's design to thwart Spanish attempts to clear the land, making this agenda the exclusive and divinely-justified right of the English. Yet while providence renders land available to the godly for cultivation, Smith's *History* also registers a gap between providence and new world practice, between the religious righteousness that endowed the English with their sense of purpose within the New World and the actual conditions of living there. European technologies of writing, military force, and exploration – such as the compass – often lacked a clear New World utility. To reconcile this gap between Smith's plantation mentality and the harsh reality of a New World existence where science becomes a site of marvel and inquiry and where indigenous technologies more effectively facilitate Smith's purpose, an intricate language of diplomacy develops within the *History*. A lengthy discussion between Powhatan and Smith, for example, concerns whether the two groups should bear arms. From the narrative record of Powhatan's speech, we learn that the Algonquians have knowledge of previous European encounters, a historical memory that either serves to augment Smith's history of his own success or prove that Powhatan may in fact be craftier that Smith originally surmised.[4]

Perhaps nowhere in the Jamestown archive are these tensions between millennial purpose and ethnographic observation, between English custom and New World circumstances, more poignantly rendered than in John Rolfe's letter of 1614, concerning his marriage to Pocahontas. Addressed to Sir Thomas Dale in England, the letter expresses Rolfe's fear of "hypocrisy and dissimulation." He writes of his own troubled soul, personalizing and particularizing through his own marriage to Pocahontas the larger cultural concerns of the English colonists. Assuaging his own anxiety and affirming his innocence, Rolfe insists that his marriage to Pocahontas did not come about through "the unbridled desire of carnal affection" but rather "for the good of this plantation, for the honor of our country, for the glory of God, for my own salvation, and for the converting to the true knowledge of God and Jesus Christ, an unbelieving creature, namely Pokahuntus [*sic*]."[5] Articulating a necessity unanticipated upon New World arrival, Rolfe explains retrospectively, in this letter written seven years after English arrival in the Chesapeake Bay, that conversion lies at the heart of the Jamestown project. This is not simply a conversion from heathen to Christian, or from unbelief to faith. Rather, Rolfe's letter establishes a format of substitution – the name Rebecca replaces Pocahontas, a Christian replaces a savage, and an English subject replaces an Algonquian (Figure 3.1). This multi-layered conversionary process ensures that the colonial encounter augments rather than depletes the national project of New World plantation, a project with clear mercantile and political dimensions that must be undergirded through the millennial vision of the rise of true knowledge of God.

Unlike the sustained trajectory of the New England colonies, the success of the Jamestown project in reclaiming divine purpose for the English nation is relatively

Figure 3.1 Pocahontas in English garb. Note the Anglicized "Rebecca" intended to replace "Matoaka" and "Pocahontas".

short-lived. Due to mismanagement, the colony loses its charter in 1624, causing tremendous financial losses to investors back in England. Among these investors were Nicholas and John Ferrar, both Deputy-Governors of the Virginia Company. Ordained in the Church of England, Nicholas Ferrar established the strict religious community, Little Gidding, in the wake of his own family's failure in the Virginia Company in a small hamlet in Huntingdonshire. The fulcrum of the community was a large manor house and a small neglected church found as a converted hay barn 30–40 feet from the house. The manor house became a site of communal living as the church became the centerpiece of a homogeneous religious life, built entirely on the principles of the Anglican Church. Both residents of the manor house, the Collet and Ferrar families parsed male and female occupants in separate rooms. They arose at four o'clock in the summer and five in the winter, making their way into the great chamber to recite biblical verses or psalms. They then retreated to their rooms for private study between seven and nine until the church bell rang, telling them to assemble for church in a procession led by three schoolmasters in black gowns.

Secular life also followed a prescribed routine of communal meals and household tasks. The community dressed similarly, read together, and collectively wrote religious storybooks for use within the little school house. Little Gidding reflected a utopian, Anglo community for over a decade until the English Civil War when Parliamentary soldiers arrived to ransack the community. "The church was despoiled, its beautiful furnishings, over which so much trouble had been spent, being ruthlessly destroyed."[6] One consequence of the English Civil War was a fear of communal fanaticism – what could potentially take place within the walls of these self-contained communities might lead to the fragmentation rather than the unification of national life. The fate of Little Gidding both emblematizes the sustainable religious vision that drove particular groups away from the shores of England to carve their own idyllic hamlet on the North American coast and forecasts the disappointment, declension, and political unrest that would plague these communities.

The Pilgrims and Puritans are the most famous of these groups. Their legacy lives on to present times in mythic proportions, symbolizing the beginnings of many of the values that we cherish as integral to American national culture. We tell ourselves that our love of freedom comes from these groups of courageous people who crossed an ocean to protect their rights from violation by a rigid religio-political order. We imagine the voluntary organization of congregationalism as an early form of what would eventually become a democratic political order. These myths must be understood as retrospective reassessments, bearing little relationship to the historical circumstances of migration. Neither the Pilgrims nor the Puritans believed in religious toleration but rather that their way was the right way and that by refusing to follow it, England was clearly moving in the wrong spiritual direction. John Winthrop and William Bradford, like Nicholas Ferrar, decided to establish strict religious communities where the right religious way could be practiced freely and collectively. If the Puritan Congregational Way was somewhat proto-democratic in its embrace of individualized and voluntary Calvinist idealism, Puritan society also instituted complex techniques for maintaining the social order. As if to ensconce their respective holy experiments within world history, Bradford and Winthrop made the writing of history central to their roles within the New World, authoring *Of Plymouth Plantation* and *The History of New England* respectively in order to leave a lasting impression upon historical memory.

We learn from Bradford that his Pilgrim group espoused a separatist vision, wishing to distance themselves from the crown entirely, to forge a new life on new soil where faith would thrive undisturbed. Arriving in the Massachusetts Bay in 1630 as part of a migration that included 20,000 people, a larger group of Puritans promoted a more complex relationship between church and state. Central to the Puritans' collective identity was a process of conversion that involved prolonged, intense, inward self-scrutiny. Puritans engaged in a daily quest for signs of grace upon their hearts in order to intuit whether they were among the elect. The Puritans believed that grace came from personal experience, supplying the convert with an "indwelling" spirit that had to be "entertained" by persons familiar with Scripture. A mark of divine election was the convert's ability to unite experiential and biblical religion. The theology of Puritan conversion was largely based on Reformation interpretations of Paul's epistles, which consisted of a belief in human depravity and the consequent human inability to know the state of the soul or instigate the conversion process. In practice, this theology of conversion proved difficult to maintain, especially as a communal form of collective identity. Calvin taught that individuals could do nothing to effect the state of their souls, espousing a doctrine of predestination in which individuals cultivated their own relationship to God without a need for recourse to ecclesiastical or social hierarchies. In England and then especially in the New World, Calvinism so privileged the spirituality of the individual as to present a challenge to any effort to form a cohesive community. In the section that follows, I dwell on Calvin's proscription for the self and the soul at some length for the purposes of elucidating how the Puritans built an improvisational New World community around this doctrine.

The Architecture of the Self and the Soul

From the 1570s through the mid-seventeenth century, Puritans responded to the dilemma that predestination posed to collective identity by adopting a "doctrine of preparation," which taught that potential converts could exercise their will by undergoing a period of introspection and self-analysis, accompanied by the rigorous study of scriptural truths. Through self and scriptural study, the prospective convert became aware of his or her own sins; this awareness led to the discovery of an innately sinful self through self-identification with Adam's original sin. Identification with Adam induced an experience known as "humiliation." Humiliation initiated the process of preparation as the individual underwent more meditations on sin and depravity, which "softened" and "broke" the heart by inculcating a need and desire for saving grace. True humility came when the Puritan realized that original sin created a debt between sinner and God that could not be repaid in good works. Paradoxically, recognizing this condition of complete debility before God was the first step that the Puritan took towards salvation. Puritans believed that a stony heart would resist grace, while a broken heart would be more receptive to divine dispensation.

Ministers emphasized repeatedly that this process of preparation did not guarantee salvation. The individual did not convert through the softening of the heart alone. Instead this initial phase lead to more introspection and self-examination as the individual became aware of an intense desire for God's saving grace. After humiliation, conversion became a process of emptying out all private feelings and ideas about individual autonomy. In his sermon, *Sincere Convert*, Puritan minister Thomas Shepard describes this process through the metaphor of melting down the tarnished inner self. The three phases described above – conviction of sin, humiliation, and then this process of self-emptying – prepared the Puritan for communion with Christ. The Puritan began to see his or herself as a hollow cast of Adam. It was into this hollow space that the euphoric, reassuring moment of Puritan conversion occurred. God's "seed" flowed into the unregenerate saint, "pricked" the sinful heart, and partially redeemed the convert from the irreparably destructive fall. Shepard described this euphoria through the metaphor of a convert as Christ's bride, drawing an analogy between this blissful spiritual moment and an idealized marital union.

Once the Puritan had experienced this feeling of assurance, he or she had hope but not proof of divine election. The elect, referred to as visible saints by the Puritans, consisted of those community members included in God's covenant of grace. Puritan covenant theology taught that the contract between God and humans was based solely on faith. Since Adam's rebellion, the covenant of works was no longer valid. The Puritan belief in the breach of this original covenant reinforced their sense that humans could do nothing to affect their conversion. Only the experience of saving grace could give Puritans a clue as to whether they might be part of the covenant of grace guaranteeing salvation for the elect. The experience of assurance necessarily recurred throughout the life of a saint, coupled with the opposing yet paradoxically complementary feeling of deep anxiety. Because the saint could never fully know the status of his or her own soul, anxiety and even despair frequently followed the experience of assurance. Through more inward searching and self-scrutiny, the saint would question whether he or she had just been deluded into thinking that the experience had been authentic. Puritan conversion was an open-ended process, patterned by a dynamic oscillation between hopeful and fearful emotions.

Even though grace was characteristically elusive and ineffable, the Puritans strove to develop a system of signs through which they could study the experience in others. What was the *ordo salutis*, or way of salvation, by which an individual realized his or her faith? Reformed interpretations of Pauline theology and the doctrine of preparation only partially answered this question. Yet the answer was central to Puritan evangelical and proselytizing goals as they tried to affect the experience of conversion in others in English and Native American communities. The testimony of faith, which became a requirement for church membership in 1635, fostered the communal study of the *ordo salutis*. It was not enough for prospective members to attest to their scriptural knowledge or belief in God; they had to display evidence of the effects of grace upon their soul before church members and ministers. Visible saints were called upon to translate the intensely inward experience of conversion and self-scrutiny into series of signs that others could recognize. The testimony of faith marked an attempt to work out the *ordo salutis* in practice, for the theology of the conversion process was an interpretive process rather than a set doctrine.

Church, State, and Gender in Puritan New England

The geographic urgency of the migration and the social and political demands of reinventing society upon New World arrival are both integral to explaining why the practice of declaring one's faith emerged in New England when it did. The Puritans arrived in the Massachusetts Bay Colony in 1630 with a vision for a godly community, most famously described in Winthrop's *Model of Christian Charity*. Preached in 1630 aboard the *Arbella* en route to the New World, the lay sermon famously imagines a godly community in which church members are the visible earthly members of the invisible body of Christ. Winthrop's sermon resolves a theological and social tension in Puritanism between an individual and a corporate identity. Born out of a Calvinist mindset that privileges an individual path to salvation, what would make the elect cohere into a uniform and cohesive community? Part of this dilemma was theological, depending on an elaborate plan for suturing the covenant of grace promised to Adam in Genesis to the notion of the federal covenant upon which the collective nature of the Puritan New World errand came to depend. Part of this dilemma was social and political as Winthrop and other first-generation magistrates sought to negotiate the complicated question of how they might implement and even mandate this theological idea in practice among a diverse group of 20,000 individuals fleeing to New England in 1630 to escape the persecution of Archbishop Laud. Relentless in their rigid commitment to doctrine and sure of the moral and divine righteousness of their faith, the Puritans nonetheless remained uncertain and deeply anxious about what governmental and ecclesiastical structures would look like. The testimony of faith stems from this sense of uncertainty rather than rigid doctrinal commitment. As described in Winthrop's *History*, the formation of the first congregation is essentially an experimental and improvisational attempt to come up with a technique for forming a church.

The journey across the Atlantic was an allegory for a spiritual journey, recorded by Winthrop as the personalized phenomenon of individuals joining the church as well as the communal pattern exhibited through the formation of new congregations where "divers profane and notorious evil persons came and confessed their sins." Following a practice quite possibly brought to the New World by John Cotton, a group of colonists "joined" in Boston in 1633 "to make confession of their faith." Winthrop defines this act of confessing as a "declaration of what work of grace the Lord had wrought in them." Six to eight individuals constituting the pillars of this new congregation gathered in the Boston town commons. In a short, succinct oral relation, probably lasting less than ten minutes, they attempted to respond to the central question of the Reformation: How do I know if I am saved? This question could not be answered with knowledge of faith or a declaration of individual belief in God. Rather, testifiers had to supply some account of what divine grace felt like upon their souls. Individual knowledge then translated into communal knowledge. Following such declarations, the church "covenant was read, and they all gave solemn assent to it."[7] A formative moment in Winthrop's *History*, this scene seems to mark the implementation of the ideal of Christian Charity into practice, linking the covenant of grace to the federal covenant as so famously imagined in his 1630 lay sermon through the image of diverse members of the elect bound collectively together through "ligaments of love."[8]

Congregationalism, as it appears in its incipient New England form as integrally connected to Winthrop's initial description of the testimony of faith, depended on some knowledge of which church members constituted the privileged body of the elect even though practitioners sought adamantly to maintain Calvin's sense of assurance as an entirely inwardly-directed, individualistic, phenomenal experience that could not be communicated to others with any degree of certainty. Sectarian disagreements over how particular doctrinal interpretations led to different forms of religious practice stemmed from subtle epistemological variations in each Christian attempt to negotiate the consequences of the fall. In Congregationalism, Reformation theology registered as a double-bind of knowledge – the social and political need to know was always coupled with a deep awareness of the theological impossibility of doing so.

This link between the individual and the community, the singular and corporate voice, was tenuous throughout the first generation of New England history, dependent as it was upon the Puritan effort to suture the theological and the political whereby the former was intrinsically focused upon the individual as well as a prominent strand of anti-authoritarianism. For first-generation Puritans, the testimony of faith stood at the heart of this effort to conjoin these competing strands, exhibiting an effort to facilitate the translation of the covenant of grace into the federal covenant whereby elect saints would share what they knew of Christ's love, tightening communal bonds. The testimony also offered visible sainthood as the preliminary stage to a supplemental form of political membership for those of the elect who were also land-owning white males. Upon declaring their faith, they merely had to give a short, succinct, and formulaic freeman's oath in order to become part of the body politic and participate in communal affairs. Due to this state-sanctioned and institutionally enforced method of excluding women from the body politic, a complex gender dynamic registers formally and rhetorically within the testimony of faith as a direct result of the genre's communal function of bridging the theological to the political, the covenant of grace to the federal covenant, and the individual voice to the corporate voice.

The 1641 *Massachusetts Body of Liberties* attempts to delineate the intricacies of the church/state relationship as it mediated between the autonomy of the individual, the liberties accorded individual congregations, and the need to maintain a social structure, hierarchically arranged according to gender and rank. A section entitled "A Declaration of the Liberties the Lord Jesus hath given to the Churches" establishes the autonomous power of the congregations. Article 4 accordingly states that "every church hath free liberty of Admission ... of their officers and members, upon due cause." However, a lengthy eleventh article qualifies this statement by explaining that the church's power is "allowed and ratified by the Authority of the General Court."[9] The law does not clearly delineate whether the authority to discern grace within the congregational system comes from the church or from the state. Returning to the still unresolved dilemma of how to balance the power relationship between church and state, the Synod of 1648 sought to narrow its focus on this question, well aware of the dangers of assigning the magistrates too much power in governing the elect. But sermons preached and documents written around the time of the Synod reveal that not only was this question of central concern but that the 1648 defense of public confession also functioned to solidify the terms of interdependency between church and state. In theological and ecclesiastical terms, a primary impetus for the testimony of faith was to create bonds within the church community, to link the individual covenant of grace to the federal covenant, and to ensure Winthrop's individual "ligaments of Christ's love" were bound to a collective sense of the whole body of Christ.

John Norton's *Of the Church Covenant* seeks to do precisely this. Norton explains that simply "dwelling together, coming together, profession, and baptism" are not enough to constitute or confirm the membership of elect individuals within a visible church, designed in its ideal form to be an external manifestation of a perfect godly community. This had been John Winthrop's ideal in 1630, but his famous sermon preached before New World arrival could not take into account the vast discrepancies between a vision of a voluntary, godly community of like-minded people and the social and political reality of implementing such a thing upon arrival in Boston. As if responding nearly twenty years later to what Winthrop could not have foreseen, Norton explains this vision of collectivity must be solidified through the "visible bond of mutual agreement" created through the public confession. Such a "visible bond" meant that male church members would take the supplemental "freeman's oath" upon giving their testimony of faith in order to become part of the body politic at the same time that they became members of the church. Once members of the General Court, they could vote for officers and magistrates and voice an opinion in town meetings.[10] What this meant, however, was that even though women, propertyless Anglo men, and Native Americans were often included in the activity of publicly professing their conversion experience, they were not formally incorporated into the visible form of the federal covenant, which could only be fully recognized through an individual's participation in affairs of the state. Until 1660, political subjectivity was tied to visible sainthood, a franchise limited to land-owning male church members.

The splintering of authority in the direction of experientially-based faith meant that Congregationalists would insist upon the voluntary nature of this testimonial practice, though, given the political stakes of visible sainthood, voluntary is not quite accurate, for not to participate meant exclusion from the visible church community, from the invisible body of Christ, and, at least for property-owning males of the first generation, exclusion from the body politic. To choose not to testify was to relinquish one's political rights. Through a correspondent mechanism of making ecclesiastical structure more democratic, women were included within the population of testifiers deemed appropriate for public reception. To invite women's experiential testimonies into the congregational setting was not simply a democratizing move. This was seen as an exclusive context for the female voice, one that took place under special conditions and followed strict rules for following theological and ecclesiastical policy. In response to the "agitation" over "women making their relations in public," John Fiske explains that testimony is a unique kind of speech that doesn't fall within the rubric of what should be kept silent. Testimony is an outwardly-directed proclamation, or "a kind of speaking by submission where others are to judge."[11] Praying Indians would soon be included as well, though their public testimonies took place through a homologous but separate structure of the Praying Town, as explored in the next section.

Praying Towns

The Puritans established what is known as the Congregational Way in order to establish what John Winthrop described as the "city upon a hill." Congregational communities modeled a particular way of faith designed to act as beacons to the world, where God would eventually reside, fulfilling the millennial biblical prophecy for all the world to see. Upon New World arrival, the Puritans encountered an indigenous population that had to be incorporated into their providential plan. The Algonquian natives of Northeastern Massachusetts were famously represented in the 1629 seal of the Massachusetts Bay Colony as a population ripe for conversion, hence justifying English purpose in migration and settlement. Yet there was a 13-year delay between the original formulation of this objective and the missionary project as it would most fully develop under John Eliot who learned to preach in Algonquin and then organized a series of settlements for Native American proselytes or "Praying Indians." These settlements were known as "Praying Towns." While maintaining some syncretic cultural and religious practices, the Praying Town functioned to indoctrinate Native Americans into English custom. As the leading missionary, John Eliot explains, the first task of the Praying Town was to construct "a very sufficient Meeting-House of fifty foot long, twenty five foot broad." Private homes and footbridges across the Charles River accompanied the meeting house, though many Praying Indians continued to reside in wigwams. In August, 1646, Puritan minister Thomas Shepard composed a list of 29 "orders" that would require inhabitants of the Praying Towns to "conform themselves to the civil fashions of the *English*. The *Society* felt that such "civilizing" institutions and laws were a necessary precondition for the conversion of Native Americans.

In 1644, the Massachusetts General Court ordered that Native American tribes in the southeastern part of the Massachusetts Bay Colony be "instructed in the knowledge and worship of God." Two years later, John Eliot went to Nonantum where he preached his first Algonquian sermon in Waban's wigwam. The court then appointed a committee to buy land for the Praying Indian towns. Land was purchased from the Native Americans at Watertown Mills, and at Nonantum, where the missionary experiment was tried at Natick, the first Praying Town. John Eliot's goal was to generate native missionaries from the structure of the Praying Town. He appointed Cutshamekin, the sachem or Indian leader, to rule over approximately 150 people in Natick. Totherswamp and Waban adjudicated legal matters initially, while Monequassun, whom Eliot had already instructed to read and write, started as teacher of the Indian proselytes. After a series of setbacks, the first Indian Church was officially formed in Natick in 1660. As such, the missionaries called upon Native people to introduce English standards of "cohabitation and labor, government and law, and church covenant" within the Praying Town.

After two years of Natick experiment, Eliot discovered the need to expand. Natick was no longer a suitable place to gather in converts from other villages, in part because the growing number of proselytes wanted to stay closer to their traditional homelands. The court's original land grant was not large enough and it was too near the English, causing tensions between Natick and the English settlers in the neighboring town of Dedham. Eliot obtained tracts of land approximating 6000 acres each and created five other Praying Towns nearby: Punkapoag, Wamesit, Hassanamesit, Okommakamesit, and Nashobahh. Magunkog followed in 1669, completing the cluster that Daniel Gookin refers to as the "old praying towns." With the exception of the Pennacook Indians in Wamesit, most of these Praying Towns were inhabited by Massachusetts and Nipmuck Indians.

The objective of the Praying Town system was to eradicate indigenous belief and custom, to create an environment where Christianity would flourish among a formerly heathen population. Indeed, the relocation of Native peoples through the Praying Town system irreparably affected kinship structures and undermined the social and political structures of Native villages. Eighty percent of the native people originally inhabiting the land where the Praying Towns were located lived by agriculture. They were not nomadic hunters but they were significantly more mobile than the British because they would move to gather and fish between harvest seasons. The English criticized the Native's relationship to the land, characterizing them as "lazy savages" who did not understand the proper use of the environment. While missionaries incorporated the political authority of sachems, they also greatly augmented the power traditionally accorded this figure within the governmental structure of the Praying Town. Conversely, the Puritans rejected the powwow, or spiritual leader's authority, reflecting their deliberate efforts to supplant Native religious custom with Christianity.

Nonetheless, the Native populations were able to incorporate some of their traditional beliefs and practices within the culture of the Praying Towns. The Algonquian language remained relatively intact among the proselytes even as Eliot used it as a tool for missionary work. Eliot even imported a printer named Marmaduke Johnson from London to publish an Indian Library in 1660. Working alongside a Massachusetts Indian named James the Printer, Marmaduke Johnson translated key Christian texts into Algonquian.[12] We do not have a lot of information on the circulation of these texts or the reading practices of Native American communities, but a few scholars have carefully sifted through the spotty archive. Hillary Wyss argues that natives redefined "literacy" to suit their own purposes, voicing their own particular relationship

to the divine. We learn from Kathleen Bragdon's archival research that "sermon deliv-
ery was a flourishing vernacular genre among the native Christians" and "several
natives enjoyed reputations as powerful and accomplished preachers."[13] For both
scholars, empowerment comes through the reappropriation of Algonquin from a
newly written and read *back* to an oral language. Powwows could be admitted into the
towns provided that they submit to the authority of the Puritans. Native interest in
Christianity was often rooted in parallels between Massachusetts creation myths and
biblical stories. Praying Indians had to alter their culture and lifestyle to subsist on the
marginalized land of the Praying Town, but the settlement system also provided a
limited avenue through which Natives could maintain a hold on ancestral land. Since
the arrival of the English, Massachusetts Bay tribes had been devastated by waves of
disease. The Praying Town presented many of them with a viable option for protecting their people and culture from further destruction.

If the Praying Town system permitted Algonquians to salvage some aspects of their
culture or acquire spiritual authority by appropriating Christian pedagogy, it also
irrevocably transformed the Christianity practiced therein. The spread of the Gospel
took place among Richard Bourne's Mashpee proselytes, the natives preaching in
Algonquin on Martha's Vineyard, and the Praying Town system established by John
Eliot in Massachusetts. Each instances a microcosm of the universalizing Protestant
spirit as it descends across sectarian divisions on both sides of the Atlantic. The aural
culture of Algonquin communication produced in each setting is evidence of this
process. Eliot "begins his prayers in the Indian's language." Then the son of Waban
reads the Proverbs from Eliot's Indian Bible, "which [according to Shepard] has been
printed & is in the hands of the Indians."[14] A native named Job prays for half an hour
in "the Indian Language" and then preaches from Hebrews 15.1. Several natives
stand up and read from the Primer or from Eliot's Bible. Shepard emphasizes that the
allure of such scenes is in hearing the aural quality of a divinely redeemed Algonquin
tongue. Such scenes serve as proof of God's presence, as the aural sound lifts the
spiritual essence from the Algonquin words printed in Eliot's library. Along with his
letter, Shepard sent a copy of the Indian Primer to the Scottish minister in an attempt
to illustrate the precision with which New Englanders pursued this Algonquin path to
a universal Protestant spirit.

The number of Praying Towns continued to expand through the 1660s. Motivated
by desire for English protection from their Narragansett enemies, eight Nipmuck
sachems requested Praying Towns. This request resulted in the formation of Quantisset,
Pakachoog, Chabanakongdomun, Wabquisset, Manchage, Maaexit, and Waeuntug.
The Mayhew family settled Praying Towns on Martha's Vineyard, home to 300
Wampanoag proselytes. Richard Bourne founded Mashpee in Plymouth Plantation
where John Cotton Jr. also preached and studied Algonquian from 1667 to 1697.
The Mohegan in Connecticut and the Narragansett in Rhode Island were generally
resistant to the mission.

During the height of the mission's success, there were between 3600 and 4000
residents in Praying Towns and thirty Indian congregations in the southern part of
Massachusetts alone. The escalating tensions between the English and the Native
Americans on the eve of King Philip's War quickly and radically changed this model
of a relatively peaceful, colonial coexistence. In June 1675, Praying Indians were relocated to only five towns. In October of that same year, the General Court moved

them to Long Island and Deer Isle. There was much suffering during the long cold, winter of the war. Eliot and Gookin were harshly criticized for defending the Praying Indians even though one-fourth of the Native Americans maintained their allegiance to the English. After the war, roughly 40 percent of the Massachusetts proselytes retained their Christian faith, but more hostile English laws and attitudes towards the Indians had a lasting and detrimental impact on the Praying Town system.

Evangelical Encounters

Colonial encounters in numerous missionary communities throughout North American transformed both indigenous religions and the Christianity that Europeans brought to the New World. As we have seen in the section above, New England's Praying Town system provided a sustainable institutional structure where this was indeed the case. Eliot's missionary project purportedly sought a complete cultural conversion from indigenous society to English civility, yet Eliot also looked to native populations for affirmation of the Christianity that he believed to be true as well as for proof that his English brethren were on the correct spiritual errand. As Jean O'Brien explains in subtle and intricate detail, the "dispossession" of the Algonquian Indians in Natick Massachusetts was incremental, occurring in "degrees" rather than according to a model of complete assimilation. The natives maintained an important connection to the land, as familiar landmarks "defined their place in a created world inseparable from an Indian spiritual realm." Key Calvinist biblical passages such as Ezekiel 37 spoke across the Indian and English cultural divide.[15] Indian preachers came to place more emphasis on religious healing, rendering sin a visibly present bodily phenomenon such that it could speak directly to the material conditions of their lives.

This pattern of intensifying the embodied elements of Christianity also appears in Kanawake, "a Christian Iroquois Community" on the St. Lawrence River. According to Allan Greer, Kanawake was a place where Christianity was not simply imposed but rather reconfigured. Through the process of her conversion, Catherine Tekakwitha turned to extreme ascetic practices of self-flagellation and bodily mortification in an attempt to transcend the contradictory categories of Iroquois, Algonquin, Christian, and feminine that defined her life. Jesuit priest, Claude Chauchtière records her conversion experience in a hagiographical account that retells the colonial encounter through the micro-history of transformations that take place within this community. Upon finishing his formal academic study in France in the early seventeenth century, Chauchtière discovered that his own spiritual quest required that he travel beyond traditional boundaries of preconceived religious truths in order to seek evidence of God in new lands. Within his small missionary community on the banks of the St. Lawrence, Chauchtière finds Christian truths that exceed the ordered world of learned rationality. Catherine Tekawitha's conversion supplies evidence of a divine encounter that augments Chauchtière's own understanding of the inward transformation of the soul as he witnesses through her embodied practices a strange blend of Christian stoicism and Iroquoian practices of self-making. Mohawk saint and Jesuit priest mutually sought to reconcile the flux and transformation of the external world through an inwardly-directed spiritual journey. Chauchtière writes Tekakwitha's life in order to communicate the wisdom gained through this individual encounter to the Christian world, transforming the genre of the Catholic hagiography in order to bridge the seemingly contradictory categories of the saint and the savage, the virgin and the cannibal, the disempowered and those with transcendent power to heal.[16]

The uneven syncretism that permits Catherine Tekakwitha to salvage some elements of her Iroquoian faith along with her exemplary demonstration of Christian stoicism bespeaks a subtle and intricate process of self-fashioning and communal remaking that I am proposing as a defining feature of New World missionary communities. If the Spanish, French, and English had distinct notions of the purpose in their respective errands and different ways of establishing godly communities upon arriving in North and Latin America, the evangelical encounter served a parallel function for each group. In colonial New Mexico, the remotest corner of Spain's colonial American empire, Christian cosmologies sat uneasily upon the cosmologies of the Pueblo Indians. Sexuality and sacred cosmic harmony blended effortlessly for the Pueblo Indians, uniting the masculine and feminine forces of the sky and the earth. The Franciscans who settled in New Mexico in the seventeenth century, by contrast, were an ascetic group who believed that the perfection of the inner self depended upon a complete expurgation of sin as well as a forsaking of the material world. From 1581 to 1680, this group of Franciscans provided the impetus for colonization in New Mexico, organizing the Pueblo Indians into a theocracy that reordered their communal life until the Pueblo Revolt of 1680. The mission church replaced the Pueblo kiva as the architecture of social hierarchy. Pueblo kastinas, or objects collected to worship the ancestral dead, were destroyed and replaced with catechistical literature such as Fray Alonso de Molina's *Doctrina Christana*. The Franciscans made memorization integral to the process of conversion, but as in each missionary community discussed in this chapter, this process of conversion was not complete. Christian cosmologies did not fit neatly on top of Pueblo cosmologies.[17] Rather, what one sees in the Christian practices of the seventeenth century, constituted as incipient modern forms, is a complex process of layering that might be best described through the metaphor of a palimpsest. Dimensions of space, objects, and time carried over from pre-contact Pueblo culture into the Franciscan present, reshaping both through a mutual encounter that defined the early American community as a site of flux, integration, and transformation upon which European and indigenous survival depended.

Notes

1　Elliot (2007), p. 41.
2　For examples of mission closings, reopening, and resitings in New France, see John Corrigan and Tracy Leavelle, *French and Spanish Missions in North America* (2004), available at: http://www.ecai.org/na-missions/maps/MissionMaps.htm.
3　Kupperman (2007), p.14.
4　Kupperman (1988).
5　Jameson (1907), pp. 237–244.
6　Collett (1925), pp.36–37.

7   Winthrop (1825), pp. 121, 312.

8   This lay sermon was "The Model of Christian Charity." Winthrop uses the metaphor of being bound together through Christ's "ligaments of love" throughout to suggest both the cohesiveness of the visible church and to announce the project of the federal covenant, or the enfolding of disparate, individual covenants of grace into a collective, corporate body. While this is a rather idealized image of a form of spiritual equality, Winthrop's sermon also famously maintains a rigid social hierarchy in which some members of Christ's body form the head and others the feet (Gunn 1994: 108–112). As the testimony of faith became codified as an official genre of church membership, the Massachusetts General Court applied this language to explain the communal function of the test of faith:

> Saints by Calling, must have a Visible-Political-Union amongst themselves, or else they are not yet a particular church: as those similitudes hold forth which the Scripture makes use of, to show the nature of particular Churches: As a Body, A building, or House, Hands, Eyes, Feet & other members must be united, or else, remaining separate are not a body. Stones, timber, though squared, hewen, & polished, are not an house until they are compacted & united: so Saints or believers in judgment of charity, are not a church, unless Orderly knit together. (*A Platform of Church Discipline: Gathered out of the Word of God: And Agreed Upon by the Elders and Messengers of the Churches* (Cambridge: Samuel Green, 1649), p. 5)

9   *The Colonial Laws of Massachusetts* (Boston: Rockwell and Churchill, City Printers, 1890) 57 and 59.

10 Waters (1905), p. 87. The freeman's oath was basically a simple supplement to the public profession of saving faith. According to Cornelia Hughes Dayton, this was also the case in Connecticut, as established by the Fundamental Agreement for laws of civil government, written and signed in June 1639. "The agreement emphasized that the franchise would be limited, as it was in the Bay Colony, to male church members, those who had made a convincing public relation of their conversion and faith and who were then the only worshipers who took communion on Sacrament Sundays and voted in church affairs" (1905: 24).

11 Pope (1975), p. 4.

12 Eliot's Indian Library included: The Bible, Bayly's *Practice of Piety*, *The Indian Primer*, Baxter's *Call to the Unconverted*, and *A Christian Covenanting Confession*, among other texts.

13 Wyss (2000); Bragdon (1996).

14 Thomas Shepard Jr. Letter, September 9, 1673, Woodrow Collection, Edinburgh, National Library of Scotland.

15 O'Brien (1997), p. 15.

16 Greer (2005).

17 The history of the Pueblo Indians has been eloquently accounted for in Ramón A. Guitiérrez, (1991) *When Jesus Came, the Corn Mothers Went Away: Marriage, Sexuality, and Power in New Mexico, 1500–1846*.

References

Bragdon, Kathleen (1996) "Gender as a Social Category in Native Southern New England," *Ethnography*, 43(4): ???.

Collett, Henry (1925) *Little Gidding and Its Founder: An Account of the Religious Community Established by Nicholas Ferrar in the XVIIth Century*, London: Society for Promoting Christian Knowledge.

Corrigan, John and Leavelle, Tracy (2004) *French and Spanish Missions in North America*, Berkeley, CA: University of California and California Digital Library.

Elliot, John H. (2007) *Empires of the Atlantic World: Britain and Spain in America, 1492–1830*, New Haven, CT: Yale University Press.

Greer, Allan (2005) *Mohawk Saint: Catherine Tekakwitha and the Jesuits*, Oxford; Oxford University Press.

Guitiérrez, Ramón A. (1991) *When Jesus Came, the Corn Mothers Went Away: Marriage, Sexuality, and Power in New Mexico, 1500–1846*, Stanford, CA: Stanford University Press.

Gunn, Giles (ed.) (1994) *Early American Writing*, New York: Penguin Books.

Jameson, Frandlin J. (1907) *Narratives of Early Virginia*, New York: Charles Scribner's Sons.

Kupperman, Karen (ed.) (1988) *Captain John Smith: A Select Edition of His Writings*, Chapel Hill, NC: University of North Carolina Press.

Kupperman, Karen (2007) *The Jamestown Project*, Cambridge, MA: Belknap Press of Harvard University Press.

O'Brien, Jean (1997) *Dispossession by Degrees: Indian Land and Identity in Natick, Massachusetts, 1650–1790*, Lincoln, NE: University of Nebraska Press.

Pope, Robert G. (ed.) (1975) *The Notebook of Reverend John Fiske, 1644–1675*, Boston: Publications of the Colonial Society of Massachusetts.

Waters, Thomas Franklin (1905) *Ipswich in the Massachusetts Colony*, Ipswich: The Ipswich Historical Society.

Winthrop, John (1825) *History of New England from 1630 to 1649*, Boston: Phelps and Farnham.

Wyss, Hillary E. (2000) *Writing Indians: Literacy, Christianity, and Native Community in Early America*, Amherst, MA: University of Massachusetts Press.

4

Practice

Tracy N. Leavelle

Over five hundred years ago in the high desert near the Rio Grande members of a Pueblo ritual society descended into their kiva, an underground ceremonial chamber. There, they conducted rituals to restore harmony in the community and in the world and to call back the kachinas who nourished the dry fields of corn with live-giving rain. The people could see in the dim light colorful figures dancing on the walls. Warriors with enormous shields. Birds, snakes, and mountain lions. Beings half-human and half-insect. Archaeologists know this ancient Pueblo village as Pottery Mound. The murals that decorated the walls of the seventeen kivas in the village reflected the intimate relationships that existed between members of this community and the powerful spirits that populated their world. The paintings also recalled the rituals that took place in those ceremonial spaces, long before the arrival of Europeans.

Images on the walls of one of the kivas show what appear to be dancers in a rain ceremony. A masked male dancer wears a patterned kilt, white shirt and sash, and feathered head dress. He carries ritual objects in his hands, a water pot and a feathered item that may have been used to sprinkle the water in simulation of rain. The flowing sash, the bent legs of the figure, and the placement of his arms, one above his shoulder and the other at his waist, suggest the movements of the dance. He is joined by a similarly attired female dancer who also seems to be wearing a mask. A bird figure, possibly a Swallow kachina, hovers between them.

In places like the Hopi Pueblos on the Colorado Plateau, kachinas have for centuries acted as mediators between the human and the other-than-human worlds. In a series of ceremonies from winter to summer, the kachinas return to the Hopi villages bearing water and gifts. In the distant past the kachinas themselves traveled from their homes in the mountains and springs, but later they came only in spirit, in the songs and dances and masks of ceremony. The dancer wearing a kachina mask becomes that being for a time and actively embodies in his ritual dress and his actions the spiritual relationships that create harmony in the world (Figure 4.1).

The murals at Pottery Mound are a testament in paint and plaster to the vibrancy of the religious life that existed in these Native villages. If the precise meaning of each of the murals remains obscure, the paintings nevertheless capture the intricate choreography of people and objects that helped establish and maintain essential connections

Figure 4.1 John Vanderlyn's *Columbus landing in the Bahamas*, 1847. Vanderlyn's Indians cower at the fringes of the piece, witnessing to the perception that Columbus' landing was a protrusion of European civilization into an otherwise uncivilized wilderness.

between villagers and the spirits that sustained them. The murals represent particular forms of religious practice, ways in which people performed or put in motion what they believed about the world and its spiritual significance. Religious practice incorporates a broad range of activities formally embedded in community traditions. Ceremonies, prayers, songs, the veneration of holy objects, ritualized suffering, visits to sacred sites, and methods of marking space and time as religiously important are all forms of religious practice. The events of everyday life, moreover, often offer opportunities for the invention of new forms of religious practice, through the adaptation of seemingly profane activities – that is, those that bear no special cosmic meanings – to religious ends. Such innovation often proceeds on a personal basis as it develops outside the familiar categories of formal religious observance. Accordingly, a strong personal attachment to certain objects – a unique stone found frozen in ice, or a feather that fell from the sky as a rainbow appeared – can form a substantial part of religious practice as it is enacted outside the usual categories of devotion. By the same token, certain activities in which people daily engage – eating, drinking, dressing, running, kissing, sneezing ("Gesundheit!"/"Bless you!"), and stepping over cracks on the sidewalk – frequently acquire an importance based on a perceived linkage of those actions to a larger cosmic scheme of things. Europeans of course arrived in North America with their own formal religious practice, and, once settled, enlarged and refined that practice with respect to everyday life, so that for them, as in the case of Native Americans, religious practice was expansive, fluid, dynamic, and at times even contradictory. In early America, encounters between Natives and newcomers were particularly important for the development of religious practice. Encounter supported the continuation of some older practices while also encouraging the creation of new ones that responded to religious needs in a changing world. Confronting differences between and within communities inspired creativity as well as reactionary violence.

Spiritual Encounters and Ceremonies of Possession

Europeans entered the Pueblo world in the 1540s, within a century or so of the creation of the last Pottery Mound mural. The oral traditions of Native peoples across North America contain prophecies and dreams that described the imminent arrival of these strangers from a distant land.

A Micmac oral tradition from the Northeast coast of the continent remembers, "When there were no people in this country but Indians, and before any others were known, a young woman had a singular dream. She dreamed that a small island came floating in towards the land, with tall trees on it, and living beings, – among whom was a man dressed in rabbit-skin garments" (Calloway 1994: 33). Dreams in many Indian cultures offered opportunities for contact with powerful spirits and also provided potential insight into future events. They required careful attention and interpretation.

In the account, the young woman consulted the healers and ceremonial specialists in her community, but they could not divine the dream's meaning. The next day they learned. "Getting up in the morning," the story continues, "what should they see but a singular little island, as they supposed, which had drifted near to the land and become stationary there! There were trees on it, and branches to the trees, on which a number of bears, as they supposed, were crawling about" (Calloway 1994: 34). The island of course turned out to be a ship and the bears were strangely bearded men. Among them was a priest in white who spoke in an unknown tongue. According to the tale, despite the opposition of traditional healers, the priest successfully introduced Christianity to the community, translating his "Prayer Book" into the Native language.

The dream and the oral tradition that preserved it provided some guidance for interpreting such moments of uncertainty and change. They fit the meeting into a larger Native cultural context and explained the results of the encounter with Europeans. The "Prayer Book" created by the priest contained Christian and Micmac influences. Such patterns of encounter and exchange were common in early American religious encounters.

Europeans also sought spiritual guidance in their affairs. The four voyages Columbus made to the Americas between 1492 and 1504 were primarily business ventures, but enlarging the empire of Christ remained an important objective. Although supporters hoped the voyages would be financially successful, Columbus and others saw divine purpose in the enterprise. Columbus refused to set sail on Sundays and looked for signs of God's will in the events of the journey. In 1501, after his third voyage, Columbus began compiling a manuscript that his son called *The Book of Prophecies*. Columbus used the collection of biblical and philosophical texts to demonstrate his prominent role in the unfolding drama of human salvation.

According to a log of Columbus's first voyage, the tired and frustrated sailors recited a Salve Regina in honor of the Virgin Mary when they finally saw signs of land. They reached a small island on 12 October and "soon they saw naked people."

The nudity of the island Natives distinguished them from the Spanish visitors, who believed absence of clothing corresponded to the absence of civilization. Columbus remarked on their physical beauty and their gentleness, but his limited understanding of the world did not allow him to see anything that he could recognize as culture. Furthermore, the people did not appear to have religion, which made them attractive targets for conversion (Symcox and Sullivan 2005: 65–71).

Columbus and his crew unfurled two banners with green crosses and the initials of Ferdinand and Isabella, king and queen of Spain, to take possession of the island. The presence of witnesses, the declarations of discovery, and written testimonials confirmed the claim. Columbus exchanged goods with the Indians, always seeking information about the location of gold. The Indians seemed content to trade spun cotton for small coins or pieces of broken glass. Columbus interpreted this as an inability to determine value, further evidence of savagery. Of course, in Native terms the objects may have had more value than the admiral appreciated. Unusual and colorful objects were attractive as decorative items, but they could also provide access to new forms of spiritual power. The exchange of gifts was not simply a trade in inanimate objects from this perspective, but rather a method of acquiring power. In any case, the Indians soon sent Columbus on his way, telling him to look elsewhere for the piles of gold he so desired.

A generation later another Spaniard applied the perceived connection between nudity and savagery to his own situation. Alvar Núñez Cabeza de Vaca was one of only four survivors of the disastrous Narváez expedition to Florida, which sailed in 1527. Narváez took possession of the region, like Columbus, by raising the banners of the king and completing other official acts. From there the situation deteriorated rapidly and around three hundred men died in the failed effort to colonize Florida. Cabeza de Vaca managed to travel along the Gulf Coast to present-day Texas, where Indians captured and held him for several years.

In the preface to his narrative of the experience, dedicated to the Holy Roman Emperor Charles V (also Charles I of Spain), Cabeza de Vaca explained that all he had to offer was the information he had gathered "in ten years during which I wandered lost and naked through many and very strange lands." Throughout the narrative he contrasted these strange and savage lands with the settled, Christian lands of Europe and the Spanish colonies in the Americas. His own nakedness marked his temporary loss of civilization, but not his faith in God. Cabeza de Vaca framed the entire experience as an expression of "the will and judgment of God," as he put it. He believed that the knowledge he acquired in the harrowing ordeal might be "of no little use to those who [in the emperor's] name will go to conquer those lands and bring them to the knowledge of the true Faith and the true lordship and service of Your Majesty" (Cabeza de Vaca 1993: 3–4).

Cabeza de Vaca survived his odyssey in part by adopting and modifying practices he witnessed in the Indian communities of the Gulf Coast region. In a reversal of intentions the Spaniard became the convert, required to learn the ways of a new culture and religion. Cabeza de Vaca escaped from one group of Indians after a year as a virtual slave and used his status as an outsider to all the communities to act effectively as a trader. He traveled for almost six years from village to village trading coastal items used in medicine and ceremonies for hides, flint, and body paint.

Eventually reunited with the only remaining survivors of the disaster, Cabeza de Vaca discovered that he and his companions could combine Christian prayer with

Native rituals to become powerful healers. One evening some Indians arrived complaining of terrible headaches and asking to be healed. One of the Spaniards made the sign of the cross and commended them to God. They recovered and rewarded the famished men with food. Later, Indians asked Cabeza de Vaca to examine a man who appeared to have died. "I took off a reed mat with which he was covered," he recorded, "and as best I could implored Our Lord to be pleased to give health to that man and all others who had need of it" (Cabeza de Vaca 1993: 72). He made the sign of the cross and blew on the man many times, as Native healers did. The Indians reported that the gravely ill man recovered, along with numerous others who received treatment. The power and prestige that came with these spectacular cures provided the means to journey from community to community until they finally found their way to the Christian lands of Mexico.

The voyages of Columbus and the failed Narváez expedition show how intertwined religion and empire were in the colonial era (Figure 4.2). The expansion of political dominion and commercial ventures took place alongside the expansion of Christendom. Ceremonies of possession reveal these close connections. In the Spanish case, colonial officials attempted to regulate the process of encounter through which new lands and peoples were brought into their possession. They issued the *Requirimiento*, a legal document read aloud in Spanish to uncomprehending Native peoples. The ritualistic reading of the *Requirimiento* explained that God had granted the Spanish, through his representative the Pope, the power to govern. The document demanded that Indians submit to Spanish rule and to the authority of God. Resistance created the necessary legal conditions for military conquest.

In 1540, Francisco Vázquez de Coronado arrived at the Zuni pueblo in New Mexico. The Zunis feared the Spanish, already having had some negative encounters with them. Warriors met the Spanish expedition outside the villages and used sacred cornmeal to make lines in the dirt, to create a powerful barrier against the invaders. Coronado identified his mission as peaceful and holy; he represented the Spanish monarchs and the God who granted them power in this world. A Native interpreter translated the words of the *Requirimiento*. The Zunis refused to submit and instead fired arrows at the outsiders. The expedition suffered casualties, but eventually defeated the Zunis and took control of their towns. Pueblo peoples have never forgotten the violence of Spanish conquests.

More than a thousand miles to the north and east the French mariner Jacques Cartier explored the bays of the Saint Lawrence River valley and made contact with the people who lived in the surrounding forests. The French dreamed of building an empire in the Americas, one that would produce the same kind of wealth the Spanish acquired. Like their colonial competitors, the French also hoped to contribute to the spread of Christianity. French ceremonies of possession were similar to Spanish ones, although they often depended on the active participation, rather than the passive acceptance, of Native peoples.

Cartier recorded that on the first of his three voyages to the region, in 1534, his men assembled and erected a 30-foot cross in the presence of Indians at the entrance to Gaspé Harbor. They attached to the cross a shield decorated with the fleur-de-lys, the symbol of French monarchs. A sign proclaimed, "Long live the King of France." Cartier recorded,

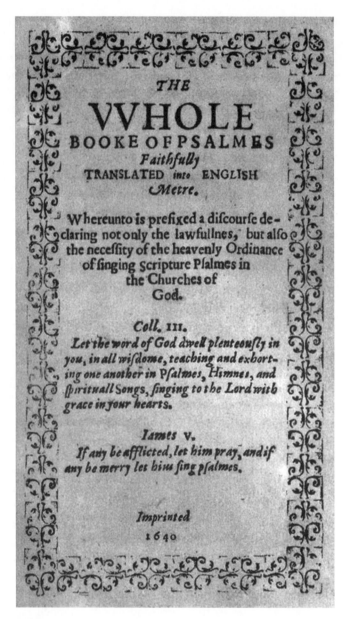

Figure 4.2 The first book published in New England, *The Whole Booke of Psalms*, more commonly known as "The Bay Psalm Book," was one of the most important elements of both private and public religious practices.

And when it had been raised in the air, we all knelt down with our hands joined, worshipping it before them; and made signs to them, looking up and pointing towards heaven, that by means of this we had our redemption, at which they showed many marks of admiration, at the same time turning and looking at the cross. (Cartier 1993: 26–27)

As it happened, Cartier's Native counterpart did not appreciate the apparent claims to the land. He complained loudly about the cross and consented to leave it standing only when the French offered gifts and the promise of alliance. The Indians wanted to trade, not become French Catholics. For the next two centuries many Indians and French found common ground through trade, the foundation for the French empire in North America, although the first permanent French settlement did not appear until 1608 at Quebec. Evangelization of Indians soon followed.

In 1675, the French missionary Jacques Marquette of the Society of Jesus (the Jesuits) started a mission among the Illinois Indians that lasted for almost a century. He orchestrated an elaborate pageant to open the mission and thus to begin incorporating the people and the place into the Christian world. Marquette covered a prairie with mats and bearskins for his guests and "stretch[ed] out upon Lines several pieces of Chinese taffeta, [and] attached to these four large Pictures of the blessed Virgin, which were visible on all Sides" (Thwaites, *JR* 59: 187–189). Hundreds of people arrived for the event and arrayed themselves around the priest. As he shared his message with the audience, he punctuated each of his major points with a gift to the leaders of the village. This method of speaking with gifts was a common practice in the region. Marquette wisely adopted the practice to demonstrate his respect for local customs and to communicate more effectively. The missionary closed the ceremony with a public mass.

The English in the seventeenth century marked their colonial possessions with settlements more often than with missions or trading posts. In New England, more families than traders and soldiers made the perilous ocean voyage, and the contours of religious life thus differed a great deal from those in New France and New Spain. John Winthrop led the Puritans to Massachusetts Bay in 1630 to create a community dedicated to holy living in a reformed church free of popish practices. Winthrop wrote in 1629:

> It will be a service to the Church of great consequence to carry the Gospel into those parts of the world, to help on the coming of the fullness of the Gentiles, and to raise a Bulwark against the kingdom of the Anti-Christ … All other Churches of Europe are brought to desolation.

He concluded, "the [true] Church has no place left to flee into but the wilderness." Winthrop proposed the erection not of a cross but of a "city upon a hill," a pious community that could act as a beacon of faith to the corrupted world (Gaustad 1982: 104–107).

Communal and Personal Practice

Winthrop's influential sermon on the *Arbella* before landing in New England offered a covenant of loving practice that would bind the members of the community to one another and to God. "That which the most (in their Church) maintain as a truth in profession only, we must bring into familiar and constant practice," he urged, "we must love one another with a pure heart fervently; we must bear one another's burdens" (Gaustad 1982: 104–107). Winthrop also warned that neglect of these Christian duties would surely ignite God's wrath. In the first generation, the era of the Great Migration, the Puritans established a rigorous routine of religious practice intended to nurture these values and sustain a community of the elect.

Winthrop was a lawyer, not a minister, but his shipboard message highlighted the providential nature of their endeavor and reminded them that God's Word ordered the covenant that bound them together. Sermons like his remained at the center of public ceremonial life in New England through several generations.

Services on the Sabbath took up most of the day, from morning to the late afternoon. Morning and afternoon sessions lasted about two hours each. A typical order included an extemporaneous opening prayer, followed by a scriptural reading and the long sermon that interpreted it. After the sermon, the congregation sang together from the psalms, another opportunity to engage with scripture. Local official and judge Samuel Sewall recorded in his diary entry for 16 September 1688 that the Reverend Samuel Willard of Boston's South Church preached from Hebrews 12:11 in the morning and Ecclesiastes 7:29 in the afternoon. The congregation sang Psalm 126 in the early service, from the 19th Psalm in the afternoon, and, finally, from the 84th Psalm in the evening. For Sewall and many others, Sunday was a highly regimented day of prayer, rest, and reflection.

Ministers preached on other occasions as well. There were sermons for weekday services, days of fasting and thanksgiving, and election days. These opportunities allowed the minister to reinforce corporate values and comment regularly on important events in the community.

New England Calvinists did not recognize the calendar of religious feasts and celebrations that so many other Europeans followed, finding no scriptural basis for it. Therefore, they refused to acknowledge such holidays as Christmas, Easter, and saints days. They readily set aside certain days for extraordinary religious practice when circumstances warranted, however. Outbreaks of disease, defeats on the battlefield, and community conflicts prompted the public observance of days of humiliation and fasting. Hours of fiery sermons documented the terrible sins that had invited suffering. Confession of these sins and rituals of self-affliction and prayerful repentance offered a chance for renewal.

A fast in May 1639 ended a drought that threatened crops. The timely rain promised a bountiful harvest. In the town of Scituate in 1637, a fast eased tensions between supporters of rival ministers. Later in the year, church members concluded a day of fasting by renewing the covenant of peace and love that bound them together. Some years after, sickness visited the town and villagers responded with a day of humiliation.

The following Spring, they thanked God with a feast for his abundant mercy in preserving the health of so many of their children. Deliverance from a drought or an epidemic or military victory called for such days of praise and thanksgiving. The highly mythologized "First Thanksgiving" celebrated at Plymouth in 1621 was not strictly speaking a religious ceremony in this tradition. The event constituted rather a harvest festival and ritual sharing of food that had more to do with intercultural relations between Europeans and Indians than with relations to God. On days set aside for religious celebration, ministers reminded their listeners that only God's freely given gift of grace – his will, not theirs – accounted for the undeserved blessings they had received. At the same time, participation in these rituals allowed people to feel that they could act in times of crisis in ways that might return individuals and communities to lives of peace and joy more properly in tune with Providence.

Samuel Sewall participated in about a hundred fasts according to his diary, many of them private and centered on the specific concerns of himself and his family. Sewall organized a private fast in his home when his son Hull became extremely ill and suffered two seizures. He invited the magistrates of the town and their wives to join his family in prayer. The well-known missionary to New England Indians, John Eliot, opened the fast with a prayer. Reverend Willard spoke on the biblical text "I am afraid of Thy judgments." The group rested for half an hour after another prayer by the minister of First Church. In the afternoon Cotton Mather led a prayer and his father Increase Mather presented another sermon, on Psalm 79:9. Finally, Joshua Moodey prayed for "about an hour and half" and the participants sang a portion of the 79th Psalm. Sewall shared some food as well as beer, cider, and wine with his guests to break the fast and end the day of prayer. Sewall closed the entry with a request that "the Lord hear [these prayers] in Heaven his dwelling place" (Sewall 1973, vol. 1: 63).

Sewall's diary also reveals in many places the intensity of the pressure some people felt in this spiritual environment of deadly and damning sin. Calvinists taught that God reserved salvation for only a few fortunate souls. Local laws required church attendance, but membership was limited to those who could demonstrate a sincere conversion experience as well as good character. In January of 1677, at the age of 23, Sewall went to the Reverend Thomas Thacher of South Church to discuss his "desire of communion with his Church." Sewall remained uncertain, however, about his spiritual fitness and "rehearsed to him some of [his] discouragements, [such] as, continuance in Sin, [and] wandering in prayer" (Sewall 1973, vol. 1: 33). Joining a church was an important step on the pilgrimage from sin to salvation, but searching the soul for signs of sanctifying grace proved difficult. Ministers and church members expected to see clear evidence that God had chosen the petitioner for inclusion in the kingdom of Heaven.

Sewall spent considerable time examining his own soul and consulting others for advice over the next two months. Doubt plagued him. He worried about his prideful nature and "startled at the daring height of such wickedness." Thacher encouraged him, saying that God seemed to be leading him to the Church, and Sewall finally joined the congregation. "I, together with Gilbert Cole, was admitted into Mr. Thacher's Church," he recorded in his diary, "making a Solemn covenant to take the [Lord] Jehovah for our God, and to walk in Brotherly Love and watchfulness to Edification" (Sewall 1973, vol. 1: 36–40). Sewall stood before the congregation and shared his relation. Standards of modesty insisted that women speak privately with the minister, rather than before the entire congregation, and their written testimonies were read aloud. On that day in Boston, all were admitted in prayer.

With his admission to the church, Sewall was ready to share communion with his spiritual brothers and sisters and to offer his children for baptism. Only the cultivation of rigorous spiritual discipline could ensure his continued growth and his desired advancement toward the Kingdom of Heaven. Sewall wrote in his diary the day after his admission to the church, "I have been, and am, under great exercise of mind with regard to my Spiritual Estate … I think I shall sit down tomorrow to the Lords Table, and I fear I shall be an unworthy partaker" (Sewall 1973, vol. 1: 41).

He had reason to be concerned. Regular Sabbath worship was an "ordinary" means of grace, celebrated regularly and open to all. The sacraments of the Lord's Supper and baptism – the only two sacraments the Puritans recognized – were "special" in that they were restricted to church members in good standing and administered only on occasion. Congregations participated in the Lord's Supper from six to twelve times per year and offered the sacrament of baptism as needed. Baptism cleansed the soul and attached the child to the savior in a holy covenant. Communion prompted engagement with the real presence of Christ, which in turn offered the renewal of faith, a strengthening of grace, and further growth of the spirit.

Ministers announced the celebration of the Eucharist in advance so people could prepare themselves with appropriate devotional exercises. On the day of the sacrament, usually during the morning service, the pastor dismissed non-members after the sermon and the psalms. Church elders went to a table in front for the blessing of the bread and wine. The minister took the bread and wine first, followed by the elders. The congregation received first the bread then the wine in their pews. They did not kneel at the altar as in Catholic practice. At the end of the performance the congregation joined in a psalm of thanksgiving. The communal rite reinforced the boundaries of an exclusive community and, for participants, perpetuated the existence of the holy remnant that maintained the ideals of the biblical church. Breaking bread and drinking from the cup, the congregation traveled together from a state of sin to union with Christ, from repentance to redemption.

Private prayer and devotional practice prepared people for these public rituals and extended the drama of salvation into the home. The home was an additional meeting-house for the practice of piety, the family a "little commonwealth" that mirrored the larger the society that surrounded it (Demos 1970). A typical pattern of family-oriented religious practice included morning and evening prayers, scripture reading, psalm singing, and thanksgiving at meals.

In the Anglican parishes of the Chesapeake Bay region, religious practice tended to center on the home out of necessity. A shortage of clergy that lasted well into the eighteenth century forced more responsibility for worship and religious education on the lay population. In the 1660s, four out of five Virginia parishes had no ministers. By 1680, the situation had improved some. Thirty-five ministers covered two-thirds of the parishes. Settlement patterns contributed to the problem. The emphasis on tobacco cultivation encouraged farmers to settle along rivers on widely scattered plots of land. Parishes generally contained more than one church, so ministers rotated services from one to the other. The Book of Common Prayer provided the order for the services as well as a strong link to the Anglican establishment in England. Yet, even essential public rites like the Lord's Supper could only be offered three or four times a year.

With opportunities for formal public worship so limited, private devotion became the foundation for Anglican practice in the Chesapeake. Members of the church read their Bibles and other religious texts, worshiped together as families, and engaged in silent prayer and self-reflection. Encouraged by their ministers and inspired by the divine example of Christ, Anglicans cultivated an active faith that emphasized the expression of virtue in daily life. Virginians frequently turned to the metaphor of the voyage, fresh in the minds of many who had made the Atlantic crossing, to describe their pilgrimage toward Heaven.

The religious lives of the slaves who began arriving in increasing numbers through the seventeenth century are less well documented. Colonists hesitated to instruct them in Christianity because they feared it would weaken the legal case for lifelong bondage that supported the emerging labor regime in the southern colonies. Africans in America also represented an amazingly diverse range of cultures and communities. Languages, social organization, and ceremonial practices differed a great deal from people to people. Many originated from Islamic societies in northern Africa. Although Africans endured what one scholar has termed "a spiritual holocaust," over time, especially in the eighteenth and nineteenth centuries, practices developed that included both African and Christian elements (Butler 1990).

Similar trends toward religious combination appeared in the encounters between American Indians and Christian missionaries. In the Illinois mission founded by Marquette, women discovered in Christianity an avenue toward increased social and spiritual power beginning in the 1690s. Marie Rouensa, the teenaged daughter of a prominent Illinois chief, was a leader of this women's movement. Taking control of their bodies and their sexuality, Rouensa and several other women refused marriages arranged by their families to men, French and Indian, who failed to accept Christianity as they did. Rouensa developed a rich Catholic spiritual practice in consultation with her Jesuit mentor that showed connections to older Illinois ways.

The Illinois and other Native peoples lived in a land populated by spirits, a world that contained great spiritual power. The Illinois used the complex concept *manitou*, translated by the Jesuits as "spirit, God … medicine," to describe these spirits as well as their power (Leavelle 2007: 376). There was also a sense in which beings, human and other-than-human, could become *manitou*, in other words, powerful or extraordinary. Productive reciprocal relationships with manitous were essential to operating successfully in the world.

Young men and women sought contact with a personal manitou when they came of age in the community. They left the village for days of fasting and self-affliction, hoping to identify and develop a strong relationship with a spirit that would guide and protect them. Illinois men relied on the manitous associated with animals for support in their activities. Men gathered in a cabin when preparing for war and spread their birds out together on a large mat. They sang and chanted over them throughout the long night, "saying: stone falcon, or crow, I pray to you that when I pursue the enemy I may go with the same speed in running as you do in flying, in order that I may be admired by my comrades and feared by our enemies" (Deliette 1934: 375–376). The skins offered access to the spirits of the birds as well as to the qualities these feathered creatures possessed.

At the onset of puberty young women left the village to fast and pray in isolation until they formed a relationship with their personal manitou. A French trader remembered, "When [the spirit] has spoken to them they are always happy and achieve the gift of great power as regards the future" (Deliette 1934: 353–354). From then on at the first sign of menstruation the women separated themselves from the community in small huts where only other menstruating women were allowed access. They renewed reciprocal relationships with their manitous through rituals of respect and exchange. Rouensa continued such practices as a Christian, isolating herself for fasting, prayer, and self-affliction, just as women had for generations. In this case, however, she directed prayers to Jesus and to her divine Mother and spiritual namesake, Mary, rather than to Illinois manitous.

Material Culture in Life and Death

For the Illinois and many other Native people, material items offered access to spiritual power. Native Catholics like Marie Rouensa rapidly incorporated rosary beads and crucifixes into their religious practices. The beads connected them with Christian religious figures in much the same way that feathers and other ritual items linked them to indigenous healing spirits. Allouez reported that a Mesquakie, or Fox, man always carried his rosary with him and used the beads to guide and concentrate his prayers. When the man's wife, children, and nephews became ill, many people in his village blamed the beads. The man argued that his continued good health was a result of his devotional practices.

Ultimately French missionaries hoped to attract such men and women to their simple wooden chapels. Consecrated to God, these rough buildings represented holy ground. In them, members of the community gathered to practice the catechism, sing hymns, and participate in the sacraments. Native people studied inexpensive printed images to learn biblical stories and contemplated the death and resurrection of Christ when they gazed on the crucifix above the altar. Even far from the towns on the St. Lawrence, priests imported ceremonial items that added beauty and drama to the primitive space. Such treasures held the wine and the sacred host for the Eucharist, a reminder of the real reward that awaited the faithful in death.

In New England, the construction of a church, or meetinghouse, in each town represented a first step toward the formation of a holy community and the sacralization of the landscape. New England towns built over 220 meetinghouses in the seventeenth century. These places of assembly and worship stood at the center of the towns, often on elevated ground, a symbol of the spiritual and communal orientation of the people. The sacred character of the meetinghouse revealed itself in the gathering of people before a minister to share the holy Word. If the succession of services guided people in time, the meetinghouse anchored the community in space.

Seventeenth-century meetinghouses in New England tended to be rather simple and plain, a physical expression of Puritan theology and evidence of what one scholar has called "a new Protestant vernacular." In this view, places and objects could not themselves become sacred. Meetinghouses merely provided the physical space for sharing the holy Word within a covenanted community. Yet, they also signified the presence of Christian civilization in a "wilderness" of sin. Builders deliberately avoided the extravagant decoration and detail of the parish churches in England, considered a legacy of Catholicism and its many corruptions. The Calvinist critique of Anglicanism is clear. The residents of Dedham, Massachusetts, constructed a wooden meetinghouse in 1638 so small that it could have fit inside the large stone structure they left behind in Dedham, Essex County, England. The dozens of churches erected in New England prior to 1680 were all built of wood. Artistic flourishes appeared not in stained glass and statues, but in the careful craftsmanship of the building itself.

The Old Ship Church in Hingham, Massachusetts (still standing, although much changed since its 1681 construction) shows that simple designs could in their execution achieve excellence and beauty. According to a recent description:

> Balconies on three sides surround a beautifully paneled pulpit … Its woodworking is as elegant as anything possible in the colony at the time. Behind it are two round-headed pulpit windows, and in front of the pulpit is a pew with a hinged table leaf for the Lord's Supper … The whole ensemble is an elaborate piece of woodworking. (Finney 1999: 462–463 and 479–485)

In these spaces, the Bible and its interpretation dominated proceedings. The Bible was a book, a physical object printed by men, but it was also the sacred vessel that carried the Word of God. Reading the Bible or hearing its words provided contact with the Holy Spirit. The Word came alive on the page and in the air, possessing the power to penetrate the heart and soul with grace. Thus, the Bible had a presence in the life of many people that helped bridge the physical world with the spiritual. The Bible was a physical reminder of God's divine presence.

Bible passages became intimately familiar, a part of daily life. Parents forged a connection with the text when they turned to the Bible to find names for their children. People searched through the book and sifted their memories for an appropriate passage during moments of difficulty or indecision. Scripture provided a text for living. Samuel Sewall recalled 1 Corinthians 10:31 when he heard about a woman who had choked to death on a piece of meat: "Whether therefore ye eat, or drink, or whatsoever ye do, do all to the glory of God." He later visited a sick woman and when they spoke about the unfortunate incident, she quoted precisely the same verse. For Sewall, this convergence was not a coincidence. It was evidence of God's voice in human affairs.

Other books also became a part of private and public worship. The Book of Common Prayer was familiar in Virginia households. In New England, *The Whole Booke of Psalms*, popularly known as "The Bay Psalm Book," was one of the most important. Psalm singing was a regular part of Sabbath services and for the devout an element of family worship in the home. Printers in New England did not have permission to print the Bible, so copies arrived by ship. "The Bay Psalm Book" appeared in 1640 and was the first book published in New England. A committee of ministers completed a new translation of the Book of Psalms and used the newly installed press in Cambridge to print it. The book was so popular that it was reprinted seven times before 1700 and even became a good seller in England.

People like Sewall turned to these sacred texts for comfort and guidance during difficult times. They thumbed well-worn pages searching for the words to heal or to inspire further devotion. At no time was this more important than when death visited a community. Puritan funerals were simple affairs in strictly religious terms. There was no sacrament that corresponded to the Catholic last rites. Yet, even in Puritan New England the compulsion to mark the transition from this world to the next was strong. Burial rituals offered an opportunity for families and communities to gather in memory of the deceased and to contemplate the questions large and small that accompanied any direct encounter with reality of death.

Families sent invitations to the funeral that often included gloves and gold rings. These symbolic items associated so closely with marriage ceremonies recalled the spiritual union of Christ with the faithful. Mourners arrived at the meetinghouse with long black mourning cloaks, large white scarves draped around their necks, and the gloves and gold rings on their hands. After a sermon, a line of wagons and coaches carried the coffin and the mourners to the burial ground. Bells tolled in the town. The community offered prayers at the grave site and the coffin was lowered into the ground. The family of the deceased often hosted a feast of food and wine afterward. The decorated tombstone stood as a record of the brief life of the deceased as well as a physical reminder of the inevitability of death itself. The funeral rites and the grave marker posed the question: would others be ready when their time came?

Winged death's heads and skulls were popular icons on New England gravestones by the 1670s. In flight at the top of the marker, they represented the ultimate triumph and the terror of death. The physical decay of the body after interment in the earth foreshadowed the eternal misery of the poor soul destined to suffer forever in hell. Imps and demons carrying arrows of death, hourglasses, and scythes were a further reminder of the intersection of temporal and spiritual concerns. On a stone carved for Thomas Call in 1676, hourglasses, crossed bones, shovels, and coffins flank a large skull crowned by another hourglass, winged and in flight. For Puritans who generally avoided such decorative symbols in other places, the funerary art they saw in the burial ground must have represented a profound expression of their feelings towards the passage of time and the significance of death.

About a year before the funeral of Thomas Call, far to the west, on the shores of Lake Michigan, the French Jesuit missionary Jacques Marquette prepared for his own journey beyond the physical world. A good, Christian death promised union with God. According to an account penned by Claude Dablon, his superior in the Society of Jesus, Marquette spent long days in prayer and reflection. As snow fell in December 1674, he participated in the annual Ignatian retreat.

Saint Ignatius of Loyola, who founded the Society in 1540, created the *Spiritual Exercises* to guide the members of his order and other pious individuals to a closer and more intimate relationship with God. The *Exercises* demanded a rigorous process of self-examination and spiritual discernment that allowed the person to understand and express fully the will of God in his or her own life. A series of intense meditations on the Passion of Christ supported identification with the suffering and sacrifice of Jesus and placed the retreatant in that story of salvation. Jesuits participated in month-long retreats twice during their formation and in shorter eight-day exercises each year thereafter. The *Exercises* were the absolute foundation of Jesuit spiritual practice. Dablon recorded that Marquette "performed [them] with every feeling of devotion, and many Celestial Consolations" (Thwaites, *JR* v. 59: 187). Finally, the missionary expired, and his companions buried him. They rang a bell to signal the occasion and planted a cross to mark the grave. Dablon believed that Marquette had experienced a good Christian death. The record would serve as an example to others.

The first sign that Marquette's life and death were remarkable came soon after his body was covered with earth. One of the missionary's companions prayed next to the grave and pressed some of the fresh soil to his breast, asking that Marquette intercede and heal a lingering illness. Dablon explained that "immediately his sickness Abated, and his sorrow was changed into a Joy."

Two years later, Ottawa Indians from the Jesuit mission at Michilimackinac arrived to retrieve the remains of the missionary. They exhumed Marquette's body and "cleansed the bones and exposed them to the sun to dry; then, carefully laying them in a box of birch-bark, they set out to bring them to [the] mission of st. Ignace" (Thwaites, *JR* v. 59: 201–205). Their treatment of Marquette's bones recalls the Feast of the Dead, a ritual practiced primarily among the Wendat (Huron) peoples but also, at least for a brief period, by Algonquian-speaking groups in the Great Lakes. During the Feast of the Dead, different groups placed the carefully washed and wrapped the bones of their deceased relatives into a communal grave, a ritual that functioned in large measure to forge or strengthen social bonds between disparate bands and nations.

In this case, the encounter of Indians and French stimulated the formation of local Christianities influenced by the traditions and experiences of Native peoples.

The Christian Ottawas carried the bark box with Marquette's bones back to the mission village in their canoes. The Jesuits exposed the relics for view in the mission church for a day and then lowered them into a vault in the chapel, where they became a destination for local pilgrimages. Christian Indians soon started traveling to Marquette's tomb for prayer and to ask for divine favors. Dablon described the case of a young woman who was cured of an illness after saying the Our Father and three Hail Mary's at the grave three days in succession. Marquette received credit for alleviating the suffering of many such petitioners.

Conflicts and Religious Violence

As he lay dying on the shore of Lake Michigan, Marquette would have recalled the other Jesuits in New France who had died in the service of God. The missionaries to the Hurons offered a particularly compelling example of sacrifice. In the late 1640s, the Iroquois attacked their traditional enemies the Hurons in an effort to control trade along the Saint Lawrence River and to replenish a declining population through adoption of captives. In the process they destroyed an extensive network of missions in Huronia. Iroquois warriors tortured and killed Jesuits, mocking Catholic ceremonies like baptism, making them martyrs for the missions of New France. Conflict was a common feature of colonial efforts at conversion and spiritual conquest. The Franciscan missions in New Mexico suffered a similar defeat.

Franciscans in the Spanish colony attempted to enforce a complete transformation in Pueblo religious life in the seventeenth century, replacing traditional religious practices with Catholic ritual. The Franciscans fought a desperate and mostly losing battle to destroy Pueblo religion. They entered the kivas to stop ceremonies, refused to allow dances on the pueblo plazas, and severely punished those who failed to obey priestly commands. In 1661, Franciscans seized and cast into a bonfire hundreds of kachina masks and prayer sticks, a direct attack on the spirits of the Pueblos. In the most closely monitored villages, Pueblo religion literally went underground, quietly back to the kivas from which it had originally emerged.

Pueblo peoples finally responded to Spanish oppression with widespread and highly effective violence in August 1680. Life had become particularly difficult in the 1670s due to drought, famine, and Apache raids. Spanish demands for labor and the suppression of Pueblo religion continued. Pueblo religious leaders advocated a return to traditional religious ceremonies as a way of combating the severe challenges. A Pueblo religious figure named Popé helped organize the revolt. According to sources, Popé communicated with powerful Pueblo spiritual beings and learned that a return to the old ways would restore order to the Pueblo world.

With well-coordinated attacks, the Pueblos quickly drove the Spanish from New Mexico in a stunningly successful operation. The Spanish needed 16 years to complete the reconquest of the northern province. The Pueblos killed around four hundred of three thousand Spanish colonists in the revolt. In the process of purifying the land of the Franciscan influence, the Pueblos killed 21 of New Mexico's 33 missionary priests and desecrated and destroyed churches throughout the region.

A Spanish inquiry into the revolt in 1681 provided some insight into the reasons for the bloody uprising and ritual violence. Colonial officials asked a Spanish-speaking Indian "why the apostates burned the images, churches, and things pertaining to divine worship, making a mockery and a trophy of them, killing the priests and doing the other things they did." He replied that as the Indians burned the church they "shouted in loud voices, 'Now the God of the Spaniards, who was their father, is dead, and Santa María, who was their mother, and the saints, who were pieces of rotten wood,' saying that only their own god lived. Thus they ordered all the temples and images, crosses and rosaries burned, and this function being over, they all went to bathe in the rivers, saying that they thereby washed away the water of baptism" (Hackett 1942, vol. 2: 238–242).

Continuing the rites of purification, they made offerings of feathers, maize, and tobacco at the center of the village. The people reopened the ceremonial kivas, violated for so long by the Franciscan priests, and started to dance once again. They reclaimed at least for a while their pueblos, the river valley, and their traditions from the oppressive rule of Spaniards. Pueblo ceremonies survived even the re-conquest as the Spaniards relented some in their efforts to end them. Over time the Pueblos found ways of accommodating practices rooted firmly in ancient traditions as well as those centered on the churches and shrines reconstructed in the aftermath of revolt.

In New England, authorities also faced challenges to their rule and to their enforcement of religious norms in the seventeenth century. Some of these crises emerged from within the community as people expressed unacceptable views or participated in unsanctioned religious practices. Colonial officials were well prepared to suppress alleged dissent and to preserve public orthodoxy. Other challenges came from people perceived as outsiders, people who threatened the purity of New England religious culture or even the survival of the colonies themselves.

The perfectionist impulse in New England made dissent all but inevitable as church members struggled to maintain consensus in a culture that celebrated direct access to the Word. Roger Williams, the minister at Salem, started criticizing Massachusetts authorities almost as soon as he arrived in the colony in 1631. Williams took a separatist position, arguing for a cleaner break from the Church of England. He also questioned English claims to Indian land, called for strict congregational independence, and, most dangerously, claimed that colonial magistrates had no right to intervene in religious affairs.

Facing arrest and deportation, Williams fled Massachusetts in 1636 and founded the town of Providence and eventually the colony of Rhode Island. There, Williams further developed his arguments against temporal interference in spiritual matters. He believed that a government of men could only corrupt a purified church based entirely on scriptural principles. His bold position on the separation of church and state meant that civil officials could not regulate religious practice. Rhode Island soon became a haven for Puritan dissenters as well as for many other religious groups, including Baptists, Jews, and Quakers.

Anne Hutchinson sought refuge in Rhode Island in 1638 after Puritan leaders in Massachusetts exiled her for threatening the social and the religious order of the colony. Hutchinson attracted the attention of local officials when ordinary prayer meetings in her Boston home grew into large public events. After she arrived in the port town in 1634, she started inviting women into her home to discuss the sermons they heard in the meetinghouse. She also served as a spiritual counselor for women in childbirth.

Hutchinson got into trouble when she started expressing "Antinomian" views that conflicted with orthodox Puritan teachings. She claimed a direct connection to the Holy Spirit, seemingly omitting the difficult introspection and public confession required to receive God's saving grace. Dozens of men and women went to hear Hutchinson's prophetic voice. She attacked her opponents as godless men whose failure to uphold Calvinist principles endangered the souls of their congregants. They in turn accused her of interpreting scripture and preaching to mixed audiences of men and women. Massachusetts officials told her, "You have stepped out of your place, you have rather been a husband than a wife, and a preacher than a hearer, and a magistrate than a subject" (Taylor 2001: 182). They banished her from the colony for her disobedience.

Rhode Island was not the only English colony that tolerated religious diversity in some form. The English inherited a very diverse community when they acquired the Dutch possessions in the 1660s. An observer some years before had noted the presence not only of Dutch Calvinists, but also Lutherans, English Puritans, Catholics, and Anabaptists. Jews arrived in New Amsterdam (present-day New York) in 1654, but struggled to maintain a stable community until later in the century. The British, like the Dutch before them, allowed Jews to practice their religion only within the confines of private homes. In some sense this was not a problem, for a Torah scroll and ten adult males was all that was required for formal Jewish worship. The Jewish home had always been a center for the celebration of holidays like Passover and for life-cycle events such as circumcision. The New York government denied a 1685 petition by Jewish families for the right to worship in public. Finally, some time in the late seventeenth or early eighteenth century, the Jews of New York secured the right to open a public synagogue.

The Puritans of New England could not tolerate this kind of diversity. Leaders resorted to state sanctioned violence to defend the boundaries of purity. Between 1659 and 1661 they executed four Quakers who returned to New England after being warned to stay away. English Quakers found a haven in the colony of Pennsylvania beginning in 1680. The Quaker proprietor, William Penn, argued for liberty of conscience as the only way to ensure the practice of true religion.

The most severe test of the Puritans' "errand into the wilderness" arrived in 1675 and 1676 with the attacks of Indian forces under the leadership of the Wampanoag sachem Metacom (Miller 1956). In what became known as King Philip's War, English colonists watched in horror as Native warriors set carefully constructed towns aflame and captured the survivors. It seemed that in this "holy war" the Indians might destroy that city upon a hill and return the region to its previous "savage" state. The colonists turned to violence to protect their communities from enemies both external and internal.

The war erupted in 1675 when three Wampanoag men were convicted of murder in the mysterious death of John Sassamon, a Christian Indian minister. Metacom responded quickly with a bloody campaign to destroy the New England colonies.

Many observers interpreted the defeats as evidence of a decline in the commitment to the moral values and religious principles of the founding generation. The English reaped in violence what they had sown in indifference. A proclamation announced that:

the Righteous God hath heightened our Calamity and given Commission to the Barbarous Heathen to rise up against us, and to become a smart Rod, and severe Scourge to us … hereby speaking aloud to us to search and try our wayes and turn again unto the Lord our God from whom we have departed with a great Backsliding. (Lepore 1998: 102)

The fragile covenant had been broken and an angry God demanded justice. The English turned to familiar rituals to cleanse themselves of the many sins that had stirred God's wrath. Official days of fasting and humiliation became common during the war.

Colonists also used the opportunity to displace Native peoples, including those who had accepted Christianity in the missions of the Puritan minister and evangelist John Eliot. In 1674, on the eve of war, over a thousand Indians lived as Christians in Eliot's Praying Towns. Their status in the colony remained ambiguous, however. For many English, they were a curious mix, both Indian and Christian, "savage" and "civilized." With the outbreak of hostilities the colonists questioned their loyalty, worrying that "Indianness" would supersede Christianity in the war. The colonial government forced them from their homes and removed them to Deer Island in Boston Harbor in 1675. Hundreds died on the bleak, windswept isle during a long, cold winter.

Late in the summer of 1676 English forces finally trapped Metacom in a swamp and killed him, bringing the war to a close and saving the colony. The English quartered his body and took the head to Plymouth. Soldiers arrived with the trophy during a day of thanksgiving held in honor of the victory. The minister Increase Mather saw the hand of Providence in the appearance of Philip's head, commenting that God had presented the offering as "meat to the people inhabiting the wilderness … the very day of their solemn Festival" (Lepore 1998: 174). The English rebuilt their towns, with meetinghouses once again at the center, signifying the restoration of the covenant and the triumph of civilization over savagery.

The witch trials at Salem in 1692 provided another spectacular example of the application of ritual violence in the attempted preservation of the religious community. Although social divisions seem to have played a significant role in the accusations of witchcraft, fear of Satan and widespread belief in occult practices made the events possible. The collection of evidence and the trials, convictions, and executions at Salem represented a public display of acute social and spiritual anxiety.

New England authorities prosecuted 93 people for witchcraft and executed sixteen prior to 1692. In these trials, judges and juries followed careful procedures to determine whether the accused was indeed guilty of casting evil spells that subjected the community to malevolent forces. Prosecutors ideally secured a confession that would lead to a pardon and the restoration of communal order.

The situation in Salem quickly got of control, however. Girls fell to the ground in convulsive fits and accused dozens of people, mostly older women, of black magic. Public trials and dramatic testimony increased the tension until finally 18 women were convicted and hanged for signing their names in Satan's book and causing the victims' diabolical possession. A man who refused to cooperate with the inquests had heavy stones pressed upon him until he suffocated. Accusations of witchcraft eventually spread from the marginalized women originally targeted to members of the elite. Fearful of the growing disorder, legal authorities halted the trials. The prosecution of witches ended in New England, although people continued to believe in witchcraft and other occult practices. The sight of women hanging from trees remained a vivid reminder, however, of the dangers of transgressive behavior, real or imagined.

References and Further Reading

Axtell, James (1985) *The Invasion Within: The Contest of Cultures in Colonial North America*. New York: Oxford University Press.

Boelter, Homer H. (1969) *Portfolio of Hopi Kachinas*. Hollywood, CA: Homer H. Boelter Lithography.

Butler, Jon (1990) *Awash in a Sea of Faith: Christianizing the American People*. Cambridge, MA: Harvard University Press.

Cabeza de Vaca, Alvar Núñez (1993) *Castaways: The Narrative of Alvar Núñez Cabeza De Vaca*, ed. Enrique Pupo-Walker, Berkeley, CA: University of California Press.

Calloway, Colin G. (ed.) (1994) *The World Turned Upside Down: Indian Voices from Early America*, Boston: Bedford/St. Martin's.

Cartier, Jacques (1993) *The Voyages of Jacques Cartier*, ed. Henry Percival Biggar and Ramsay Cook, Toronto: University of Toronto Press.

Deliette, Pierre (1934) "Memoir of De Gannes Concerning the Illinois Country," in *Collections of the Illinois State Historical Library*, vol. 23, ed. Theodore Calvin Pease and Raymond C. Werner, Springfield, IL: Illinois State Historical Library.

Demos, John (1970) *A Little Commonwealth: Family Life in Plymouth Colony*, New York: Oxford University Press.

Finch, Martha L. (2006) "Pinched with Hunger, Partaking of Plenty: Fasts and Thanksgivings in Early New England," in Etta M. Madden and Martha L. Finch (eds.) *Eating in Eden: Food and American Utopias*, Lincoln, NE: University of Nebraska Press.

Finney, Paul Corby (1999) *Seeing Beyond the Word: Visual Arts and the Calvinist Tradition*, Grand Rapids, MI: Eerdmans.

Gaustad, Edwin S. (ed.) (1982) *A Documentary History of Religion in America*, Grand Rapids, MI: Eerdmans.

Griffith, R. Marie (ed.) (2008) *American Religions: A Documentary History*, New York: Oxford University Press.

Gutiérrez, Ramón A. (1991) *When Jesus Came, the Corn Mothers Went Away: Marriage, Sexuality, and Power in New Mexico, 1500–1846*, Stanford, CA: Stanford University Press.

Hackett, Charles W. (ed.) (1942) *Revolt of the Pueblo Indians of New Mexico and Otermín's Attempted Reconquest, 1680–1682*, 2 vols, trans. Charmion Clair Shelby, Albuquerque, NM: The University of New Mexico Press.

Hall, David D. (ed.) (1997) *Lived Religion in America: Toward a History of Practice*, Princeton, NJ: Princeton University Press.

Hall, David D. (2004) *Puritans in the New World: A Critical Anthology*, Princeton, NJ: Princeton University Press.

Hambrick-Stowe, Charles E. (1982) *The Practice of Piety: Puritan Devotional Disciplines in Seventeenth-Century New England*, Chapel Hill, NC: University of North Carolina Press.

Hickerson, Harold (1960) "The Feast of the Dead among the Seventeenth Century Algonkians of the Upper Great Lakes," *American Anthropologist*, 62(February): 81–107.

Knaut, Andrew L. (1995) *The Pueblo Revolt of 1680: Conquest and Resistance in Seventeenth-Century New Mexico*, Norman, OK: University of Oklahoma Press.

Leavelle, Tracy Neal (2004) "Geographies of Encounter: Religion and Contested Spaces in Colonial North America," *American Quarterly*, 56(December): 913–943.

Leavelle, Tracy Neal (2007) " 'Bad Things' and 'Good Hearts': Mediation, Meaning, and the Language of Illinois Christianity," *Church History*, 76(June): 363–394.

Lepore, Jill (1998) *The Name of War: King Philip's War and the Origins of American Identity*, New York: Knopf.

Ludwig, Allan I. (1966) *Graven Images: New England Stonecarving and Its Symbols, 1650–1815*, Middletown, CT: Wesleyan University Press.

Miller, Perry (1956) *Errand into the Wilderness*, Cambridge, MA: Harvard University Press.

Schaafsma, Polly (ed.) (2000) *Kachinas in the Pueblo World*, Salt Lake City, UT: University of Utah Press.

Sewall, Samuel (1973) *The Diary of Samuel Sewall, 1674–1729*, ed. Milton Halsey Thomas, 2 vols, New York: Farrar, Straus and Giroux.

Sewall, Samuel (1998) *The Diary and Life of Samuel Sewall*, ed. Melvin Yazawa, Boston: Bedford/St. Martin's.

Simmons, William Scranton (1986) *Spirit of the New England Tribes: Indian History and Folklore, 1620–1984*, Hanover, NH: University Press of New England.

Stout, Harry S. (1988) *The New England Soul: Preaching and Religious Culture in Colonial New England*, New York: Oxford University Press.

Symcox, Geoffrey and Sullivan, Blair (eds.) (2005) *Christopher Columbus and the Enterprise of the Indies: A Brief History with Documents*, Boston: Bedford/St. Martin's.

Taylor, Alan (2001) *American Colonies*, New York: Viking.

Thwaites, Reuben Gold (ed.) (1898–1901) *The Jesuit Relations and Allied Documents 1610–1671*, Cleveland, OH: Burrows Brothers.

Todorov, Tzvetan (1984) *The Conquest of America: The Question of the Other*, New York: Harper & Row.

Vecsey, Christopher (1996) *On the Padres' Trail*, Notre Dame, IN: University of Notre Dame Press.

Vecsey, Christopher (1997) *The Paths of Kateri's Kin*, Notre Dame, IN: University of Notre Dame Press.

Weber, David J. (1992) *The Spanish Frontier in North America*, New Haven, CT: Yale University Press.

II
The Atlantic World
(1692–1803)

5

Politics

Jon Sensbach

The political orders of North American societies were profoundly shaped by the fact of their participation in a dynamic Atlantic world. Political developments in Europe were keenly felt in North America, particularly as the spillover of religiously-framed wars in England, France, Spain, and the Netherlands. The rhetoric of the American Revolution, in its effusive religious rhetoric and Christian symbology, reflected the European conceptualization of the relationship of political order to religion. It did so even as it set the stage for a national separation of church and state, a development influenced by the rise of Deism, other kinds of rational religion, and outright skepticism. In the colonies, political conflicts between whites and African Americans, Catholics and Protestants, and Native Americans were shot through with religious arguments. Political inequality, and its most extreme manifestation, slavery, were fashioned from biblical materials. By the same token, the emergent emphasis on democracy and "republican virtue" was strongly influenced by a religious approach to conceiving political order. Confident that they had been awarded the land by a God who approved of their piety and would bless them through their practice of it, colonists, and then the citizens of the early American Republic, joined a sense of cosmic destiny to a program of inspired political consolidation and continental domination.

Religion and politics were intimately joined in early America. From colonization through the age of revolution, religion framed the way nation-states, communities and individuals understood themselves and their relationship to the social and political order. In the broad scope of Atlantic and global geopolitics, religion was a cornerstone in the architecture of empire and nation-building as Europe's wars of the Reformation spun themselves out on American soil. On the more intimate level of personal politics, early Americans of Native, European, and African descent drew on religious ideology to anchor themselves within, or often to define themselves against, prevailing power relations in the secular world. Religion and religious hatred also fueled some of the most violent episodes in early American history. For many people in the early modern Atlantic world who drew no line between sacred and secular, religion *was* politics, and that connection signified a literal battleground in the realm of the spirit and in the flesh.

In 1692, the most visible religious battleground in colonial America was, of course, Salem, Massachusetts, where a famous series of witchcraft trials left an indelible mark on American history, becoming synonymous with mass hysteria and a desire to target scapegoats for social or political ills. When, in May of that year, several adolescent girls experienced fits and trances, the local physician diagnosed them as bewitched, setting off a frenzied fear of sorcery and black magic resulting in a long series of witchcraft accusations against scores of Salem residents. By October, more than one hundred and fifty people had been tried, more than 50 convicted, and 19 executed, in what court magistrates and clergy deemed a war against Satan. Most of those executed were hanged, and one man was pressed to death by stones. Salem, it seemed, would devour itself. But when the charges were aimed at some of the village's most prominent residents, judges began to realize they had convicted people on flimsy spectral testimony that did not meet the standards of court evidence. They suspended the trials in tacit admission that their battle against the devil had claimed innocent victims.

Historians have suggested many explanations for this outbreak of witch-hunting violence, most of which have to do with a sense of social unease and spiritual purpose under siege in Salem from within and without. One reason may have been tensions between the commercial town of Salem and the adjacent agrarian Salem village, since many of those accused of being in league with the devil lived in a part of the village closest to the town, while the accusers lived farthest away. Since the majority of the accused were women, another reason might have been a tendency on the part of accusers to target vulnerable older women, many of them single or widowed, who through unconventional behavior seemed to defy social norms or otherwise lie outside the bounds of male control. And while the Salem witch hunts were certainly the largest in the history of Massachusetts, they had been preceded by many smaller ones in previous decades, usually triggered by anxiety that the colony's special godly mission was eroding or being undermined by malignant forces. Fearing the devil's implacable power to infect a vulnerable person or community, colonists remained ever alert for signs of his work.

Given all these factors, the events of 1692 are best understood in the larger context of events in the English Atlantic world during the last quarter of the seventeenth century, when a new relationship between religion and politics emerged in England and her American colonies. Sometimes in step with the changes and sometimes not, Massachusetts and the other colonies were bound up in this new relationship, which was characterized by a desire to promote Protestantism as a foundation of empire, and a corresponding hostility toward Catholicism and its imperial champions, England's enemies France and Spain. Accompanying these goals was an increasing trend toward toleration of religious dissenters, which came to be regarded in England as a way to diminish strife and strengthen the empire, but which caused resentment in Massachusetts, where dissenters had long been persecuted as anathema to the colony's original vision from the 1630s of a "city on a hill."

The Protestant-Catholic rivalry had split Christendom since the Protestant Reformation of the sixteenth century, when England, along with other nations and principalities in northern Europe, seceded from the authority of the Roman Catholic

Church and established their own churches free of papal authority. The Reformation's chief theological instigator, the German former monk Martin Luther, had insisted that salvation came through faith alone rather than "works," or the Catholic emphasis on good deeds. His concept of the "priesthood of all believers" meant that everyone was entitled to seek a personal relationship with God independently rather than depend on the intercession of priests. Luther's translation of the Bible from Greek and Latin into German soon after the invention of the printing press made the sacred text more accessible to ordinary readers, giving them greater authority to interpret it themselves and participate in worship.

The new doctrines appealed to many northern European rulers who resented Rome's powerful hold on court politics and the draining away of taxes to support the Catholic Church bureaucracy. But their split from the Vatican plunged Europe into a cycle of destructive religious wars as Catholics and Protestants accused the other of heresy, each claiming to be the one true church. Hundreds of thousands on both sides died from warfare and persecution during the sixteenth century. The quest to root out heretics reinvigorated the medieval practice of witch-hunting on a scale that dwarfed the Salem witch trials more than a century later, claiming thousands of victims who were tortured, hanged, or burned at the stake. Predictably, religious warfare followed European colonizers to America. In Florida, Spanish Catholic colonists massacred several hundred French Huguenot Protestant settlers in 1565. The desire to colonize America for the glory of Protestantism or Catholicism and convert Native Americans to those faiths helped fuel the imperial competition between England, Spain and France. Settled in 1630, the Puritan colony of Massachusetts was a western Atlantic outpost of radical Protestantism that condemned the doctrine of the divine right to royal authority, opposed the Church of England and its monarch, and considered Catholics the devil's agents.

England was itself thrown into turmoil in the 1640s by civil war between royal and parliamentary forces, which was also largely a religious war between radical Puritans who supported Parliament and Anglican supporters of the king. Victory by the parliamentarians led to the execution of King Charles I in 1649 and eleven more years of Puritan rule under the protectorate of Oliver Cromwell. With the restoration of royal authority under Charles II in 1660, the Church of England once again became the established, or official, tax-supported church of the nation, reaffirming the close longstanding relationship between church and state that had been sundered by the civil war.

The Glorious Revolution of 1688–89 set England and her colonies on a new political course with religion at its core. The overthrow of Charles II's son James II, who was Catholic, and the accession of William III afforded a moment of national consolidation combining toleration for some religious dissenters with imperial expansion fueled by renewed anti-Catholicism. These seemingly paradoxical aims were intended as perfectly complementary. Decades of civil war and upheaval in England throughout the seventeenth century had shown that strife between Protestants undermined national unity and confirmed the impossibility of enforcing orthodox religious belief. As the anti-James conspirators of 1688, and the Revolution's chief political philosopher, John Locke, equated the king's Catholicism with tyranny, so Protestantism correlated with political liberty. William's own battle standard during his invasion of England in November 1688 proclaimed: "The Liberties of England and the Protestant Religion I Will Maintain." The new ethos of Protestant unity was bolstered by the recognition that the empire need not be weakened, and indeed might be strengthened, by an accommodation with Protestant dissenters. "Toleration," wrote Locke in *A Letter Concerning Toleration* in 1689, "is the chief characteristic mark of the true church."

Accordingly, a counterpart to the political rights enshrined in the new constitution, the Toleration Act of 1689, stated that "some ease to scrupulous consciences in the exercise of religion may be an effectual means to unite their Majesties Protestant subjects in interest and affection." Embodying the *Zeitgeist* of 1689 in its evocation of British, and Protestant, providentialism, the Act guaranteed freedom of worship for Protestant nonconformists, though they were still denied some political rights. In the aftermath of the Revolution, Catholics were denied all political rights, they were purged from the many posts in government and the military they had held under James, and the Constitution guaranteed a Protestant succession to the throne. In league with the Dutch Republic, England declared war against France in what Protestant champions hailed as a struggle against reinvigorated worldwide Catholicism under Louis XIV.

While anti-Catholicism became a great rallying cry after 1688, it was also a device to be deployed selectively against Britain's greatest threats to imperial hegemony, particularly France, since the British on occasion made convenient alliance with other Catholic nations such as Austria, which were seen as less intent on reimposing Romish rule on the world. Nonetheless, imperial ideology was grounded on the symbiotic connection between British imperial ascendancy and the victorious destiny of God's chosen Protestant champions. "Protestantism determined how most Britons viewed their politics," historian Linda Colley has written. "And an uncompromising Protestantism was the foundation on which their state was explicitly and unapologetically based." Popular culture drove home this lesson. The perennial popularity of John Foxe's sixteenth-century *Book of Martyrs* and John Bunyan's *The Pilgrim's Progress* (1678–1684), both of which featured cruelties and obstacles faced by Protestant protagonists at the hands of Catholic oppressors, confirmed the widespread belief that the Popish menace was a trial to be transcended on the way to spiritual and national triumph (Colley 2005: 18).

In England's American colonies, anti-Catholicism was nothing new and had in fact intensified throughout the 1680s, dovetailing with the Glorious Revolution and paralleling, in places, an increasing religious toleration. The anti-popish sentiment was particularly vehement along the northern and southern imperial fringes where the threat was most conspicuous from England's rivals for New World supremacy, France and Spain. In New England, memories of King Philip's War of 1676 remained fresh among Anglo-American colonists fearful of a French and Indian union on their borders. Militant Puritans regarded the war as evidence of divine displeasure with their colony's ungodliness, and saw the Catholic power of New France to the northwest as no less than an agent of the Antichrist bent on undermining God's work in America. But the Puritan leadership also opposed toleration for Protestant religious dissenters such as Quakers and Baptists, even though they themselves had once been persecuted in England. They believed adherence to the congregational order laid out by the colony's founders was part of their collective covenant with God that could not be undermined by alternative religious viewpoints. Through the years dissenters had been banished or silenced and several Quakers had been executed as heretics.

To the south, the relatively new proprietary colony of Carolina, founded in 1670 on land once claimed by Spain, also saw itself on the frontier of struggle against the

Catholic bastion of Florida, though in somewhat less apocalyptic terms than did New Englanders. The colony excluded Catholics, but unlike Massachusetts, it established the Church of England and provided toleration for Protestants of all kinds even before the Glorious Revolution. The proprietary colony of Pennsylvania, founded in 1682, went one better, with no church establishment and granting toleration of dissenters, propelled by William Penn's vision of pacifist Quakers co-existing amicably with Native Americans.

The climate of anti-Catholicism became further aggravated when Louis XIV revoked the Edict of Nantes in 1686, ending limited religious toleration in France and sending thousands of Huguenot refugees to America. The presence of these displaced Protestant dissenters, many of them radical Calvinists who settled in New York, New Jersey and South Carolina, reaffirmed the benefit of religious toleration as a practical matter of invigorating imperial policy and colonial defense by attracting Protestant settlers eager to partake in the civic, religious, and even military life of their new homes. It also confirmed the sense of America as a haven for spiritual fugitives in an international Protestant movement united against Catholic aggression, reinforcing the longstanding Puritan belief in the providential destiny of the New World. "The overruling *Providence* of the *great God* is to be acknowledged, as well in the *concealing* of America for so long a time, as in the *discovering* of it, when the fulness of time was come for the discovery," wrote Cotton Mather in 1702, conceiving of America as a sacred space, or *"Christianography,"* whereon God would etch his favored design (Elliott 2006: 184).

As in England, anti-Catholic suspicion in the colonies was also linked to fears of political repression by royal authority. In the northern colonies, these combined resentments focused on the figure of Edmund Andros, governor of the unpopular new administrative entity called the Dominion of New England, formed by James II in 1686 out of the Puritan colonies as well as New York and New Jersey. James's intent was to bring these colonies under closer royal control by enforcing the Navigation Acts and revoking colonial charters. Andros was seen, especially in Massachusetts, as the stooge of a Catholic monarch, too conciliatory toward the French, too dismissive of colonial liberties, and too supportive of the Church of England. In the aftermath of the Glorious Revolution, a series of three popular anti-royalist uprisings deposed colonial officials regarded as conspirators in a papist plot to impose absolutist rule. In Boston, a coalition of merchants and ministers raised troops, arrested Andros and deported him to England. In New York, merchant Jacob Leisler denounced Dominion officials as "Popish Dogs and Devils," unseated Governor Francis Nicholson, and seized power. And in the Catholic-controlled colony of Maryland, a small-time planter, John Coode, formed "An Association in Arms for the Defense of Protestant Religion," seized control of the colonial government, expelled Catholics from office and prohibited Catholics from worshiping publicly. In each case, by 1692, the government of William III reasserted crown control over the rebellious colonies, installing royal governors and representative assemblies, restoring some liberties, and enforcing grudging religious tolerance of Protestant dissenters.

The Salem witchcraft trials in 1692, then, can be seen as a product of, and outlet for, the anxieties caused by the multiple pressures of the previous twenty years (Figure 5.1). A colony whose identity derived from a special covenant with God now saw that covenant in danger–from Indians, from Catholics who might infiltrate and try to take over the government, from Quakers and other dissenters who were now

Figure 5.1   The Salem witch trials provide an enduring example of American history of violence in the name of religious devotion.

to be tolerated, from lax morals and other ungodliness. The struggle against perceived internal and external religious foes prepared colonists to see and believe evidence of the devil's machinations through witchcraft. Only after the nineteenth victim dangled from the gallows did they realize they had accepted that evidence too easily, by which time they had left an enduring example of American history of violence in the name of religious devotion.

In unusually dramatic fashion, the Salem trials telescoped a set of local and colonial tensions in one corner of the Atlantic world in the era of the Glorious Revolution. The larger lesson of the revolution in both England and the colonies was that anti-Catholicism served as a potent mobilizing force for nationalist and colonial activists seeking to preserve British political liberties and to project a transatlantic vision of imperial power and militant Protestantism. The 1690s and the early decades of the eighteenth century saw the vigorous joining of this international imperial and religious struggle by Britain, France and Spain, contested on multiple fronts in North America and the Caribbean.

Religion, in the service of an absolutist state, had long been the cornerstone of French and Spanish colonial policy in the Americas; the New World was both a battle line in the global cause of Counter-Reformation and a field for commercial exploitation. Since the sixteenth century, Jesuit and Franciscan priests had sought to use the mission system to incorporate Indians into the Spanish imperial orbit in New Spain and along the North American edge of the empire in Florida and New Mexico. No less than militant Puritans, millennialist friars regarded the New World as sacred ground upon which to project their providential vision. In their minds, Indians were prelapsarian agents of worldly regeneration through whom paradise might be restored in America, ushering in God's kingdom. The missions thus expressed an inclusive policy of assimilating Indians into the realm through forced acculturation, as opposed to the English policy of excluding them from colonial society. Though seventeenth-century rebellions against the severity of the priests' methods by Indians in both Florida and New Mexico indicated that the vision of earthly paradise had fallen short, missions were still considered the frontline of Spain's North American defense network against Protestantism and a vital part of Spanish imperial strategy.

Jesuit missions in New France served a similar purpose, and the colonization of Louisiana in 1699 by Louis XIV opened another strategic geopolitical front at the mouth of the Mississippi in the struggle to contain and encircle Anglo-American empire. The colony's audacious claim to the enormous middle third of the continent was intended to link Canada to the Gulf and to France's sugar colonies in the West Indies, a plan in which religion figured prominently. Though missionary outreach to Indians ultimately played a smaller role in Louisiana than in Canada, the Catholic presence, especially in New Orleans, visibly anchored a colony considered an undesirable imperial outpost populated by soldiers, traders and scofflaws.

The outbreak of the War of the Spanish Succession in 1701 (known in British America as Queen Anne's War), a compact of European states opposed to the union of Spain and France, brought the enduring imperial rivalries between those nations and Britain into open hostility in America. The war emerged as a contest over many things – territorial and geopolitical supremacy, trade, Indian allegiances, even slaves – but fundamental to it as well were competing visions of empire rooted in religious identity. Thus it was seen on both sides as a continuation of the long-running Protestant-Catholic holy war over imperial politics and cosmic hegemony. As during the previous quarter-century, the war was waged particularly bitterly in contested borderlands regions. French and Mohawk raids decimated Puritan communities in western Massachusetts, taking hundreds of captives. To the south, combined forces of South Carolina militia and Creek Indians raided the Spanish missions in northern Florida in 1702 and 1704, destroying the mission system that had been the bulwark of Spanish colonization in the Southeast for more than a century. Hundreds of Catholicized Apalachee and Timucua Indians as well as several Spanish friars were killed in the assault, including many who were burned alive by Creek captors. In one mission, seventeen prisoners were tied to stakes or "stations of the cross" in the town plaza and set alight. Thousands more Indians were taken captive and sold into slavery in Carolina and the West Indies. On a far greater scale than in New England, violence of both a political and religious nature transformed the southeastern frontier by annihilating the great majority of the region's Catholic adherents.

The Carolina–Florida border region remained a volatile disputed zone, becoming, from the British perspective, a test case of the mixed political objectives of anti-Catholic militancy, limited toleration, and imperial expansion. The new colony of Georgia was founded in 1732 to serve as a buffer against the lingering Spanish threat to South Carolina and as a deterrent against escape by enslaved Africans, who were tempted by Spanish promises of freedom to flee Carolina and seek refuge in Florida, converting to Catholicism in the bargain. Unlike its neighbor to the north, Georgia had no established church, opening itself instead to Protestant dissenters of all stripes and even to a small community of Jews who were deemed worthy colonial citizens. The colony's principal founder, James Oglethorpe, immersed in evangelical and Pietist communication networks with correspondents in Britain and Europe, envisioned Georgia as a link in a transatlantic Protestant chain, in which British imperial strength derived from religious diversity. Thus, one of his most important groups of recruits were Lutheran Pietist Salzburgers who, after their expulsion from Austria, immigrated to Georgia and eagerly embraced the founding vision of tolerance, humanitarian philanthropy, and antislavery that for a time made the colony quirkily unique in British America.

The outbreak of the War of Jenkins' Ear between Britain and Spain in 1739 renewed a British sense of resurgent Protestant unity and global struggle against Catholic aggression. That year Anglican bishop Isaac Maddox applauded the "amiable Candour and Condescension" with which his church "abhors all the Methods of Violence, and all the Influence of Persecution" perpetrated by Catholicism. "With other gross Absurdities of Popery," he continued, "[our church] most cordially rejects that cruel Spirit, which spreads Devastation and Misery upon Earth, and calls down Fire from heaven." His church, by contrast, "*in meekness instructing those that oppose* ... endeavors their Conviction, pities their Mistakes, but desires not to awaken any terrors of the Secular Arm" (Gould 2000: 19). For James Oglethorpe, Georgia's position on the southern frontier of the continuing struggle against perceived Catholic tyranny was both a matter of survival for the fledgling colony and an affirmation of its strategic political and religious importance. His defeat of a Spanish attack from St. Augustine on Georgia in 1742 preserved the colony as a Protestant stronghold anchoring Britain's southern mainland claim, though as an unintended consequence the quelling of the Spanish threat perhaps hastened the end of the ban on slavery in 1750 and ushered in the colony's headlong rush into slaveholding.

The first half of the eighteenth century was characterized by the increasing integration of Britain's North American and West Indian colonies into the imperial orbit, driven by defensive needs and commercial expansion. Though the colonies exercised some measure of autonomy through their elected legislatures, their essential relationship to the empire was one of political unity and commitment to British conceptions of liberty. Paradoxically, the relationship between religion and politics, in the colonies and the empire, was much more diffuse as a result of the changing nature of the colonies after 1689. By the late seventeenth century, the demographic growth of colonial British North America had become the fastest in the world, at 3 percent annually, driven by natural increase, the African slave trade, and the voluntary migration of British, Scots-Irish, and Germans eager for land. A population of 50,000 in 1650 rose to more than two million by 1750, 20 percent of whom were enslaved Africans. This explosive growth made the British colonies among the most culturally heterogeneous places in the world and, in conjunction with growing religious toleration, strengthened dissent while working against the full religious integration of the colonies into the empire.

To be sure, there was broad allegiance to the advancement of Protestantism as an imperial aim and in opposition to the specter of Catholicism on the borders. On the other hand, no consistent pattern of church–state relations prevailed as in New France or New Spain; in British America, Congregationalism was established in some colonies, the Church of England in others, and Pennsylvania and Georgia had no state church (though the latter established Anglicanism in 1756). Within these various enclaves, there tended to be a close correspondence between elected officials and the dominant church of their colony – Puritan office holders in Massachusetts, Quakers in Pennsylvania, and Anglicans from the Virginia planting oligarchy. The founding of the Society for the Propagation of the Gospel in Foreign Parts in 1701 marked an aggressive effort by the Church to expand its hitherto limited reach in the colonies. But with no American bishops, a chronically underdeveloped infrastructure that was inadequate to meet the needs of parishioners, and a diverse colonial population from numerous dissenting traditions, Anglicanism remained weak even in some places where it did have a foothold, as in the Carolinas. The church's missionary outreach to Native Americans and enslaved Africans met limited success. In short, to the extent that there was any unified policy toward religion and politics in the colonies, it was that religious diversity, limited toleration, and decentralization strengthened the empire more than did adherence to a state church.

Debates over toleration, pluralism, and religion's relationship to politics gained radical new force in the 1730s with the advent of the evangelical revivals that came to be known as the Great Awakening. Because of the powerful effect of the revivals in colonial America, which many historians have argued were a precursor to the American Revolution, it is easy to overlook the connections between evangelical Protestantism in Europe, Britain, and America, which its proponents considered key nodes in a resurgent transatlantic, if not global, fellowship. Much of this revivalist spirit bore the imprint of continental Pietism, which, originating within the Lutheran Church in the late seventeenth century, deemphasized the finer points of formal theological doctrine and elevated an emotional religion of the heart and the need for spiritual rebirth in Christ. This approach proved influential in Britain and made its way to the colonies, to resurface in localized revivals, first in Dutch Reformed congregations in New Jersey and slightly later in western Massachusetts under the auspices of Jonathan Edwards. Across the Atlantic, then, by the 1730s thousands of Protestants eagerly embraced, and in turn disseminated, some version of teaching that encouraged them to bypass orthodox religious authority and take charge of their own salvation through a close relationship with Jesus. In this emphasis, the needs and abilities of the individual rose above those of the organic church community.

This revision, while by no means new to the history of Christianity, raised familiarly difficult questions – posed ever more regularly since the Reformation – about the relationship of faith to politics and to civil authority. The ideological leap from spiritual empowerment to religious liberty, and thence to social liberty, had ample precedent in Christian reform movements, but across the Atlantic the age of evangelical renewal evoked different responses to that challenge. In German-speaking lands on the Continent, Pietism did not originate as a popular movement but as a reform movement by church leaders wishing to reinvigorate interest in religion while carefully cultivating aristocratic favor. Zeal for an emotional connection to Christ, they taught their flocks, must be accompanied by submission to worldly authority, an accommodation that enabled the nobility to preempt Pietism for their own purposes, enlisting it as a crucial mechanism of social control and state building. In Britain, high church and civil leaders regarded evangelical stirrings as uncomfortably reminiscent of radical dissenting social levelers like Ranters and Quakers during the Civil War a century earlier. In British North America, where civil and ecclesiastical authority was weaker, the Great Awakening generated, or revealed, new layers of religious, social and political division that established churches had always sought to subsume under their hierarchy.

The revivals did not begin as explicit attempts to foster social divisions or to redefine the link between religion and politics in colonial America, but they quickly achieved that effect. By the late 1730s, itinerant evangelical preachers such as George Whitefield, Gilbert Tennent and James Davenport took their preaching out of the pulpit and directly to the public, addressing crowds of thousands in town squares, fields and barns. The evangelicals, or "New Lights," portrayed themselves as champions of the people seeking to revive moribund Christianity and undermine the stodginess of church authorities who jealously guarded their prerogative to interpret and control

God's word. Accusing the "Old Lights" of spiritual lifelessness and insufficient piety, the New Lights urged listeners to make their own choices, to take a greater role in church affairs. Tennent's inflammatory pamphlet of 1742, *The Danger of an Unconverted Ministry*, compared the established clergy to Pharisees, calling "ungodly ministers" a "great curse" on righteousness, "caterpillars [who] labor to devour every green thing," constantly "driving, driving, to duty, duty" as a substitute for real Christian conversion. This condemnation was cast as a matter of spiritual freedom, as an "unscriptural infringement on Christian liberty" for false ministers to deny authentic teachers of the Gospel at the people's expense. The effect of such language was to encourage ordinary people, especially social marginal groups such as the laboring poor, slaves, and women of all classes, to begin challenging authority and to participate eagerly in congregational life, even to preach and exhort others (Tennent 1742: 1).

The dispute sharply divided Presbyterian, Baptist, and Congregational churches, and as the revivals surged up and down the Atlantic seaboard from New England to Georgia, factions repeatedly split off from the "spiritual tyranny" of their parent congregations and set up as regenerate new apostolic churches. As the Old Lights feared, religious schism and the questioning of ecclesiastical authority fostered calls for social equality and resentment against civil authority. Some New Lights denounced wealth and social hierarchy as ungodly, and ostentatious luxury as a sign of corruption. Others decried slavery as an abomination of God's law. Threatened by the breakdown in religious and social deference, the Old Lights responded vigorously, denouncing the "enthusiastic, factious, censorious Spirit" of the evangelicals and accusing itinerants such as Tennent for sowing "the Seeds of all that Discord, Intrusion, Confusion, Separation, hatred, Variance, Emulations, Wrath, Strife, seditions, Heresies, &c that have been springing up in so many of the Towns and Churches thro' the Province." One minister, Charles Chauncy, contended that "Good Order is the Strength and Beauty of the World," which was threatened, wrote Isaac Stiles of Connecticut, when "Contempt is cast upon Authority both Civil and Ecclesiastical" (Bonomi 2003: 150, 151).

Working closely with the old guard, the Connecticut legislature passed a series of laws in the early 1740s to restrict evangelical preaching and to expel radicals deemed too threatening (Figure 5.2). In Virginia, New Lights were attacked by mobs, arrested and fined, and forbidden from preaching. As established religion and orthodox political authority became directly implicated in the maintenance of social order, the religious awakenings forced a dispute on the meaning and limits of religious toleration. Anticipating language that would become famous a generation later, Connecticut cleric Elisha Williams drew on John Locke in *The Essential Rights and Liberties of Protestants* (1744) to argue that the objective of civil government was the "greater Security of Enjoyment of what belongs to everyone," and that "*this Right of private Judgment, and worshipping* GOD according to the *Consciences*" was the "*natural and unalienable Right of every Man*" (Williams 1744: 324). For George Whitefield, likewise, it was a question of liberty – religious, political and social liberty, bound up together, a British imperial birthright that Americans shared. "We breathe indeed in a free air," he told an audience in Philadelphia in 1746, "as free (if not freer) both as to temporals and spirituals, as any nation under heaven" (Gould 2000: 20).

For many evangelicals, the question of religious freedom assumed a larger political dimension when they linked the swelling of revivalist fervor with the larger cosmic

Figure 5.2 Tennent's *The Danger of an Unconverted Ministry*, published by Benjamin Franklin in 1740, represented the "New Lights'" criticism with stodgy orthodoxy and the injustices of ecclesiastical and popular hierarchies.

struggle against the Antichrist. In this radical millennialist outlook, religious enthusiasm presaged the advent of Christ's kingdom and the defeat of the wicked, who might be not only the ungodly in colonial society but also the traditional and convenient enemy of Catholicism. Williams's "unalienable right" to freedom of conscience was grounded in the warning of what followed in the absence of toleration:

> the clergy through Pride and Ambition assumed the power of prescribing to, imposing on and domineering over the Consciences of men; civil Rulers for their own private Ends helping it forward; which went on 'till it produced the most detestable *Monster* the Earth ever had upon it, the *Pope*, who has deluged the Earth with the Blood of Christians.

Thus was revealed the "true Spirit of *Popery*, to impose their Determinations on all with their Power by any Methods" necessary, and any "*civil magistrates* that suffered and helped that *Beast* to invade this Right, did therein *commit Fornication with her, and give her their Strength and Power*" (Williams 1744: 325). Evangelicals throughout the Protestant world saw the new spiritual fervor as evidence of God's mighty dealings against the Catholic beast, and several British military victories against the French during the 1740s gave comforting reassuring worldly confirmation of divine favor in the struggle.

Given new vigor by the awakenings, this strain of conventional British anti-popery found further reinforcement in the prophetic view, advanced perhaps most forcefully by Jonathan Edwards, that America stood poised to realize its special destiny as the site of Christ's new kingdom on earth. Echoing the providential certainty of the Puritan founders' vision of America as the New Jerusalem, Edwards saw the revivals as God's sign of the approaching millennium which, unfolding in the New World, would sweep the Antichrist to final doom. From his reading of the Book of Revelation, Edwards construed the likelihood "that this work of God's spirit, that is so extraordinary and wonderful, is the dawning, or at least, a prelude of that glorious work of God, so often foretold in Scripture … And there are many things that make it probable that this work will begin in America." Noting that the end time was prophesied to begin "in some very remote part of the world" accessible only by sea, he concluded that America must be the site of divine intent, and "it gives more abundant reason to hope that what is now seen in America, and especially in New England, may prove the dawn of that glorious day," the beginning "of something vastly great" (Edwards 1742: 270, 273). Historians have identified Edwards's writings as fundamental to an emerging kind of religious nationalism which, when mixed with Whiggish constitutionalism, marked a potent marriage of religion and politics in the mid-eighteenth century that emphasized the language of American rights and freedom.

Though the first blush of revival enthusiasm had passed by the 1750s, many New Lights saw the advent of war with France in the 1750s as the culmination of eschatological politics, the moment of God's final reckoning with the Antichrist. Though the war was to be waged on a global scale, many evangelicals saw the American theater as the essential struggle for the soul of the continent and the confirmation of American providential destiny. Endorsing violence in a righteous cause, preachers urged their flocks to take up arms in the cosmic battle with the Catholic Whore of Babylon. A successive string of British defeats in the early years of the war was as disheartening to evangelicals as to other Anglo-American colonists, but some reminded downhearted listeners that the righteous must endure God's stern test before claiming prophetic victory. "The Destruction of *Antichrist*, and the End of this Night of *Popish Darkness*, is near at hand," to be followed by God's "*plentiful, outpouring* of the Spirit of all Grace," assured one writer. In Virginia, New Light Presbyterian Samuel Davies wondered in 1756 whether "the present war is the commencement of this grand decisive conflict between the Lamb and the beast, i.e. between the protestant and the popish powers?" He felt certain that it was: "However bloody and desolating this last conflict may be, it will bring about the most glorious and happy revolution that ever was in the world." Throughout the Protestant Atlantic, Britain's victory in 1763 was hailed as a glorious defeat of militant Catholicism; for evangelicals and even many mainstream liberal Protestants in British America, the eviction of Britain's great foe from the continent – along with the takeover by the British of Spanish Florida – confirmed God's glorious plan to use America to usher in the millennium (Bloch 1985: 40).

In the aftermath of the war, religion also inspired a sense of cultural revival and political resistance for Native Americans, many of whom were less happy with Britain's triumph. Many Indian nations who had long-established trade relations with New France and sided with the French during the war now found themselves facing the British victors. These included Ottawas, Ojibwas, and Hurons in the Great Lakes area, Miamis and Kickapoos in the Illinois Country, as well as Senecas in Western New York and Delawares, Shawnees, and Wyandots in the Ohio Country, who were not long-term allies of the French but had fled to the west to escape Anglo-American encroachment on their land. They were unhappy with a sharp reduction in the quality and quantity of trade goods from the British and with Britain's new claim on all the land east of the Mississippi River, which they feared opened the way for a flood of new settlers into their territory. Besides these material grievances, native people were inspired by a Delaware prophet named Neolin, who led a religious revival urging them to shun the influence of western trade goods, particularly alcohol, and return to traditional ways. Only by purifying themselves of corrupting habits could they restore spiritual balance to their disrupted universe.

For the first time, this Indian equivalent of the Great Awakening helped many native people overcome traditional rivalries and unite in common cause against an Anglo-American enemy. In 1763, a coalition of native people organized by the Ottawa chief Pontiac attacked British forts throughout the Great Lakes area, the Illinois and Ohio country all the way to western Pennsylvania. They captured several forts, slaughtering garrisons and civilians. The violence cut both ways, when a group of Scots-Irish vigilantes called the Paxton Boys, angry at Indian attacks on frontier homesteads, massacred a settlement of noncombatant, Christian Conestoga Indians in Pennsylvania. While Pontiac's Rebellion was not exclusively a religious war, religion did help shape a sense of ethnic identity on both sides of the conflict. In the case of the unfortunate Conestogas, even their Christianity was not enough to save them from the perception that they were savage Indians to be eliminated. Though Pontiac's Rebellion ended in 1765 without a clear military victory, the uprising did stir Britain to pass the Proclamation Act of 1763 which, to protect Indian lands, barred Anglo-American settlement west of the Appalachians. Along with the Stamp Act and other taxes Parliament levied on the colonies, the Proclamation proved another source of colonial resentment against Britain during the 1760s.

The changes to early American society and religion wrought by the Great Awakening found ample expression in the emerging disputes with Britain. The incipient revolutionary movement involved a rich intertwining of religion and politics. In broad terms, the awakening had sowed in large cross-sections of the colonial public a suspicion of power, producing a skeptical and even harshly critical anti-authoritarianism that was easily transferred from church figures to imperial government officials. "The common people now claim as good a right to judge and act for themselves in matters of religion as civil rules or the learned clergy," wrote Isaac Backus in 1768. Evangelical religion and classical republican theory shared common ground not only in the language of "unalienable rights," as one historian has written, but also in "the revolutionary appeals to a virtuous citizenry, the ethic of self-sufficiency and frugality ... [and] the characterization of the royal ministers as greedy, self-interested, dissolute, and even Catholic at heart" (Bloch 1985: 15).

Beyond the dispute over imperial authority and colonial rights, several specific religious issues added to colonists' pique on the eve of permanent political rupture. One was the fear that the Anglican Church would install a bishop over the American colonies in an effort to enforce religious conformity and fasten imperial control all the tighter. To many, perceived British political tyranny equated to an attempt to deprive religious freedom. "Let the pulpit resound with the doctrines and sentiments of religious liberty," John Adams wrote in 1765. "There is a direct and formal design on foot to enslave America." Second was the resurgent fear of Catholicism now represented by Britain's acquisition of Quebec in the Seven Years' War, which had forced British authorities to leaven the empire's traditional anti-Catholic policies with a more tolerant approach to newly conquered territories. To ensure that some 70,000 French Quebecois would not join the growing revolutionary movement to the south, parliament passed the Quebec Act in 1774, which permitted office holders to practice Catholicism, eliminated references to Protestantism in the imperial oath of loyalty, and allowed state support of Catholic schools. The presence of an established Catholic state within British imperial borders only intensified colonial Anglo-American resentment against the crown.

As they had done a generation earlier, many American evangelicals focused apocalyptic expectations on the dispute with Britain, redirecting their former rage for the French against their own empire. The crown now became the Antichrist, coddler of Catholics, destroyer of natural liberties. Preachers urged support for boycotts to purge the sin of luxury and purify the country for the day of reckoning with the Beast. They equated armed resistance to tyranny with godliness and attacked the Anglican Church for an unholy relationship to the state. In pamphlets, broadsides and sermons, New Light clergy breathed life into Jonathan Edwards's millennial nationalism, comparing America to Israel and Britain to Egypt while proclaiming America the world's last best hope for freedom. Imagining the eyes of the world on the colonial struggle, evangelicals described it as a cosmic drama, the chosen moment in divine time that would banish the stain of sin and hasten Christ's kingdom.

Such prophetic calculations also informed other political protests that had less to do with British tyranny than with personal injustices. In the late 1760s and early 1770s, a group of farmers in central and western North Carolina called Regulators protested what they saw as unfair taxation, predatory land speculation by wealthy investors, and a corrupt colonial administration dominated by eastern elites. Many of these protestors were Scots-Irish Presbyterians and New Light Baptists, and their leaders included a millennialist Quaker from Pennsylvania, Hermon Husband. Much as radical religious groups like the Ranters and Diggers had done during the English Civil War of the 1640s, the Regulators invoked biblical language to decry social injustice and gross imbalances in wealth, but their military defeat by the colonial governor in 1773 ended the movement.

In another kind of revolution within the revolution, enslaved African Americans employed the language of evangelicalism to invoke a day of reckoning and God's deliverance for them as well. Since the 1730s, the awakenings had drawn in slaves and free blacks with the language of egalitarian universalism and the suggestion of worldly power relations turned upside down through a new birth in Christ. As a result, a new, specifically African American, kind of Christianity had taken root throughout the colonies and in the Caribbean in which the enslaved saw themselves as chosen people redeemed and liberated by the prophetic power of divine justice. The vigorous rhetoric of freedom during the revolutionary era intensified this sense that a time of Christian deliverance was at hand. "We have in common with all other men a natural right to our freedoms without Being deprived of them by our fellow men as we are a freeborn Pepel and have never forfeited this blessing by any compact or agreement whatever," a group of slaves petitioned the governor of Massachusetts in 1774. "There is a great number of sincere members of the Church of Christ, how can the master be said to bear my Burden when he bears me down with the chains of slavery?" In Virginia in 1777, a newspaper advertised for the recapture of a runaway slave, Jupiter, "a great Newlight Preacher," who had escaped after his master had whipped him for "stirring up the Negroes in insurrection." Many evangelical churches nurtured both a sense of biracial Christian fellowship as well as antislavery politics, but those religious impulses were insufficient to make antislavery a goal or projected outcome of the Revolution for most white Americans. In fact, for most revolutionaries, the idea of America as a place of divinely-ordained rights and liberties simply did not apply to Americans of African descent.

The tumult of the era drew the cords between religion and politics tighter as people turned to faith for guidance in the decision over independence. In truth, the Revolution split religious communities as it did the general population, demonstrating that religion was no reliable predictor of political allegiance. Strong religious voices spoke out unequivocally on both patriot and loyalist sides. On the other hand, one alliance that proved crucial to the outcome was evangelical support for independence, which involved an important religious and political compromise. Evangelicals had directed their critique of the sins of luxury, unholiness and corruption against not only the crown and its colonial representatives but also against Anglo-American merchants, planters, lawyers and other elites, many of them leaders in the revolutionary movement. To court evangelical support for independence, elites promised more electoral representation from ordinary folk as well as a greater degree of toleration and freedom for religious dissenters. With these concessions from influential leaders, many evangelicals backed the revolutionary cause, believing independence offered the best chance for religious and political reform. Anglican officials repeatedly accused New Light clergy of "breathing the spirit of rebellion on the people," and one churchman contended that "religion itself, or rather the Appearance of it, [has been] humbly ministered as an handmaid to Faction and Sedition" (Gould 2000: 189).

There was no consensus within the revolutionary movement, however, on what religious liberty meant or how far it was to extend. In fact, it varied state by state as the Anglican establishment disintegrated and as the states drew up new constitutions after 1776. Each confronted, in different ways, the question of whether freedom of conscience was compatible with a state religion. Some states such as New York explicitly banned any connection between church and state; others such as Maryland, Georgia and South Carolina, while not establishing a specific church, passed state taxes "for the support of the Christian religion." Pennsylvania required public office holders to acknowledge the divine origins of the New Testament. Virginia's "Declaration of Rights" in 1776 agreed that "all men are equally entitled to the free exercise of religion" and suspended tax support for a state Episcopal church, but did not disestablish it. Massachusetts, Connecticut, and New Hampshire tried a version of multiple establishment, maintaining Congregationalism as a state church and taxing citizens for the support of religion, but allowing them to choose which church their money should support.

After the war Virginia became the central battleground over multiple establishment as Episcopalians lobbied for a tax or "general assessment" to be distributed among churches. In his "Memorial and Remonstrance" of 1785 James Madison argued that religion was "the gift of nature" that "must be left to the conviction and conscience of every man," and that religious establishment of any kind was tantamount to coercion. Swayed in part by the intense organizing and petition-gathering of evangelicals, particularly Baptists, who gathered thousands of signatures in favor of disestablishment, the Virginia legislature in 1786 adopted Thomas Jefferson's "Statute for Religious Freedom," which guaranteed freedom of worship and affirmed that no one "shall be compelled to frequent or support any religious worship, place, or ministry."

In addition to pressure from evangelicals and other religious dissenters, the move toward separation of church and state reflected the influence of Deism and religious skepticism among prominent Founders like Madison and Jefferson. Deism, a religious philosophy that rose to prominence during the Enlightenment of the late seventeenth and early eighteenth centuries, favored reason over faith. Deists acknowledged divine creation of the universe but deemphasized God's active hand in the affairs of mankind, arguing that humans' free will and intellectual rigor were more reliable guides to social, political, and moral behavior than nebulous divine intent. Deism denied the divinity of Christ and was skeptical of the divine inspiration of the Bible, though many Deists agreed the Bible contained some useful lessons. Deism, then, was a religious counterpart to the Enlightenment political theory of checks and balances: God provides balance in the cosmos and provides humans with the tool of reason to maintain balance in government. Accordingly, religion and government should be kept apart.

As an expression of this philosophy, the Virginia Statute for Religious Freedom proved a model for the First Amendment to the Constitution, which reflected a broad commitment to separate church and state: "Congress shall make no law respecting an establishment of religion, or prohibiting the free exercise thereof." The apparent ambiguity and elusive meaning of the establishment clause in modern interpretation reflect the divided opinion of the founders themselves on the relationship between church and state. While everyone agreed that the government should not support a state religion, there was no consensus that government should be completely divorced from anything to do with religion. Could the government aid religious groups, as long as it did not discriminate among them? Were states permitted to support a church? In fact, several states maintained multiple establishments until the 1820s. Whether by flexible interpretation of the Bill of Rights or simply common agreement of the founding generation, moreover, the government took on a religious persona and actively promoted the observance of religion. Following the passage of the Bill of Rights, Congress passed a resolution for a "day of public thanksgiving and prayer to be observed for the many signal favors of Almighty God." Congress observed the Sabbath and religious holidays, and chaplains led prayers in the army and in both houses of Congress. In public addresses, presidents and other officials routinely sought God's blessing for the country. While these forms of civil religion endorsed no specific faith, in practice they promoted the worship of Protestant Christianity, the heritage in which all the founders were raised. Whether they considered themselves Deist or church men, whenever someone invoked God in an official government setting the earliest generation of elected representatives shared a common understanding of a God loosely or entirely embedded in a Protestant context. Thus, religion was central to the conduct of government as a performed set of political rituals designed to reinforce the ideological shape of the nation-state.

In a broader sense, the place of religion in the early republic as delineated in the First Amendment encapsulated broad changes in the relationship between religion and politics in Atlantic America during the previous century. The anti-Catholicism and limited religion toleration of the British Empire had given way to full official religious freedom in the US, though of course popular intolerance and discrimination against religious minorities and perceived outsiders continued. Established religion, chronically weak in colonial America outside of New England, was undermined further by religious pluralism, revivalism and dissent, making the creation of a state church impossible in the new nation. Yet, in very different ways, religion remained as central to the sense of American nation-state as it had to the British Empire whence it emerged. Whereas once the colonies had embraced and expressed the religious nationalism of the British Empire, many religious folk, including elected officials and church leaders, now projected on the United States a sense of divine national destiny in spiritual and global affairs. To many, the post-revolutionary world was simply that much closer to God's kingdom than the pre-revolutionary one; a new generation of radical apocalyptic prophets urged the nation to purify itself and return to an unadulterated religion of the soul in preparation for the coming millennium.

In the late eighteenth and early nineteenth centuries, as denominations flourished in the sunlight of religious freedom and evangelical revival, churches expanded their traditional roles as centers of community life, education, social services – and political action. Religion suffused politics in the new republic, as in the intensifying debate over role of slavery in American life, and burgeoning political and social reform movements such as abolition, temperance, and prison reform drew their moral strength from post-revolutionary religious idealism. Even as slaveholders used the Bible to defend bondage, energetic resistance to slavery and racism radiated from African American churches, which claimed thousands of new members by the early nineteenth century. Slavery, they insisted, was unchristian and had no place in a country supposedly shining with the promise of God's favor. From the West Indies and United States to Canada and Britain, black Atlantic Protestants envisioned Africa as a spiritual homeland to be settled and evangelized by God's redeemed people, a project they began in the new West African colony of Sierra Leone. In Richmond, Virginia, in 1800, a thwarted rebellion led by a slave named Gabriel Prosser contained an explicit prophetic call for the enslaved to throw off their shackles and claim their destiny in freedom as God's chosen people. As he went to the gallows, one slave rebel said that in striking a blow for liberty he had only done the same as George Washington. Many years would pass before the religiously-inspired abolition movement and a bloody war would bring the dream of African American freedom to fruition.

Native Americans, too, looked to prophetic religion as they faced dispossession and dislocation after the American Revolution. Fearing that a victory by the revolutionaries would open up the trans-Appalachian west to settlement, most Indians had supported the British during the war, and with the British defeat, their fears were realized. Hundreds of thousands of settlers streamed across the mountains into Ohio, Kentucky, Illinois, Alabama and Mississippi territories, displacing many Native groupings who were forced by the federal government to cede their lands to make way for a Christian, white man's nation. The familiar problems of land loss, trade dependency, alcoholism and the erosion of traditional cultures again gave rise, as in the 1760s, to a new series of religious revivals led by holy men who called for Indians to purify themselves and shed pernicious Anglo-American influences, including clothing, Christianity, and education. In the 1790s such leaders as Handsome Lake of the Senecas and Tenskwatawa of the Shawnees ("The Prophet") invoked divine revelation through dreams and trances to urge a return to traditional ways through spiritual renewal. For Tenskwatawa more than for Handsome Lake, that awakening held the key to Indian unity in resisting white encroachment. Together with his brother, Tecumseh, Tenskwatawa organized diverse Indian peoples from the Great Lakes to the Gulf Coast into a pan-Indian confederacy, ready to defend Indian lands and rights with armed force. A united Indian army was defeated at Tippecanoe, Ohio, in 1811, and a force of Creeks with a similar prophetic outlook, called Red Sticks, was likewise defeated in 1814 in Alabama. Though many Indians allied with the British during the War of 1812, the outcome of the war left them more vulnerable than ever to white pressures, against which religious revivalism offered little protection.

By the time of the Lewis and Clark expedition in 1803, many in the United States had shifted their Atlantic gaze to the west where, it seemed, an inexhaustible wealth of land to the far reaches of the continent would guarantee the fulfillment of a divinely-ordained rise of American liberty, empire and global power. In this triumphal vision, the destiny of the nation went hand in hand with religious chosenness, a revitalized sense of America as the new Israel. As long as slavery endured, however, and as long as that westward-seeking drive meant the dispossession of native people from their own land, that vision remained imperfect. For millions, religion and politics remained intertwined and indistinguishable, but in different ways. As religion supplied a moral justification for national power, it also reinforced a sense of purpose for those who did not share in that power. The tension between those competing views guaranteed the vibrancy, and the discordant jarring, of religious expression in the political and moral life of the New Republic.

References and Further Reading

Bloch, Ruth (1985) *Visionary Republic: Millennial Themes in American Thought, 1756–1800*, New York: Cambridge University Press.

Bonomi, Patricia U. (2003) *Under the Cope of Heaven: Religion, Society and Politics in Colonial America*, 2nd edn, New York: Oxford University Press.

Butler, Jon (1990), *Awash in a Sea of Faith: Christianizing the American People*, Cambridge, MA: Harvard University Press.

Colley, Linda (2005) *Britons: Forging the Nation, 1707–1837*, New Haven, CT: Yale University Press.

Dowd, Gregory Evans (1993) *A Spirited Resistance: The North American Indian Struggle for Unity, 1745–1815*, Baltimore, MD: The Johns Hopkins University Press.

Edwards, Jonathan (1742) *Some Thoughts Concerning the Present Revival of Religion in New England*, Boston, quoted in Alan Heimert and Perry Miller (eds.) (1967) *The Great Awakening*, Indianapolis and New York: Bobbs-Merrill.

Elliott, J.H. (2006) *Empires of the Atlantic World: Britain and Spain in America, 1492–1830*, New Haven, CT: Yale University Press.

Frey, Sylvia, and Betty Wood, Betty (1998), *Come Shouting to Zion: African American Protestantism in the America South and British Caribbean to 1830*, Chapel Hill, NC: University of North Carolina Press.

Gould, Eliga H. (2000) *The Persistence of Empire: British Political Culture in the Age of the American Revolution*, Chapel Hill, NC: University of North Carolina Press.

Kidd, Thomas S. (2007) *The Great Awakening: The Roots of Evangelical Christianity in Colonial America*, New Haven, CT: Yale University Press.

Lambert, Frank (2006) *The Founding Fathers and the Place of Religion in America*, Princeton, NJ: Princeton University Press.

Sidbury, James (2007) *Becoming African in America: Race and Nation in the Early Black Atlantic*, New York: Oxford University Press.

Tennent, Gilbert (1742) *The Dangers of an Unconverted Ministry*, Boston.

Williams, Elisha (1744) *The Essential Rights and Liberties of Protestants*, Boston, quoted in Alan Heimert and Perry Miller (eds.) (1967) *The Great Awakening*, Indianapolis and New York. New York: Bobbs-Merrill.

6

Cosmology

Stephen A. Marini

As the imagined worlds that people inhabit, cosmologies affect human behavior in many ways, and often underlie political decision-making, community organization, and religious practice. For many Americans after 1692, cosmologies changed to reflect increasing interest in the individual's place in the world. During the next century, politics reflected new concerns about citizenship, the natural rights of man, and the individual nature of religious opinion, and religious communities paid increasing attention to individual experience, and the practice of religion focused more on methods to attain personal piety and moral virtue. These changes occurred as people moved away from inhabiting medieval worlds defined by beings external to the individual toward modern, secular worlds in which individual feeling and individual choice attained greater prominence

British and European historians write about "the long eighteenth century" as a single period stretching from the Glorious Revolution of 1688 to Napoleon's defeat in 1815 and even beyond (O'Gorman 1979). These years constitute a unified era, they say, because of closely interwoven developments in war, political affairs, and dynastic fortunes. American religion had a long eighteenth century too, but it was marked by the quite different episodes of the Salem Witch Trials, the Great Awakening, the Revolutionary Crisis, and the Second Great Awakening. Yet the long eighteenth century in America arguably produced more fundamental change in religion than the British or Continental one did in politics, for between 1692 and 1805 the religious identity of the United States took shape. The Protestant communities of British North America were transformed from a collection of communions rooted in doctrinal systems of the Reformation into a pluralistic Evangelical majority counterbalanced by a small but influential Liberal minority. At the same time, diverse communities of Catholics, Jews, Native Americans and African Americans developed their religious traditions amidst complex interactions with Protestants, and all religious groups had to deal with changing political circumstances impinging on them from colonial governments, the Revolutionary movement, and the constitutional order of the new American republic.

Visible and Invisible Worlds

At the end of the seventeenth century, the Tudor Reformation and the English Civil War still powerfully shaped the religious world of British North America. Henry VIII and Elizabeth I had created the Church of England in the sixteenth century and mandated it as the religion of their realms. By 1692, Anglicanism was legally established in Virginia, constitutionally privileged in the Carolinas, dominant in Maryland, and powerful in all major colonial port cities. Its core beliefs and practices, as defined in the *Thirty-Nine Articles of Religion* (1563), had been engrained for nearly a century in the South, where they powerfully legitimated British colonial governments. The English Civil War and Commonwealth (1640–60), however, had facilitated the creation of other American colonies by Separatists and Puritans in New England, Quakers in Pennsylvania and West Jersey, and Catholics in Maryland. All the leading religious factions of the English Civil War – Anglican, Puritan, Radical, Catholic – had found hegemonic colonial niches in colonial America.

Important non-English ethnic religious enclaves diversified these rival colonial regimes. The Dutch Reformed in the Hudson Valley and East Jersey were the largest of them, with a small community of Swedish Lutherans in Delaware and West Jersey and an increasing number of German communions – Lutheran, Reformed, Mennonite – migrating to William Penn's "holy experiment" in Pennsylvania after 1681. Nearly every colony in British North America also harbored at least a sprinkling of Huguenot refugees, French Calvinists who fled France following Louis XIV's 1685 revocation of the Edict of Nantes (1598) that had granted limited religious toleration to Protestants. A handful of diasporic Sephardic Jewish communities, emigrants from Brazil and other Iberian colonies to American port cities, completed the religious spectrum.

This was a profoundly Protestant religious world whose people lived in a deeply traditional and hierarchical sacred cosmos inhabited by spiritual presences and omens heavy with prophetic and apocalyptic meaning. The Salem Witch Trials were a spectacular instance of this religious mentality in its Puritan inflection. What began in January 1692 as the perplexing illnesses of the daughter and niece of Samuel Parris, Salem Village's controversial new minister, culminated a year later in the arrest of dozens of local people and the trial and execution of 19 of them as witches (Figure 6.1). Many factors contributed to this heinous outcome. Its root cause was a tangled web of familial rivalry, economic competition, political conflict and ministerial allegiance, but other all-too-human elements were also present (Boyer and Nissenbaum 1974).

A clash of healing cultures separated Tituba, the Parrises' female slave who practiced an indigenous South American healing cure on the girls, from William Griggs, Salem's new physician who first suggested a supernatural cause for the maladies. Conflicted relationships between Salem mothers and daughters worked powerfully on the alleged victims. The girls' guilt and fear of punishment took hold when adults began to take seriously their perhaps playful but certainly untrue allegations. Broader influences were also at work. Salem was reeling from the renewal of Indian wars in nearby Maine, and the entire colony was anxious about the outcome of distant negotiations in London for a charter under new monarchs William and Mary. From a still larger perspective, Salem was a transatlantic manifestation of what historian Hugh Trevor-Roper called "the European witch craze of the sixteenth and seventeenth

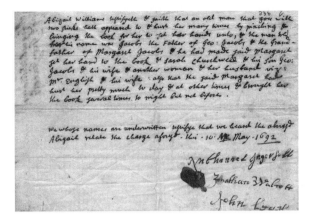

Figure 6.1 Abigail Williams' testimony to the charge of witchcraft leveled against Reverend George Jacobs, Sr.

centuries," a protracted episode of violence, especially against women, that reflected changing gender roles and power relationships in early modern Atlantic society (Trevor-Roper 1967: 90–193).

As colonial cosmology, however, the most important aspect of the Salem Witch Trials was their articulation of a potent system of popular Puritan beliefs that explained physical, psychological, and social disorder through a combination of confessional Protestant theology and traditional magic. When the girls' illness, trance, hysteria, and apparent spirit possession could not be dealt with by usual medical means, religion's capacity to explain anomaly through sacred symbols came to the fore. As Salem Village descended into a welter of internecine accusation and inexplicable behavior, Samuel Parris turned to a Puritan worldview capable of interpreting it as the work of Satan, loosed by the permissive will of God to test the faith and order of his community. There was a rich heritage of Puritan demonology and witchcraft lore for him to call upon. Just 15 years earlier, John Milton had crafted a superb portrait of the Prince of Darkness in *Paradise Lost* (1676) that conveyed both Satan's raging quest for vengeance against God and his alluring temptation of Adam and Eve. Closer to home, Cotton Mather, young minister of Boston's Second Church, had recently published an account of sorcery against four young parishioners in *Memorable Providences Relating to Witchcraft and Possessions* (1688). Mather's eyewitness narrative contained many elements that would subsequently appear in Salem. Samuel Parris had a copy in his library.

Symbolically, witchcraft took place in the shadowy borderland where spiritual realities made contact with the physical, sensory and moral world of human experience. To Puritan understanding, it was precisely in this liminal realm where the saints fought a constant war against Satan, whose supreme strategy was disobedience of the laws of God and nature. Hence the bodies of the possessed moved in impossible ways, they saw preternatural visions of "the invisible world," and they spoke in moral riddles. All of this was called "spectral evidence," testimony of witchcraft victims still under spell. One of the most difficult cosmological dilemmas facing Puritan authorities was whether such claims were admissible as testimony in civil courts. Accusation of witchcraft by godly members of the community carried the presumption of guilt. The only recourse for an accused witch was to confess and plead for forgiveness, an option that Tituba took early in the Salem proceedings. Many accused church members denied they were witches, however, thereby forcing the issue of spectral evidence's credibility. If the evidence was true, the denials of the accused were lies and therefore proof of their witchcraft. If it was false, however, then the accusers were lying and guilty of profound sin that also deserved punishment. There was no cosmological middle ground here, no escape from theological and legal tautology. And when "innocent" children made the accusations, the presumption of guilt from spectral evidence was difficult to resist.

As the trials began in May 1692, Chief Judge William Stoughton allowed great leniency that looks today like blatant violation of the rights of the accused. Cotton Mather, eager to validate his credentials as resident expert in witchcraft, preached in favor of spectral evidence and wrote to the judges urging that they admit it. He obtained the records of their deliberations, which he used in a new book advocating the Salem trials called *The Wonders of the Invisible World*. Mather wrote at the height of the frenzy, which finally broke in September 1692 when Lady Mary Phips, wife of Governor William Phips, was accused as a witch. The governor promptly revoked the court's powers, declared the inadmissibility of spectral evidence, halted the executions, prohibited further arrests, and released the remaining accused.

The Witch Trials plainly showed religion's potential to inflame public fear and to persecute the innocent during times of uncertainty. They were a textbook example of the fatal religious construction of otherness, cast in the form of spiritual others who were identified as both external enemies and internal betrayers of the faith. But in the long run, Salem's primary result was to invalidate spectral evidence and the magico-religious lore that accompanied it. Puritanism benefited from the dismantling of its traditional tenets about witchcraft, emerging with a clearer cosmological distinction between the invisible world of spirits and the visible world of human affairs, the better to interpret both of them. The Salem Witch Trials did not shatter the traditional worldview of Puritanism so much as they amended it.

Medieval and early modern beliefs continued to flourish in New England for decades more, however, continually rehearsed by Congregational ministers' sermonic interpretations of storms, earthquakes, public executions, and wars (Hall 1989). A similar popular religious mentality informed Anglican Virginia, and in the rice and indigo plantations of the Lower South, West African slaves blended their traditional beliefs with Barbadian plantation culture to create a cosmos in which the spirits were very much alive in everyday experience (Isaac 1982; Sensbach 2005). The influence of religious "steady sellers" also molded the popular worldview. Classics of seventeenth-century English Puritan piety continued to circulate widely in all the colonies through the ensuing century. Books like Lewis Bayly's *The Practice of Piety* (1611), Richard Baxter's *The Saints' Everlasting Rest* (1650), and Joseph Alleine's *Alarm to the Unconverted* (1672) joined John Milton's *Paradise Lost* and John Bunyan's *The Pilgrim's Progress* (1678) in detailing a program of prayer, meditation, and moral duty for the devout (Brown 2007). Underpinning these features of popular cosmology were confessional doctrinal systems in all of the major Protestant churches, complex formulations that had emerged from decades of fierce debate after the Reformation and continued as official standards of belief and practice well into the eighteenth century.

These traditional and confessional worldviews were strongest in rural and frontier settlements, but new currents of scientific and philosophical inquiry began to develop in the rising colonial cities, stimulated by the British Enlightenment. The powerful examples of John Locke, Robert Hooke, and Isaac Newton influenced American investigators to explore human nature and the physical universe through philosophical reasoning and scientific observation. The paradoxical Cotton Mather also shared this interest, beginning with his youthful preparation of almanacs and extending to later experiments in corn hybridization and advocacy of smallpox vaccination. In 1721, he published *The Christian Philosopher*, the first American book to use evidence from celestial and terrestrial sciences in arguing for divine creation. He had come a long way since Salem.

The experimental method thrived among educated elites in all the colonies, nowhere more than in Philadelphia. There John Bartram, a Quaker farmer, developed America's first botanical garden in 1729 and soon gained transatlantic fame as a chronicler of North American plants. Appointed Royal Botanist to King George III in 1765, Bartram (1699–1777) took an active part in promoting science throughout the colonies. He joined with Benjamin Franklin, himself a noted experimenter in electricity, to found the American Philosophical Society in 1743. Later in the century, figures like the astronomer David Rittenhouse, the physician Benjamin Rush, and Bartram's botanist son William cemented Philadelphia's reputation as an international center of scientific research. With the success of the scientific method in solving some perennial mysteries of the natural world came Enlightenment skepticism about traditional Protestant teachings, like the biblical miracles or the doctrine of the Trinity, which seemed to defy natural laws and the canons of logic. At coffee houses, taverns, and Masonic lodges in America's urban centers, a younger generation of Enlightenment-influenced intellectuals began voicing doubts about the confessional systems of doctrine upon which the major colonial religions were based.

The Great Awakening

Significant groups of immigrant Protestants continued to diversify colonial religion, producing a bewildering array of confessional communities in British North America by the early 1720s. They could easily have remained disparate ethno-religious enclaves governed by local leaders or distant European authorities. Soon, however, they were swept into a transatlantic religious movement that eventually altered the worldview of most American Protestant communities. That movement is variously known as Pietism in its Continental form and Evangelicalism in its Anglo-American manifestation. It exploded spectacularly onto the American cultural landscape in a massive popular religious revival called the Great Awakening.

Pietism began in Frankfurt, Germany, where in 1670 a Lutheran scholar, teacher, and minister named Philip Jacob Spener organized small groups of parishioners to study the Bible together and share their spiritual experiences. Spener (1636–1705) called these meetings "collegia pietate," in Latin "gatherings of the pious," from which Pietism took its name. Pietist meetings swept across the Lutheran and Reformed churches of Germany and the Netherlands, kindling intense lay spirituality and moral fellowship. The influence of Pietism greatly increased in Anglo-America with the accession in 1714 of Georg Ludwig, Prince-Elector of Hanover in Lower Saxony, to the British throne as George I. Almost immediately the movement's spiritual influence began to be felt in the United Kingdom, where it melded with Anglican and late Puritan piety in figures like William Law, author of *A Practical Treatise on Christian Perfection* (1726) and *A Serious Call to a Devout and Holy Life* (1728), and powerfully affected the rising generation of Presbyterian ministers in Scotland and Ireland.

By the early decades of the eighteenth century Pietism had intensified from a spiritual renewal movement into a call for experiences of spiritual rebirth and sanctification as signs of true Christianity. The first major American advocate of this more extreme form of Pietism was Theodorus Jacobus Frelinghuysen (1691–1748), who emigrated from Germany in 1719 to serve four Dutch Reformed congregations in the Raritan Valley of East Jersey. Frelinghuysen's uncompromising demand for personal conversion and strict moral discipline proved controversial, but by the mid-1720s his effective evangelism had energized his congregations. At the same, an Anglophone form of conversionistic religion arrived in America, brought by the Scots-Irish Presbyterian William Tennent. Called in 1726 to serve the congregation at Neshaminy, Pennsylvania, Tennent (1673–1746) began preaching a highly emotionalized version of Calvinism that found many converts. He also opened a theological school for prospective ministers, derisively known as "the Log College," that drew dozens of talented young men. William's student and eldest son Gilbert Tennent (1703–64) was installed as Presbyterian minister at New Brunswick, New Jersey, in 1726, where he immediately joined his neighbor Frelinghuysen to promote the doctrine of "the New Birth," the requirement that Christians must experience conscious regeneration by the Holy Spirit. Their message gained new converts while also producing intense spiritual fervor and moral quickening among older members of their congregations.

The New Jersey ministries of Frelinghuysen and Tennent opened the Great Awakening, but it flowered fully in the 1734–1735 revival at Northampton, Massachusetts. The Northampton revival was occasioned by the sudden death of an adolescent boy who had been challenging the town's traditional Puritan moral and behavioral norms. The death fostered deep religious concern among the community's young people, furthered by the emotional preaching and frequent family visits of its minister Jonathan Edwards (Marsden 2003). Soon parishioners both young and old began to experience the New Birth. Virtually the entire town was eventually converted before the revival ended with the despairing suicide of one of Edwards's own uncles, who feared he would not be saved.

Edwards (1703–58) made the Northampton revival internationally famous in *A Faithful Narrative of the Surprising Work of God* (1737). He offered the Northampton experience as a blueprint for promoting religious renewal, calling it a "revival of religion" because it affected all aspects of congregational life, from preaching and spirituality to moral discipline and worship. Edwards also gave compelling accounts of regeneration as experienced by two converts, Abigail Hutchinson, a young woman, and Phebe Bartlet, a 4-year-old girl. His tragic portrayal of Abigail followed her from the heights of ecstatic spiritual experience to an agonizing death through which she persevered sanctified, while his portrait of Phebe invented the infant Evangelical saint who precociously possessed every spiritual attribute of the elect adult. Through these two examples Edwards presented a new Evangelical archetype of spiritual rebirth that gained enormous popular influence. *A Faithful Narrative* not only brought Edwards acclaim, it also marked the beginning of a controversial

Figure 6.2 Rev. George Whitefield's American tours during the Great Awakening drew large crowds from all walks of colonial life.

Evangelical strategy of validating their revivals by publishing highly partisan accounts of them. This savvy editorial presentation of individual and community religious experience as the act of God galvanized the rising Evangelical movement to expect revivals and promote them relentlessly (Butler 1982; Lambert 1999).

As revival fervor grew, the Awakening entered its climactic phase with the inter-colonial preaching tours of the English itinerant George Whitefield from 1738 to 1744 (Figure 6.2). Whitefield (1714–70) was a newly ordained 23-year-old Anglican protégé of John and Charles Wesley when he sailed for Georgia in 1738 on a personal mission to evangelize America. Immediately after his arrival, he unleashed an intensely emotional preaching style as a "divine dramatist," aimed at facilitating the New Birth in his hearers (Stout 1991). In a short time his controversial revivalism had been rejected by Carolina Anglicans and warmly embraced by Charleston's Baptists, Congregationalists, and Presbyterians. Before returning to England the young preacher took his message to Philadelphia where he enjoyed a resounding response.

Once home, Whitefield, like Edwards, wrote about his experience in the mounting revival. But Whitefield's *Journals* gave a fiercely partisan report of his religious adventures, specifically naming those who had sustained and resisted God's cause. Anglican authorities on both sides of the Atlantic were unable to contain the indefatigable Whitefield. Three more times before 1745 he traversed the entire eastern seaboard from south to north, preaching at Dissenting meetinghouses and public venues in port cities and smaller towns. Everywhere "the Grand Itinerant" drew extraordinary crowds. He attracted extensive newspaper coverage and continued to publish his inflammatory *Journals*. In many places Whitefield's powerful preaching was enough to bring conversions and charismatic exercises on the spot; in others, his visit touched off subsequent revival campaigns by local ministers. Such ripple effects spread out across the Jerseys and much of New England, creating the sort of generalized religious concern that Edwards had described at Northampton.

An analogous movement of revivalistic Pietism flourished among the German churches of Pennsylvania, complementing the Anglophone Awakening that thrived there in Presbyterian and Baptist communities. Led by the aggressive efforts of the Moravians, a radical Pietist sect founded in 1727 by Saxon nobleman Count Ludwig von Zinzendorf, Pennsylvania Germans developed a distinctive focus on the wounds of Christ and an intimate child-like relationship to the Savior in their prayer disciplines and hymnody. Zinzendorf (1700–60) also used his charismatic leadership in an attempt to fashion an interdenominational Pietist union among seven German communions. His "Synod of the Holy Spirit" got off to an encouraging start in the early 1740s but foundered on charges of Moravian heterodoxy and deception.

As the Awakening grew in scope and intensity, it spawned an exclusionary wing of radical Evangelicals who demanded that their religious communities, including ministers, be composed entirely of the regenerate. Gilbert Tennent gave definitive literary expression of this separatist imperative in his October 1740 sermon *The Dangers of an Unconverted Ministry*. Tennent said that ministers who had not experienced the New Birth were "Pharisees" and "blind guides" incapable of leading their people to God's salvation. He instructed congregations afflicted with such unconverted ministers either to remove or to separate from them. Tennent's criticism of his fellow Presbyterian ministers was the last straw for the anti-revival party, known as "Old Sides." By the narrowest of margins they excluded Tennent's "New Sides" from the Synod of Philadelphia in 1741, a schism of the fourth-largest colonial communion that continued until 1758. Radicalism and separatism quickly spread to the New England Congregationalists. Jonathan Edwards, leader of the Evangelical "New Lights," sought successfully to maintain communion with the anti-revival "Old Lights," but New Light extremists led by James Davenport took the further step of schism, forming themselves into "Separate" or "Strict" Congregational churches. By the 1750s there were more than more than one hundred of these schismatic churches, producing a complex division of Congregationalists in which roughly one-third were Old Lights, one-third New Lights, and one-third Separate.

The radicalism of the Separates also provoked theological debate in New England about the validity of the revival. In his 1741 Yale commencement address *The Distinguishing Marks of a Work of the Spirit of God*, Edwards took a careful middle ground, arguing that while such disruptive Separate hallmarks as crying, shouting, vision, and trance were not necessarily marks of the Spirit's presence, they could accompany a genuine infusion of grace. On the other hand, he positively asserted that certain spiritual states, especially a sense of God's supreme "excellency," were scripturally mandated indicators of the New Birth. Edwards's carefully wrought position drew a heated reply from Charles Chauncy, minister of Boston's First Church. Harvard-educated scion of a noted Anglo-American clerical family and pastor of one of the most Enlightenment-influenced congregations in British North America, Chauncy (1705–87) declared in his 1742 sermon *Enthusiasm Described and Caution'd Against* that the New Birth and its effects were delusional "heats of the imagination" more akin to mental illness than the regenerating actions of the Holy Spirit. The two leaders traded polemics on the revival and by 1743 a new theological battle line had been drawn, with Edwards and Chauncy established as the respective New Light and Old Light champions.

As theological stalemate loomed and controversy over New Light itinerancy increased, Harvard's faculty publicly condemned Whitefield in 1744 as "an Enthusiast, a censorious, uncharitable Person, and a deluder of the People," whose 'going about, in an itinerant way ... [is] utterly inconsistent with the Peace and Order, if not the very Being of [the] Churches of Christ' (Holyoke et al. 1744: 3) Yale's faculty soon followed, along with several Congregational ministerial associations, and in 1745 Davenport published his *Retractations*, apologizing for any harm his radicalism might have caused and begging for reinstatement. By the time an exhausted Whitefield sailed to Bermuda for his health in the spring of 1748, the tide of revival had long since ebbed.

Evangelical Calvinism and Liberal Arminianism

It was not clear in the mid-1740s whether Old Lights or New Lights would emerge as the dominant religious faction in British North America. Over the next 15 years Edwards earned his lasting reputation as America's greatest theologian by fashioning a brilliant synthesis of Evangelical Calvinism. Chauncy proved to be his most able liberal respondent, the chief formulator of what was called Arminianism. The adjective referred to the Dutch theologian Jacobus Arminius (1560–1609) whose dissent against orthodox Calvinist doctrines of predestination and election was repudiated at the Synod of Dortrecht in 1618–19. Arminian ideas migrated into British and Continental philosophy during the seventeenth and eighteenth centuries, where they powerfully reinforced Enlightenment rationalism in theology as well as philosophy. Edwards and Chauncy were hardly alone in this great debate – Presbyterian and Baptist writers in the Middle Colonies and the South also took it up – but the New England rivals gave it the most sophisticated and systematic American articulation.

Edwards had already begun his construction of Evangelical Calvinism in a series of 1739 sermons later published as *A History of the Work of Redemption* (1774), the goal of which was to understand how God had fashioned his church through human history as the vehicle for realizing his sovereign will to save the elect. Not surprisingly, Edwards included the Northampton revivals as one of the defining episodes of this sacred chronology, a sign pointing to the near dawn of the thousand-year reign of Christ on earth before the Last Judgment. *Redemption*'s optimistic cosmology, called post-millennialism, suffused all of Edwards's writings, giving revivals an aura of divine purpose that became a staple of Evangelical self-understanding. For Arminians, however, Edwards's view of history betrayed a Puritan providentialism and biblical literalism they sought to dispel with a "scientific" Enlightenment historiography of cause and effect.

More central to Edwards's synthesis was his interpretation of the New Birth, the definitive analysis of which appeared in *A Treatise on Religious Affections* (1746). In good Calvinist fashion, he argued that, while rational understanding was necessary for the soul to comprehend the terms of God's covenant, regeneration came only by sovereign grace bestowed upon the elect through the Holy Spirit. Edwards insisted that the will was the human faculty through which regeneration occurred, moved to receive saving grace by religious affections or emotions supernaturally infused into it through a new "spiritual sense" created during the New Birth. "True religion, in great part, consists in holy affections," he proclaimed, joining Calvinist cosmic determinism to Evangelical religious experience (Edwards 1746: 3). Edwards's argument turned on identifying reliable signs of regeneration, which he described in strongly aesthetic and even mystical terms. A spiritual sense of divine "excellency, beauty, and symmetry" was the hallmark of authentic religious experience, he argued, the affective response of the soul to being ineffably bound to God's own spiritual essence. Against this affectional theory of religious experience, Arminians insisted that way to religious truth led through the careful application of logic and scientific empiricism to the evidence of scripture, nature, and traditional doctrine. Chauncy's *Twelve Sermons* (1765) was the most direct and complete statement of this "supernatural rationalism" applied to faith, works, and justification (Wright 1955).

Edwards turned next to the composition of the church. In *A Humble Inquiry into … the Qualifications Requisite to Complete Standing and Full Communion in the Visible Church* (1749) he endorsed the ecclesiology of the "gathered church" made up of the regenerate elect who alone could take the Lord's Supper. Edwards's efforts to enforce these standards at Northampton failed, leading to his dismissal in 1750 to the frontier settlement of Stockbridge, Massachusetts. By contrast, Chauncy made standards for the Lord's Supper more inclusive at Boston's First Church. In *The Breaking of Bread* (1772) he presented communion as an "obligation" that all should undertake, not only committed Christians but also the "securely wicked, careless and indifferent, and those who are hindered by doubts, fears, and spiritual difficulties" (Chauncy 1772: 33–34).

At Stockbridge, Edwards completed treatises on the thorny theological issues of human free will and original sin. *A Careful and Strict Enquiry into the Modern Prevailing Notions of … Freedom of the Will* (1754) is considered his masterpiece of philosophical theology. It addressed the allegedly Arminian tenet that the will was free because it was governed by aspects of the human mind – ideas, sense perception, affections – rather than external forces such as God's will. Edwards pointed out that this premise still entailed a will determined by something other than itself and asked what caused the ideas, perceptions, or affections that thus moved it. With each answer he asked again about its cause, producing an infinite regress or *reductio ad absurdum* of the claim to self-determination that eventually ended in God as First Cause. Constructively, Edwards argued that the will in fact was free in a different sense – it was free only to choose that which produced the most pleasure or avoided the greatest pain. Given the Christian assumption that God was by definition the supreme source of pleasure, it followed for Edwards that the will must always choose what God intends for it.

This argument secured a determinate Calvinist universe while granting a certain freedom to human will, and at the same time it demolished some of the more extreme Enlightenment alternatives being debated by elite colonial Americans. The New England Arminians, however, did not recognize themselves as holding the "modern notions" of freedom of the will that Edwards condemned. They were not rationalists and they certainly did not hold the sort of radical self-determination that he so opposed. In fact, Arminians like Chauncy were inclined to agree that the will naturally pursued pleasure and avoided pain and that some spiritual dimension was involved in turning it to God. They thought of that influence as more intellectual than emotional, but for them, as for Edwards, it required deep engagement with the scriptures and the sacraments.

Edwards's treatise *The Great Christian Doctrine of Original Sin Defended* was in press when he died in 1758. In it, he asserted a deeply Augustinian view of human nature as innately depraved, bringing scripture, history, and theological reasoning to support his case. He argued the traditional Calvinist positions on original sin and added a new one, that God had actively "constituted" the sinful nature of Adam and later humanity as a consequence of the Fall. Arminians readily acknowledged the reality of sin, but they denied that it totally pervaded the human character. They argued instead that an element of Adam's innocence survived the Fall, which in turn helped humans to embrace the gospel and perform at least some good works. Chauncy outlined this view in his *Five Dissertations on the Scripture Account of the Fall*, written during the 1750s or 1760s but not published until 1785.

Edwards also left incomplete a short treatise on *The Nature of True Virtue*. Published in 1765, it represented his only major venture into theological ethics. Edwards defended the proposition that "true virtue most essentially consists in benevolence to Being in general." Good will is the moral attitude of Christian love, which Edwards defined as selflessness or "disinterested benevolence." Instilled in the souls of the elect by the Holy Spirit, disinterested benevolence extends first to God in grateful thanks for salvation, then to other humans as God's created immortal souls, and thence to "the degree of being" in all other creatures great and small (Edwards 1765: 117 and 189). *True Virtue* looked back to the classical cosmological concept known as the Great Chain of Being for its vision of regenerate good will extending from the godhead to the lowest point of the created order. Like his teachings on original sin, Edwards's view of good works and true virtue reduced the significance of human agency nearly to the vanishing point. Arminians responded by agreeing with him that good works did not earn salvific merit but contesting his concept of disinterested benevolence. Good works were a product not of some mysterious grace, they argued, but of sound religious education and moral training, crucial elements of Christian culture upon which a proper social order should be built.

Evangelical Pluralism and Narrative Theology

The great majority of people in Revolutionary America lived in frontier settlements, small agricultural communities and market towns. Among this rural population a different kind of cosmological development took place after the Great Awakening grounded not in confessional disputation but in competing versions of Evangelicalism. After the French and Indian War secured the frontier, a flood of settlers occupied newly available land in Maine, the Connecticut, Hudson and Susquehanna Valleys, and the vast southern Piedmont from central Pennsylvania to Georgia. Much of this migration occurred in ethno-religious groups. In some cases entire congregations relocated to the new settlements, while others came in family or neighborhood groups. The religious combination was different on each frontier, yet though these communities were divided by ethnic traditions, their communities shared deep Reformation roots and powerful Pietist and Evangelical influences. During the pre-Revolutionary decades this intensive process of settlement created a uniquely American mosaic of religious cultures into which two new radical Evangelical movements, the Separate Baptists and the Methodists, entered decisively.

The Separate Baptists developed in New England after the Great Awakening. By the early 1750s, many Separate Congregationalists had come to accept believer's baptism by immersion, even as they retained their other radical New Light sectarian imperatives of extempore preaching, charismatic gifts, gathered church, and separation from the world. A party of these Separate Baptist radicals, led by Elder Shubael Stearns, arrived at Sandy Creek, North Carolina, from Connecticut in 1755. They immediately began evangelizing in every direction. By 1758, they had gathered enough churches to form the Sandy Creek Baptist Association under Stearns's charismatic direction, and at the time of his death in 1771 their New Light revivalism had gathered dozens of churches north to Virginia and south to Georgia. Stearns was a unique American religious hybrid, a blend of New England Congregational and Presbyterian roots, Whitefieldian charisma, and Arminian theology from the General Baptists who had ordained him. Stearns and his convert preachers delivered their message in vernacular language without formal training, which produced a blend of Calvinist and Arminian teaching and a popular religious mentality that they deployed to potent evangelistic advantage.

The Methodists began organized evangelism in America with the arrival of John Wesley's deputy Francis Asbury in 1771. They proclaimed an Evangelical Arminian gospel of New Birth, sanctification, and Christian perfection. They organized small separated communities of intense discipline and spiritual fellowship built on Spener's Pietist model. And their preachers were lay elders whose ministry was certified by their Whitefieldian charisma and the conversions they gained, not their mastery of systematic theology. Their founder John Wesley provided guidelines for faith and practice, his brother Charles wrote their hymnals, and Asbury administered the movement in America. By 1774, the Methodists were concentrating their efforts on the Virginia and North Carolina Piedmont, where revivals had again intensified. There they competed furiously with Separate Baptists, Regular (Calvinist) Baptists, and Presbyterians. On the eve of political revolution itinerants little known today, such as Methodists Robert Williams and William Glendenning and Separate Baptists Samuel Harriss, John Waller, and Jeremiah Walker transformed the emerging religious culture of the Piedmont. They introduced hugely popular Evangelical Arminian alternatives to the region's older Anglican and Presbyterian communions. As the revivals continued nearly unabated through the Revolutionary and Constitutional crises, they filled the Piedmont and the Shenandoah with Methodist chapels and Baptist churches and followed ever-increasing migration west to the Ohio and Mississippi Valleys.

This intense infra-Evangelical competition began to dissolve traditional doctrinal and denominational boundaries and create a new theological framework for American Evangelicalism. Unlike the polarizing controversies of the Great Awakening, Piedmont contestants debated Calvinist and Arminian variants within a shared Evangelical consensus. Put another way, New England and port cities moved toward speaking two different and mutually exclusive theological languages, while the Piedmont and other frontier regions developed multiple dialects of a common Evangelical tongue. Cosmological discourse shifted from the logic of rival confessional systems to a shared narrative of the economy of grace, the soul's progress from sin to regeneration to sanctification.

This development altered the significance of many doctrines. The New Birth, for example, over which Edwards and Chauncy had struggled so mightily, was a theological given for Piedmont Evangelicals. Whether it entailed spiritual assent to divine "excellency" or possession by charismatic gifts was no longer a burning issue. The urgent theological question instead became whether the soul was able freely to offer itself to God in the process of regeneration. Evangelical Arminians said yes, Evangelical Calvinists no. Arminians offered human free agency to accept or reject God's grace with the prospect of gaining – but also losing – sanctification and even Christian perfection, while Calvinists countered with a deterministic universe and original sin but also the absolute assurance of salvation for God's elect. This turn toward the human dimension of salvation, or "anthropology" in the language of eighteenth-century theology, also had Christological implications. Reformed theology considered Christ as the divine agent of the Father's decrees of election and reprobation, whose death on the cross provided a "limited" atonement only for the sins of God's elect. By contrast, Evangelical Arminians taught what the Methodists called "universal redemption" and the Separate Baptists "general provision," whereby Christ's death paid the price for the entirety of human sin. Grace, as John Wesley said, was "free in all and free for all" (Wesley 1739: 5).

These issues proved to be the flashpoints of the Piedmont cosmological debate. No faction had clinching doctrinal answers to these great questions of Evangelical religion, but every party had formulations of them that coalesced into competing forms of salvation narrative, a mythic arc that joined Adam and Eve and Christ's ministry to their own human destinies. So they debated creation and fall, human nature and atonement endlessly, creating a new narrative discourse for American Evangelical cosmology. And the longer the revivals continued, the more urgently contested yet inconclusive the debate became.

The furious cosmological disputes in the Piedmont and on the other Revolutionary frontiers also produced the apparently paradoxical consequence that as rural religious culture became more solidly Evangelical, it also diversified institutionally with the rise of new schisms and sectarian movements. Some leaders saw in this situation a Whitefieldian vision of potential Evangelical union. North Carolina Presbyterian Henry Pattillo gave early expression to this hope in his 1788 sermon *On the Divisions among Christians*, but the sectarian impulse largely prevailed. The Methodists, for example, experienced a double division in 1792 when James O'Kelly and William Hammett led their followers out of Wesley's fellowship in Virginia and South Carolina respectively. Both leaders protested Asbury's centralization of authority, but they also voiced doubts about the Trinity and denounced Methodist compromises on slavery.

The Separate Baptists spawned several more sects. After the Revolution, John Waller formed a body of Arminian Separate Baptists in Virginia as did his colleague Jeremiah Walker in the Carolinas and Georgia. In New England, the original stronghold of the Separates, the leaven of Evangelical Arminianism produced Benjamin Randel's Freewill Baptists and varieties of Universalism founded by Caleb Rich, a Separate Baptist, and John Murray, one of Whitefield's English preachers. Mother Ann Lee's Shakers, also founded by radical English Whitefieldians, converted thousands of New England Separate Baptists who in 1787 elevated one of their former elders, Joseph Meacham of Enfield, Connecticut, to the sect's supreme leadership. In the Middle Colonies, Separate Baptist Elhanan Winchester established yet another variant of Universalism in Philadelphia while among the Pennsylvania Germans the hybrid Brethren in Christ movement emerged under Mennonite pastor Martin Boehm and German Reformed minister Philip Otterbein.

The New Divinity, Enlightenment Liberalism, and Revolutionary Ideology

No great confessional theologians followed Edwards and Chauncy in the second half of the long religious eighteenth century. An often-cited reason for this cessation is the supposed "desacralizing" effect of cultural disruption during the Revolutionary crisis and the turbulent 1790s. From a cosmological perspective, however, the late eighteenth century seems more a period of transition than one of increasing secularity. After Edwards's death in 1758, his students Joseph Bellamy (1719–90) of Bethlehem, Connecticut, and Samuel Hopkins (1721–1803) of Newport, Rhode Island, developed his teachings on church membership, holiness, and the millennium but they encountered difficulties in working out the metaphysical implications of his determinism. The titles of Bellamy's *The Wisdom of God in the Permission of Sin* (1759) and Hopkins's *Sin, thro' Divine Interposition, an Advantage to the Universe* (1773) suggest the sort of intractable philosophical and moral puzzles they undertook to solve. Even among the Reformed intellectual elite, this Edwardsean "New Divinity" did not dominate, though Bellamy and Hopkins trained dozens of ministers during their long careers. At Yale, President Ezra Stiles (1723–95) maintained a moderate "Old Calvinist" orthodoxy until nearly the end of the century. A similar development took place at Princeton under the presidency of John Witherspoon (1723–94), a leading Scottish Evangelical who did not endorse the Edwardsean views of his predecessors.

Arminians, on the other hand, moved rapidly toward Enlightenment liberalism and even Deism. Before his untimely death in 1766, Jonathan Mayhew of Boston's West Church published *Two Sermons on the Nature, Extent, and Perfection of the Divine Goodness* (1763) in which he argued that benevolence, not justice, was God's principal moral quality. Charles Chauncy agreed, and drew the inference that such a God would not condemn his own human creatures to eternal punishment for sin. He prepared a treatise during the early 1760s arguing for Universalism, which finally appeared in 1784 as *The Mystery Hid from Ages and Generations, ... or, the Salvation of All Men*. The most controversial development in Arminian theology, however, was its emerging critique of the Trinity. Chauncy and other Boston-area ministers cautiously explored Arianism, an ancient heresy that held the Son of God to be a created being and not fully divine. It followed for them that if Christ was not a divine person, the already dubious logic of the Trinity collapsed altogether. Amidst these liberal Congregationalist speculations, in 1785, the former Anglican parish of King's Chapel in Boston became the first American congregation formally to embrace Unitarianism under its lay leader James Freeman.

Enlightenment religious thought also spread among mercantile and plantation elites outside New England. Philadelphia sustained a particularly important circle of religious liberals around the College of Philadelphia (1755) that included Anglican William Smith, its first provost, and Old Side Presbyterians Thomas Ewing, Francis Allison, Benjamin Rush, and Benjamin Franklin, all of whom served it as instructors, administrators, or trustees. Franklin, the city's leading intellectual, carried the Enlightenment critique of Christianity to the point of denying biblical miracles and most doctrinal assertions. Declaring for Deism, Franklin gave a classic summary of that small but influential elite movement's beliefs in his *Autobiography*.

> That there is one God, who made all things; that he governs the world by his providence; that he ought to be worshiped by adoration, prayer, and thanksgiving; but that the most acceptable service of God is doing good to man; that the soul is immortal; and that God will certainly reward virtue and punish vice either here or hereafter. (Franklin 2003: 146)

Deistical ideas also attracted many nominally Anglican southern planters, most notably Thomas Jefferson, who by the 1770s had joined with Philadelphia Deists and Boston Arminians to form a powerful intercolonial network of elite Enlightenment religious liberals.

Today we rightly highlight the liberal religious principles of Founders like Franklin, Adams, and Jefferson, whose belief in free will, human rights, moral perfectibility and a benevolent deity underpinned the cosmic optimism of their Revolutionary ideology. While often considered Deists, however, most of the major founders are better understood as sharing Arminian, Unitarian, or Arian theological opinions (Holmes 2006). The cosmological roots of Revolutionary ideology, however, reached far back to Calvinist justifications for the Dutch Revolt (1568–1648) and the English Civil War (1642–51) and more recently to New England debates over religious dissent in the Great Awakening. In 1742, the Connecticut legislature passed a law requiring Separate Congregationalists to pay taxes for orthodox ministers, forbidding them to itinerate across town lines, and prescribing fines and imprisonment for noncompliance. This act drew the ire of Elisha Williams, orthodox Congregational minister, former rector of Yale College, and respected Connecticut legislator. His scathing 1744 pamphlet *The Essential Rights and Liberties of Protestants* denounced the law as a tyrannical abuse of political power and made an impassioned case for the inalienable right of religious liberty. A landmark in American political thought, Williams's essay was one of the earliest expressions of the natural rights theory that so deeply informed the Revolutionary movement. A few years later Boston Arminian Jonathan Mayhew gave another early expression of Revolutionary rights theory from the other side of the theological divide in his *Discourse Concerning Unlimited Submission and Non-Resistance to Higher Powers* (1750).

A quite different scenario played out in Pennsylvania, where the long-standing political dominance of the Quakers was challenged by the outbreak of the French and Indian War in 1756. Pacifist Quaker leaders faced the choice of marshalling a military defense of the colony or giving up political power. They chose the latter course, resigning from the colony's legislature and turning it over to their militant opposition most of whose leaders were Scots and Scots-Irish Presbyterians. In Virginia, the Anglican establishment reached a compromise with Presbyterian New Sides after the Awakening, agreeing to license their churches in return for their oath to uphold the government. This arrangement worked well until the Separate Baptists brought their brand of social and religious radicalism into the Commonwealth in the 1760s. By 1770, converted planters like Samuel Harriss and John Waller were openly violating Virginia's laws against dissenting preaching, for which they were repeatedly arrested and imprisoned. Turning the tables on the Anglican authorities, Harriss and Waller preached from jail, drawing large crowds who joined the Separate Baptists and intensified the social and religious ferment.

Separate Baptist radicalism met even more hostility in North Carolina, where thousands fled to Tennessee after the defeat of the Regulators at the Battle of Alamance

(1771) fearing loss of property and religious persecution at the hands of victorious Governor William Tryon. Separate Baptists were also the leading controversialists for religious liberty. Isaac Backus of Middleborough, Massachusetts, made the denomination's most accomplished public argument for an inalienable right to freedom of conscience in his *Appeal to the Public for Religious Liberty* (1773). In Virginia, the Baptists' protest for freedom of conscience had grown so strong that they were able to mount the largest petition drive in the history of the American colonies to press their case. Their efforts resulted in Thomas Jefferson's *Virginia Statute for Religious Freedom*, first proposed in 1779 and finally passed in 1786 with the help of James Madison's brilliant advocacy in his *Memorial and Remonstrance* (Isaac 1982).

Meanwhile, as the American colonies plunged toward war with Britain, Congregational and Presbyterian ministers, Evangelical and Arminian alike, came to their defense with an American version of Reformed political theology. In dozens of published sermons they depicted the colonies as godly, virtuous and innocent communities whose divinely mandated rights and political consent had been violated by a corrupt ministry, an ungrateful Parliament, and a tyrannical king. British commanders called the New England ministry "the Black Regiment" for the effectiveness of the religious propaganda they preached in their black Geneva gowns. When the protracted conflict ended in colonial victory, these same ministers hailed American independence, as Edwards might have, as the dawn of Christ's millennial kingdom in the New World. Just a few years later, however, they were resorting to jeremiads decrying the loss of virtue and political discipline evidenced by public disorders like Shays's Rebellion of 1786–87. Some Federalist Congregational ministers even offered biblical commentary on the new federal and state constitutions, as did Harvard president Samuel Langdon in *The Republic of the Israelites an Example to the American States*, his 1788 New Hampshire election sermon on the Book of Judges.

Catholics and Jews, First Nations and African Americans

The post-Revolutionary constitutional order mitigated centuries of legal sanction against Catholics and Jews, who responded with democratic experiments on their own traditional institutions. During the eighteenth century Maryland's Jesuit community had established some of the best grammar schools in the colony, through which generations of prominent families had maintained their Catholic identity. The most important of these families was the Carrolls, whose patriarch Charles Carroll of Carrollton was reputed to be Maryland's wealthiest man on the eve of the American Revolution. In 1773, Pope Clement XIV suppressed the Society of Jesus, leaving the Maryland Jesuits without hierarchical supervision. John Carroll, Charles's cousin, assumed informal leadership of the Jesuit community and the two kinsmen played crucial roles in gaining American Catholic support for the Revolution. In 1784, John Carroll drafted a *Constitution of the Clergy* that stipulated democratic decision-making for the Maryland community and recommended against appointment of an American bishop by Rome. Despite this protest, Carroll himself was named the first Catholic bishop in the United States in 1790. Headquartered at Baltimore, he founded Georgetown College in 1791, managed controversies over local control of church property in Philadelphia, and arbitrated ethnic parish conflicts in New York. By 1805,

Catholic growth had spread north and west in the new nation spurred by Irish and German immigration and frontier expansion. In 1808, Carroll was elevated to Archbishop of Baltimore and four new dioceses were established in Philadelphia, New York, Boston, and Bardstown, Kentucky. As the nineteenth century began, American Catholics had emerged as a large, multi-ethnic, and largely urban religious community whose tendencies toward independence and democratic experiment had already been noticed by the wider Catholic world.

Catholic cosmology, however, stood in fundamental tension with the Protestant culture majority of the new nation. (Dolan 2002, 13–46) Its sacramentalism and Eucharistic piety recalled central conflicts from the Reformation, and its Latin liturgies seemed linguistically exclusionary. Catholicism's centralized ecclesiology of bishops, cardinals, and pope also ran against the democratized church orders of American Protestants. Even the Episcopalians and Methodists elected their own bishops. More basically, American Catholics had to negotiate the dilemma of lining in a new nation whose political principles of republicanism and religious liberty had been condemned by the Vatican. Above all, Catholics struggled against the widespread belief that the Pope was the Antichrist. This traditional Protestant belief was incorporated into millennial expectations for the new republic, creating deep suspicion of American Catholics. The memory of Catholic patriotism during the Revolution and Carroll's sure administrative hand kept these tensions in check through the turn of the nineteenth century, but the vulnerable and paradoxical situation of the American Church would remain permanent.

While constitutional guarantees of religious freedom allowed American Catholics to emerge from centuries-long antipathy rooted in the British Reformation and imperial wars against France, it had an even more remarkable effect on American Jews who had suffered from centuries of Christian oppression and exile. The tiny American Jewish community – just 2500 in 1776 – suffered heavily during the Revolution due to its overwhelming concentration in the port cities that were the chief targets of British military strategy. The military struggle recalled painful memories of persecution in the Old World, but it turned suddenly into "the revolution in American Judaism" (Sarna 2004: 31–61). One feature of that revolution was the rewriting of traditional synogogue covenants as "constitutions," with affirmations of democratic principles and the inalienable right of religious conscience. Another element was experimentation with English as a liturgical language. Most important perhaps was the challenging of Sephardic control of American synagogues. In colonial times the Sephardic founding elites, like the Seixas family of Philadelphia, had controlled synagogue leadership and represented entire local Jewish communities. Under the new conditions of religious liberty, however, competing synagogues were organized in Philadelphia and New York by a younger and more recently arrived Ashkenazic minority, Jews from Central Europe who observed alternative liturgical and lifestyle practices. This process of diversification mirrored that of Protestants, placing Jews in a similar situation as the American religious majority and facilitating their integration into the new nation's emerging culture.

Jewish cosmology changed along with these organizational experiments. The commandments given to God's people on Mt. Sinai, and the sacred obligation to observe them, remained central to how Jews pictured the world. But their diversity and greater freedom to interpret Jewish law and practice led to new American versions of this centuries-old cosmology and to conflicts over the extent to which it should be changed. While some American Jews celebrated similarities between ancient Israel and the new Israel of America and interpreted their destiny and obligations in that context, others pulled back from adjustments that seemed to remake Judaism into an extension of American Protestantism.

Very different kinds of religious and cultural interaction took place between non-white populations and the Evangelical and Pietist missionaries, ministers, and masters through whom they encountered Anglo-American cosmology. After the Awakening, Evangelicals undertook a concerted effort to missionize indigenous peoples. During the 1740s, Eleazar Wheelock, a staunch New Light Congregationalist, founded a Latin grammar school – later Dartmouth College – for Native Americans in Lebanon, New Hampshire. Among his most talented students was Sampson Occom, a Mohegan, who in 1759 became the first Native American ordained by the Presbyterians. Occom (1723–92) broke with Wheelock over the latter's use of Indian School funds to support white students, then pursued an indigenized Christian ministry at Mohegan, Connecticut, and Brothertown, New York. Other New Lights and New Sides also engaged in Native American missions including Jonathan Edwards, who was appointed missionary to the Mohicans of Stockbridge, Massachusetts, in 1750, and his friend David Brainerd, who served among the Delaware of Pennsylvania and was the subject of Edwards's popular *Account of the Life of the Late David Brainerd* (1749).

Among the Pennsylvania Germans, the Moravians' missionary identity took them to the forefront of evangelistic efforts with First Nations. Led by the indomitable David Zeisberger (1721–1808), Moravian missionaries gathered small Christian settlements among the Delaware in New York and Pennsylvania and the Mohicans in Connecticut during the 1740s. They followed the Delawares west to Ohio and Canada and during the 1790s made lasting contact with the Cherokee. The 1792 massacre of 90 Moravian Native Americans at Gnadenhutten, Ohio, by white militiamen, however, marked a violent and tragic turning point in Evangelical missions to First Nations from which they never recovered.

The post-Revolutionary period was a devastating time for Native Americans. The new United States government regarded First Nations as conquered enemies and pursued a series of aggressive "conquest-theory" treaties that restricted them to reservations. Continuing resistance by the trans-Appalachian tribes of the Western Lakes Confederacy led to the Northwest Indian War (1790–95) in which indigenous forces were decisively defeated on 20 August 1794 by General Anthony Wayne's troops at the Battle of Fallen Timbers. Decades of war, displacement, and Christian missions had undermined traditional Native American cultures, but after the Northwest War prophetic figures sparked religious renewal and adaptation in some indigenous communities. The most noted of these prophets was the Seneca warrior and shaman Handsome Lake.

In 1799 and 1800, Handsome Lake (1735–1815) experienced visions of the spirit world guided by sacred beings including four angels and Jesus. He saw an apocalyptic judgment coming upon the Seneca and proclaimed that to be saved from everlasting torture by the Punisher they must confess their sins to the Creator, give up the evils of whiskey, witchcraft, love magic, and abortion, and scrupulously perform the rituals of their ancient ceremonial tradition. Most of the Seneca embraced Handsome Lake's mandates, to which he added a series acculturationist social teachings in 1802 including temperance, peace, preservation of tribal land, acquisition of American farming skills, English literacy, the sanctity of marriage and parental obligation to children. Later cast into elaborate written form, the Code or *Gaiwiio* of Handsome Lake played a crucial role in "the renaissance of the Iroquois" in the early nineteenth century (Wallace 1972: 239–302).

From a cosmological perspective, Handsome Lake's movement asserted traditional Iroquois religious culture while adapting to the Quaker missionary Christianity taught at the Seneca reservations. The attributes of his two great spirit beings, the Creator and the Punisher, closely resembled those of the Seneca culture hero Tarachiawagon and his evil twin Tawiskaron, and his demand that traditional ceremonials be performed probably saved them from extinction. Yet Handsome Lake also added heaven and hell to Seneca cosmology where no such eternal realms had existed before, and his visionary Jesus taught acceptance of whites as equals. Handsome Lake's movement was one of religious revitalization that honored the continuity and efficaciousness of Native American religious cultures in an era of relentless violence and exploitation.

Evangelicals had a quite different and more complex encounter with African Americans. In the Great Awakening, George Whitefield had preached salvation to African slaves and antislavery to their masters. Many planter converts accepted their regenerate responsibility to offer the gospel and even biblical literacy to their slaves. Some went further. In 1773, George Galphin, a Separate Baptist planter, permitted the gathering of what seems to have been the first Afro-Baptist slave congregation at his plantation in Silver Bluff, South Carolina. At least three notable slave preachers served Silver Bluff. George Leile (1750–1828) was converted, freed, and licensed as a Separate Baptist itinerant in 1773 and ordained in 1775. He helped to organize the Silver Bluff congregation, which he served intermittently for several years, then founded the First African Baptist Church of Savannah, the oldest permanent Afro-Baptist community in America. Leile, a Loyalist, left Savannah in 1784 for Kingston, Jamaica, where he established and ministered to the first Baptist church in that colony until his death. David George (c. 1742–1810), the first pastor of the Silver Bluff congregation, joined Leile in ministering to the Savannah church. Jesse Peter was another early member of Silver Bluff who returned after the war, was probably ordained by Separate Baptist Elder Abraham Marshall, and revived the slave congregation there from the late 1780s to 1792.

The most successful early Afro-Baptist minister of this period, however, was Andrew Bryan, coachman and body slave of Jonathan Bryan, a wealthy Low Country planter, fervent patriot, and radical Evangelical, whose name he took. Andrew was converted in 1782 by Leile and ordained by Abraham Marshall and Jesse Peter to succeed him as minister of the First African Baptist Church of Savannah. After he was freed under the terms of Jonathan Bryan's will, Andrew built Bryan Street African Baptist Church in Savannah in 1794, ministering to its large interracial congregation of 700 members until his death in 1812. Other Separate Baptist slave churches were organized in Georgia during the 1780s and 1790s at Springfield and Beaverdam, establishing the Savannah River country as a major center of Afro-Baptist religious culture.

Interpreters have puzzled over the attraction of Baptist beliefs and practices for slaves in the Lower South, most of whom had West African provenance. Scholars have identified two powerful sources of Afro-Baptist religious synthesis in spirit possession and water rituals. West African societies had a rich pantheon of ancestral and totemic sacred beings who were understood to communicate with humans through spirit possession or ecstatic trance. The tropical environments from Cape Verde to the Bight of Biafra also inscribed West African religions with sacred powers of initiation and immortality associated with rivers and water symbolism. The Separate Baptist gospel of spiritual rebirth expressed in charismatic gifts, with a dramatic initiation ritual of immersion in local rivers and streams, appealed to slave communities who still preserved analogous elements of West African religions. They readily embraced the Separate Baptist message but infused it with their own symbolic and ritual meanings, generating a distinctive New World Afro-Baptist religious tradition (Sobel 1979).

The Methodists gathered even more converts than the Separate Baptists among slave and free African Americans. Preaching that slavery was a sin not to be tolerated among believers, Methodist itinerants like Freeborn Garrettson and Jesse Lee gained speedy access to the slaves of planter converts in the Upper South, whom they successfully evangelized. When Francis Asbury began publishing racially categorized membership statistics in 1786, "blacks" accounted for less than 10 percent of the Methodists. By 1793, that proportion had risen remarkably to 24 percent, where it settled for the rest of the period. While African Americans were a majority in some Methodist circuits and an occasional class leader was appointed from their number, the first black Methodist elder, Richard Allen, was not ordained until 1799. Born a slave in Philadelphia, Allen was converted in 1777, purchased his freedom, and began touring as a Methodist itinerant. After leading segregated dawn services for several years at St. George's Methodist Church in Philadelphia, Allen joined Absalom Jones and several others in 1787 to form the Free African Society, a mutual aid organization. Allen also purchased a lot nearby, on which he built the Bethel Church in 1794, the first African American Methodist house of worship. After Asbury finally ordained Allen, he gathered several dozen congregations in the Northeast to form the African Methodist Episcopal Church in 1816, the first African American denomination.

Leadership by free blacks and uniform institutional discipline gave African Methodism a somewhat different character than the Afro-Baptist movement. Spirit possession and charismatic gifts were salient in both traditions, but African Methodists enjoyed greater social and spiritual fellowship in class meetings, and through Charles Wesley's hymns they were able to restore traditional elements of music and chant more readily than Afro-Baptists. Most fundamentally, however, all African Evangelicals found in the Genesis narrative of Israel in Egypt a hope for their own liberation that extended far beyond matters of spirit alone.

The Second Great Awakening

The Establishment and Free Exercise clauses of the First Amendment are often credited with the luxuriant growth of American religious diversity after the Revolution. Their grant of religious liberty, as James Madison had argued in the *Memorial and Remonstrance*, not only promoted religious competition but also strengthened what he called "religion in general," a force believed necessary to provide the moral discipline of citizens requisite for republican government. A national explosion of religious revival known as the Second Great Awakening did follow a few years after the Bill of Rights, but whether the First Amendment was its ultimate or even proximate cause may be doubted. The First Amendment only affected the laws of a weak and still experimental national government, not the states. And while most of the states out-side New England granted some form of religious liberty in their new constitutions, they had already become religiously diverse during the Evangelical revivals and Enlightenment experiments of the late eighteenth century. A more likely cultural source for renewed revivalism among Evangelical leaders was the perceived threat of secular radicalism stemming from the French Revolution. Its descent into fratricidal violence and the outspoken Deism and anti-clericalism of its principal Anglo-American apologist Thomas Paine in *The Age of Reason* (1793) alarmed many Evangelicals. They feared that anti-Christian forces were threatening the much-touted virtue of the American citizenry and turned to revival as a remedy after the failure of the Alien and Sedition Acts of 1798 to quash radical dissent.

In Federalist New England, the French threat played a prominent role in the revival strategy of Timothy Dwight, a grandson of Jonathan Edwards who was elected presi-dent of Yale College in 1795. Dwight (1752–1817) was a leader of the New Divinity faction that had continued to develop Edwards's theology during the Revolutionary decades. From his Evangelical Calvinist perspective, the French Revolution had embraced an "infidel philosophy" that he condemned in print and from the pulpit. By the turn of the century Dwight had recruited a new generation of revivalists from Yale to ride circuits throughout New England bringing the New Divinity's message of intense Evangelical spirituality and tightly controlled emotion. During the first dec-ade of the new century his young recruits, led by Lyman Beecher and Asahel Nettleton, sparked the Second Great Awakening in New England.

Dwight's strategy did revitalize New England Congregationalists, and his advocacy of the 1801 Plan of Union with the Presbyterians aligned them with their denomina-tional cousins to the south and west. But once again the renewal of revival also strengthened New England's dissenting Evangelical groups, especially the Separate Baptists and Methodists. More New Light sects also appeared, the most important of which was Elias Smith's Christian Connection. Smith's central theological goals were to free Evangelicals from the historical constraints of Reformation confessionalism and to unite them in one non-creedal fellowship. In publications like his popular reli-gious newspaper *The Herald of Gospel Liberty* (1808), Smith (1769–1846) published accounts of the Awakening and promoted his cause of ecumenical Evangelicalism. Although Smith's movement remained small, it served as an important unifying force for a popular Evangelical culture that turned increasingly away from traditional doc-trinal systems and toward the compelling narrative of salvation.

The *locus classicus* of the Second Great Awakening, however, was the trans-Appalachian West. There apprehension about French radicalism and the disruptions of the Northwest Indian War combined with an acute shortage of ministers to create a sense of religious crisis among Evangelical leaders. Notable revival campaigns began in 1799 in the Gaspar River country of western Kentucky and gradually built in inten-sity. The landmark episode of the Second Great Awakening was the Cane Ridge Revival. In July 1801, Barton W. Stone, a Presbyterian minister, announced that he would conduct a quarterly sacramental meeting the following month for preaching, prayer, singing, and the Lord's Supper at Cane Ridge, near Lexington, Kentucky. Similar mass sacramental meetings, popular among the Scots and Scots-Irish, had drawn large crowds who set up tents and camped near the proceedings (Schmidt 1989). No one was prepared, however, for the twenty or thirty thousand people who descended on Stone's farm for a "camp meeting" that became nine days of intense preaching, singing, exhortation and charismatic "exercises."

Camp meetings quickly became the distinguishing ritual feature of the Second Great Awakening, with revival preaching, all-night prayer, praise and lay exhortation, and spectacular charismatic manifestations of trance, glossolalia, laughing, crying, and singing. In a matter of months camp meetings had spread back east across the Appalachians to the Piedmont, where they continued to flourish through the first decade of the century and beyond. Cosmologically speaking, the camp meetings further blurred the doctrinal and denominational differences among rival Evangelical communions. As competition intensified and popular interest soared, preachers found themselves pressed to find doctrinal articulations that could persuade "the sovereign audience" of Evangelicals, who continued to abandon confessional traditions in significant numbers (Hatch 1989).

As the revival progressed, Stone (1772–1844) and some of his Presbyterian colleagues became convinced that formal doctrinal creeds were not part of biblical Christianity. They withdrew in 1804 to form their own Presbytery of Springfield, then dissolved it a year later because they had concluded that denominational factions were also not part of the apostolic faith. In the *Last Will and Testament of the Springfield Presbytery* (1805) they made a classic argument for restorationism, the claim that believers should return to the original form of Christianity as depicted in the New Testament without any extra-biblical elements whatsoever. While several Springfield Presbytery ministers joined the Shakers, Stone became leader of a larger group known simply as "Christ-ians" because they rejected all non-biblical names for the disciples of Christ. A further implication of anti-creedalism and restorationism was the rejection of the classical education that Presbyterians required for ordination. Knowledge of the scriptures and preaching that brought converts were the only apostolic requirements for ordination, they said. Claiming that a saving knowledge of the scriptures and an internal spiritual call to preach were the only requisites for ministry, Finis Ewing (1773–1841), a prominent critic of traditional educational standards, led his followers out of the Transylvania Presbytery in 1810 to form the Cumberland Presbyterian Church in Kentucky and Tennessee (Boles 1972).

The Long Eighteenth Century

American cosmology in 1805 would have been unrecognizable to Cotton Mather, Samuel Parris, and the Salem judges viewing it from the other end of the long American eighteenth century. The enchantments of their visible and invisible worlds had long since been broken, first by Enlightenment science and philosophy and then by the American Revolution. Only their own Massachusetts, with neighboring Connecticut and New Hampshire, still harbored vestiges of religious establishments and the systems of confessional orthodoxy that had supplied cosmological justifications to Puritan and Anglican political regimes of the colonial era. The new nation had enshrined religious liberty as an inalienable right and swept away most legal constraints on religious belief and worship. Thomas Jefferson, the most outspoken public advocate of religious freedom and the Enlightenment principles underpinning it, had been elected president of the young United States in 1800, swept to victory by votes of Baptists and

Methodists, Catholics and Jews for whom his *Virginia Statute for Religious Freedom* was a beacon to full participation in American religion and politics.

And yet spiritual enchantment had not disappeared in America. It had taken new form in the ravished souls of Evangelicals and Pietists regenerated by the atoning blood of Jesus and the charismatic powers of the Holy Spirit. Since the ministries of Frelinghuysen, Tennent, Edwards, Davenport, and Whitefield in the Great Awakening, their numbers had grown constantly and their gathered churches of the reborn had spread to every corner of the land. During the revivals of the 1760s, 1770s and 1780s their existential quest to understand spiritual rebirth had grown so intense that it overwhelmed the traditional Reformation systems of doctrine that had presided over British North America since colonization and replaced them with ceaseless inquiry into the nature and destiny of the individual soul. The myth of redemption – the narrative articulation of the economy of grace from creation to Last Judgment – became the new cosmological framework for Evangelicals. 1805 marked the zenith of yet another massive revival, the Second Great Awakening, whose camp meetings and new sects made permanent the narrative cosmology of Evangelical pluralism that had emerged during the Revolutionary Era.

By 1805, Evangelicals had launched a cultural campaign to create a Christian America, but for many others their spiritual enchantments and political agenda were bittersweet at best. Enlightenment liberals found refuge in New England Unitarianism and the capacious traditions of the Protestant Episcopal Church, independent America's revitalized Anglican communion. Even Thomas Jefferson discovered unmatched divine wisdom in the moral teachings of Jesus. For African Americans, however, Evangelical cosmology remained unrealized hope and tragic consolation. Still groaning under the oppression of co-religionist masters, Evangelical slaves hoped to cross over Jordan to real freedom, while their free brethren struggled with racism deeply inscribed in white Evangelical beliefs and practices. Catholic immigrants faced an increasingly powerful and hostile Evangelical establishment that suspected their capacity to be be good Americans. Jewish immigrants also faced discrimination, but along with it they found greater freedom in the United States than in Europe to express, adapt, or lose their religion. And in the vast unquiet woodlands and prairies of the Old Southwest, Old Northwest, and the new Louisiana Purchase, First Nations watched with growing apprehension as those same Evangelicals approached their land, hungry for its rich bounty and certain in their regenerate souls that God had given it to them.

References and Further Reading

Andrews, Dee (2000) *The Methodists and Revolutionary America, 1770–1800*, Princeton, NJ: Princeton University Press.

Balmer, Randall (1989) *A Perfect Babel of Confusion: Dutch Religion and English Culture in the Middle Colonies*, New York: Oxford University Press.

Boles, John B. (1972) *The Great Revival, 1787–1805: The Origins of the Southern Evangelical Mind*, Lexington, KY: University Press of Kentucky.

Bonomi, Patricia U. (2003) *Under the Cope of Heaven: Religion, Society, and Politics in Colonial America*, updated edn, New York: Oxford University Press.

Boyer, Paul S. and Nissenbaum, Stephen (1974) *Salem Possessed: The Social Origins of Witchcraft*, Cambridge, MA: Harvard University Press.

Brown, Matthew (2007) *The Pilgrim and the Bee: Reading Rituals and Book Culture in Early New England*, Philadelphia, PA: University of Pennsylvania Press.

Butler, Jon (1982) "Enthusiasm Described and Decried: The Great Awakening as Interpretative Fiction," *The Journal of American History*, 69(2): 305–325.

Chauncy, Charles (1772) *The Breaking of Bread in Remembrance of the Dying Love of Christ*, Boston: D. Kneeland.

Corrigan, John (1987) *The Hidden Balance: Religion and the Social Theories of Charles Chauncy and Jonathan Mayhew*, Cambridge: Cambridge University Press.

Dolan, Jay P. (2002) *In Search of an American Catholicism: A History of Religion and Culture in Tension*, New York: Oxford University Press.

Edwards, Jonathan (1746) *A Treatise Concerning Religious Affections*, Boston: S. Kneeland and T. Green.

Edwards, Jonathan (1765) *Two Dissertations: I. The End for which God Created the World; II. The Nature of True Virtue*, Boston: D. Kneeland.

Ellis, John Tracy (1965) *Catholics in Colonial America*, Baltimore, MD: Helicon.

Franklin, Benjamin (2003) *The Autobiography of Benjamin Franklin*, ed. Leonard Labaree, et al., New Haven, CT: Yale University Press.

Goen, C.C. (1969) *Revivalism and Separatism in New England, 1740–1800*, New Haven, CT: Yale University Press.

Hall, David D. (1989) *Worlds of Wonder, Days of Judgment: Popular Religious Belief in Early New England*, New York: Knopf.

Hall, Timothy D. (1994) *Contested Boundaries: Itinerancy and the Reshaping of the Colonial Religious World*, Durham, NC: Duke University Press.

Hatch, Nathan O. (1989) *The Democratization of American Christianity*, New Haven, CT: Yale University Press.

Heimert, Allan (1966) *Religion and the American Mind: From the Great Awakening to the Revolution*, Cambridge, MA: Harvard University Press.

Holifield, E. Brooks (2003) *Theology in America: Christian Thought from the Age of the Puritans to the Civil War*, New Haven, CT: Yale University Press.

Holmes, David L. (2006) *The Faiths of the Founding Fathers*, New York: Oxford University Press.

Holyoke, Edward, et al. (1744) *The Testimony of the President, Professors, Tutors and Hebrew Instructor of Harvard College in Cambridge, against the Reverend Mr. George Whitefield, and his Conduct*, Boston: T. Fleet.

Isaac, Rhys (1982) *The Transformation of Virginia, 1740–1790*, Chapel Hill, NC: University of North Carolina Press.

Kidd, Thomas S. (2007) *The Great Awakening: The Roots of Evangelical Christianity in Colonial America*, New Haven, CT: Yale University Press.

Lambert, Frank (1999) *Inventing the "Great Awakening,"* Princeton, NJ: Princeton University Press.

Longenecker, Stephen L. (2002) *Shenandoah Religion: Outsiders and the Mainstream, 1716–1865*, Waco, TX: Baylor University Press.

Lyerly, Cynthia Lynn (1998) *Methodism and the Southern Mind, 1770–1810*, New York: Oxford University Press.

Marini, Stephen A. (1982) *Radical Sects of Revolutionary New England*, Cambridge, MA: Harvard University Press.

Marsden, George M. (2003) *Jonathan Edwards: A Life*, New Haven, CT: Yale University Press.

Mulder, Philip N. (2002) *A Controversial Spirit: Evangelical Awakenings in the South*, New York: Oxford University Press.

Noll, Mark A. (2002) *America's God: From Jonathan Edwards to Abraham Lincoln*, New York: Oxford University Press.

O'Gorman, Frank (1997) *The Long Eighteenth Century: British Political and Social History, 1688–1832*, London: Arnold.

Rhoden, Nancy L. (1999) *Revolutionary Anglicanism: The Colonial Church of England Clergy during the American Revolution*, New York: New York University Press.

Sandoz, G. Ellis (1990) *A Government of Laws: Political Theory, Religion, and the American Founding*, Baton Rouge: Louisiana State University Press.

Sarna, Jonathan D. (2004) *American Judaism: A History*, New Haven, CT: Yale University Press.

Schmidt, Leigh Eric (1989) *Holy Fairs: Scottish Communions and American Revivals in the Early Modern Period*, Princeton, NJ: Princeton University Press.

Sensbach, Jon F. (2005) *Rebecca's Revival: Creating Black Christianity in the Atlantic World*, Cambridge, MA: Harvard University Press.

Sobel, Mechal (1979) *Trabelin' On: The Slave Journey to an Afro-Baptist Faith*, Westport, CT: Greenwood Press.

Stout, Harry S. (1991) *The Divine Dramatist: George Whitefield and the Rise of Modern Evangelicalism*, Grand Rapids, MI: W.B. Eerdmans.

Trevor-Roper, H.R. (1967) *The European Witch-Craze of the Sixteenth and Seventeenth Centuries and Other Essays*, New York: Harper & Row.

Valeri, Mark (1994) *Law and Providence in Joseph Bellamy's New England: The Origins of the New Divinity in Revolutionary America*, New York: Oxford University Press.

Wallace, Anthony F.C. (1972) *The Death and Rebirth of the Seneca*, New York: Vintage.

Walters, Kerry S. (1992) *The American Deists: Voices of Reason and Dissent in the Early Republic*, Lawrence, KS: University Press of Kansas.

Wesley, John (1739) *Free Grace: A Sermon Preach'd at Bristol*, Bristol: S. and F. Farley.

Wills, Gregory A. (1997) *Democratic Religion: Freedom, Authority, and Church Discipline in the Baptist South, 1785–1900*, New York: Oxford University Press.

Wright, Conrad (1955) *The Beginnings of Unitarianism in America*, Boston: Starr King Press.

7

Community

Kenneth P. Minkema

Community structures changed dramatically in the course of the eighteenth century, especially in North America, where many different ethnic and religious groups were moving in, and moving around. Individuals detached from ethnic and religious groups also moved around at unprecedented rates, challenging the strength of existing social structures, founding new communities, and coping with the disintegration of older patterns of bonding, social hierarchy, and interaction. Meanwhile, newspapers and other forms of print culture, including religious publishing, expanded at an amazing rate, supporting virtual communities drawn together around the printed word. Out of these virtual communities supported by print media, political and religious movements grew alongside face-to-face communities, and many face-to-face communities formed or reformed in response to larger political and religious movements. The American Revolution and the founding of the United States were part of this wholesale transformation in community structures taking place in eighteenth-century America. Newspapers and printed sermons stirred up patriotic and religious enthusiasm for independence and a new American nation. They also warned of the dangers of democracy and religious freedom, stimulating conservative efforts to preserve traditional community structures and moral efforts to reform them.

The eighteenth century brought incredible changes to communities in the New World, particularly in terms of the interaction of religious assumptions and social and political mores. This chapter examines key changes and continuities among peoples of the New World on familial, communal, tribal, and colonial levels, and shows how religious belief and practice reflected those changes and continuities. We cannot pretend to treat every ethnic and national experience in the colonization period, but here we will consider groups that played major roles: Native Americans, and Europeans including the Spanish, French, and British, and Africans.

One important point to keep in mind is that while we distinguish between these various groups for the sake of convenience, their stories are intertwined with each other, as well as with the broader Atlantic, transatlantic, and even global story. Indeed, it is impossible to fully understand the experiences of any one group without the others, or without that larger perspective.

Native Americans

While there were continuities in Indian life from the sixteenth and seventeenth centuries into the eighteenth, the general picture is one of decline, adaptation, retrenchment and retreat. Tribes remained organized according to clans and families, usually with loose or conciliar, or, in the case of the Iroquois, a matrilineal, leadership. Occasionally, a leader, such as Pontiac among the Ottawas in the 1760s, or Tecumseh among the Shawnee (1808–12), or Ocseola among the Seminoles, would emerge in a dire time.

One particular factor that tragically changed Indian life was disease. European diseases had of course contributed to native decline in the previous two centuries, and even before, when colonists marveled at how (they believed providentially) the land had been emptied, the previous inhabitants leaving only abandoned villages. But European diseases, such as smallpox, continued to ravage native populations – sometimes unknowingly through natural spread and contact, and sometimes deliberately by colonists who distributed pathogen-laden blankets or clothing. In an epidemic ending in 1738, for instance, about one half of the entire Cherokee tribe died. By the early 1760s, the Nantuckets, once several thousand strong, numbered less than 350. And beginning in the late 1770s, a smallpox epidemic, beginning in Mexico, swept through native populations in New Mexico, Texas, and eventually northward to Hudson's Bay. Faced with this mortality, remnants of tribes would merge to form new ones. Over the course of the century, disease, poor nutrition, and forced migrations decreased native resistance to disease and lowered birthrates.

War was another means of attrition. For protection, Indians would make alliances with colonizers. However, these alliances often resulted in conflict with other colonizers who had treaties with other tribes. In the eighteenth century, there was a series of imperial wars that usually began in Europe but had their American theaters as well. These wars included the War of Spanish Succession, the War of Austrian Succession, the War of Jenkins' Ear, and the Seven Years' War, pitting English against French or Spanish along with allied Indian tribes on both sides. Even in the American Revolution, Indian alliances played an important role in both British and American strategies. Of course, the reasons Indians fought wars, whether against Europeans or against other Indians, were often their own. Certainly alliance obligations were important, as well as revenge. But Indians often fought wars to take captives, in order to adopt them into the tribe and replace members they had lost through war and disease.

Some tribes, such as the Apaches and the Sioux on the Great Plains, remained relatively isolated through the century, but, for the majority, adaptation to and adoption of Europeans ways was the norm. Because of shrinking numbers and loss of tribal lands, traditional skills and knowledge were forgotten. Indians became party to the larger European economy of barter as they came to rely on European (later American) items such as clothing, cooking utensils, and weapons. Some Indians, such as the ones attached to missions established by the Catholics in California, wore European-style clothes, lived in European-style houses, and ate a European diet. But this was only a small fraction at any time. Generally, adaptation was not wholesale but rather a hybrid of Indian and European ways – in dress, tools, practices, and beliefs. It was helpful to be multilingual, and many Indians were, more so than whites away from the frontier (and even more than some who were not). At Indian meeting places could be heard many different languages, or even fusions of two or more languages. For their parts, colonizers also adapted to Indian ways, including the custom of long speeches at councils, giving presents as a means of securing allies, making or accepting retribution for a death by "covering the grave" (which again involved presents), the use of medical treatment with herbs and native plants, cultivation of native crops, and hunting and martial techniques, to name a few.

Another means of mixing was intermarriage of natives and colonizers. Within English culture, miscegenation was frowned upon – especially after King Philip's War – though inter-racial marriages were not unheard of. In French and Spanish colonies, where the ratio of men to women was high, the practice was more accepted, even expected. Within the French and Spanish spheres, the offspring of such unions were called, respectively, *creoles* or *mestizos*; among English, they were known more derogatively as "half-breeds."

This hybridization of two cultures, Indian and European, was especially true in religious practice. Christianity and native beliefs were often mixed syncretistically. Many Indians found a "middle way" between traditional animism and Christian doctrine. On the other hand, some Indians compartmentalized their religion, practicing both indigenous practices and Christianity alongside each other. Among these, some, such as the Housatonic Mohicans, became Christian, in order to acquire the education necessary to possess the literary and diplomatic skills needed to retain their lands and to act as intermediaries between the English and other tribes. Of course, it is difficult to fully assess the extent to which Indians and Europeans understood the teachings of Christianity in the same manner. What did "conversion" mean to an Indian in the Northwest, or in upper New York State, or in Florida, or in New Mexico? For some, it simply mean adding God and Christ to the world of *manitou*. The Indians of New Spain typified tribal belief systems of the New World in conceiving of deities as combining both good and evil, benevolence and maliciousness. Meso-Americans went further than most others of their race in seeking to appease the gods' anger and to insure prosperity and victory in regularly offering human sacrifices. If the Meso-Americans, previous to Spanish incursion, had lived in a virtual theocracy, the Nachez of present-day Mississippi, constructed a theocratic state in which religious figures ruled and the tribe maintained ceremonial mounds and decorated temples, and sacrificed a chief's servants upon his death. For Indians under Catholic influence, too, Christian saints were identified with indigenous deities.

Even so, some Indians became zealous Christians, such as those proselytized by Moravians in the British colonies, or individuals such as the Mohegan preacher Samson Occom, or the Iroquois woman Katherine Tegakovita, later canonized by the Catholic Church. Groups of Indians also accepted offers to live in mission communities from Massachusetts and Pennsylvania to Florida and California. Indians could achieve full status within churches such as at the English mission at Stockbridge, Massachusetts, or become members of a Moravian *brudergemein* in Pennsylvania, North Carolina, or the island of St. Thomas, zealous utopian celibate communities segregated by gender. Under Spanish rule, Indians in Florida, New Mexico, or

California could be compelled to become members of a mission, at which they were forced to live European style and follow the dictates of the church, including the daily and seasonal rituals.

If some Natives, creoles, and mestizos lived in virtual bondage to their Christian leaders, they did find ways of using the morality of their colonizers against them. For example, in the Yucatan, Mayan proselytes under Spanish rule found a way to remove priests who used their authority to demand sex of their communicants, kept concubines, or were pederasts. By supplicating to the bishop or higher authority, they were able to remove, temporarily or permanently, an increasing number of priests. During the eighteenth century, in fact, more than twice as many abusive priests were removed than in each of the previous two centuries.

Dreams and visions had always been a central part of Indian religion. Neolin during the 1760s, or Elskwatawa of the Algonkians, or Kennebuk the Kickapoo, and later, Handsome Lake of the Seneca, who formulated what was called the "Longhouse Religion" in the 1790s, called for a return to traditional beliefs and practices, promising that if this reformation occurred, the colonizers (in their cases, the British and, after them, the Americans) would disappear. Advocating what has been called a theology of separation, they taught that Indians and whites were created differently and by different gods, and that they therefore could not take the same path to the afterlife – a backhanded way of saying that Indians should not convert to Christianity. Though this was a denunciation of Christianity as taught by missionaries, it nonetheless did co-opt elements of Christianity, such as the notion of hell. For the Indian prophets, this place of eternal suffering was reserved for those who accommodated to the whites and adopted their religion. For still other tribes, this "nativism" amounted to a religious revival (something like the Ghost Dance of the late nineteenth century) in fervor. A civil war among the Creeks in 1811, for example, was caused by prophetic teachings that through purification and rituals such as the Green Corn ceremony, they could eliminate white influence and regain their lands.

West of the Mississippi, on the Great Plains, lived the Souian tribes. A mixture of sedentary and nomadic groups, these tribes, many of which were matriarchal, shared a reliance on the buffalo. Religion was characteristically individual. Young men would go off alone to engage in a quest, during which they would hopefully receive a vision that would reveal to them their guardian spirit. Spiritual power was also vested in medicine bundles, collections of natural and man-made items that were of special meaning to the individual.

The horse changed these native cultures significantly. First re-introduced to America by the Spaniards, Indians began to acquire them in numbers during the early eighteenth century. Along with guns provided mostly by the French, the speed and carrying power of the horse enabled much more efficient and broad-ranging hunting by Plains tribes, greater number of buffalo killed, and easier mobility from one place to another. The natives' diets improved, their numbers increased. But a warrior cult evolved, which focused on success in battle and the hunt; with it came lower life expectancy for men. Accompanying the rise of the warrior cult, inequities in the social structure developed among men. Ownership of horses and other property, as well as wives, became sources of competition. But while the horse allowed for the development of what has come to be remembered as the classical image of the Indian on horseback, the dependence on the animal came at a cost. Environmental degradation occurred as a result of over-grazing. Plains grasses were depleted, which decreased the buffalo population. Thus, there was escalating competition for buffalo resulting in intertribal conflicts through this period.

Turning to the European colonizers, there are several general eighteenth-century trends to note. First, transatlantic communication was improving. More ships were making the cross-ocean trek, and in faster time. This allowed for more correspondence between mother countries and colonies in the form of letters – the eighteenth century was the great age of letter-writing. The proliferation of printing presses also encouraged communication. Improved travel meant improved commerce. As the century progressed, the colonies – with the exception of New France, which was a constant drain on the royal treasury – gained a larger place in the imperial economy. For example, in 1700, the British colonies accounted for 4 percent of the gross national product, but by the verge of the American Revolution they accounted for 40 percent. The growing importance of colonial holdings for the great European powers of Spain, France, and Great Britain in particular entailed keeping those holdings, deriving the most profit from them, and, if possible, expanding them. Finally, the eighteenth century in Europe was the Age of Enlightenment, of new ideas, scientific discoveries, and exploration, and this new intellectual environment had profound effects on politics, religion, and other areas, making itself felt in the colonies in revolutionary ways.

New Spain

The ambivalent perception of Native peoples on the part of the colonizers of what became New Spain, stretching from Central America to Florida, New Mexico, and California in the north, was typical of colonizers from other European countries: they were at once primal innocents and bestial pagans to be subjected under the Catholic (and Spanish) banner or to be exterminated. As with the Puritan settlers of New England, the conquistadores carried with them an "errand mentality," that is, the conviction that they had a special divine mission to bring God and the sword. Any indigenous religious practice among Indians was almost universally seen as bearing the influence of Satan to set up perverse imitation of true religion. Religious leaders such as Bartolomé de las Casas, who defended native rights, were an exception. Into the early eighteenth century, a policy of idolatry extirpation was in force. In some places, such as Villa Alta in southern Mexico, natives resisted surrendering their indigenous specialists, implements, and texts. Such resistance testified to the perpetuation of traditional ways of belief.

In colonies such as Portuguese Brazil and Spanish Mexico, Indians were ultimately linked in Spanish minds with diabolism. We often associate the year 1692 and witchcraft with the famous incident in Salem, Massachusetts. However, an equally dramatic incident occurred in Querétaro, Mexico, in that same year: the possession of several Native women who manifested convulsions and distended stomachs and who expelled pins. The victims themselves and their own priests believed this was true demonic possession, but they were accused of faking by church inquisitors and the priests involved were condemned. Thus this incident did not end in executions as the one well to the north in the English sphere.

The number of Spaniards who actually took up residence in New Spain amounted to a quarter million by the end of the sixteenth century, but up north, on the frontier, the emigrant population was tiny, much like the French in North America. Under a policy of pacification, Hispanicization and Christianization implemented by political and military leaders and by Jesuit priests and friars, the colonizers relied on Natives to labor in the mines and on the plantations, and to build and attend the churches. Villages of Natives, and later, Natives and mestizos, under the *encomienda*, were set up to provide labor in return for education; under the *repartimiento*, they were also required to provide a specific proportion of labor based on population.

Mission strategies utilized an array of devices to bring the Native converts fully into the Christian fold. If the conquistadores saw themselves as God's conquerors, the priests often had the zeal of martyrs, working in difficult conditions (others were simply corrupt). They lived among the Natives and mestizos, helping to build their churches, and they learned native dialects – though with the goal of ultimately teaching them Spanish and becoming "civilized." The priests made use of visual elements such as images and paintings, and of gifts, to secure the converts to their interest.

Native and Spanish ideologies, similar in some respects but quite different in others, bred cultural and religious syncretism. While Indians of Mexico, such as the Nahua, held animistic notions about spirits relating to the human body quite different from the idea of the Christian "soul," there was enough similarity – or mutual miscomprehension – to allow blending of the two cultures. Religious precepts wove together with assumptions about honor, reputation, status, and prerogatives, which were conveyed through use and decoration of the body: length and treatment of hair, aversion of the eyes, adornment or hiding of the face, ornaments and jewelry, and clothing (for example, trousers vs. loincloths). The Spanish, like their Native subjects, were hierarchical, valuing bloodlines, primogeniture, and elderly power, among other structuring factors. Thus colonizers and colonized came to have similar social assumptions about the body, but for different reasons.

This system of mission outposts, isolated forts, and *presidios* prevailed in northern New Spain into the eighteenth century, though on the northern frontier from Florida to New Mexico there were threats to Spanish hegemony. In 1680, the Pueblo Indians revolted in New Mexico, killing several hundred Spanish settlers and forcing the Spanish out of the province for more than a decade. In Florida, in the meantime, the English from the Carolinas attacked Spanish posts in the Guale region (present-day Georgia) and in Florida itself. By 1706, only St. Augustine itself was left in Spanish possession in that area.

As a result, Spanish strategy changed. Peaceful settlement in the north would end. Instead, they would attempt to challenge the British on the east coast, the French coming down the Mississippi, and, later in the century, the Russians coming south from Alaska down the coast of California. The Spanish maintained a larger (at least, relative to the scant forces hitherto) military presence and adopted a more lenient Indian policy. In the very early decades of the century, they expanded into present-day Texas, establishing missions and forts, and eventually they were able to regain some of what they had lost in Florida. In the 1760s, under the leadership of the Franciscan Junipero Sierra, the Spanish set up a string of missions in the San Francisco area, and the Spanish colonized the Baja peninsula. Two decades later, there were 21 in California, housing some twenty thousand neophytes. In the 1780s, a *rancho* system was established around Los Angeles, consisting of large tracts of land for livestock.

Spanish policy, in the end, only temporarily staved off incursion by other nations and by Natives. The English founded the colony of Georgia in 1730, claiming northern Florida as well; with the establishment of the United States several decades later, the threat was only more insistent. The French, too, had secured their hold on the mouth of the Mississippi River and the surrounding region, and only a handful of missions were still running in Texas, where the Spanish had been virtually run out by the Tejas Indians. And in California, inhabitants of the missions suffered high mortality and were treated like slaves. Many ran away, others fought back, as in the San Diego rebellion of 1775. In short, Spain's hold on its northern frontiers, while it persisted into the early nineteenth century, was increasingly tenuous. All the same, Spanish culture exerted a lasting influence on the American southwest in terms of religion, language, and other factors.

New France

The French plan of colonization, formulated in the seventeenth century, remained basically unchanged into the eighteenth, to France's eventual loss of a potentially huge segment of the North American interior. France was able to establish small colonies, never amounting to more than 50,000 souls – a mere fraction of their British neighbors to the south and the Spanish in Mexico – along the St. Lawrence Seaway and in Louisiana. (The French also possessed the islands of Domingue, Martinique, and Guadeloupe in the West Indies.) Few incentives were offered for emigrants, and reasons to leave France – whether economic, religious, or otherwise– were not as compelling as they were for the Spanish or English. Not to mention that it was a cold, dangerous place to live, with bitter winters and even bitterer Indians, such as the Iroquois.

Instead, French reliance continued to be placed on trading and military posts – such as Michilimackinac, Detroit, and St. Louis – placed strategically in a huge arc from the Canadian Maritimes, through the Great Lakes area, and down the Mississippi to Louisiana. French presence was reliant on the toleration of an array of Indian tribes over this vast area, so the French always had to be constructing uneasy alliances and treaties between shifting groups. But Indians were more prepared to indulge the French than perhaps most any other colonizers. The French did not force-feed Christianity, they recognized the autonomy of Indian authority, and they were willing to learn the languages and adapt to the cultures of natives in a way that the Spanish, English, or Russians were not. The French traders, too, were willing to trade for items that became highly prized, particularly guns and ammunition and metal implements. This endeared them to their Indian clients and provided them with means to attack the Spanish (for example, in Texas) and the English (in New England and the Carolinas).

The porosity of the interior was demonstrated in the *pays d'en haut*, the "Upper Country" around the Great Lakes. Here existed what historian Richard White has called the "Middle Ground," where neither Algonkians nor the French completely dominated. What emerged here by the eighteenth century was a culture of diplomacy and accommodation in which both sides crafted new customs and a new system of meaning. For a time, this "middle ground" allowed both sides to view each other as humans and as equals. However, it was a constant struggle of definition and re-definition that eventually disintegrated with the retreat of the French and the arrival of the British in the early nineteenth century.

Most French colonists, or *habitants*, lived along the St. Laurence Seaway in the area from Montreal to Quebec. These plantations were imitations of French rural villages, only smaller and more spread out. Most colonists were tenant farmers, who had to adapt to a very short Canadian growing season – often only a couple of months. Thus, they planted fast-growing crops, such as wheat, or raised livestock, or sought other ways to diversify their income. Lacking a cash crop like tobacco, they were mostly subsistence farmers, which disappointed the monarchy hoping to make some profit from the colonies. Overall, though, colonists in New France enjoyed more freedom and more land than their counterparts in the old country.

Towns were arranged in *seigneuries*, provinces usually awarded to a member of the nobility (though on rare occasions a commoner would accede to that status) who leased land to families. The *seigneur* collected rents and fees on land purchases and milling. Working for a *seigneur* – often in an uneasy alliance – was a military force, miniscule and under-equipped, ruled by a military governor. Common soldiers were subject to abuse and neglect by their officers, who, with the belief that they were owed privileges, sought ways to make money from their men through graft or extortion.

Colonies cost money, however, and New France was as constant drain on the royal treasury. What the French sought in particular to offset these costs were furs, which fetched large sums on European markets. A class of French colonists who played a vital role in this trade were the *coureurs de bois*, a sort of renegade assemblage of trader-explorers who ventured far into Indian country to barter, live with Indians, and marry their women. They irked French officials because they ignored orders limiting their activities and preferred a lifestyle that bordered on the "savage" (hence the saying, "Gone Indian"), which was a particular horror to Europeans who considered theirs the highest and best culture of all.

Women enjoyed some economic benefits in French society over their English or Spanish counterparts. In contrast to English colonies such as Massachusetts and Connecticut where families and sometimes entire church communities emigrated, women made up only a small percentage of French colonists. But there were advantages. French law treated women as co-equal in marriage. When her husband died, a widow inherited half of his estate. Women – particularly elite women – in a Catholic colony such as New France also had the option of joining a convent in Montreal or Quebec, where nuns supervised education, hospitals, and other social services.

The Catholic Church dominated religion in New France. No dissent was tolerated. The bishop was one of the three ruling figures, along with a military and civil representative. Most *habitants* were nominal or indifferent members of the church, but recognized and participated in Catholicism as a marker of their identity. Missions among the Indians were conducted by Jesuit priests. Rather than trying to draw Indians into sequestered missions or Praying Towns and forcing them to become "civilized" (i.e. Europeanized), as did the Spanish and English, the Jesuits went out to the villages and lived among the tribes, learning Indian languages and customs, and allowing Indians to draw their own parallels between their traditional beliefs and Christianity. They made headway among tribes such as the Huron and the Abenaki, but met resistance, or only measured cooperation, as often as not. Still, Francophilic, Catholicized Indians became fast allies of the French due in large part to the effort of Jesuit missionaries. It was these Indians who formed the core of raiding parties during the War of Spanish Succession (1702–13) and later conflicts such as the French and Indian War (1754–62).

Louisiana formed the southern touchstone of the French Empire in America. Following the expeditions of La Salle down the Mississippi and later along the Gulf of Mexico, the D'Iberville expedition in 1702 established more towns and began the process of developing the city of New Orleans. Louisiana was a racially mixed colony, and for some time a rather miserable one at that. It was, in part, a penal colony, that is, prisoners were sent here from France as punishment instead of going to jail. Also, Louisiana was the only French colony on the mainland to import slaves, and in the early eighteenth century there were several thousand African as well as Indian slaves there. Prisoners, slaves, and commoners worked to clear the forest and drain the land in and around New Orleans, which formed the settled core of the colony. The interior, however, was dominated by Indians, and there the French pursued their policy of pacification and open trade. Given the makeup of the colony, the Church had little influence. St. Louis Cathedral and an Ursuline convent were constructed in the early eighteenth century. The Ursulines assumed responsibility for educating and caring for the population as they were able, and even accepted black novitiates into their midst, but the community remained small.

British America

One of the key social factors that distinguished the British colonies in the New World was sheer growth in numbers, through natural increase and immigration. In 1650, there were just over 50,000 British settlers; a century later, there were over a million, lending a permanence that the much smaller population of New France could not achieve. In Pennsylvania alone, for example, the number of inhabitants grew six times in the four decades after 1720; by the Revolution, the colony's population had risen to a quarter of a million (not including slaves) – which rivaled all of New Spain.

Too, the economic situation of the British colonies flourished, affording its inhabitants a better standard of living than their seventeenth-century predecessors, and, for that matter, of their French and Spanish contemporaries. With improvements in communication and commerce, with the development of cash crops such as tobacco, rice, and indigo through a massive importation of African slaves, and with England and its colonies more closely intertwined following the Glorious Revolution, English colonial culture began, in the early decades of the eighteenth century, to rival that of the mother country. Provincial elites sought to emulate the genteel, cosmopolitan lifestyle of London. This "refining" of the colonies brought the acquisition of luxuries that were not possible before the subjection of the Natives or the development of home economies. Colonials began to adopt the latest fashions in architecture, household accessories such as fine china and tea sets, coaches, clothes, and other marks of wealth, including slaves. The demand for these products created a consumer revolution that brought the proliferation of stores, advertising, traveling salesmen, and other aspects of commercialism.

This consumer revolution was largely limited to the affluent, though people from lower classes too engaged in conspicuous consumption in order to appear genteel. The quarter century before the Revolution saw the growth of poverty, particularly urban poverty, in the British North American colonies. The increasing number of poor was a result of the series of debilitating and expensive imperial wars, increasing emigration (for example, Scots-Irish and German in the Middle Colonies), and the vulnerability of colonial markets – and their currencies – to fluctuations. The rise in the number of poor paralleled a rising inequality of wealth, that is, the concentration of wealth and land in fewer hands.

Despite emerging inequities and the turmoil and controversies of the late seventeenth and early eighteenth centuries, both in the mother country and in her colonies, Anglo-American society generally remained hierarchical and deferential. The social ladder extended from religious and political leaders down to male heads of families, to women, children, and servants or slaves. Within this system of the "little commonwealth," individuals on each rung were to pay due submission to those above them. As well, youth were to heed the middle-aged, and all were to heed the elderly. Religion bolstered this ideal through sermons, catechizing, printed tracts, poetry, and other means. Although by the end of the seventeenth century the political franchise was no longer connected to church membership, ecclesiastical practices continued to lend credence to a class-based social structure. In New England Congregationalism and Middle Colonies Presbyterianism, full church membership meant not only the privilege of having access to sacraments, but also the opportunity to serve in lay offices, such as elder or deacon, and more of a likelihood to be selected for civil officers, such as delegate, constable, or assessor. Ministers, whether New England Congregationalists or Virginia Anglicans, also exhorted their hearers and readers to avoid materialism, to be "weaned from the world," and to concentrate on becoming rich in spirit.

In some ways, however, this picture of society as portrayed in sermons and printed tracts was an ideal only. As the "refinement" of the colonies suggests, a theology of prosperity – that God blessed those who prospered because they deserved it – pertained, and charity was only obtained with difficulty (for example, support for Indian missions came not from colonists but from overseas philanthropists). In some respects, women enjoyed more rights in the English colonies than those prescribed by the traditional notion of the division of gender roles into "domestic spheres." To varying degrees from colony to colony, women could inherit portions of their husband's estate, sue in court, and more easily obtain a divorce than in the mother country. Courtship patterns were shifting from pre-arranged matches or strict requirement of parental permission to matches in which individuals chose their own mate. Young people were given freer rein for socializing, engaging in "frolicks" and other extra-ecclesial activities. Pre-marital sex was increasingly the norm among young people; illegitimate births were on the rise through the century, so that in New England by the Revolution, as an example, fully a third of the children born were conceived out of wedlock (though, to be fair, a significant number of couples were "published," or engaged, at the time of conception). In rural areas especially, parents sought to supervise courtship and to determine compatibility by employing a custom called "bundling," in which a young man and woman could sleep together in a bed in the woman's home, separated by a board, or with the man sewn into a sack. A growing emphasis on youth was accompanied by a decrease in respect shown to the elderly. Generational tensions developed over land, inheritance, occupational choices, and religious affiliation.

The early eighteenth century did, however, see the beginnings of religious toleration. The colonies had already been established in the seventeenth century with a variety of established or semi-established churches: the Congregationalists in New England, the Quakers in Pennsylvania, the Church of England in Virginia and the Carolinas, and even – for a time anyway – Catholicism in Maryland. In the wake of the

Restoration and Glorious Revolution, religious requirements for voting and office-holding were rolled back, and hitherto non-tolerated religions – such as Quakerism and Anglicanism in New England and Protestant dissenters in the South – were recognized by royal mandate (usually in form of being excused from paying taxes to support the established religion). Intolerance, of course, did not, and never would, entirely disappear; for example, the British colonies and their religious culture had by the early eighteenth century become secure in the "Protestant interest," and so continued wary, even hateful, of Catholicism, and radical and non-English movements were persecuted. But in being forced to recognize the legitimacy of hitherto "heretical" religions, the transition from state-sponsored to voluntary religion had begun. Also, the relative openness of English colonial religious culture attracted adherents from several European nations – from Protestant refugees of Salzburg and German Pietists to French Huguenots and Dutch Labadists – representing a broadening range of beliefs that made these colonies a religious potpourri.

The single most important religious phenomenon in the English-speaking world during the long eighteenth century was the so-called "Great Awakening," which began in the 1740s. "Awakenings," or revivals, involved the conversion of significant numbers of people, usually assembled in large crowds to hear a popular preacher. The most popular preacher of the time was George Whitefield, an ordained minister of the Church of England, who had no settled parish but instead itinerated, or traveled, through England and the North American colonies on extended tours, preaching the "New Birth" – a decisive, often convulsive moment of surrender of one's soul to Christ. Gifted with a voice that could carry for hundreds of yards, a theatrical, extemporaneous style, and media-savvy, he was instrumental in the introduction of modern evangelicalism.

Whitefield and his many imitators used a highly affective language that not only reintroduced the role of emotions in religion but also brought with it subversive implications for traditional social order. The clergy, in New England, the Middle Colonies, and the South alike, divided over the legitimacy of the revivals as a work of God, with Old Lights or Old Siders denouncing them, and New Lights or New Siders promoting them. Critics of the revivals were not only suspicious of the self-promoting Whitefield; they also were horrified by the effects of the revivals among the populous, which included bodily manifestations, "crying out," and trance-like states. Churches split over the meaning of "true" religion; pastors and congregations argued; laymen and women derided and deserted their ministers if they were thought to be unconverted; radical, controversial leaders arose – such as the Reverend James Pierpont, who led book- and clothes-burning meetings; and new voices were heard – women, young people, and slaves and free blacks began "exhorting," or preaching, signaling the beginning of new movements and sects. During and in the wake of the Great Awakening, the Congregational and Presbyterian dominance in the north and the Anglican dominance in the south were challenged, furthering religious pluralism and diversity. Baptists made new inroads into the colonies, followed later in the century by Methodists. With its antiauthoritarian, proto-democratic impulse, the Great Awakening reflected a growing egalitarianism in the British colonies.

The American Revolution was the result of and brought with it a constellation of social and religious changes. Though some states did not abolish state-supported religion until the early nineteenth century, the Revolution did bring with it freedom of religion that made voluntary involvement in religion the norm. Individuals could choose from a marketplace of religious options. For their part, religious leaders worked to convince their hearers and readers that religious piety and practice were essential to national virtue and progress. But lest we take away too rosy a picture of the new republic as a haven of religious liberty, the post-Revolutionary decades also saw religious and racial conflict in cities between whites and blacks, and between natives and immigrants, as well as violent suppression of new religious movements and ideas, such as the Shakers. Denominational educational institutions sprouted up around the country dedicated to inculcating their own particular creed and confession against rivaling institutions. One important site of religious competition was in the new western territories, which saw Methodist circuit riders and missionary representatives from other denominations make the rounds to new settlements, creating an amalgamation of religious communities and loyalties. The end of the eighteenth century marked the beginning of a new period of revivals, called the Second Great Awakening. Rural areas and the frontier in particular became the scene for new episodes of revival such as seen during the Great Awakening, a famous example being the revivals held at Cane Ridge, Kentucky, in 1800.

Africans

The eighteenth century saw the importation of Africans into the New World increase dramatically to fill the growing demands of the slave trade. During this one century alone, an estimated two and half million were taken forcibly to the New World. The majority went to British colonies, reflecting the leadership that England took in the transportation of slaves over the course of the century.

In the terminology of historians, "push" and "pull" factors for emigrating shifted at the end of the seventeenth century. At that time, the number of white indentured servants coming to the colonies decreased because of improving conditions in England. Yet, the development of cash crops, such as rice, indigo, sugar cane, and later, cotton in the deep South, Lowcountry, and Caribbean created a demand for slaves that could not be filled by the diminishing stream of white servants – and, even more, casting whites into the sort of abject slavery required to work the plantations made their fellow colonists uncomfortable.

The solution was to turn to Africa as a source for plantation labor. In the English colonies especially, a racial system of slavery developed. Where in the previous century racial associations were not hard and fast, in the eighteenth century the identification of slavery with blackness became firm. Race and slavery became equated. In the English colonies writ large and even in French Louisiana, where creole populations constituted a significant minority, owning slaves became a mark of social status as well as affluence, and the racialized system of slavery masked growing class irregularities among whites, in which wealth was increasingly concentrated in fewer hands. Only in New Spain, in colonies such as Florida, where mestizos and mulattos were accepted, were African slaves manumitted – drawn to Spanish territory by offers of freedom, and given the opportunity to fight in wars against their former masters.

Most Africans who became New World slaves were from tribes of western Africa, whose cultures were sedentary and agricultural. They came to be victims of the slave

Figure 7.1 A New Orleans slave market. In the relatively relaxed environment of New Orleans, slaves developed relationships at markets which could open doors to new work prospects.

trade through a variety of means, such as war with other tribes in which the conquered were sold into slavery, or kidnapping by African or European traders. They would be taken from the interior in groups, chained together, and marched to the coasts, where they would be held till a ship came to take them across the sea.

Having left their homeland, the dreaded Middle Passage, or crossing between the two continents, began. To maximize their profit, traders would cram as many individuals into the holds of their ships, resulting in dismal, inhuman conditions. Shackled together, with no sanitation, little food, and only occasional respites on deck, mortality through disease, malnutrition, or other causes was high. Some, in despair or refusal to be subjected, committed suicide. Occasionally, however, the imprisoned would manage to free themselves from their chains, rise up to kill or capture the crew, and take over the ship.

Once ashore, at any number of ports from New England to the West Indies, the enslaved were sold at auction (Figure 7.1). Here commenced the "seasoning" stage, during which the slave was exposed to New World diseases. Surviving this, the slave became part of the household or plantation community, serving as a domestic (usually women), fieldhand, or, more rarely, an artisan. The number of slaves in a given estate varied from one or two to hundreds. Whatever the size, slaves were generally mixed with individuals from different tribes, originally speaking different languages, observing different customs. Thus occurred in the slave community a blending of cultures that varied depending on the region.

This mixing – deliberately observed by masters to deter slaves from joining together to rebel – resulted, over time, in the formulation of a distinct culture, the "world that the slaves made." Initially unable to speak English, and often knowing only their own tribal or regional dialect, slaves developed a *patois* of one sort or another, a fusion of pigeon English and African along with new words (the dialect called Gullah, spoken by residents of islands off South Carolina, is a survival from this period). Common folkways included music in the form of task-oriented worksongs and sacred pieces, dances, healing techniques that blended traditional and European methods, and use of magic and the occult, either personally or through the use of a conjurer. A body of tales developed also, with themes that included the victory of the underdog, the trickster, and the weak over the strong.

Generally speaking, rural areas, particularly within the English colonies, came to contain either relatively few slaves in the Northeast, or the majority of them in the South and Islands. However, there was a small minority of slaves, along with an equally small community of free blacks, that lived in cities, especially seaports. Urban markets created unique opportunities for these Africans and African-Americans to develop and offer artisanal skills and to take up different sorts of labor than strictly agricultural. Urban slaves of course lived with their masters' families, and free blacks congregated in their own sections of towns; but even so, they had more freedom to venture forth on their own and to mingle with the general population and build social networks. These cosmopolitan slaves and freepersons lived in proximity to white elites and emulated their tastes and ways. Urban blacks, for example, made their own festival days, such as Negro Election Day (in New England) or Pinkster Day (in New York and New Jersey). During the Revolution, many urban blacks took up the British offer of manumission and land if they fought for the Crown against the rebellious colonies; by the same token, many fought with the patriot forces, only to be denied the benefits of the cause for which they had fought.

In Louisiana, within the French domain, several thousand slaves were imported during the early eighteenth century. In the wake of the fierce Nachez Indian revolt in 1729, however, the French authorities realized they must provide the slaves with a better standard of living – including healthier quarters and diets – if they were to avoid a slave uprising. Also, the lack of a cash crop, as in the English southern colonies, alleviated the demand for concentrated, plantation-style slave labor, which allowed slaves to disperse, diversify and enter various occupations. Here, black marriage and family status was accorded more respect than in English colonies. By the 1760s, the black creole population outnumbered whites. The city of New Orleans became the center for slave life, where they lived under the close scrutiny of their masters but were able to mix in the streets, hire themselves out for labor, and develop relationships at events such as market days.

The family was a vital "survival mechanism" among slaves. Marriage for slaves was illegal in many colonies, but, as the century went on, slave and free black weddings became more common, especially in colonies where the slave trade was in question, and common-law matches were encouraged. Couples worked together to supplement their diet by keeping vegetable gardens or livestock, hunting and fishing. They also could earn money by making furniture, or fixing shoes, or practicing other skills for their fellow slaves, their master's family or, when permitted to leave the estate, other whites and slaves in their area. Often, this income was kept in a fund to buy their freedom, or the freedom of a family member; otherwise, the coins could be used to purchase necessary items or even the occasional luxury. Similar to Native cultures, children were given nearly free reign; narratives by former slaves nearly all state that, as children, they hardly recognized themselves as enslaved, and played with the children of their owners. Despite hard conditions, Africans and African-Americans on the mainland saw their population increase through childbirth; by the 1730s, beginning in the Chesapeake, African-Americans eclipsed African-born due to acquired immunities to diseases, population growth, and expanding familiarity of English, the landscape, and the economy. By contrast, in the West Indies, where the harshest of climates and most merciless of drivers prevailed, the black population decreased through disease, punishment, and poor nutrition.

Ironically, the family was the strongest aspect of slave life, but at the same time it was the most fragile. The family could be torn apart at any time by the sale of one or more of its members, and females were subject to forced concubinage or rape by their masters. White attitudes towards children resulting from such relationships varied: some masters loved and cared for their mistresses and mulatto children, while others viewed them merely as sources of labor and profit. Meanwhile, male slaves could engage in polygamy or adultery by keeping wives and mistresses on different estates, whom they would visit with a pass from their master or in a covert nighttime rendezvous. When slaves died, they were given elaborate, lengthy funerals by their families and friends, and were buried with personal effects that they could use in the afterlife. Many slaves who were native Africans believed that when they died, their souls returned home.

Many Africans brought with them religious beliefs that posited a Creator and lesser gods. Sacrifice was a way of obtaining forgiveness and favors. Spiritual powers were accorded to certain healers and prognosticators, who were believed to be able to cast and ward off spells, promote health, and even protect from the overseer's lash. In the New World, Africans and their descendants tended to resist Christianity, since it was the oppressors' religion and colonial ministers emphasized submission to masters as the will of God. As with Native Peoples, the offer of Christianity to slaves was accompanied with the expectation that they would also be "civilized," that is, adopt European assumptions and habits. Liberty was strictly a spiritual state, to be obtained in the hereafter. Missionaries sent to bring the gospel to slaves beginning in the early eighteenth century were largely ineffectual.

However, the religious revivals of the mid-eighteenth century, known as the Great Awakening, were fundamental in changing black attitudes towards Christianity. New Light ministers – those most active in promoting the revivals – did not initially differentiate black from white in their preaching, which promised freedom through grace and spiritual equality, and criticized authority. A number of slaves and free blacks were attracted by these revivalist itinerants, predominantly Congregational and Presbyterian in the north, Baptist and Methodist in the south. In New England, for instance, it was not until the 1740s that, in many churches, blacks were first baptized and even admitted to full church membership. The Baptists in Virginia at first welcomed blacks into their midst, which made them a target of abuse for local slaveholders. The implication of having people of color as fellow church members, however, was disturbing for many colonists, who balked at the notion that they were to be treated equally as children of God.

If slaves and free blacks began to be brought in, however slowly, into the established churches, the Great Awakening also encouraged the earliest stages of the formation of distinct black churches and black forms of Christianity. They began the process of interpreting the gospel for themselves, creating new forms of worship. An extemporaneous, emotional preaching style emerged, along with a distinct body of sacred hymns. Themes that especially spoke to blacks were those of the Old Testament, such as Exodus and the Promised Land. In rural areas, religious communities were independent and unique. In urban areas, black churches were formally established. By the end of the century, the African Methodist Episcopal Church in Philadelphia was thriving under the leadership of ministers like Richard Allen. Free black communities in other urban areas also constituted a growing body of dedicated church members. In Vermont, a white congregation even hired a black ordained minister named Lemuel Haynes.

Slaves, sometimes in cooperation with free blacks and even with whites, could offer resistance. One option was to escape. Some slaves simply left the plantation following harsh punishment, to return only after they had run out of food. Escaped slaves could find a new home in "maroon" communities, hidden in forests and swamps; these groups relied on raids of surrounding areas for supplies. Other escapees would take up residence with Native tribes, such as the Seminoles in Florida. Yet another option was rebellion. Outnumbered, whites were terrified by the prospect of slave revolts. A full-fledged slave rebellion, called the Stono Rebellion, occurred in South Carolina in 1739, in which slaves attempted, unsuccessfully, to march to freedom in Florida. All too often erroneous rumors led to severe punishments of slaves. One such case was the so-called New York Slave Revolt of 1741, in which slaves, free blacks, and poor whites were reportedly planning to burn the city; the "conspiracy" was detected, and blacks and whites alike were burned at the stake and hung. The most famous and successful slave rebellion occurred on the French-held island of Saint Domingue in the Caribbean, where, beginning in 1794, slaves rose in insurrection under the leadership of Toussaint L'Ouverture and established the new, independent nation of Haiti.

Further Reading

Anderson, Fred (2000) *Crucible of War: The Seven Years' War and the Fate of Empire in British North America, 1754–1766*, New York: Knopf.

Berlin, Ira (1998) *Many Thousands Gone: The First Two Centuries of Slavery in North America*, Cambridge, MA: Belknap Press.

Blassingame, John W. (1972) *The Slave Community: Plantation Life in the Ante-bellum South*, New York, Oxford University Press.

Brooks, James F. (2002) *Captives and Cousins: Slavery, Kinship, and Community in the Southwest Borderlands*, Chapel Hill, NC: University of North Carolina Press.

Butler, Jon (1990) *Awash in a Sea of Faith: Christianizing the American People*, Cambridge, MA: Harvard University Press.

Cervantes, Fernando (1994) *The Devil in the New World: The Impact of Diabolism in New Spain*, New Haven, CT: Yale University Press.

Clark, Emily (2007) *Masterless Mistresses: The New Orleans Ursulines and the Development of a New World Society, 1727–1834*, Chapel Hill, NC: University of North Carolina Press.

Corrigan, John (1991) *The Prism of Piety: Catholick Congregational Clergy at the Beginning of the Enlightenment*, New York: Oxford University Press.

De Mello e Souza, Laura (2003) *The Devil and the Land of the Holy Cross: Witchcraft, Slavery, and Popular Religion in Colonial Brazil*, trans. Diane C. Whitty, Austin, TX: University of Texas Press.

Dowd, Gregory Evans (1992) *A Spirited Resistance: The North American Indian Struggle for Unity, 1745–1815*, Baltimore, MD: Johns Hopkins University Press.

Gibson, Arrell Morgan (1980) *The American Indian: Prehistory to the Present*, Lexington, MA: D.C. Heath & Co.

Gray, Colleen (2007) *The Congrégation de Notre-Dame, Superiors, and the Paradox of Power, 1693–1796*, Montreal: McGill-Queen's University Press.

Greer, Alan (1997) *The People of New France*, Toronto: University of Toronto Press.

Heyrman, Christine (1997) *Southern Cross: The Beginning of the Bible Belt*, New York: Knopf.

Isaac, Rhys (1982) *Transformation of Virginia, 1740–1790*, Chapel Hill, NC: University of North Carolina Press.

Juster, Susan (1994) *Disorderly Women: Sexual Politics and Evangelicalism in Revolutionary New England*, Ithaca, NY: Cornell University Press.

Kidd, Thomas (2007) *The Great Awakening*, New Haven, CT: Yale University Press.

Lepore, Jill (2005) *New York Burning: Liberty, Slavery and Conspiracy in Eighteenth-Century Manhattan*, New York: Knopf.

Porterfield, Amanda (1980) *Feminine Spirituality in America: From Sarah Edwards to Martha Graham*, Philadelphia, PA: Temple University Press.

Raboteau, Albert J. (1978) *Slave Religion: The "Invisible Institution" in the Antebellum South*, New York: Oxford University Press.

Richter, Daniel K. (1992) *The Ordeal of the Longhouse: The Peoples of the Iroquois League in the Era of European Colonization*, Chapel Hill, NC: University of North Carolina Press.

Schroeder, Susan and Poole, Stafford (eds.) (2007) *Religion in New Spain*, Albuquerque, NM: University of New Mexico Press.

Stout, Harry S. (1986) *The New England Soul: Preaching and Religious Culture in Colonial New England*, New York: Oxford University Press.

Sweeney, Kevin and Haefeli, Evan (2003) *Captors and Captives: The 1704 French and Indian Raid on Deerfield*, Amherst, MA: University of Massachusetts Press.

Taylor, Alan (2001) *American Colonies*, New York: Viking Press.

Taylor, Allan (2006) *The Divided Ground: Indians, Settlers, and the Northern Borderland of the American Revolution*, New York: Knopf.

Weber, David J. (1992) *The Spanish Frontier in North America*, New Haven, CT: Yale University Press.

Wheeler, Rachel (2008) *To Live on Hope: Mohicans and Missionaries in the Eighteenth-Century Northeast*, Ithaca, NY: Cornell University Press.

White, Richard (1991) *The Middle Ground: Indians, Empires, and Republics in the Great Lakes Region, 1650–1815*, Cambridge: Cambridge University Press.

8

Practice

Martha L. Finch

Over the course of the eighteenth century, devotion to the subjective aspects of religion influenced many different forms of religious practice in the Atlantic world. Often called Pietism, this devotion to religious subjectivity and to methods for cultivating and shaping religious subjectivity developed among German-speaking Protestants in Europe and swept from there through the English-speaking world on both sides of the Atlantic. Coinciding with an equally forceful movement to apply reason to all aspects of life, Pietism in Britain and the Americas resulted in new methods of religious discipline aimed at methodically infusing individual feeling and behavior with Christian virtue. Pietism brought new scrutiny to, and enthusiasm for, the process of religious conversion and resulted in new forms of pious exercise in a variety of different religious groups. In a highly important development, African Americans began to embrace Pietistical Christianity in the eighteenth century, and in so doing contributed new forms of practice drawn from African religions to the Pietistic movement. Pietistical devotion to the subjective aspects of religious discipline also affected Catholics, Jews, and Native Americans, contributing both to the heterogeneity of Pietism in the Atlantic world and to an emerging emphasis on individual persons as the common denominators of religion.

The year 1692 was explosive in the New England Puritan colonies. In Salem, Massachusetts, dozens of people – most of them lower-status or unmarried women, like Tituba, an African or Native American servant – were accused of witchcraft and hauled into court, where they were grilled by church ministers and civil magistrates regarding their alleged activities. As the drama unfolded, embodied practices, including magic, healing, food, sex, dress, and ritual worship, played their roles on center stage as the critical signs and promoters of both godliness and sin. Accusers claimed they had been physically assaulted by the ghostly specters of neighbors who had compacted with the devil, and court-appointed investigators inspected the naked bodies of the accused for signs of that compact, such as witches' teats – small growths of skin in hidden areas of their bodies indicating they had engaged in sexual activity with the devil. Ministers called for days of fasting, which required all community members to avoid food, sex, expensive dress, and labor in order to attend services in the meeting-house, where they sang psalms, listened to sermons condemning the devil's activity, and prayed for divine mercy and healing of the evil scourge. God, however, seemed to close his ears to their desperate pleas. By October, 19 convicted witches had been executed by hanging, one man had been pressed to death with boulders, and several people had died in prison. Governor William Phips, whose own wife now stood accused of witchcraft, Reverend Increase Mather, Judge Samuel Sewall, and other church and court authorities acknowledged that the devil could, in fact, cause a specter of an innocent person to appear, and besides, it seemed unlikely that "so many in so small compass of land should abominably leap into the Devil's lap at once." The wily devil, they determined, had bamboozled them; they suspended the trials permanently.

The witchcraft trials of 1692 caused early New Englanders to question the divine meaning and purpose of their presence in North America as they moved into the eighteenth century. The unsettled feelings were compounded by changes throughout the British colonies, as British and European Protestants, Catholics, and Jews arrived in rapidly growing numbers, Native Americans stepped up their struggle to resist and adjust to the impact of colonization, and the African slave population multiplied. Practice – what people *did*, more than what they thought or believed – allowed groups to establish their presence, resist others, and adapt to the changing social and cultural landscape that culminated in the War for Independence and the founding of the American Republic. This chapter considers religious practices – rituals, including communal worship and domestic devotions, and bodily practices such as sexuality, food, dress, and healing – among Protestants, Jews, Catholics, Native Americans, and Africans in the British colonies during the eighteenth century.

Protestants

The 1700s saw radical shifts in Protestantism, as religious revivalism swept through the colonies, Methodism, founded by John Wesley in England, arrived and with the Baptists rose to prominence, and Enlightenment philosophy and Freemasonry shaped the religious beliefs and practices of many of the nation's "founding fathers." During the revivals of the 1730s and 1740s, often called the Great Awakening, evangelists identified not only religious conversion but also preaching itself with emotional experience and physical expression. Descended from intellectually oriented Puritan New England ministers, Jonathan Edwards introduced a new preaching style with vivid illustrations, such as an image of the sinner as a spider dangling by a thread over the raging fires of hell, intended to engage his listeners' "affections," or emotions, and bring about an intense awareness of sin, repentance, and, eventually, divine mercy and forgiveness. Other evangelists, such as George Whitefield from England, refined the art of preaching as a skillfully embodied performance, which attracted thousands to his outdoor meetings. The physical self-presentation of the preacher himself became critical for Whitefield's success. He was reportedly young and slender with a "bold countenance." He gestured theatrically while preaching and dramatically modulated his "deep-toned, yet clear and melodious" voice to capture the affections of his audiences. He also was cross-eyed, which fascinated his followers, who saw this as a sign of divine blessing. The attraction Whitefield's body held for devotees was such that following his death and burial in Newport, Massachusetts, in 1770 until at least the 1830s ministers periodically opened his coffin to observe the decomposition of his corpse, remove his clerical collar and wristbands to distribute them among patriot soldiers, or meditate upon his skull.

Publicly in revival gatherings and privately in their homes, those who attended Whitefield's meetings expressed their conviction of sin by weeping uncontrollably, collapsing to the ground, or falling into psychologically and physically incapacitating depressions. After hearing Whitefield preach in Connecticut in 1739, farmer Nathan Cole struggled for two years to receive God's grace until he became deeply depressed and physically ill. One evening when he was curled up in bed, staring at the hearth-fire and contemplating his death, God finally appeared to him in a vision. When the convicted experienced God's forgiving mercy, like Cole they often felt "lightness," burst into laughter, and were healed of emotional and physical maladies. Edwards, Whitefield, and others viewed these bodily manifestations as desirable signs of the Spirit of God working. However, well aware that anti-revivalists like Charles Chauncy saw "gross disorders" and "wantonness between the sexes" when those overcome by divine power fell upon each other and often ended up embracing, they also strove to balance intense emotionalism and physicality with a true working of the Spirit in one's heart.

While Congregationalist Edwards and Anglican Whitefield depended on dramatic preaching to move their audiences, Presbyterians brought from Scotland the use of food, as well as preaching, to revive religious enthusiasm in the middle colonies. The "sacramental season" gathered remote settlers, and sometimes Indians, from miles around for several days of services that began with fasting and prayer and culminated in the distribution and ingestion of the bread and wine, which often elicited "divine Power" and "affectionate sobs, sighs, and tears" among the communicants, as missionary David Brainerd described in the 1740s. Even more than these evangelists, founder of Methodism John Wesley grounded salvation in the body, including the use of food, by promoting perfection of the spiritual self through bodily disciplines. Wesley wrestled with doubts regarding whether those who cried out, trembled, and fell to the ground during Methodist revival meetings were truly inspired by divine power, but he settled on neither promoting nor rejecting such expressions and instead developed practical "methods" for regularizing and perfecting public and private life.

Two Methodist practices, love feasts and fasting, employed food as a means for uniting the community of believers and disciplining the self. On Wesley's first visit to the American colonies in 1737, he participated in a German Moravian love feast in Georgia. The experience made such an impression on him that he incorporated love feasts into Methodist practice, and Methodists lacking ordained clergy often replaced the Lord's Supper with love feasts. The gatherings, intended to bond committed members of the community to each other and God, involved the ritual sharing of water and "a little plain cake" or bread, testifying, praying, and almsgiving. Like the Puritans of the previous century who had called for public and private fasts, Wesley also promoted fasting as a means of denying oneself worldly pleasures in order to pray more effectively. But unlike New England Puritans and their spontaneous fasts,

Wesley followed the Anglican liturgy of regularized weekly or monthly fasting and he linked the practice of fasting not only to spiritual but also to physical health.

Debilitating diseases were common and much feared during the eighteenth century, and new developments in medicine attracted ministers like Wesley, Whitefield, and Cotton Mather. Most people continued to practice folk healing with herbal and more bizarre remedies, such as applying animal feces to cure sores, and magical charms, but ministers educated in Enlightenment science embraced new medical models of the human body, while continuing to attribute spiritual meanings to physical illness and health. During the winter of 1713–14 a measles epidemic in Boston took the lives of several hundred people, including Mather's wife and three children. In a sermon preached in January, Mather argued that sin was the cause of sickness, although sometimes God allowed illness to afflict the godly as a test of their faith. Thus, those who were ill should repent of their sins, be thankful, and recognize that God was the one who healed, directives that Jonathan Edwards's sister Hannah would follow when she contracted diphtheria in 1736. Smallpox ravaged Massachusetts in 1721, and Mather was soon at the center of a major controversy regarding the newfangled medical practice of inoculating against the disease, which he and other educated ministers endorsed as God's means of working in the natural world, but the majority of New Englanders feared was from the devil. The practice of inoculation was new, but other forms of preventive health practices, especially dietary regulations, were not. Like seventeenth-century Bostonian John Winthrop, Whitefield and Wesley, who both read Scottish-born physician George Cheyne's popular and influential writings on mental, spiritual, and physical health, advocated an abstemious diet in order to have a lean body, cure illness, maintain health, control "sensual pleasures," and "promote Christian Purity." Wesley's *Primitive Physick* (1747), based on Cheyne's principles, became the most widely read medical text of the 1700s, and American Methodists advocated its prescription to eat only food that "fits light and easy to the stomach" in order to avoid sinful excesses and have the energy to serve God.

Another means of disciplining one's fleshly yearnings, promoted by evangelical Methodists, Baptists, and Presbyterians, Puritan Congregationalists, Moravians and other German Pietists, and Quakers, was clothing. Dress displayed social status in the colonies. Wearing fashionable garb of expensive fabrics like fine linen, velvet, and silk ornamented with embroidery, ribbons, lace, and gold and silver jewelry demonstrated wealth and social power. For Protestants who promoted inner "modesty" through outer "plainness" it also exhibited sinful self-indulgence and pride. Thus, when John Wesley called upon his followers to avoid "costly and delicate food," he also condemned "costly apparel." By the 1690s New England had abandoned sumptuary laws regulating dress, but some Boston ministers, like Cotton Mather, continued to attack "proud rayment," especially on women. Others, like George Colman, in response to a troubled request from Lydia George (who, incidentally, would become Mather's third wife) for specific guidelines regarding appropriate dress, allowed that godly women of wealth and status like George might chart their own middle paths between the undesirable extremes of asceticism and overindulgence. For Quakers, or Friends, early in the 1700s, plain dress, which primarily meant clothing with simple lines and somber colors, reflected their growing emphasis on quietism, or the suppression of all "creaturely activity" during religious meetings so that one might sit silently until divinely inspired to speak. Plain dress served not only as a sign of quiet inner godliness but also as a bonding and a boundary-making device; it united members by equalizing their social status while distinguishing them from "the world." By the mid-1700s, however, many Quakers, especially those in Philadelphia, had acquired considerable wealth, which they displayed in expensive clothing and other material extravagances. Such falling away from the Discipline – Quaker laws regulating individual and group conduct – motivated a reform movement among some Friends, who feared the loss of God's blessing.

One practice that concerned Quaker reformers was the rise of promiscuous sexuality, both extramarital sex and intermarriage with non-Quakers. In the late 1700s, for example, wealthy Philadelphia merchant William Wister, a bachelor, had four mistresses; when he died in 1801 in the home of one of them, Quaker leaders refused to allow his burial in the Friends' graveyard. Controlling sexual activity was always a concern for Protestant ministers. John Wesley advocated celibacy, believing that when a person embraced Christianity he or she lost all lustful desires, but he modified his view over time to say that celibacy was the ideal, but for most people their desires returned, in which case they should marry. For most Protestants, heterosexual marriage, which ideally reflected the loving relationship between Christ the Bridegroom and the Church, his Bride, was the expected norm; extramarital sex was a sin of the lustful flesh. As in the seventeenth century, church congregations, especially in New England, strove to regulate the sexual activities of their members by watching for indications of immoral sexual behavior – a child born out of wedlock or fewer than nine months after marriage was the most obvious sign. By the mid-1700s civil courts no longer prosecuted such indiscretions, although churches continued to require public confessions of sexual sins before the entire church body. With the increasing privatization of the individual during the eighteenth century, however, private confessions and admonishments gradually replaced the shameful humiliation of public confession. Moreover, as Jonathan Edwards and other ministers noted, sexual promiscuity, especially among young people, was on the rise. In 1744, Edwards feared that the popular practice of groups of young, unmarried men and women "frolicking" together until late at night would lead to "lasciviousness, both in talking and acting."

Indeed, the 1700s saw a remarkable rise in premarital pregnancy. The common practice of "bundling," condoned by parents, allowed a young man and woman to sleep together before marriage. The expectation was that the couple would remain at least partially clothed while sharing a bed, but the reality was that many engaged in sex. Needless to say, ministers condemned the practice. In 1738, Edwards complained about "young people of different sexes reclining together," and in a 1753 sermon Samuel Hopkins attacked the practice of "lying on the bed of any man with young women" as a visible "act of uncleanness." By the end of the eighteenth century, however, such sexual activity seemed innocent when compared with the rise of prostitution in urban areas, to which Reverend William White, bishop of the Episcopal Church in Philadelphia, physician Benjamin Rush, and others responded by forming the first organization in the United States dedicated to reforming prostitutes, the Magdalen Society, in 1800.

Ministers considered heterosexual sex, either within or outside of marriage, as "natural"; that is, it was sex as God intended it, to produce children. More serious acts of sexual uncleanness – masturbation, same-sex relations, and bestiality – were "unnatural," for they were non-procreative: occurring with oneself (masturbation), with one's "own kind" (men with men and women with women), or with "other" (animals). Eighteenth-century men were expected to achieve "self-mastery," and masturbating indicated a lack of power over one's lustful desires. Furthermore, medical theories posited that masturbation would cause sexual impotency. In his diary from the 1720s, New Englander Joseph Moody agonized over his "sin of self-pollution," as he called it; he worried that the depraved practice threatened both his spiritual salvation and his physical health. Sodomy and bestiality were even more serious, for they undermined the natural social order. Yet concern about these sex acts radically declined from the seventeenth century, when being convicted of such acts had brought public whippings or executions by hanging upon the perpetrators; there are apparently few recorded cases of sodomy in eighteenth-century church records and no cases of bestiality. In 1732, Ebenezer Knight merely lost his church membership for repeatedly engaging in "uncleanness" with other men and was allowed to rejoin the church six years later. In 1756, Baptist minister Stephen Gorton, whom church members knew had been attracted to men for several years, was finally suspended from his position for "unchaste behaviour with his fellow men when in bed with them." And anti-revivalists accused Dutch Reformed evangelical Theodorus Jacobus Frelinghuysen of attempting "scandalous undertakings" with men he "happened" to be sleeping with. As the Gorton and Frelinghuysen cases demonstrate, beds were luxury items, few in number in colonial homes and inns, and men commonly slept with other men while traveling on business or visiting friends and family, which provided opportunities for those with same-sex proclivities to explore their desires, though often to the dismay of their bedmates.

Less orthodox groups, such as the Immortalists and the Shakers, rejected the heterosexual marital and procreative norm. They distinguished themselves from mainstream Protestants by claiming to receive divine revelations that practicing celibacy purified the body and produced spiritual perfection in this world. The Immortalists, a network of individuals who had experienced dramatic conversions during the revivals of the 1740s, believed that God had freed them from their earthly marriages to non-believers in order to join with partners in celibate "spiritual marriages." Outsiders were skeptical, suspecting that Immortalists like Sarah Prentice were, in fact, engaging in "criminal Freedoms with the other sex, under the splendid Guise of Spiritual Love and Friendship." While this was true of at least some of them, others like Prentice were committed to renouncing sex in order to achieve spiritual perfection and an incorruptible body that would live until Christ returned to earth. The United Society of Believers in Christ's Second Appearing, more commonly known as the Shakers for their trembling when overcome by the power of the Holy Spirit, sailed from England to New York in 1774. In dreams and visions, God had revealed to their leader, Mother Ann Lee, that sexual intercourse between Adam and Eve was the original sin, lust the root of evil, and henceforward she and her followers must renounce all carnal desires and activities. The Shakers organized themselves into communities with the intention of creating the kingdom of God, in which "there is no giving or taking in marriage," on earth. Members shared all material goods and labor and sublimated their sexual impulses and desires by allowing "all the faculties of soul and body" to be fully absorbed in "energetic" and ecstatic worship, song, and dance.

The first company of Shakers arrived in the colonies when Revolutionary fervor was reaching its peak. Unlike those attracted to the enthusiasms of evangelical revivalism, who often were from the lower classes, less educated, and rural, those who led the charge for American independence from Britain tended to be among the colonial elite. Men like George Washington, Thomas Jefferson, John Adams, James Madison, and Benjamin Franklin, educated in the Enlightenment principles of deism, rationalism, natural law, and moral virtue, participated to varying degrees in denominations emphasizing the intellectual rather than the emotional, especially Congregationalism, Anglicanism (after the Revolution, the Episcopal Church), and Unitarianism. The practices in these churches and after the War during sermons delivered in Congress reflected this emphasis on rational religion. In Anglican churches the congregation sat quietly, respectfully attending to a well-constructed sermon of about twenty minutes in length that emphasized "sound morality, or deep studied Metaphysicks," rather than hellfire and salvation, and then solemnly filed to the altar to participate in communion. Ministers like Jonathan Mayhew, pastor of the West Congregational Church of Boston, furthered the Revolutionary cause by preaching patriotic sermons arguing that it was only "reasonable," when a king "turns tyrant and makes his subjects his prey to devour and destroy," to "throw off our allegiance to him and to resist."

Many colonial gentlemen, including several signers of the Declaration of Independence and, later, men from the middling and lower classes, including African Americans, also were members in a new fraternal order from England, Freemasonry. First established inthe colonies in the 1730s, it brought together "ancient" wisdom, Enlightenment values, and, after the Revolution, Christian principles to exert great influence in American public life by the 1790s. Based on brotherly love, the biblical story of the building of Solomon's Temple (viewed as a model of both the human being and the universe), and the "Three Great Lights" (the Bible and the two symbols of geometry and architecture, the square and compass), Masonic lodges and their secret rites promised intellectual, emotional, and social enlightenment and access to esoteric knowledge, including the secret name of God, the Grand Architect of the Universe (Figure 8.1). Moving through "degrees" of membership required participation in complex ceremonies in lodge rooms elaborately decorated with symbolic imagery, the central symbol being the square and compass surrounding a G (signifying Geometry and God). Over their clothing, ritual participants wore white aprons, derived from the stonemason's apron, richly embroidered with colorful symbols indicating one's degree of membership. On the apron owned by George Washington (Figure 8.2), committed Episcopalian and active Mason, was the square and compass, the beehive (representing industry and cooperation), Noah's Ark (representing "man's journey over the sea of life"), the all-seeing eye of God (which also appears on the reverse side of the Great Seal of the United States), and dozens of other symbols.

Masonic culture permeated American life from the 1790s into the first decades of the 1800s. Engravings of Washington in his Masonic regalia were popular; symbols adorned quilts, drinking glasses, and shopkeepers' signs as well as the Great Seal; and cornerstone ceremonies dedicated schools, churches, and government buildings. The most public Masonic ceremony was the dedication of the "Temple of Liberty," the United States Capitol, led by President Washington on September 18, 1793. Attended by large crowds and accompanied by "music playing, drums beating, colours flying,

SHAKERS.
their mode of Worship.

Figure 8.1   Shaker worship services often involved "all the faculties of soul and body."

Figure 8.2   *George Washington as a Master Mason*, 1856, by Emanuel Gottlieb Leutze, American oil on canvas. Courtesy of the 32nd Degree Masons, Valley of Detroit, Michigan.

and spectators rejoicing," the procession of city commissioners, the Virginia Artillery, and Masonic brothers "in all their elegant regalia" marched "in the greatest solemn dignity" to the southeast corner of the Capitol building, where Washington placed an engraved silver plate upon the cornerstone and poured over it the Masonic biblical symbols of consecration: corn, wine, and oil, representing nourishment, refreshment, and joy and invoking fruitful abundance for the new nation.

Catholics and Jews

At worst vigorously persecuted and at best suspiciously tolerated in most of the colonies, Catholics and Jews struggled to establish their communities and accommodate to Protestant-dominated life. Both groups were in a very small minority, even in Maryland, which had been established in the mid-1600s as a joint Catholic-Protestant venture. In fact, Catholics, the primary focus of Protestant ire since the Reformation, had a harder time of it than Jews until the revolutionary changes that swept across the colonies, affecting all Americans, during the latter decades of the 1700s. During the 1600s Jews had practiced their rites and ceremonies privately, in their homes, quietly going public with the erection of the first synagogue, Shearith Israel in New York City, at the turn of the eighteenth century. None of the five urban synagogues built by the 1750s bore any outward signs, such as a Star of David or Hebrew lettering, to indicate their Jewishness. Catholics in Maryland, on the other hand, had experienced some religious freedom until the late 1600s, but with rising persecution and an ongoing dearth of clergy primarily practiced their religion privately, in homes or on Jesuit plantations, during most of the 1700s. They fared better in Quaker Pennsylvania, the most religiously tolerant of the British colonies, where they were able to build churches and set up a parish system. During the final decades of the century Catholics and Jews opened their places of worship to prominent Protestants, inviting them to observe firsthand their religious practices in order to garner understanding and support.

Jewish ritual life was based in homes and synagogues. The majority of the two thousand colonial Jews were Ashkenazim, from Germany and Eastern Europe, but because the first Jews in North America were Sephardim, from Spain and Portugal by way of South America, all American synagogues until the 1790s followed the Sephardic rite in architecture, music, and Hebrew pronunciation. No rabbis settled in North America until the 1840s, so synagogues were lay-run, functioning as hubs of Jewish life where Sephardim and Ashkenazim together, although not always peaceably, attended religious services, circumcised and educated their boys, purchased kosher meat, married, were buried in their own cemeteries, and, sometimes, were excommunicated for violating Jewish law. Gender and social status determined seat assignments within the synagogue, with men seated on the main floor at the center of ritual practice, the most elite near the eastern wall, and women in the upstairs gallery behind the men, also according to rank and status. Such rigorous guidelines could be challenged, although not without censure. Echoing Protestant church practice, far more women attended synagogue in colonial America than they did in Europe or Britain, and so many women attended Shearith Israel that battles ensued over women's seating in their small gallery. In 1760, Miss Josse Hays sat in the seat of prominent member Judah Mears's daughter, to which the father responded by entering the women's gallery during worship and kicking Hays out of his daughter's seat. Mears was fined for violating the law of separate gendered seating; eventually, Shearith Israel abandoned seating by social rank, although it continued the practice of seating men and women separately.

The laymen who ran the synagogues sometimes ruled with iron fists as they strove to determine that all Jews were observing the body of laws, or *halakah*, both publicly and privately. Nevertheless, many Jews, with no rabbis to answer to as they accommodated to colonial society, did not feel obligated to follow the letter of the law. In 1757, Shearith Israel excommunicated Jews living on the outskirts of New York City who had been "Trading on the Sabath, Eating of forbidden Meats & other Heinous Crimes." In 1774, synagogue leaders took innkeeper Hetty Hayes to task for serving *treyf*, or nonkosher, food. Despite the fact that these individuals had broken *kashrut*, the dietary laws, most colonial Jews considered keeping kosher by following *kashrut* among the most important of their daily practices. In order to blend in with the rest of colonial society, they shunned many traditional external signs of Jewishness, such as beards on men and wigs on women, dressed like other colonists of their social rank, and sometimes married non-Jews. Observing the dietary laws became an important means of embodying Jewish identity, but *kashrut* was difficult to maintain outside the home. Most Jewish men were merchants and tradesmen, who had regular commerce with non-Jews in their homes and businesses, and Jewish women socialized with Protestant women. Many, perhaps most, Jews likely maintained a double standard, keeping kosher at home but when out in the world eating pork "or any other meat that was put before them," as one observer noted of young men in New York.

Avoiding work on the Saturday Sabbath and observing Jewish holidays such as Passover and the High Holy Days of Rosh Hashanah and Yom Kippur also posed practical difficulties. Christian colonists regularly transacted business on Saturdays, observing Sunday as the day of communal worship and rest from worldly activities. Individual Jewish merchants had to decide whether to observe the Sabbath and holidays properly or to comply with the dominant social mores. Some were like wealthy Aaron Lopez, who "rigidly observed … Saturday as a holy time" by closing his business for both the Jewish and the Christian Sabbaths, from Friday sundown until Monday morning. Others traded and traveled on Saturdays, which could bring the threat of excommunication from the synagogue upon them but likely became the norm for many colonial Jews. Such expressions of individual freedom that challenged traditional Jewish practices only increased after the Revolution. More people, even some supposedly kosher butchers, ignored *kashrut*, fewer men prayed with *tallisim*, or prayer shawls, fewer women used the ritual purification bath, the *mikveh*, following their menstrual periods, and intermarriage with non-Jews increased. As a Philadelphia synagogue reported in 1785, "In this country … everybody does as he pleases."

Like Jews, Catholics in the British colonies struggled to maintain their practices, centered on Mass and the seven sacraments of Baptism, Eucharist, Reconciliation, Confirmation, Marriage, Holy Orders, and Anointing of the Sick, during the eighteenth century. Earlier, French and Spanish missionaries had experienced remarkable success baptizing Indians. By the 1770s, following the removal of the French from Maine, Penobscot Indians demonstrated their commitment to French Catholicism when they requested that the Provincial Congress send them a French priest, for they refused to "hear any prayers that come from *England*." The Congress complied, and in 1791 Indian Agent John Allen wrote that the Penobscots he knew were "very exemplary" in their Catholic practice. They were "zealous and tenacious of the rites of the church, and strictly moral, cautious of misbehaving in point of religion ... Their performances, chants in latin, etc. were in most instances superior to any," and they diligently taught their children the service. When English priests arrived in the British colonies, however, they encountered resistance from both the Indians and the Protestants who already lived there. The largest numbers of Catholics settled in Maryland and Pennsylvania. In 1704, the Maryland Assembly enacted a law intended to restrain virtually all Catholic practice, forbidding priests to exercise any priestly functions other than baptizing children whose parents were Catholic. Two months later, however, the Assembly softened, allowing priests to say Mass in private homes, which became law in 1707, but all public chapels and churches were closed. At the same time the practices of English Catholics in Maryland were being restricted, German and Irish Catholics in Pennsylvania enjoyed a fair amount of religious freedom and erected a public chapel in Philadelphia in the 1730s.

Throughout most of the eighteenth century there were few priests to serve a growing Catholic population that ranged from cities to remote rural areas. Catholics, including slaves, who lived on or near the Jesuits' plantations in Maryland, where priests held Sunday services twice a month followed by a meal and socializing, or in urban centers like Philadelphia had more ready access to Mass and the sacraments. However, most Catholics were scattered across the countryside on isolated farms, which resulted in the two primary characteristics of colonial Catholic practice: priests rode circuits on horseback to reach isolated Catholics, and families led their own private home devotions. The life of a Jesuit circuit rider was rigorous; he traveled sometimes 60 miles to spend a few days or a week in a region serving rural Catholics in their homes. The priests celebrated Mass, preached, visited the sick, baptized and catechized children, heard confessions, and performed weddings. John Carroll, who would become the first American bishop in 1789, described caring for his "very large congregation" in Maryland: he often rode 25 or 30 miles to visit the sick and once a month traveled fifty or sixty miles to another congregation on a plantation in Virginia. When the priest was not available, families practiced their own domestic devotions, fasting once a week to discipline fleshly desires, reciting the prayers of the Mass, and reading from devotional manuals. Catholics were to attend confession and Mass at least once each year, during the Easter season, but it is likely that most colonial Catholics did not attend even that often. Popular devotional manuals may have contributed to such negligence, for they emphasized internal, private devotions over external, public rituals and an over-dependence on the sacraments. The authors allowed that when one was unable to attend Mass, a half hour privately reciting prayers would suffice. They also expected parents to instruct their children in Catholic faith and morality.

By the 1760s, private, domestic Catholicism became more public and congregational, as persecution declined and churches were built. Jesuit plantations in Maryland began to function like parish churches, which emphasized the congregational over the individual through such communal rituals as adoration of the Blessed Sacrament. In the 1770s, the largest and most active Catholic congregation was in Philadelphia, at St. Mary's and St. Joseph's Church, where John Adams and George Washington attended an evening service in 1774. For stoic Congregationalist-Unitarian Adams, the pomp and ceremony, especially the assault on the physical senses, of Catholic practice was "awful and affecting." The priest's vestments were "rich with lace" as he preached from a pulpit covered with "velvet and gold." The altar "was very rich, little Images and Crucifixes about" and "Wax Candles all lighted-up." Most distressing was "the Picture of our Saviour in a Frame of Marble over the Altar, at full Length, upon the Cross in the Agonies, and the Blood dropping and streaming from his Wounds!" During the Mass Adams observed "the poor Wretches fingering their beads, chanting Latin, not a Word of which they understood; their Pater Nosters and Ave Marias, their holy Water, their Crossing themselves perpetually; their Bowing to the Name of Jesus, whenever they hear it, their Bowings, Kneelings and genuflections before the Altar." Adams reflected common anti-Catholic sentiments when he summarized that the Mass had "everything which can lay hold of the eye, ear and imagination – everything that can charm and bewitch the simple and the ignorant." In spite of Adams's biting commentary, during the final decades of the 1700s Catholics began to feel comfortable mingling more freely with the rest of society – as demonstrated by their willingness to invite Adams and Washington to a Mass. By 1800, the United States had its first bishop, the number of American priests had increased dramatically, and, with the growing ethnic diversity among American Catholics, English, rather than Latin, had become the common language for Mass.

Native Americans and African Slaves

During the eighteenth century the indigenous population in North America, ravaged by poverty, disease, alcoholism, and warfare, continued to decline. Meanwhile, the African immigrant population increased exponentially, from 27,000 people of African birth or descent in 1700, to over a million, nearly 90 percent of them enslaved, in 1800. Each group – Indians and Africans – was internally culturally diverse, yet both struggled with similar challenges and threats to their physical and cultural survival. "Race" developed as a means of defining and distinguishing individuals and groups based on inherited physiological features, in part in order to explain the decline of Native peoples and to justify the increased importation of African slaves. Skin color was the first bodily trait colonists used to identify racial categories and create social hierarchies, as they connected whole sets of intellectual and moral characteristics with the color of one's skin. Ministers and missionaries typically related lighter skin to Christian purity, enlightened intellect, and industrious labor and "tawny," "dusky," or "black" skin to heathen sinfulness, dark ignorance, and lazy indolence. Such rhetoric justified beatings and whippings, economic exploitation, and social discrimination against darker skinned peoples, as well as the destruction of their traditional cultures and practices. Native Americans and Africans often refused to accept such treatment silently and developed a variety of practical strategies to aid them in both resisting and adapting to colonial pressures.

Euro- and Anglo-American attempts to civilize and Christianize the Indians of North America, begun well before 1700, continued in the eighteenth century but with some changed attitudes on both sides. Along the eastern seaboard, Indians who still resided in areas dominated by English and European settlers had adjusted, more or less, to colonization. Some attempted to live "in the manner of Christian Englishmen"; in New England this primarily occurred in "praying towns," although by the American Revolution most had been overrun by land-hungry colonists. Others rejected both English and Christian practices and sustained their traditional ways of life as best they could within constrained circumstances. The likely majority engaged in a variety of practices that allowed them to piece together aspects of Anglo, European, Christian, and Native cultures in the typically pragmatic, flexible, and inclusive Indian style of cultural adaptation. Those on the western edges of the British colonies and in western territories became more resistant to European encroachment and suspicious of entering into social or political relations with colonial powers. Yet most had learned something of Christianity, which often shaped their religious responses to the impact of colonization, especially in Native revitalization movements beginning in the mid-1700s.

Until at least the 1760s, missionaries continued to believe that in order to convert Indians to Christianity, they must first be "civilized" according to English customs, a process that was grounded in the alteration of Native bodies and practices, such as hairstyle, dress, sexuality, and language, to conform to English modes of embodiment. Reverend Cotton Mather wrote in 1721 that before the New England Indians were civilized, they were clothed in "Rough Skins with which they hardly covered themselves" and lived in "squalid and dark *Wigwams.*" "The best thing we can do," he proclaimed, "is to Anglicize them in all agreeable Instances," including requiring them to speak English, for when they retained their own languages, they retained "other Salvage Inclinations" that undermined Christianity. But Mather complained that "humanizing," "taming," and "civilizing" these "Miserable Animals" was "a work of no little difficulty." Indians typically saw no need to give up their practices for uncomfortable and impractical English clothing or to reject their spiritual traditions, grounded in their sacred lands and histories, for a religion foreign and insensible to them. When missionary David Brainerd attempted to gather some Iroquois in New York for Sunday meetings in 1745, the Indians responded that they did not wish to be "transformed into white men." Ten years earlier in Connecticut, Richard Treat had attempted to infiltrate Niantic dance and divination ceremonies in order to preach, to which the Indians responded with "rage" and "fury," telling him on no uncertain terms to "begone."

By the early 1700s, Congregational, Presbyterian, and Anglican missionaries in New England and the middle colonies realized that converting adult Indians was something of a lost cause and turned their attention more fully to the conversion of young people, primarily by building mission schools dedicated to the thoroughgoing "reeducation" of Native children, especially boys. A primary strategy of the boarding schools was to civilize the children by physically isolating them from the "savage" ways of their families and tribal communities. The initial requirement upon entering a school entailed bodily alterations – donning English garb (missionaries often offered clothing as an enticement to attract children to the schools), cutting hair in the English style, eating English-style food with English utensils, rising early in the morning, and so on. Then they learned to speak, read, and write in English while being instructed in Christian doctrine, with the ultimate goal of conversion and baptism. Colonists tended to view Indians as unsettled, indolent, and lazy; thus, also critical for the civilization of the missionaries' charges was that they learn to engage in industrious labor in order to be "useful" in the world. The standard means of discipline was corporal punishment, a childrearing practice unfamiliar to Indian children. In some schools boys were whipped and beaten daily, as missionaries attempted to inculcate civilized Christian values and grew frustrated with their homesick and disoriented charges.

Many of the children at the mission schools contracted contagious diseases to which they had no immunities. The missionaries prescribed common European medical procedures, such as "purges" by vomiting, but many boarders died, whether by illness, an unfamiliar diet, or other aspects of rigorous boarding school life. Those who survived tended to run away; as Virginia governor Robert Dinwiddie noted in 1756, Cherokee boys who had left the Anglican William and Mary College in Williamsburg "did not like Confinement." Missionaries complained that when students escaped the schools to return to their families they typically fell back into their heathenish ways, unable to remain "unstain'd either by a course of intemperance [drunkenness] or uncleanness [sex], or both," as Reverend Eleazar Wheelock opined in 1771 about several Iroquois boys who had returned to Quebec after leaving his school in Connecticut. They had "sunk down into as low, savage, and brutish a manner of living as they were in before." Many runaways were rejected by their tribal communities, for they were no longer able speak the languages or practice the traditions and often became objects of contempt. At the end of the eighteenth century, Scottish American missionaries described the conflict experienced by the former Native student: "He is neither a white man nor an Indian."

On the northern and western edges of colonial settlement English Quaker, German Moravian, and French Catholic missionaries found better success in civilizing and Christianizing Indians due to their generally more benevolent approaches. French Jesuits along the Canadian border lived among the Indians, sharing their food and learning from their healing and other practices. They adapted Catholic rituals and material culture to Native ones, requiring far fewer changes in Native modes of embodied life. In Pennsylvania, peace-loving Quakers attempted to treat Indians fairly and focused on proselytizing by example, although they did hope, in vain, to civilize Delaware Indians by turning them into industrious English farmers. Most successful were German Moravian missionaries, who first arrived in North America in 1735 in Savannah, Georgia, and soon established Indian mission towns in the middle and southern colonies. By 1772, the pressures of colonial encroachment and discrimination pushed the Pennsylvania missionaries westward with their Delaware converts into Ohio and then, during the Revolution, to Ontario, Canada. Moravians built neatly laid-out, orderly, and protective mission towns in which they lived with their proselytes. The Indians learned civilized Christian modes of life, such as farming fruits and vegetables, raising cattle and hogs, spinning and weaving, and reading and writing, as well as ingesting Moravian religious beliefs, and they became, according to one missionary, "robust and strong and enjoy[ed] good health." Moravian communities were organized on more benevolent principles than were other Protestant missions, although the missionaries outlawed extramarital sex, alcohol, murder, lying, and idleness. Like the Jesuits, the Moravians were deeply interested in all aspects of Native life and willingly learned from the Indians with whom they lived. For example, in eastern Ohio during the 1770s missionaries David Zeisberger and John Heckwelder recorded in great detail the illnesses and healing practices of Lenni Lenape converts, even using some of the remedies themselves. Heckwelder noted, "I have myself been benefited and cured by taking their emetics and their medicines in fevers," and, when beset by a "stubborn rheumatism," he found relief in the "sweat oven" the Indians had built for the mission. Notably, while Moravians like Heckwelder rejected the spiritual beliefs behind Native practices, such as the sweat, they nevertheless had no qualms about embracing the practices themselves.

The linkage between civilization and Christianization promoted by missionaries ultimately contributed to the destruction of Native cultures but also, for some Indians, paradoxically helped to mitigate the negative effects of that destruction by allowing them some means to adapt to the radical changes brought about by colonization. In response to the pressures brought by disease, alcoholism, loss of land, warfare, and dependence on European material goods like weapons and cloth, several Indian "prophets" arose during the middle and later decades of the eighteenth century. Receiving divine revelations through dreams and visions, they preached their messages and incited revitalization movements intended to encourage Indians to reject Christianity and all other aspects of "white" culture and return to their traditional customs and practices. The messages typically accused whites of causing the suffering of Native people and outlined specific codes Indians must practice in order to heal themselves and their lands. In the 1760s, Neolin, known as the Delaware Prophet, promoted a code of conduct given to him by the "Master of Life" in a vision of heaven, where there were Indians but no whites. Neolin's code limited alcohol intake to one or at most two draughts per day, promoted monogamous marriage, outlawed fighting with each other and engaging in trade with whites, and provided guidelines for how to greet another Indian: "bow, and give one another the hand of the heart." Yet it also admonished his listeners against traditional practices: they were not to sing "the medicine song" or practice "witchcraft," for by doing so they were "speak[ing] to the evil spirit." Instead, they were to pray to the "Son or Little God," who took their prayers to the Great Being. From 1799 into the early 1800s, Handsome Lake, a Seneca, also codified his visionary experiences into a message of moral reform similar to that of Neolin. The prophets intended their messages and the practices they encoded to promote and strengthen Indian independence from colonial oppression, but they were shot through with Christian images, metaphors, symbols, and language, which created a synthesis of Indian and English worldviews that tapped into the power Christianity carried in the colonial world.

Africans transported across the Atlantic and enslaved in the British colonies also tapped into the power of Christianity later in the eighteenth century, fully shaping it to their own purposes by the mid-1800s. Two sets of practices – African and Christian – contributed to slaves' religion, which would produce distinctively African American forms of Christianity. The institution of slavery became far more oppressive in the early 1700s than it had been during the previous century, and the experience of forced migration and enslavement dissolved African social and cultural systems, including religious systems. However, discrete African practices survived; although eighteenth-century sources reveal few, they were undoubtedly far more common than white observers saw, were able to make sense of, or bothered to mention. Court records note conjurors accused of using magical charms and practices, such as concocting a potion out of dried salamanders, to poison both white masters and fellow slaves; it is likely that black conjurors also used their skills for healing, as they would in the nineteenth century. Reverend John Sharpe described the burial practices of slaves in New York in 1712 as "heathenish rites" performed at the graveside. Ministers also complained about slaves gathering on Sundays and other holidays for "dancing, feasting, and merriment." To the twang of banjos and the rhythm of drums, described a visitor to Virginia in the 1770s, slaves danced "with astonishing agility, and the most vigorous exertions, keeping time and cadence, most exactly." One minister observed slaves meeting for "*Idolotrous Dances* and *Revels*" on Sundays "as a *means* to *procure Rain*." However, it is unclear how often slaves engaged in their frequent dance gatherings for spiritual purposes derived from African traditions, rather than simply entertainment.

Arguments concerning whether slaves should convert to Christianity consumed many southern slave owners and ministers; both sides grounded their arguments in the slave's body. Masters claimed that slaves were too much like animals to convert: their manners were "rude" and "bestial," their languages "strange," and their minds "weak" and "shallow." Ministers like Morgan Godwin and Cotton Mather took the other side, arguing that one need only consider "the shape and figure of our Negroes Bodies, their Limbs and Members, their Voice and Countenance" to recognize that they were just like other "rational" human beings. Nevertheless, southern slave owners, who often did not hold strong religious commitments themselves, tended to deny their slaves Christian instruction, for fear its inherent message of divine grace and freedom would make them "proud and saucy." Indeed, slaves were not attracted to the formal, liturgical style of Anglican worship that dominated in the southern colonies or the requirements of catechetical learning that church membership entailed. Other denominations met with a bit more success, such as the Quakers and Presbyterians. In New England there were relatively few slaves, who labored in private homes or on small farms rather than the large plantations of the south; they participated in the domestic religious practices, such as evening prayers, Bible reading, and religious instruction, of the Puritan families who owned them. Nevertheless, throughout the British colonies very few African Americans had embraced Christianity by the first decades of the eighteenth century.

With the Protestant revivals of the 1740s, however, slaves began converting in larger numbers. Edwards and Whitefield, who both owned slaves, happily noted that "negroes" often attended their meetings and "were wrought upon and changed." But it was the rise of Baptists and Methodists in the South after the 1760s, with their fundamentally embodied experience of salvation, that softened slaves' resistance to Christianity. A revival during the 1770s in Virginia and North Carolina attracted "hundreds of Negroes … with tears streaming down their faces" to evangelist Devereux Jarratt's meetings. African Americans' practices in earlier revival meetings may have mirrored those of white participants, but by the 1790s there was a noticeable difference, according to Baptist preacher John Leland, between Afro and Anglo conduct. Blacks were "more noisy, in time of preaching, than the whites, and … more subject to bodily exercise." Methodist ministers noted that blacks often broke out in shouting during meetings, which could sometimes drown out the preacher. And at the turn of the nineteenth century a slave woman named Aunt Katy, "with many extravagant gestures" during a Methodist meeting in North Carolina, cried out that she was "young King Jesus," demonstrating the African tradition of spirit possession. All of these practices – energetic participation, the "shout" indicating being overcome by the Spirit, and spirit possession – were characteristic of African spiritual traditions, which slaves in the heat of the revival meeting melded with Protestant revival elements to birth the distinctive African American worship style that would come to full fruition during the antebellum period.

White ministers, however, strove to squelch practices that indicated obvious African influences. Joseph Travis, the preacher present when Aunt Katy claimed to be young King Jesus, ordered her to be seated and publicly retracted her membership in the church, saying that "we would not have such wild fanatics among us," for "such expressions were even blasphemous." Even as they encouraged godly physical and emotional release in spiritual exercises, white Baptists and Methodists promoted disciplined codes of conduct intended to separate believers from "the world" – and slaves from their African past. Given Methodists' rejection of extravagant dress and ornamentation, in 1783, Maryland minister Freeborn Garrettson confronted a slave woman who attended his meeting with "her ears, nose, and hands ... loaded with gold." She explained that she was an African king's daughter and thus entitled to wear jewelry, but she removed it, handing it to a friend who would give her a traditional African burial when she died, which included interring her jewelry with her body so that she could wear it in the afterlife.

There were some Baptist and Methodist practices that challenged whites' notions of appropriate relations with blacks. The tumultuous drama of revival meetings often broke down participants' racial prejudices, generating a sense of social egalitarianism. Outsiders often criticized Baptists for accepting into their communities slave converts as "brothers" and "sisters." Their central ritual – adult baptism by full immersion, called "dipping" – was available to white and black converts alike. During mass baptisms following a revival, new converts, dressed in white robes to indicate their sinless purity, lined up according to social status, white men first, at the river's edge. One at a time they waded out to meet the minister, who held them in his arms as they fell backwards into the water and then lifted them out again, laughing, crying, shouting, and wiping water from their faces. Other rituals also involved physical contact between blacks and whites: the "devoting of children," in which ministers laid their hands on children's heads and prayed for them; the "laying on of hands" to ordain preachers; greeting each other with "the right hand of fellowship" or "kiss of charity"; footwashing, a rite demonstrating humble service; and anointing the sick with oil for healing. During Methodist love feasts, participants shared physical and spiritual food. Some white Baptists and Methodists, but especially outsiders, questioned such physical intimacy between whites and blacks, for it challenged fundamental notions of propriety regarding the "commingling" of the races.

By the late 1700s, slaves had linked the physically and emotionally liberating experience of evangelical conversion and the Revolutionary values of liberty and social equality with freedom from slavery. One way this played out was through the practice of black preaching, which began during the revivals of the 1740s and allowed some slaves new positions of authority. Critics, such as Charles Chauncy, were disgusted by the sight and sound of uneducated blacks doing "the Business of Preachers." But by the 1790s dozens of black preachers, many of them recognized and supported by white Protestant organizations, preached to both whites and blacks. However, although the latter decades of the eighteenth century saw African Americans preaching and embracing Christianity in much larger numbers than previously, in 1800, the number of black church members was still low, less than five percent of the total black population in the southern colonies.

References and Further Reading

Axtell, J. (1985) *The Invasion Within: The Contest of Cultures in Colonial America*, New York: Oxford University Press.

Bonomi, P.U. (2003) *Under the Cope of Heaven: Religion, Society, and Politics in Colonial America*, updated edn, New York: Oxford University Press.

Bowden, H.W. (1981) *American Indians and Christian Missions: Studies in Cultural Conflict*, Chicago: University of Chicago Press.

Bullock, S.C. (1996) *Revolutionary Brotherhood: Freemasonry and the Transformation of Social Order, 1730–1840*, Chapel Hill, NC: University of North Carolina Press.

Butler, J. (1990) *Awash in a Sea of Faith: Christianizing the American People*, Cambridge, MA: Harvard University Press.

Carroll, B.D. (2003) " 'I Indulged My Desire Too Freely': Sexuality, Spirituality, and the Sin of Self-pollution in the Diary of Joseph Moody, 1720–1724," *William and Mary Quarterly*, 60: 155–70.

Chireau, Y.P. (2003) *Black Magic: Religion and the African American Conjuring Tradition*, Berkeley, CA: University of California Press.

Diner, H. (2004) *The Jews of the United States, 1654–2000*, Berkeley, CA: University of California Press.

Dolan, J.P. (1985) *The American Catholic Experience: A History from Colonial Times to the Present*, Garden City, NY: Doubleday and Company.

Foster, L. (1984) *Religion and Sexuality: The Shakers, the Mormons, and the Oneida Community*, Urbana, IL: University of Illinois Press.

Godbeer, R. (2002) *Sexual Revolution in Early America*, Baltimore, MD: Johns Hopkins University Press.

Griffith, R.M. (2004) *Born Again Bodies: Flesh and Spirit in American Christianity*, Berkeley, CA: University of California Press.

Hamm, T.D. (2003) *The Quakers in America*, New York: Columbia University Press.

Hennesey, J. (1981) *American Catholics: A History of the Roman Catholic Community in the United States*, New York: Oxford University Press.

Heyrman, C.L. (1997) *Southern Cross: The Beginnings of the Bible Belt*, New York: Alfred A. Knopf.

Isaac, R. (1982) *The Transformation of Virginia, 1740–1790*, Chapel Hill, NC: University of North Carolina Press.

Karlsen, C.F. (1987) *The Devil in the Shape of a Woman: Witchcraft in Colonial New England*, New York: W. W. Norton and Company.

Kidd, T.S. (2007) *The Great Awakening: The Roots of Evangelical Christianity in Colonial America*, New Haven, CT: Yale University Press.

Mahr, A.C. (1950) "Health Conditions in the Moravian Indian Mission of Schönbrunn in the 1770s," *Ohio Journal of Science*, 50: 121–131.

Minkema, K.P. (2001) "The Spiritual Meanings of Illness in Eighteenth-century New England," in C. McDannell (ed.) *Religions of the United States in Practice*, vol. 1, Princeton, NJ: Princeton University Press, pp. 269–298.

Raboteau, A.J. (2004) *Slave Religion: The "Invisible Institution" in the Antebellum South*, updated edn, New York: Oxford University Press.

Reis, E. (1999) *Damned Women: Sinners and Witches in Puritan New England*, Ithaca, NY: Cornell University Press.

Sarna, J.D. (2004) *American Judaism: A History*, New Haven, CT: Yale University Press.

Schmidt, L.E. (1989) "'A Church-going People Are a Dress-loving People': Clothes, Communication, and Religious Culture in Early America," *Church History*, 58: 36–51.

Schmidt, L.E. (2001) *Holy Fairs: Scotland and the Making of American Revivalism*, 2nd edn, Grand Rapids, MI: Eerdmans.

Wallace, A.F.C. (1970) *The Death and Rebirth of the Seneca*, New York: Alfred A. Knopf.

White, R. (1991) *The Middle Ground: Indians, Empires, and Republics in the Great Lakes Region, 1650–1815*, New York: Cambridge University Press.

III

American Empire
(1803–1898)

9

Politics

Mark A. Noll

Two great constellations of political issues shaped American religious life in the nineteenth century – slavery and race segregation, on one hand, and nationhood and national unity, on the other. The politics of slavery and race segregation loomed over American religious life throughout the century; in villages and cities, farms and plantations, and borderlands across the continent prior to the Civil War, Americans took religious stands on political questions regarding legal protection for slavery. After President Lincoln emancipated slaves in the United States and its territories in 1863, Americans took religious stands on political questions about the ways and degrees to which government should uphold black segregation in a white-dominated society. The politics of nation-building were as much wrapped in religion as the politics of race; religious pronouncements about national destiny and America's God-given role in world history drove the politics of territorial and industrial expansion as much as the politics of expansion shaped religion. On both issues of race and nation building, religion mediated politics in increasingly strategic ways as people became more manipulative and self-conscious about deploying the Bible to defend their political views. At the same time, public figures who disagreed about slavery and race often agreed that Protestantism was a marker of American political identity. The idea of America as a Protestant nation worked to some extent to cover deep problems of race, even as it forced Catholics and Jews to defend their religions and their patriotism.

In the presidential contest of 1800, vocal Protestants campaigned against Thomas Jefferson as an "infidel" whose election would doom the new United States to the anticlerical mayhem of the French Revolution. Much would change over the next century, as the United States grew from a fragile ocean-facing nation of barely five million souls to a continent-wide empire of over seventy-six million. But what did not change was the constant interplay between religion and politics. For Jefferson's part, by 1800, he had already begun his lifelong adult habit of daily reading from a New Testament he had edited for himself – with the text in Greek, Latin, French, as well as

English, but with the miracle stories excised. After he was elected, in 1802, this "infidel" expressed his opinion in a letter to Baptist political allies in Connecticut that the United States Constitution had erected "a wall of separation" between church and state. Yet during his two terms in office Jefferson often attended the Sunday services of Protestant worship that were conducted in the US House of Representatives, he authorized religious societies to act for the government in dealing with Native Americans, and he did not oppose government-sponsored chaplains in Congress or the military.

Half a century later, the presidents of North America's two constitutional republics – Abraham Lincoln for the Union and Jefferson Davis for the Confederacy – each proclaimed multiple days of national fast and national thanksgiving. These proclamations, which reflected the pervasive American belief in God's providence, were intended to encourage their respective "Christian nations" in fighting a religiously-charged civil war over slavery and state's rights. In the early days of the war, a Southern spokesman, Presbyterian minister John H. Rice, drew on widespread convictions to explain why the slave system of the American South was as indubitably the result of "certain providential conditions" as was "the wonderful providence of God" that had made possible European colonization of America and, later, the unexpected American victory in the Revolutionary War (Rice 1861: 40). At about the same time, Bishop Daniel Alexander Payne of the African Methodist Episcopal Church, preached a sermon that celebrated the ending of slavery in the District of Columbia. His belief in providence was just as strong as Rev. Rice's, but now it was the termination of slavery that demonstrated divine activity: only God "alone could … have moved the heart of this Nation to have done so great a deed for this weak, despised and needy people!" (Payne 1861: 10–11).

While opinions about slavery divided them, people on both sides drew from shared notions of American providential destiny rooted in Protestant interpretations of America as a latter-day manifestation of biblical history. This underlying, shared commitment to America as a biblically grounded Protestant nation continued to develop after the Civil War, even as new waves of immigration challenged Protestant religious dominance.

In 1900, for example, when over 200 Protestant agencies met in New York City for what was at the time the largest missionary gathering ever assembled, honored guests who were warmly welcomed as speakers included the sitting US president (William McKinley), a former president (Benjamin Harrison), and a soon-to-be president (Gov. Theodore Roosevelt of New York). Each of these leaders assured the meeting that its general Protestant goals and the general purposes of the United States ran on parallel lines. Yet even as the presidents gave their benediction to this very Protestant convention, Roman Catholics had become the most numerous religious body in the country, Jews were mounting increasingly successful efforts at ending readings from the Protestant King James Version of the Bible in the nation's public schools, and the strongly Mormon population of Utah was for the first time overcoming the hurdles that had heretofore prevented a Mormon from representing that state in the US Senate.

The interweaving of religious and political history was affected by many factors. Region, for example, mattered hugely. In 1900, Catholics and Jews in the urban Northeast had come to occupy an essentially different religious universe from the white Baptists and Methodists of the South, though these Catholics, Jews, and white southern evangelicals were all loyal supporters of the Democratic Party. Above all, the dynamics of race exerted an immense influence on the ever-shifting American confluence of religion and politics. Yet great differences marked how that influence came to bear from the organization of the African Methodist Episcopal Church as the first self-standing black denomination in the 1790s to the anguished complaints against systemic racial discrimination voiced at the end of the nineteenth century by black leaders for whom religion was central, including W. E. B. DuBois, the first African American to earn a Ph.D., and the Rev. Francis Grimké, a distinguished Presbyterian minister in Washington, D.C. The conflicts of the Jefferson administration begin this enduring, yet tangled story.

The Reconfiguration of Religion, Politics, and Society

In 1800, the new nation's main religious trajectory was just coming into view against an ever-expanding national landscape. The Lewis and Clark Expedition of 1803–06 was President Jefferson's initiative for exploring the vast terrain of the Louisiana Purchase that had more than doubled the land area of the United States. Although few could have realized it at the time, the explorers' successful journey, which documented the immensity of the country and the scarcity of its population, also described an environment for which the emerging religious mainstream was ideally suited.

During the late eighteenth century, the churches in the new United States existed in a state of confusing transition. The colonies' one total religious system, New England Puritanism, survived only in fragments and as a lingering belief in God's ability to covenant with nations. The tumultuous upsets of the War for Independence had also seriously disoriented the main religious traditions of the colonial era. To be sure, local religious revivals promoted by evangelical Protestants were taking place at many locations from the 1780s, but these revivals were on the margins. Uncertainty also attended the denominations' efforts to bring their teachings to the huge open spaces of the new nation, and in their efforts to compete with each other for adherents. They were also trying to cope with the fact of disestablishment, which represented a nearly unprecedented innovation in the long history of Western Christianity.

From time out of mind, churches had been supported (and regulated) by the European states, as had been the case also in most of the American colonies. But now, with the pluralistic religious situation of colonial Pennsylvania, New Jersey, and New York as precedent, the United States as a whole was moving rapidly toward a free market in religion. At first the move was pragmatic, since how could a state support one denomination when its people belonged to several denominations, or where large numbers did not practice any religion? But soon practice gave way to principle. The "free exercise" of religion and the prohibition of a national state church prescribed by the First Amendment of the Constitution set a pattern for the states. As promoted effectively by Baptists like Isaac Backus of Massachusetts and John Leland of Virginia, alongside noted founders like Thomas Jefferson and James Madison, the federal stance soon became an ideal throughout the nation.

After leaving behind religious establishments, and in response to the challenge of the nation's wide open spaces, religious life on the ground underwent a transformation.

Methodists under the leadership of Bishop Francis Asbury, Baptists instructed by countless local preachers, and Disciples and "Christians" guided by the creative leadership of Alexander Campbell and Barton Stone took the lead in preaching the salvation of souls, organizing congregations, and recruiting young men (also a few young women) to serve as itinerants. With these upstarts in the lead, the more traditional churches of the colonial era (Congregational, Episcopal, Presbyterian) also accommodated themselves to the new religious style.

Politics during this period of concentrated evangelization and voluntary moral mobilization was mostly incidental. The Congregationalists and Presbyterians who for religious reasons supported the Federalists in the battle against Jefferson in 1800 soon quieted when Jefferson's tenure proved inoffensive to the churches. For some Baptists and most Methodists, especially so long as Asbury lived (he died in 1816), politics became nearly invisible. For them, narrowly religious concerns were all-consuming. For other Baptists and the followers of Campbell and Stone, the Christian message was mixed with the ideological legacy of the Revolutionary era. But in general, for about a quarter century after the 1800 election, Protestants mostly retreated from active involvement in elections and partisan politics.

Yet the American religion that flourished in the early nineteenth century was still political in broader ways. Most importantly, it was intensely republican because it had internalized the fear of unchecked authority and the commitment to private virtue that drove the ideology of the political founding. But it was also "Christian republican" because the virtue that the United States' energetic itinerants promoted was not classical manliness but humility in Christ. The religion that came to prevail was more anti-formal than formal – it did not trust ascribed authority or inherited bureaucracies, but rather achieved authority and ad hoc networking. It was populist or democratic – it championed the ability of any white man to assume leadership in any religious assembly. And it was biblicistic – it spoke of the Scriptures as a supreme authority that trumped or even revoked all other religious authorities.

Above all, the religion that came to prevail so vigorously in nineteenth-century America was voluntaristic. Voluntarism was a mind-set keyed to innovative leadership, proactive public advocacy, and entrepreneurial goal-setting. Voluntarism also became an extraordinarily influential practice that, beginning with church organization, soon mushroomed to inspire mobilization on behalf of myriad social and political causes. Not government, not an inherited church, not the dictates of Big Business, but enterprising connections forged voluntarily built American civilization in the first decades of the new century.

A few small-scale voluntary societies had been formed in United States before 1800, but as self-created vehicles for preaching the Christian message, distributing Christian literature, encouraging Christian civilization, and networking philanthropic activity, voluntary societies came into their own after about 1810. The best funded and most dynamic – like the American Board of Commissioners for Foreign Missions (1810), the American Bible Society (1816), or the American Education Society (1816) – were rivaled only by the Methodist Church in their shaping effects on national culture.

With this new mode of organization, a period of tumultuous, energetic, contentious innovation first reversed the downward slide of religious adherence and then began to shape all of American society. Most remarkably, evangelicals even conquered the South, where an honor-driven culture of manly self-assertion had offered a more difficult challenge than regions to the North. In demonstrating how religion could thrive despite the absence of an establishment, the period's dynamic evangelicals established an enduring pattern for the future. Other religious movements that differed greatly in belief and practice from Protestant evangelicals would flourish in the United States by adopting, to at least some degree, many of the free-form and populist traits that evangelical Protestants pioneered.

The institutional results of this transformation were remarkable. Between 1790 and 1860, the United States population increased eight-fold; the number of Baptist churches increased fourteen-fold; the number of Methodist churches twenty-eight-fold, and the number of Disciples or Restorationist churches cannot be figured as a percentage, since there were none of these churches in 1790 and over two thousand in 1860. The 1860 census found 77 places of Jewish worship in the United States, which represented a doubling from only ten years earlier. The number of Roman Catholic places of worship had risen even faster, from about 1200 in 1850 to over 2500 in 1860. But still the nation's formal religious life was dominated by Protestants: over 83% of the value of church property and over 95% of the churches themselves (about 50,000 of them). And the combined budgets of the churches and religious voluntary agencies came close to matching the income of the federal government.

Alexis de Tocqueville, the period's most famous foreign observer, dwelt at length on how he thought Protestantism had shaped the nation's political course. During his visit to the United States in the 1830s, Tocqueville observed what he described as a conundrum: why did religion, which because of the Constitution's separation of church and state "never mixes directly in the government of society," nonetheless exist as "the first of [the nation's] political institutions"? His explanation centered on how Protestant faith had aligned itself with republican principles of liberty: "if [religion] does not give them the taste for freedom, it singularly facilitates their use of it." In particular, Tocqueville pondered the "great political consequences" that "flowed from" the flourishing of disestablished Protestant churches. His final judgment was comparative: In Europe, "I had seen the spirit of religion and the spirit of freedom almost always move in contrary directions. Here I found them united intimately with one another: they reigned together on the same soil" (Tocqueville 1835/1840 [2000]: 281–282).

Religious voluntarism became more broadly influential when religious practices inspired mobilization on behalf of social and political causes. When in the 1830s, national political parties reinvented themselves as voluntary societies for organizing local campaigns and national conventions, they did so on the model of religious revivals and religious societies.

By the 1830s and 1840s, the nation's religious situation was also changing rapidly, especially with the dramatic increase of Roman Catholic immigration from Germany and Ireland. Yet because of evangelical success at adapting so well to the ideology and social circumstances of the new nation, the decades from 1830 to 1860 witnessed the most comprehensive Protestant impact on politics in all American history. Except for debate on tariffs and the national bank, the era's most visible social and political conflicts were all colored by Protestant concerns. In the 1830s, protest against removal of the Cherokee from Georgia to Oklahoma, efforts for temperance reform, and debates over moving the mails on Sunday brought Protestants back into the political arena.

Of these issues, temperance reform extended over the longest time. From the early nineteenth century, temperance societies made up an important component of the

American voluntary empire. But not until the 1840s did voluntary persuasion spill over into direct political action; the Maine prohibition law of 1846, which was strongly supported by many of the state's Protestant churches, became a model for how to channel private reform into public legislation.

More broadly, strong Protestant associations with the Whig, Liberty, Free Soil, American (or Know-Nothing), and Republican parties – along with a reciprocating Catholic loyalty to the Democratic Party – transformed national elections and many local contests into occasions for religious tension. By the 1830s, the country's most consistent Whig, and then Republican, voters were northern Protestants, with Congregationalists, Episcopalians, Presbyterians, and Methodists providing near unanimous support. Baptists and other sectarian Protestants in the North leaned to the Whigs and Republicans. Many southern Protestants were also Whigs, until sectional division over slavery drove these voters toward the Democratic Party. Catholics of all ethnic backgrounds were strong for the Democrats against the Whigs and became even more ardent in opposing the Republican Party. Some sectarian Protestants, especially Baptists and especially in the South, along with a few members of Lutheran and Reformed churches who found "Yankee meddling" obtrusive, objected to this Whig/Republican vision and also voted Democratic.

The ideological affinity that drew evangelicals, especially in the North, to the Whigs and Republicans, was a formal congruity between political activism and evangelical voluntarism. Protestants and Whigs shared a common approach to public life: self-realization linked to care for community along with personal liberty coordinated with self-discipline. Inner ties between evangelicals and Whigs help explain why Abraham Lincoln, though never a church member and more church-friendly rather than an active Christian, enjoyed such strong support from northern Protestants in his two Republican campaigns for president in 1860 and 1864.

These campaigns marked the height of religious influence in the political sphere, but also the collapse of that influence. The reason in both cases was the same: religious-backed disputes over slavery, race, and the national union.

Religion, the Civil War, and Race

From its earliest days, the political history of the United States was driven by debates over slavery; from the 1830s these debates became more intensely religious. As they did so, considerations of race and considerations of slavery became hopelessly confused, with results that decisively shaped later American history. The Civil War – as a conflict to define the Union, determine the legitimacy of slavery, and specify the limits of states rights – was also fundamentally a religious battle over how to interpret the Bible and how to promote moral norms in public life.

By the early 1830s, the simmering mixture of race, religion, and politics was coming to a boil. In 1829, the free black, David Walker, published the era's most incendiary attack on slavery in his *Appeal ... to the Coloured Citizens of the World*. A major element in this work was Walker's charge that white America was hypocritical in proclaiming a love for Scripture while violating the Scriptures in supporting the slave trade and the institution of slavery. If Walker's message was mostly shrugged aside, it was not as easy to shrug aside the rebellion led by Nat Turner in Southampton

Figure 9.1 Alexis de Tocqueville remarked in *Democracy in America* on the peculiar place of religion in American politics.

County, Virginia, two years later. The confession that Turner made before his execution used the language of Christian apocalypse to justify his revolt. If few Americans conceded that Turner had grounds for rebellion, the strength of his biblical vision did reveal how thoroughly at least some of the nation's slaves had internalized at least some Christian elements in their own understanding of human bondage.

In response to Nat Turner, legislatures cracked down on slaves in many southern states and restricted rights of free blacks in some Northern states. In reaction to this response, anti-slave reformers greatly increased their efforts to contest what they called "sin" or an "evil in itself." They were led in this charge by William Lloyd Garrison, whose newspaper, *The Liberator*, first published in 1831, defined anti-slavery as a higher law than even the Scriptures. Also, 1831 was also the year of Charles G. Finney's revivalistic conquest of Rochester, New York, and the emergence of Finney as the North's most visible promoter of evangelical Christianity. A year after Parliament outlawed slavery in the British Empire in 1833, Finney published a widely read series of lectures, *Revivals of Religion*, in which he proclaimed that "slavery is, pre-eminently, the *sin of the church*," while he held out the hope that if believers mobilized against this "great abomination," there would soon "not be a shackled slave, nor a bristling, cruel slave-driver in this land" (Finney 1835 [1960]: 301–302).

Predictably, such charges produced outrage in the slaveholding South, as well as among Northerners who felt Finney was abusing Scripture. In particular, abolitionist appeals to Christian principles as support for emancipation produced detailed scriptural arguments defending slavery as a divinely sanctioned institution. Abolitionists who turned to Scripture for the attack on slavery were chagrined to find that the defenders of slavery could quote many more texts that simply took the institution for granted, or even regulated its operation, than there were passages that, even by implication, questioned its propriety. When, in 1837, one of Finney's converts, Theodore Dwight Weld, published *The Bible Against Slavery*, abolitionists applauded Weld's passionate efforts to force the semantics of ancient Hebrew into an anti-slave posture. But pro-slavery advocates like Thornton Stringfellow of Virginia positively rejoiced. As Stringfellow demonstrated in 1841 with *A Brief Examination of Scripture Testimony on the Institution of Slavery* and then in numerous later adaptations of this work, it was relatively easy to show that Abraham, Moses, the Apostle Paul, and even Jesus himself either took the existence of slavery for granted or made no obvious moves to eliminate it.

From the early 1830s, when these positions on the Bible were staked out, until the early months of 1861, when the last round of published conflict took place between self-confident biblical anti-slavery and even more self-confident biblical pro-slavery, the question of slavery was debated vigorously as a theological as well as a political problem.

The ecclesiastical schisms that paralleled these debates exerted an unusual impact on the nation. When John C. Calhoun in March 1850 addressed the United States Senate for almost the last time, church splits weighted heavily on his mind. Calhoun described the major Protestant denominations as providing powerful cords of "a spiritual and ecclesiastical nature" that had greatly strengthened the political bonds of the nation. But then he issued the doleful prediction that when these church bonds snapped, "nothing will be left to hold the States together except force" (Crallé 1854: 557–558).

Calhoun in 1850 was reflecting on a dismaying recent history of religious fragmentation. In 1845, there had been about as many Methodist clergy as postal employees, who made up the largest non-military department of the United States government. Were it not for the military buildup occasioned by the Mexican War, there would have been more active Methodist and Baptist ministers than US military personnel. Along with Methodist churches, the churches of the Baptists and Presbyterians were distributed more widely in the nation than any single organization of any kind. The only national institutions that came close to the denominations were religious voluntary agencies like the American Bible Society. In 1845, the Methodist and Baptist churches could seat at one time well over half of the nation's population. Yet by the end of 1845, the national organizations of Methodists, Baptists, and Presbyterians were divided. A Presbyterian schism in 1837 was prompted only in part by disagreements over slavery. But then in 1844–45, the Methodist and Baptists divided expressly over this issue. For Methodists the question was whether a bishop could hold slaves, for the Baptists a missionary. The result was the same. Slavery had divided the churches at a time when the churches were the nation's strongest inter-sectional institutions.

Conjunctions of religious history and political history during the period 1830 to 1860 show how these realms were intertwined. In 1836 and 1837, Congress enacted a Gag Rule to table the accumulating pile of petitions from abolitionists; Elijah Lovejoy became the first abolitionist martyr when he was killed by a mob attacking his printing operation in Alton, Illinois; and the Presbyterian denomination divided into New School and Old School factions. In 1844, John C. Calhoun used his office as Secretary of State under President Tyler to promote slave-state interests, and the Baptists and Methodists divided over slavery. In the early 1850s, Congress hammered out a compromise to deal with the new territories of Nebraska and Kansas, and Harriet Beecher Stowe's novel, *Uncle Tom's Cabin*, with its overtly religious attack on slavery, was published to great acclaim in the North and great disdain in the South. In 1854 and 1855, Know Nothings won elections throughout the North with a strong anti-immigrant, anti-Catholic platform; and Kansas suffered bloody lawlessness as guerillas battled over whether to permit slavery in the new state. In 1859, John Brown's raid on Harper's Ferry piled up economic, political, social, and religious responses all on its own. Brown, who was known to be a reader of Jonathan Edwards and a fervent

Calvinist, hoped his effort would inspire slaves to seek their own liberty. He was universally noticed, but judged with sharply antithetical opinions.

By the time of the Civil War, the potent mix of race, politics, and religion was also at work among American Catholics, who had become a major presence. For the most part, American Catholics were not as concerned about questions of race and slavery in themselves as they were about how race and slavery affected integration into American society and the church's ability to maintain its internal unity along with its ties to Rome.

In the early history of the United States, Catholics faced the daunting task of making their way in a nation that had been founded by largely Protestant interests and in which a strong revival of evangelical Protestantism was underway. In this setting, the American church tried to provide cohesion and stability for its relatively small number of traditional adherents as well as for the great burgeoning of Irish and German immigrants who poured into the country from the 1840s. Within the large population of Catholic immigrants, the Irish were especially wary of abolition because the British, who had oppressed them, were viewed as strong against slavery. America's large population of German Catholics reacted against the abolitionism, liberalism, and anti-clericalism of the European supporters of the 1848 Revolutions, who had also migrated to America in great numbers. In this era, the church's main goals were conservative: to achieve social stability for its often impoverished adherents, religious stability through the promotion of traditional Catholic teaching, and cultural stability through its opposition to radicalism and revolution.

These tasks were being carried out while evangelical, reforming, and nativist forces, which were all hostile to Roman Catholicism, grew in strength. The career of the American Party (known popularly as "Know Nothings") was emblematic as it rode an anti-immigrant, anti-Catholic stance into brief political prominence during the mid-1850s. Moreover, of all "Yankee" reforms, abolition was the most radical for its potential to disrupt social order and threaten communal unity. Given these American dynamics, Catholics were pushed ineluctably toward the pro-slavery Democratic Party. Although this party also harbored some evangelical and nativist elements, it was organized to protect local interests, especially the interests of slaveholders in the South.

American clerics did attempt to promulgate traditional Catholic teachings on slavery, which had never considered slave-holding a sin, but which did include strict guidelines for protecting slave marriages, demanding slave religious instruction, and maintaining the mass as a rite to which all (black and white) were called for common worship. The apostolic letter, *In Supremo* (1839) from the conservative Pope Gregory XVI pointed the way with its strong denunciation of the slave trade and its strict instructions about humane treatment of the enslaved. In addition, a traditional wariness about unrestrained capitalism came into play when the church criticized the notion of chattel slavery (treating humans as objects) and the lust for profit that seemed to drive American society as a whole, including the slave system.

If, however, Catholic teaching offered a powerful, if moderate voice against the abuses of slavery, that voice never exerted much influence on the Catholic faithful. Rather, Catholics remained more concerned about the threat of radical reform than the abuses of the slave system. No Catholic came out unambiguously for abolition until the Civil War was well underway. Especially Irish Catholics were key participants in riots and other violent resistance to the slavery reforms promoted by the Republican Party. After the War, while the Bishops maintained their position of apolitical conservatism, lay voices spoke out forcefully against passage of the Thirteenth, Fourteenth, and Fifteenth Amendments.

For all Americans, the disjunction between consideration of slavery and consideration of black people was a fixture in the nation's charged ideological history before, during, and after the War Between the States. Yet it was a disjunction difficult to recognize at the time. On the eve of conflict in 1861 the émigré historian and theologian, Philip Schaff, highlighted this difference when he wrote that "*the negro question lies far deeper than the slave question*" (Schaff 1861: 316). Because solutions to economic and political problems of slavery differed from solutions to the social problems of race, repeated efforts by both whites and blacks to differentiate issues of slavery from issues of race exercised almost no influence. Even when writers and speakers pointed out that the slavery described in Scripture was almost entirely the enslavement of Caucasians, it made little difference.

African Americans most aggressively stressed the incongruity of the fact that the American debate over slavery was simply assumed to be also a debate about race. As the noted black abolitionist, Frederick Douglass, wrote in March 1861, "nobody at the North, we think, would defend Slavery, even from the Bible, but for this color distinction … Color makes all the difference in the application of our American Christianity" (Douglass 1861: 417).

In the event, it proved quite easy for both North and South to defend slavery from the Bible and not to differentiate between slavery and black slavery. Throughout the South and in many places of the North, it was widely assumed that since Scripture did not condemn the institution as such, it thereby sanctioned the form of black-only slavery that prevailed in the United States. Countless works – arising almost as frequently in the North as in the South – casually transposed the terms "slaves" and "Africans" as if they were simply equivalent. The result was that slavery, debated as a religious matter, became the crux of national political development, but statements about slavery were confused with statements about the nature of African Americans.

The fact that religion was so central during the war was a direct result of how important religion had become before the war. Both Northerners and Southerners, hard-line abolitionists along with hard-line pro-slavery advocates and the many who vacillated in between, almost all had looked for a word from God to resolve their dilemmas about slavery. Many had reached expressly for the written Word of God. This depth of religious conviction helps explain how the Republican administration in the North could succeed in its unprecedented expansion of centralized government authority, first, to save the Union and then to exterminate slavery. It explains as well how the classically republican South, with its deep commitment to severely limited government, could allow the central Confederate state to become almost as vigorous as its northern counterpart. It was warfare that allowed deep-seated republican scruples to be set aside, but warfare defined in strongly religious terms.

Before and during the Civil War, advocates on all sides eagerly deployed the Scriptures to defend their own convictions and skewer the convictions of their opponents. But this deployment was directed overwhelmingly to the question of slavery, only rarely to the question of race (even though the Bible is much clearer in its teachings against racism than it is about its permission of slavery). As a result, when the Civil War decisively settled the questions of national unity and slave legality, and when public religion became the servant of national civil religion, the public use of the Bible became much tamer than it had been before the war. There remained only a small and marginal interest, mostly expressed by African Americans, about what the Bible had to say about racism. And because African Americans were progressively deprived of a public voice in the decades after the war, national politics reflected scant influence from the only constituency that thought it was important to understand the Bible for its message on race as well as its implications for American national destiny.

Reconstruction and Political Retreat

The effect of the Civil War with the most momentous long-term consequence was the opening of space for African Americans to direct their own churches and other institutions. While the full political effects of that opening would not be apparent until the civil rights movement of the mid-twentieth century, the energy displayed after the Civil War began a process that, decades later, brought about a religious-inspired transformation of American public life.

Organizationally, the Civil War was immensely significant for the opportunity it afforded African Americans to establish their own churches, schools, and publishing houses. Even before the war was over, previously existing northern denominations like the African Methodist Episcopal Church were expanding into a liberated black South. Immediately after the war, another kind of ecclesiastical organizing took place as former slaves began to establish new denominations like the Colored Cumberland Presbyterian Church, the Colored Methodist Episcopal Church, and (a few years later) the National Baptist Convention and the Church of God in Christ. Stride for stride alongside the emergence of black denominations came black educational institutions, some founded with the help of white Protestants and the Freedman's Bureau, many others established through the initiative of African-American churches.

In the first years after the war, the newly organized or expanded churches and the educational institutions were joined by the Republican Party in providing opportunities for black leadership. As Reconstruction was slowed and then overwhelmed by the reinstatement of racially exclusive white regimes, these opportunities were pulled back to churches, schools, and a very limited range of businesses serving an exclusively black clientele.

In the wake of the Civil War, the churches faced the enduring reality of racism. They also confronted the expansion of consumer capitalism that was creating unprecedented opportunities for wealth but also large-scale alienation and new depths of poverty. For religion to have addressed these two problems constructively, America's believers needed the kind of vigor that had been brought to bear on so many tasks in the generations between the Revolution and the Civil War.

Instead, the Civil War was won and slavery was abolished by an unprecedented expansion of central government authority and by a hitherto unimaginable degree of industrial mobilization. If the war freed the slaves and gave African Americans a constitutional claim to citizenship, it did not provide the moral energy required for securing equal rights for all. If the war showed what could be accomplished through massive industrial mobilization, it did not offer clear moral guidance for using industrialization for the good of all citizens.

In general, the receding national authority of British-origin evangelical Protestants was a good thing. Protestants not of British origin, Roman Catholics, Jews, Eastern Orthodox, free-thinking secularists, and a host of smaller religious bodies all came to enjoy more practical freedom. The complicated maneuvers by which the Mormons abandoned their earlier practice of polygamy as the price for nearly unlimited liberty to fashion a Latter-day Saints culture in Utah illustrated the space that non-evangelical groups could win.

With the relative decline of evangelical Protestantism as a *national* public force, the central government for a brief period became the dominant influence in the nation's public life. So long as central government retained the capacity to act nationally, it was conceivable that the abolition of slavery accomplished by the Thirteenth Amendment (1865) and the guarantee of full civil rights set forth in the Fourteenth Amendment (1868) and Fifteenth Amendment (1870) might truly apply to the freed slaves. But by the early 1870s, national willingness to support an active national government failed.

The graphic presence of naked terror in Mississippi during elections in 1874, 1875, and 1876 became a template that inspired other aggrieved white Democrats throughout the South. The national election of 1876 and its aftermath sealed the retreat from active Reconstruction. In exchange for the votes from four contested states, the Republican Party and its standard bearer, Rutherford B. Hayes, agreed to end the military occupation of the South. The southern "redemption" that resulted violently transferred power from liberated slaves and their Republican allies to an all-white Democratic Party. Unwillingness to support national enforcement of civil rights once again drew on the interaction of race and religion, acting this time negatively in promoting social passivity, instead of positively in promoting social change.

Throughout the South, almost all strands of white religion accepted or supported the efforts of vigilantes, mobs, and lynching to win a victory in peace that armies could not gain in war. Religious leaders were especially active in promoting the specter of white Christian womanhood threatened by rapacious African sexuality. This specter throve on a bad historical conscience, since it overlooked the generations during which white masters had sexually preyed on black slave women. Yet it nonetheless became a powerful instrument for mobilizing whites and controlling blacks.

Religious-inspired actions were usually passive, as pastors and church leaders stood by silently while the Ku Klux Klan, the Knights of the White Camellia, and other organized mobs menaced, assaulted, or murdered African Americans and the whites who, however cautiously, supported their efforts. Occasionally, church leaders could be more active, even to the point of sometimes approving the most vicious actions of lynch mobs.

From the North, the willingness of well-known religious figures to sacrifice black civil rights for other religious goals, made an important contribution to the "redemption" of the South. Examples included Henry Ward Beecher, minister of the Plymouth Congregational Church in Brooklyn, and his sister, the novelist Harry Beecher Stowe (Figure 9.2). During the War, Beecher had been the best-known Northern minister supporting the emancipation of slaves. By the late 1860s, however, he had become an

Figure 9.2 Harriet Beecher Stowe. Along with her brother, Henry Ward Beecher, Stowe was a well-known religious figure from the North, willing to sacrifice black civil rights to contribute to the "redemption" of the Reconstruction-era American South.

advocate of southern home rule and an opponent of federal authority to enforce Reconstruction. For her part, when Harriet Beecher Stowe began spending winters in Florida during the 1870s, she rapidly became a proponent of sectional reconciliation and white supremacy.

A different motive worked among some evangelicals, including Dwight L. Moody, the leading revival preacher of the late nineteenth century. As much reflecting as guiding the white evangelical spirit of his age, Moody seemed to react against the political over-commitments of evangelicals during and after the Civil War. Instead, he guided his audiences away from social duties toward a consideration of personal states of being. Innovative groups like the Salvation Army were an exception as the Army marshaled its strong Holiness piety to promote aggressive social service. But Moody and his supporters represented a wide swath of Northern Protestant religion in speaking much about evil reflected in sins of the flesh, little about sins of greed, and almost nothing about sins of social domination.

As such leaders successfully distanced racial issues from religious examination, they also promoted a new sense of divine providence. Their goal was to use the massive blood-letting of the Civil War to create a new sense of national destiny that stressed God's providential design for the whole nation, South and North reunited as one. This form of civil religion was traditional in stressing the United States as God's "chosen people" and in its use of biblical metaphors. But ultimate concern was shifting from a transcendent deity to an immanent nation. The new civil religion supported the suspension of concern for black civil rights. It also undergirded the nation's willingness to embark on imperial adventures in the Caribbean and the Pacific that would come to a head with the Spanish-American War in the late 1890s.

For Catholics, the post-war decades witnessed stronger identification with the Democratic Party. Especially lower-class Catholics, often Irish, who were economic competitors with liberated slaves, found themselves pulled along as the Democratic Party allied itself with the Ku Klux Klan and other racist movements to strip blacks of their newly won civil rights. In these circumstances, it was a short step for some

Catholics to move from a religiously based ideological anti-abolitionism to a racially grounded opposition to black civil rights.

Eventually, this general Catholic position also came to prevail in the unusual racial configuration of Louisiana where Catholics had long practiced an unusual triracialism – blacks, whites, creoles – that had moderated at least some of the nation's black-white racialism. By the end of the nineteenth century, however, the Catholic Church in New Orleans brought its traditional racial flexibility into line with the nation's hardening racial categories. In the mid-1890s – at the very time when the Supreme Court sanctioned the segregationist regime of "separate but equal" in *Plessy v. Ferguson*, a case involving a Louisiana creole – Catholics in New Orleans opened their first church designated for blacks only. Over the next two decades, the forces that had led Louisiana's large Methodist population to sanction Jim Crow discrimination also came to prevail in the state's Catholic churches.

From the end of Reconstruction until well into the twentieth century, organized religion gradually receded as a force in national politics. While local religious enclaves decidedly shaped local politics – like Catholics in New York, Boston, or Chicago; or Lutherans in Minnesota and the Dakotas – on the national level the Northern (Republican) versus Southern (Democratic) division resulting from the Civil War remained firmly in place. This division meant that Protestantism as a whole could not exercise a determinative force on public life, as it had done before the sectional crisis. Still, Protestant personalities played a large role in both Populist and Progressive political movements, and Protestant factors came directly to the fore in the crusade for prohibition, continuing opposition to Roman Catholicism, and various efforts at social reform.

William Jennings Bryan, three-time Democratic nominee for president (1896, 1900, 1908) and later Secretary of State under Woodrow Wilson, was an active Presbyterian who promoted public morality defined by both Christian and American ideals. For Bryan, the Populist desire to protect the farmer, the wage-laborer, the women and children working in factories, and the hard-pressed debtor represented moral as well as political imperatives. His memorable speech against the gold standard at the Democratic Convention in 1896 ("You shall not press down upon the brow of labor this crown of thorns, you shall not crucify mankind upon a cross of gold") exemplified both his economic policies and the Christian overtones of his thought. Yet Bryan's reformist campaigns on behalf of ordinary Americans never gained wide success. They failed, in part, because the racist Democratic regimes in the South made all Democrats suspect to the rest of the nation, and in part because many Democrats, especially in the South, were suspicious of Bryan's willingness to use large-scale government action for social change.

Only when populist pressure within the South could be harnessed to reforms like the income tax and the popular election of Senators, or when evangelical causes, like support for prohibition, gained southern backing, was it possible to give national government broader authority over national life. Otherwise the race-protected facts of regional politics hamstrung efforts at national reform.

The more progressive segments of the Protestant world, which retained an interest in social justice, did not always include racial matters in these concerns. Notable social reformers who otherwise worked to embody biblical values in their reforms regularly turned aside from racial problems. Bryan, who was the era's most consistent political

Christian, may have hinted at the need to address racial injustice, but those hints were overwhelmed by his need to maintain good relations with the Democratic power base in the South. Especially as Jim Crow hardened during Bryan's repeated campaigns for president, he acceded more and more to external realities and so paid less and less attention to African Americans.

The Social Gospel movement of the late nineteenth and early twentieth centuries did include a few figures who consistently struggled for racial transformation. Among them the mid-western Congregational minister, Harland Paul Douglas, author in 1909 of *Christian Reconstruction in the South*, was the most active opponent of the nation's ingrained pattern of racial discrimination. But for the most part, leaders of the Social Gospel focused their attention on problems of urban poverty and class alienation among whites rather than on racial injustice.

Walter Rauschenbush, the movement's most profound theologian, was representative. He saw much in American society that needed the rebuke of Christian reform, but felt no particular urgency to challenge the era's conventions about race. For Rauschenbush, the sad plight of African Americans would be rectified by the same sort of economic improvements and Christianizing impulses that he felt were improving the circumstances of at least some immigrant communities.

To be sure, some Progressive reforms eventually became law, including the national income tax, the direct election of senators, prohibition, and women's suffrage. All of these reflected some of the goals of the Social Gospel. Yet although the energies of Populist and Progressive Protestants were not insubstantial, they fell far short of meeting the needs of a rapidly changing nation. Residual anti-Catholicism, which was kept alive by organizations like the American Protective Association and the Ku Klux Klan, undercut the ability to work with the large Catholic populations in the urban North and the Midwest.

More importantly, intra-Protestant strife between progressive factions (or modernists) and their conservative counterparts (or fundamentalists) was beginning to absorb religious energy and move attention away from society as a whole. The fundamentalist-modernist battles that eventually divided Baptist and Presbyterian denominations seemed to draw down the curtain on more than a century of active Protestant efforts at shaping the nation's social fabric and influencing its political agenda.

At the end of the century, the Spanish-American War reflected the ongoing complexity of religion and political connections. President William McKinley spoke with genuine altruism when he assured a delegation of Methodists that his decision to enter war with Spain had come from a desire to provide Christianity, education, and civilization to the Filipinos who came under American jurisdiction because of that war. At the same time, American commitment to this war was fueled by the kind of civil religion that had taken shape after the Civil War and that exploited religion for injustice even as it enlisted religion to support American ideals.

References and Further Reading

Bennet, James B. (2005) *Religion and the Rise of Jim Crow in New Orleans*, Princeton, NJ: Princeton University Press.

Blight, David W. (2006) *Race and Reunion: The Civil War in American Memory*, Cambridge, MA: Harvard University Press.

Blum, Edward J. (2005) *Reforging the White Republic: Race, Religion, and American Nationalism, 1865–1898*, Baton Rouge, LA: Louisiana State University Press.

Carwardine, Richard A. (1993) *Evangelicals and Politics in Antebellum America*, New Haven, CT: Yale University Press.

Crallé, Richard K. (ed.) (1854) *The Works of John C. Calhoun*, vol. 4: *Speeches of John C. Calhoun, Delivered in the House of Representatives and the Senate of the United States*, New York: Appleton.

Douglass, Frederick (1861) "The Pro-slavery Mob and the Pro-slavery Ministry," *Douglass' Monthly*, March: 417–418.

Finney, Charles Grandison (1835 [1960]) *Lectures on Revivals of Religion*, ed. William G. McLoughlin, Cambridge, MA: Harvard University Press.

Fox-Genovese, Elizabeth, and Eugene, D. (2005) *The Mind of the Master Class: History and Faith in the Southern Slaveholders' Worldview*, New York: Cambridge University Press.

Goen, C.C. (1985) *Broken Churches, Broken Nation: Denominational Schisms and the Coming of the Civil War*, Macon, GA: Mercer University Press.

Gordon, Sally Barringer (2002) *The Mormon Question: Polygamy and Constitutional Conflict in Nineteenth-Century America*, Chapel Hill, NC: University of North Carolina Press.

Hatch, Nathan O. (1989) *The Democratization of American Christianity*, New Haven, CT: Yale University Press.

Hochgeschwender, Michael (2006) *Wahrheit, Einheit, Ordnung: Die Sklavenfrage und der amerikanische Katholizismus, 1835–1870* [Truth, Unity, Order: The Question of Slavery in American Catholicism, 1835–1870], Paderborn: Ferdinand Schöningh.

Howe, Daniel Walker (2008) *What Hath God Wrought: The Transformation of America, 1815–1848*, New York: Oxford University Press.

Kazin, Michael (2006) *A Godly Hero: The Life of William Jennings Bryan*, New York: Knopf.

Lemann, Nicholas (2006) *Redemption: The Last Battle of the Civil War*, New York: Farrar, Straus & Giroux.

Luker, Ralph (1991) *The Social Gospel in Black and White*, Chapel Hill, NC: University of North Carolina Press.

McGivigan, John R. and Snay, Mitchell (eds.) (1998) *Religion and the Antebellum Debate over Slavery*, Athens, GA: University of Georgia Press.

McGreevy, John T. (2007) "Catholics and Abolition: A Historical (and Theological) Problem," in Wilfred McClay (ed.). *Figures in the Carpet: Finding the Human Person in the American Past*, Grand Rapids, MI: Eerdmans, pp. 405–427.

Miller, Randall M., Stout, Harry S. and Wilson, Charles Reagan (eds.) (1998) *Religion and the American Civil War*, New York: Oxford University Press.

Miller, Robert J. (2007) *Both Prayed to the Same God: Religion and Faith in the American Civil War*, Lanham, MD: Lexington Books.

Noll, Mark A. (2006) *The Civil War as a Theological Crisis*, Chapel Hill, NC: University of North Carolina Press.

Noll, Mark A. (2008) *God and Race in American Politics: A Short History*, Princeton, NJ: Princeton University Press.

Noll, Mark A. and Harlow, Luke (eds.) (2008) *Religion and American Politics: From the Colonial Period to the Present*, 2nd edn, New York: Oxford University Press.

Payne, Daniel Alexander (1861) *Welcome to the Ransomed; or, Duties of the Colored Inhabitants of the District of Columbia*, Baltimore, MD: Bull & Tuttle. Collected in Payne, D.A. (1972) *Sermons and Addresses, 1853–1891*, ed. Charles Killian, New York: Arno.

Raboteau, Albert J. (2004) *Slave Religion: The "Invisible Institution" in the Antebellum South*, 2nd edn, New York: Oxford University Press.

Rice, John H. (1861) "*The Princeton Review* on the State of the Country," *Southern Presbyterian Review*, 14: 33–40.

Schaff, Philip (1861) "Slavery and the Bible," *Mercersburg Review*, 13: 316–317.

Stout, Harry S. (2006) *Upon the Altar of the Nation: A Moral History of the Civil War*, New York: Viking.

Stowell, Daniel W. (1998) *Rebuilding Zion: The Religious Reconstruction of the South, 1863–1877*, New York: Oxford University Press.

Tocqueville, Alexis de (1835/1840 [2000]) *Democracy in America*, ed. and trans. Harvey Claflin Mansfield and Debra Winthrop, Chicago: University of Chicago Press.

10

Cosmology

Robert Fuller

Cosmologies became more elaborate and more varied with immigration, religious innovation, the challenge of the Enlightenment, and the increasing complexity of everyday life. Many denominations undertook more detailed articulation of doctrines in response to debates about how to live a virtuous life, the nature of religious authority, the fate of the soul, and the legitimacy of competing cosmologies. The experience of westward movement and of life on the frontier shaped religious thinking about space, time, identity, and destiny. As Americans built empire, they experimented with new visions and created new religions. For some devoted to the authority of "principles" and "laws," spiritual principles harmonized with natural laws in grand systems of cosmic order. For others, a fresh embrace of supernatural power and expectations of its miraculous flashes informed religious ideas. And between these two ends of the spectrum a multitude of groups hammered out their own distinctive understandings of cosmology in connection with the unfolding of their lives in a rapidly growing, diverse, conflicted, and ambitious nation.

Expectations ran high as citizens of the fledgling republic greeted the nineteenth century. These expectations were raised even further by the continent's sheer geographic expanse. The Louisiana Purchase in 1803 sparked Americans' interest in pursuing the economic and cultural opportunities awaiting them on the frontier. The Lewis and Clark Expedition (1803–06) strengthened the United States' claim to the entire reach of the continent. Lewis and Clark's explorations opened diplomatic relations with several of the Native American tribes, gave rise to more accurate maps, and generated geographical knowledge enabling the new nation to set its sights on an empire stretching all the way to the Pacific Ocean.

The nation's population ventured progressively westward. Following closely behind the new states of Kentucky (1792) and Tennessee (1796), Ohio became a state in 1803, Louisiana in 1812, Indiana in 1816, Alabama in 1817, Illinois in 1818, and Missouri in 1821. Nor was the nation's growth limited to territorial expansion. It also included unprecedented rates of urbanization. At the century's outset the nation had only six cities with a population of at least eight thousand. Within a few decades, urban populations had multiplied not only along the Eastern seaboard, but across the expanding republic. America's geographical, economic, and political boundaries were thus stretching in seemingly unlimited directions.

By the 1820s, the idea of a national destiny began to emerge. The nation's sixth president, John Quincy Adams, gave voice to what became known as the belief in "Manifest Destiny" when he proclaimed that the United States would become "coextensive with the North American Continent, destined by God and by nature to be the most populous and powerful people ever combined into one social contract." The core tenets of faith in America's manifest destiny – geographic expansion, divine mission, chosen status, and moral virtue – were rooted in a biblically based worldview that placed Americans at the forefront of a new era in salvation history. Many of the early colonists had viewed themselves as conducting "an errand into the wilderness" through which they would create a civilization wholly obedient to God's will. The most literate of these colonists were well acquainted with biblical themes and interpreted the settling of North America as the final and most significant chapter in God's plan for consummating world history. The long journey toward the establishment of a true kingdom of God on earth was, it seemed, moving steadily westward. Beginning with Christ's resurrection, the providential movement of history shifted from Jerusalem to Rome, then to the Protestant portions of western Europe, and finally to the North American continent. Biblical imagery thus framed Americans' understanding of themselves as the people who were called upon to be "a light unto all nations." The Age of Empire was therefore more than an age of expanding national boundaries. It was also understood to be the extension of true religion and true government across the continent in anticipation of the millennial rule of Christ over all humankind.

The nation's religious outlook was gradually reshaped by the very growth and progress it encouraged. Citizens of the expanding empire imaginatively understood themselves as inhabiting a variety of supernatural worlds that all in some way encouraged them as they set about the task of civilizing this one. Most of the nineteenth-century's religious cosmologies assured Americans that God's universe was both lawful and orderly, and that by adapting to these lawful structures they were assured of personal and national progress. Precisely how these lawful structures were described or how progress was to be measured were matters that varied according to ethnic, geographical, and temporal circumstances.

Shifting Paradigms in Protestant Thought

At the onset of the age of expanding empire, American culture rested on what historian William McLoughlin (1978) describes as a cluster of interrelated beliefs: the chosen nation; the covenant with God; the laws of nature, presumed to be from God, and evolutionary or progressive in purpose; and the work ethic which holds that hard work will bring both success and respect to all who discipline themselves. These concepts had roots in both the religious (Protestant) and nonreligious or humanistic (Enlightenment rationalism) strands of American life. Enlightenment rationalism, for example, had done a great deal to incite confidence in the nation's destiny as an agent of worldly progress. Rationalists believed the universe to be thoroughly lawful and therefore malleable under the direction of human reason. Advocates of Enlightenment rationalism tended to embrace the relatively nonreligious philosophy known as Deism that removed God from the sphere of everyday life. Many of the nation's leading political architects had an abiding faith in the power of reason to lead a democratic nation toward virtually unlimited growth and progress. Yet for reasons that are not completely clear, nonreligious humanism receded from the forefront of American thought in the first half of the nineteenth century. It seems that Protestantism was more in touch with the nation's expansive mood and took the lead in rephrasing these core cultural concepts in ways that better guided Americans to the new opportunities that awaited them.

In 1802, Yale president Timothy Dwight was distraught over the student body's "freethinking" religious views. He sensed that the nation's youth were torn between an outmoded Calvinism and the anti-biblical rationalism that had become fashionable among many of the new republic's cultural elite. Dwight was correct that Deism and outright infidelism had won over many of the educated citizenry during the previous few decades. Thomas Jefferson, Benjamin Franklin, and Thomas Paine were but a few of the founding generation who in varying degrees either denied biblical religion outright or at least conceptualized God in such rational terms as to make religion more or less irrelevant to everyday life. Dwight consequently considered it his mission to rescue the next generation from the radicals whose freethinking views would destroy what he considered to be the nation's moral and religious foundations.

In a series of sermons delivered in the college chapel, Dwight encouraged students to return to both God and the Bible. Much to his surprise, they did. A full third of the Yale student body claimed to undergo a religious conversion and subsequently joined the student "Moral Society." Dwight's success led him to conclude that revival meetings were an effective means of restoring persons' relationship with Christ. He was thus one of the first prominent New England clergy to break with American Protestantism's earlier understanding of conversions. Following the lead of the early Protestant theologian John Calvin, conservative Protestants believed that humans are separated from God by a chasm that cannot be bridged from the human side. The salvation of a human soul was thought to be initiated by God, not humans. Calvinism's emphasis on human depravity and the predestination of souls implied that all individuals could do was to repent as sincerely as possible and then wait in hope that God would send them assurance of their salvation. Dwight, however, put a slightly new slant on this inherited model of salvation and emphasized humanity's own role in choosing or procuring salvation. This new confidence in human ability and choice meshed perfectly with the new and expanding contours of a society committed to democracy, freedom of choice, and economic opportunity.

Other theologians emerged as champions of this new strategy for winning souls. A generation younger than Dwight, Lyman Beecher inched the theological climate even further from traditional Calvinism when he emphasized that human nature is open to immediate and total renovation. This confidence in personal agency symbolized the perfectionism and millennial optimism that pervaded the nation by 1830. Nathaniel Taylor, meanwhile, conducted a series of revivals based on his premise that "sin is in the sinning." Like Edwards, Taylor was principally concerned with converting "the multitude of the ungodly" – including the ungodly who attended orthodox churches. Taylor never abandoned traditional Calvinism's insistence upon humanity's dependence on the sovereign grace of God. He did, however, shift the emphasis away from human dependency to humanity's capacity for moral agency, making it possible for him to argue that it is our own acts that make us sinners. The implication was that we have the power to quit sinning and make ourselves again worthy of God's grace. The further implication was that revival meetings could hasten this process and thereby serve as instruments for procuring conversions. James McGready, Barton Stone, and numerous other preachers soon followed Dwight's and Taylor's lead and began orchestrating revival meetings to bring pressure to bear upon potential converts. What many scholars call the "Second Great Awakening" gave rise to a series of revivalist meetings held in Kentucky, Tennessee, and western New York.

Revivalist religion expressed the subtle adjustments that Americans were making in their conceptions about God's relationship to the universe. Compared to previous generations, Protestants in the Age of Empire were inclined to believe that God had had imparted mechanisms for regenerating humans right into nature itself. As a consequence, the means by which a person might be saved are potentially subject to human control. The individual who most clearly symbolized the new theological mood was Charles Grandison Finney. A lawyer, Finney understood salvation as a legal or contractual agreement between two parties. If one willfully accepts Christ's offer of salvation, he or she in turn will be accepted by God. In his *Lectures on Revivals*, Finney proposed that a conversion "is not a miracle or dependent on a miracle in any sense … it consists entirely in the right exercise of the powers of nature." By implication, the experience of salvation can be humanly engineered. He believed that he had hit upon a series of "new measures" that turned the conversion process into a lawful science. "New measures," he wrote, "are necessary from time to time to awaken attention and to bring the gospel to bear upon the public mind." Finney's new measures consisted of persuasion tactics that adapted old-time revivalism to the nation's new urban audiences. The success of his carefully orchestrated revival meetings symbolized Protestantism's mid-century swing to a new theological model that emphasized humanity's role in regenerating the world through the right exercise of lawful principles.

Evangelical religion directs its message to individuals. Its goal is to save the world by saving individual persons one at a time. This is not, however, to suggest that nineteenth-century Protestants were uninterested in the moral renovation of society. Revivalist ministers counted selfishness as one of humanity's most egregious tendencies. Conversion, therefore, was understood as a transformation of the heart that leads to a revitalized concern for the welfare of others. Toward this end the churches began organizing a variety of missionary societies aimed at promulgating the gospel. At first the societies focused on explicitly evangelical goals: distributing Bibles, forming Sunday schools, and sponsoring foreign missions. With time the goals became more ambitious. Converted individuals formed "voluntary societies" to establish grammar schools, colleges, and seminaries. Even more ambitious was the formation of societies aimed at reorganizing the whole fabric of society in accordance with biblical principles. Temperance societies promoted restraint from the consumption of alcohol. Other societies helped establish hospitals, provide relief for the poor, and promote international peace. Perhaps the most ardent of all voluntary societies were the abolitionist groups that endeavored to harness the forces of evangelical religion to rid the nation of slavery (an effort that eventually led to bitter disputes between northern and south-ern wings of the established denominations). The "voluntarism" spawned by the Second Great Awakening established long-lasting patterns whereby American religious organizations have exerted significant, though indirect, influence on American social and political life.

Slavery, Emancipation, and the Rise of Free Black Churches

An estimated 596,000 Africans were brought to North America before the close of the slave trade in 1808. As the slave population grew to approximately 4.5 million by the onset of the Civil War, intricate religious patterns began to emerge. African and Caribbean influences persisted in the cosmology of black Americans throughout the nineteenth century, whether expressing themselves autonomously or by gradually mingling with Christian belief and ritual.

African-born belief in the spirit world suffused a complex of beliefs and rituals that oriented black Americans to everyday life. Many black Americans in the nineteenth century took great efforts to honor the spirits of their ancestors; most consulted con-jurers to procure charms or to seek omens understood to be disclosing supernatural influences in worldly affairs. Conjuring took many forms, all based on the belief that particularly adept individuals can control supernatural powers for such worldly pur-poses as healing, resolving disputes, or procuring revenge. Voodoo is another prime example of the creative syntheses that emerged as West African belief in the spirit world mingled with Roman Catholic belief in saints and the power of sacraments. Emerging first in the Caribbean, voodoo eventually took root both in the Georgian Sea Islands and the Mississippi Delta region where it promulgated its distinctive con-ceptions of the forces that govern the universe as well as its practices for influencing these forces in such a way as to produce desired worldly outcomes. Yet another exam-ple of how West African systems of belief and ritual influenced African-American relig-iosity is the emergence of the "ring shout" often performed in areas of Georgia and South Carolina. Group dance traditions of African origin merged with revivalist Christianity to produce a distinctive dance performed by shuffling counterclockwise in a circle, clapping in a complex counter-rhythm, and singing in a liturgical or respon-sive pattern all in an effort to produce ecstatic religious fervor. The process whereby African singing and dancing traditions were progressively Christianized was acceler-ated by the many Baptist and Methodist revivalists who sought to win converts on the southern plantations. Evangelical Protestantism readily appealed to the slave popula-tion as it offered impassioned preaching, made use of emotionally evocative hymn singing, incorporated rhythmic dancing, and encouraged ecstatic possession by the Holy Spirit.

The gathering of black Baptist congregations continued throughout the nineteenth century, culminating in the formation of the separate black National Baptist Convention in 1895. Meanwhile the creation of the African Methodist Episcopal Church in 1816 and the African Methodist Episcopal Zion Church in 1822 furthered the process whereby African Americans gathered religiously in racially segregated Protestant denominations. These churches provided the principal vehicle through which a struc-tured social life originated among black Americans and through which black Americans oriented themselves to the broader patterns of American life. Churches provided opportunities for social and economic networking, published the most influential periodicals, and promoted education more effectively than any other cultural institution.

Because most political or economic leadership roles were closed to black Americans, the ministry emerged as a significant source of moral and cultural authority in African-American communities both before and after the Civil War. As W. E. B. DuBois noted in his *The Souls of Black Folk*, "The Preacher is the most unique personality developed by the Negro on American soil. A leader, a politician, a 'boss,' an intriguer, an idealist – all of these he is, and ever, too, the center of a group of men, now twenty, now a thousand." The precise nature and significance of African-American preaching in the nineteenth century are, however, a matter of considerable dispute. To be sure, many preachers taught a message of consolation and passive accommodation. The gospel was frequently seen as extolling submissiveness and humility, a willingness to endure the burdens of worldly life in the hope of earning eternal reward in the hereafter. A great deal of African-American preaching throughout the century had a decidedly other-worldly focus, ultimately reinforcing the ideal of the "suffering Christian servant." Yet other slave preachers insisted that both spiritual and human equality is a fundamental principle of Christian belief. Drawing upon the Exodus story of deliverance from bondage, slave preachers taught that black slaves were a chosen people and have a special role in God's providential plans for humanity. God would not only protect his children, but act decisively to set them free. As evidenced in Nat Turner's slave revolt in 1831 that resulted in the death of over 60 whites and 100 blacks, faith in a future millennial rule of Christ on earth could inspire bold action to bring unjust social arrangements to an immediate end.

The institution of slavery was without question the most divisive issue facing white churches during the Age of Empire. The reformist spirit born of nineteenth-century Protestant faith led many – particularly in the North – to join the ranks of the abolitionist cause. Slavery, it was argued, violated Christian morality predicated as it was on the cardinal principle that we should do unto others as we would have done unto ourselves. Yet Southern clergymen were quick to point out that slavery was fully consistent with God's law as revealed in the Bible. The Israelite patriarchs (Abraham, Isaac, and Jacob) all had slaves. Mosaic law supported the idea that slavery was a permissible human institution. In his New Testament letter to Philemon, Paul urged the slave Onesimus to return to his master and in his letter to the Colossians he commanded slaves to obey their masters. Thus even though the Bible demands that slave owners treat their slaves fairly, it implicitly suggests that slavery is consistent with religiously based morality.

The nation's churches initially confined themselves to roles as indirect rather than direct champions of either the abolitionist or anti-abolitionist causes. It was, however, only a matter of time before they found themselves to be participants in the national fray. Although the ecclesiastical division within the Presbyterian church occurring in 1837 was not explicitly about slavery, it signaled the beginning of North-South divisions within the established denominations. Methodists, like Presbyterians, experienced numerous confrontations between Northern and Southern wings of their denomination throughout the middle decades of the century. It was the Baptists, however, whose unity was most clearly splintered over the issue of slavery as evidenced by the formation of the separate Southern Baptist Convention in 1845 (Figure 10.1).

Figure 10.1　The institution of slavery was without question the most divisive issue facing white churches in the Age of Empire.

Voices of moderation or compromise within the churches were eventually drowned out and intellectual dialogue all but disappeared. When the firing on Fort Sumter began in 1861, the churches had long since lost much of their national unity. Most of these schisms proved irreparable and henceforward American Protestantism would forever be divided along theological, geographical, and racial lines.

Sectarian Voices and Religious Innovation

Charles Finney's use of "new measures" to awaken religious enthusiasm was but one example of the period's experimental approach to religion. In an age undergoing geographic and cultural expansion, evangelical faith readily sought innovation and adaptation. The 1830s and 1840s witnessed a particularly strong outburst of innovative religious practices that contemporaries often referred to as *ultraism*. Ultraism, in the words of historian Whitney Cross (1950), consisted of a "combination of activities, personalities, and attitudes creating a condition of society which could foster experimental doctrines." Up to this point in American history virtually every religious organization had originated in Europe and had been carried to the New World by immigrants. The spirit of ultraism, however, inspired the formation of wholly new Christian sects that were uniquely American. These newly emerging sects, though having different origins and theologies, typically emphasized three revivalism-inspired themes: (1) experientialism – a desire for intense religious experiences that may afford personal revelation of God's plan for humanity; (2) perfectionism – the quest for complete holiness and moral purity; and (3) millennialism – strong belief in the imminent Second Coming of Christ and the establishment of a thousand-year reign of righteousness preceding final judgment.

John Humphrey Noyes illustrates the ultraistic temperament of the era. After graduating from Yale Divinity School, Noyes became convinced that the established denominations were in error when they asserted that conversion releases one from sin. He envisioned God's demand that we strive for moral perfection as requiring the further step of separating ourselves from the world's sinful ways. In 1848, he gathered

June 26 1907

Oneida Community, Home Building, Kenwood, N. Y.

McGuinness, Oneida, N. Y.

Figure 10.2 The Oneida Community, Mansion House, where Noyes and his followers practiced "complex marriage," a marital structure where each adult member was a spouse to every other adult member.

a community of about 200 together at Oneida, in western New York to put his theological vision into practice. The Oneida Community proved to be economically viable, relying first upon farming and logging and later upon light industry that produced silver-plated flatware. Noyes's most distinctive teaching was his view that romantic relationships are too possessive to embody true Christian love. For this reason he institutionalized a system of "complex marriage" in which each adult was a spouse to every other adult (Figure 10.2). This included sexual relations. The Oneida Community's practice of "complex marriage" – while intended to further humanity's moral perfection – drew persistent scorn from surrounding neighbors, eventually forcing the experimental commune to disband.

Another fascinating example of religious innovation during the Age of Empire is the case of the Millerites. A farmer from upstate New York, William Miller underwent a thoroughgoing conversion while attending a revival meeting and committed himself to a disciplined course of daily Bible reading. He soon found himself obsessed with the millennial or apocalyptic message found in the Books of Daniel and Revelation. Miller devoted countless hours trying to decipher the cryptic passages that he thought would shed light on the precise moment at which Christ would return to pass judgment on the human race. He gradually came to the shocking conclusion that the Bible clearly and unequivocally indicates that the Second Coming was scheduled for 1843 – just 25 years from when he made this startling discovery. Miller soon published a pamphlet aptly titled "Evidences from scripture and History of the Second Coming of Christ About the Year A. D. 1843." A year later he was granted a license to preach as a Baptist minister, and his apocalyptic message began to attract the attention of ministers and laity alike. With the help of a Boston minister by the name of Joshua Himes, Miller set out across the country with his exciting message of the imminent end of the world and the need to make oneself pleasing to Christ in anticipation of final judgment.

It is estimated that 50,000 Americans became committed Millerites. Thousands more were fascinated by his predictions and were consequently filled with religious excitement. It is easy to understand why so many were attracted to his teachings. A large number of Americans had already become "born again." When Miller came along they were eager for someone to light the fires of enthusiasm again. Many had joined one of the voluntary societies spawned by the Second Great Awakening, but had become discouraged by the slow progress being made toward renovating the world. It was only natural that they would be enchanted by a message promising an immediate and total resolution of the world's imperfections. This was particularly the case given the financial panic of 1837 that had set off a widespread economic depression and thus dashed the worldly hopes of farmers and businessmen alike. Miller's message was perfectly suited to persons experiencing such spiritual and economic doldrums. He told how, in the twinkling of an eye, every last problem in the world would be magically solved. The disintegrating kingdoms of earth would magically give way to the glorious Kingdom of God. Such belief in the imminent Second Coming of Christ – generally referred to as millennialism – fit neatly with the Age of Empire's expectation of growth and progress. Nineteenth-century millennialism generally embraced American hopes for expansion and world leadership, adding its distinctive promise that Christ has His eyes firmly fixed on those Bible-believing Americans certain to become the vanguard of a purified earth.

As 1843 approached, millennial fever soared. Some Millerites even gave away all their possessions and gathered on hilltops to await Christ's descent from the clouds. When the predicted date came and passed, Miller made new calculations and reset the date to October 1844. But still there was no cataclysmic destruction nor any appearance of Christ. Hopes were dashed. The "Great Disappointment" of 1844 dealt a serious blow to the adventist cause (named for the expected return or advent of Christ). Some followers became bitter and wary of all forms of enthusiastic religion. Others did not readily concede error but instead maintained that their basic prophetic scheme was still valid; they had erred only in relying upon inaccurate dates supplied by shoddy biblical scholars.

The most innovative of Miller's followers was Ellen Gould White. White's numerous visions afforded her the certain knowledge that October 1844 had indeed been a signal moment in the end-times scenario. Her revelations indicated that this was the date that Christ ascended to a heavenly sanctuary, where He is even now making His final preparation for His return. White's visions had the effect of keeping Miller's general framework intact while simply lengthening the timetable a bit. In a further revelation she learned that Christ will not return until more Christians live up to His moral demands, which include keeping the true, biblical Sabbath on Saturday. White's charismatic prophecy prompted the formation of a new Protestant church, the Seventh-Day Adventists. Seventh-Day Adventist theology manages to balance messages of asceticism and pre-millennial piety with an emphasis on physical health and worldly vigor – a combination that has allowed it to grow into the second largest denomination to have originated on American soil.

Unquestionably the most impressive episode of religious innovation during the Age of Empire was the long saga eventuating in the triumphant success of the

Church of Jesus Christ of Latter-day Saints. In 1816, Joseph Smith's family moved to western New York State in pursuit of economic opportunity. The region turned out to be an epicenter of frontier revivalism, exposing the young boy and his family to the religious excitement and theological controversies of the era. After a rather uneventful adolescence marked by sporadic interest in magic and divination, Joseph was visited by an angel named Moroni who led him to a site containing a glorious book etched on strange golden plates. The text inscribed on these tablets wasn't in English, but Joseph was eventually able to translate them with the aid of two "ancient seer" stones provided by Moroni. In 1830, at the age of 25, Joseph published the finished translation – the *Book of Mormon* (named after the text's original author who had buried the tablets centuries before).

The *Book of Mormon* tells the story of a small group of Hebrews who escaped the Babylonian invasion of Jerusalem about 600 B.C.E. by building a boat and journeying to North America. These people settled in what is now the northeastern United States, constructing quite advanced cities and temples. The most amazing part of the story comes when Christ, following His resurrection and ascension in Jerusalem, appeared before these people and organized His church among them. A soldier-statesman by the name of Mormon etched Christ's teachings onto a set of tablets and buried them to ensure they would survive an impending war. And there these tablets remained until the angel Moroni led Smith to uncover them almost two thousand years later.

It is easy to understand the spiritual excitement felt by the six elders and approximately fifty others who joined together in 1830 to form "the only true and living church upon the face of the whole earth." Calling themselves the Church of Jesus Christ of Latter-day Saints, they were full of millennial enthusiasm and lived in expectation of their Lord's return amid the tribulations that would destroy unbelievers. Latter-day Saints were not the only group emphasizing inner experience and a close relationship to God. Nor were they the only group claiming that some of their members entered into ecstatic states and were thus empowered to offer private interpretations of biblical writings. But the Saints possessed a new scripture miraculously translated from plates of gold, a new prophet called by God Himself, and a new church restoring the ancient order of things under the direction of ongoing divine revelation. The discovery and translation of the *Book of Mormon* would alone have set Joseph Smith apart as a religious genius. Yet a few years God sent a revelation explaining that He had sent "his servant Joseph to be a presiding elder over [the] church" and that he had chosen Joseph "to be a translator, a revelator, a seer, and a prophet." Smith responded to this special mission by receiving a continuing stream of divine revelations that reassured church members that they had a special role in building the Kingdom of God on earth.

The people Smith ministered to were optimistic, hard-working, and held high hopes for their worldly futures. Smith's revelations embraced these hopes and gave them new theological expression. Those who joined the Church of Jesus Christ of Latter-day Saints identified with the cultural patterns of the biblical Hebrews. Much as Moses had been selected by God to reveal the terms of the covenant to ancient Hebrews, Joseph Smith was thought to be revealing the moral or spiritual practices that would enable nineteenth-century citizens to live in accordance with divine law and to thereby create a "New Israel" on the North American continent. Smith explained that spiritual progress is ongoing and extends well beyond this lifetime. The highest degrees of glory, reserved for Latter-day Saints, provide continuing opportunities for spiritual progression.

This doctrine of eternal progression raised a number of theological questions that were addressed in continuing revelations. The Saints learned that there are many gods, all of whom were once human and evolved to their divine status through ongoing moral perfection. They learned that while salvation is available to all, there are three distinct degrees of glory: terrestrial, telestial, and celestial. Part of the path to godhood consists of developing the special creative powers made possible by marriage. Joseph's revelation on "celestial marriage" disclosed that temple ordinances can seal a marriage for eternity, permitting married couples to continue to evolve toward godhood in their future state. This doctrine of celestial marriage in turn connects with the single most distinctive Mormon tenet – that of plural marriage (polygamy). Smith announced that God was reinstating the ancient biblical custom of males having more than one wife. Many Saints were themselves scandalized by Smith's announcement (and even before the church reversed its position on this issue and officially denounced plural marriage, polygamy was never practiced by more than 5% of male and 12% of female members). Yet Smith's revelations were sensitive to the role that sexual disorder and family disorganization played in tearing frontier communities apart – particularly when females outnumbered males. Plural marriage actually desexualized the family structure and bound men and women together in loyalty to the long-term purposes of the gathered community of saints. The revelation of plural marriage thus pointed to a new form of kinship ties that could potentially strengthen social bonds.

The Mormons' bold religious innovations were destined to stir up resentment and acrimony among their neighbors. Even as their settlement in Nauvoo, Illinois grew to a population of over 10,000, disputes with outsiders led to Joseph Smith's arrest and confinement in a jail in the nearby town of Carthage. There, in 1844, a mob of about 150 armed men attacked the jail and murdered both Joseph and his brother. Shortly after Smith's death, Brigham Young led the majority of Saints to Salt Lake City, where they would begin another phase in the creation of their own religiously charged vision of an American empire.

The Flourishing of Metaphysical Religion

Some of the most creative theological constructions during the Age of Empire emanated from the fringes of the nation's formal religious institutions. The principal reason for this was that many who styled themselves as progressive thinkers found themselves in a spiritual predicament. On the one hand, they yearned for a form of religion that might offer them a felt-sense of connection with a higher spiritual reality. Simultaneously, however, they demanded a form of religion that could fully embrace the era's scientific discoveries. Neither the liturgical model (churches that emphasize personal renewal through ritual and worship) nor the evangelical model (churches that emphasize personal renewal through conversion and biblical piety) quite satisfied their spiritual needs.

It was among these unchurched seekers that an alternative model of spiritual emerged in American life: the metaphysical model. The term "metaphysical" refers to a loosely organized range of beliefs concerning the existence of a more-than-physical reality surrounding everyday existence. As such, metaphysical religion thrives in a cultural territory that exists somewhere between conventional religion and conventional science. Some forms of metaphysical religion are more overtly mystical than conventional churches insofar as they encourage belief that humans can make direct connection with invisible spiritual realms. Other forms of metaphysical religion are less concerned with inner experience than they are with establishing "objective" evidence for the existence of nonmaterial realities that conventional science normally dismisses, ignores, or even denies. The common aim of metaphysical religion is to understand how human life is affected by spiritual forces in ways that bypass both biblical religion and materialistic science. In contrast to either liturgical or evangelical models of piety associated with the nation's churches, metaphysical religion promotes what historian Sydney Ahlstrom (1972) termed harmonial piety. Harmonial piety comprises a wide range of beliefs and practices predicated on the conviction that spiritual composure, physical health, and even economic well-being flow automatically from a person's inner rapport with a metaphysical reality.

One of the earliest spokespersons for American metaphysical religion was the Harvard-trained Unitarian minister, Ralph Waldo Emerson. Just three years into his ministry, Emerson resigned because he was uncomfortable with public prayer and with administering the Lord's Supper to his congregations. Yet, in 1836, he published a slim volume entitled *Nature* that ignited a fire in his contemporaries' religious imaginations. In this book Emerson held out an exciting vision of God's presence in our world. He explained that divine spirit surrounds us, awaiting our recognition. We need only put aside our worldly rationality and open our inner spiritual faculties. A mystical encounter with God is thus an imminent possibility of human experience. The key is cultivating spiritual receptivity. He wrote that when alone in nature, "All mean egotism vanishes. I become a transparent eyeball; I am nothing; I see all; the currents of the Universal Being circulate through me; I am part and parcel of God." Emerson had forged a new spiritual path that avoided the limitations he perceived in both the science and biblical religion of his day. His vision of God's presence in the natural world did not ask people to denounce scientific rationality; only to expand it. It didn't require belief in the Bible. Nor did it portray humans as wretched sinners in desperate need of forgiveness. It asked instead that we temporarily set aside the egocentric rationality of everyday life and become receptive to God's in-streaming presence.

The same year that Emerson published *Nature,* a group comprised mostly of rebellious Unitarian preachers gathered with Emerson in the home of George Ripley. The group called themselves "The Transcendental Club." The club included some of the period's greatest thinkers: Theodore Parker, James Freeman Clarke, Frederic Hedge, William Henry Channing, and Orestes Brownson. Shortly thereafter they were joined by Henry David Thoreau, Bronson Alcott, Margaret Fuller, and Elizabeth Peabody. In truth, the Transcendentalists didn't even try to forge consensus among themselves. They were far too independently minded to expect conformity. The group could, however, agree upon four basic principles: (1) the immanence of God; (2) inward experience as the primary conduit of spiritual truth; (3) that there are "higher" spiritual levels of the universe than are recognized by conventional science; and (4) that these various levels of the universe are fundamentally in correspondence with another such that the possibility exists for a lawful "influx" of energies from higher to lower metaphysical levels. These principles in turn became the common denominator in terms of which nineteenth-century spiritual seekers understood the message of other metaphysical systems such as mesmerism and spiritualism.

While Transcendentalism cut a new cultural path for many members of high-brow American society, groups such as mesmerism and spiritualism disseminated a harmonial spiritual outlook among a wider segment of the population. Throughout the 1830s and 1840s dozens of mesmerists toured New England giving lecture-demonstrations of the wondrous new science of animal magnetism. The science they extolled stemmed directly from the Viennese physician Franz Anton Mesmer's "discovery" of an ultrafine fluid that he termed animal magnetism. Mesmer postulated that animal magnetism constituted the etheric medium that links the physical universe together. He further claimed that he could put people in a sleep-like trance state that would render them especially receptive to the inflow of this invisible spiritual energy. Astonishingly, a significant number of mesmerized patients testified that they had spontaneously developed extraordinary mental powers such as telepathy and clairvoyance. Some even claimed to become filled with the Holy Spirit, undergoing an immediate moral and spiritual transformation. The mesmerists, it seemed, had tapped into the era's penchant toward ultraism and gone the revivalists one better. In the twinkling of an eye they could effect a person's total renewal – physical, mental, and spiritual. And this was accomplished without asking persons to repent, to accept any formal religious doctrine, or to join any religious institution.

In many ways the mesmerists offered a concrete and therapeutically practical variation of Transcendentalist principles. Being mesmerized enables a person to become inwardly receptive to the "influx" of energies ostensibly emanating from some higher, invisible metaphysical realm. The era's foremost mesmerist, a clockmaker from Maine named Phineas P. Quimby, was especially instrumental in adapting metaphysical religion to the everyday needs of middle-class Americans. Quimby proposed that our thoughts and attitudes function like control valves or floodgates: They determine the degree to which our minds are open to flow of vital energies emanating from higher spiritual realms. Positive, optimistic, and spiritual thoughts establish the harmonious flow of vitality into our lives. Quimby asserted that if he could just show his patients "that a man's happiness is in his belief, and his misery is the effect of his belief, then I have done what never has been done before. Establish this and man rises to a higher state of wisdom, not of this world, but of that World of Science ... the Wisdom of Science is Life eternal."

Quimby's references to the Wisdom of Science symbolized his commitment to the metaphysical model of spiritual piety. One of Quimby's students, Mary Baker Eddy, gave her own slant to Quimby's teachings and turned them into the fundamental principles of the Church of Christ, Scientist (commonly known as Christian Science). Several of his other students, notably Anetta Dresser, Julius Dresser and Warren Felt Evans, amplified this harmonial message in a new middle-class philosophy variously known as the mind-cure philosophy or New Thought. The New Thought movement provided an optimistic philosophy anchored in the conviction that "thoughts are forces." Books, pamphlets, and public lectures reached millions with the message that by controlling our thoughts and attitudes we can gain inner-access to unlimited spiritual power. As New Thinker Ralph Waldo Trine put it:

The great central fact in human life is the coming into a conscious vital realization of our oneness with the Infinite Life, and the opening of ourselves fully to the Divine inflow … in the degree that thought is spiritualized, does it become more subtle and powerful … this spiritualizing is in accordance with law and is within the power of all.

The New Thoughters and Transcendentalists studiously avoided making any reference to the existence of angels, spirits, or any other kind of personal entities who might be residing in higher metaphysical realms. Most of them considered such belief to be crass superstition, wholly incompatible with their progressive and co-scientific spiritual outlook. But as fate was to have it, an apprentice shoemaker by the name of Andrew Jackson Davis allowed himself to be mesmerized only to enter a trance state within which he began receiving messages from the spirit world. Claiming that he had come into contact with the spirit of the famed Swedish mystic Emanuel Swedenborg, Davis helped reconnect the American metaphysical movement with its earlier Swedenborgian roots. Davis's trance-channeled revelations depicted a universe that is both structured and lawful. The basic principles of the universe, not surprisingly, are correspondence and influx. It seems that the universe is comprised of a series of concentric "spheres" of increasing beauty and wisdom. These spheres are ordered hierarchically. At the top of the hierarchy is God, the source of all life and force. God's spiritual influence permeates the universe, communicated to each sphere through an electricity-like ether. Occupying the spheres between earth and God are spirit beings of progressively higher levels of spiritual attainment. Each of these spirit beings – including each human being – is on his or her own spiritual journey toward perfection and increasing proximity to God. Humans, who occupy the lowest sphere, can avail themselves of wisdom and support from spirit guides immediately above them in the cosmic order. Upon death, humans ascend to a higher spiritual sphere in direct accordance with the spiritual progress achieved during their earthly life.

Just four years after Davis began the spiritualist movement, two young girls named Maggie and Kate Fox also claimed the ability to communicate with the spirit world. The Fox sisters charged admission to their spiritualist séances and soon spiritualism proved to be a lucrative enterprise. Spiritualists' séances were part sideshow entertainment, part shaman-like encounter with awesome supernatural powers. Despite its frivolous excesses, spiritualism was an early champion of nearly every theme that was later to become central to liberal Christianity: renewed emphasis on the immanence of God, a tendency to view the Bible as symbolic rather than literal, a concern for progressive social causes, and a call to seek God both in nature and within the self.

Particularly prescient in terms of anticipating later theological trends were the ways that nearly all forms of nineteenth-century metaphysical religion imaginatively reconceptualized gender. Most religious thinking in the Age of Empire unquestioningly assumed the male gender of God, the central importance of God's son to human redemption, and the normative role of males as religious authorities. True, Ellen Gould White helped pioneer new religious roles for women as she became a living symbol of humanity's capacity to receive direct revelations from God. And, too, Shakers believed in the dual nature of God as embodying a complementary and equal expression of both male and female elements. But neither the Shakers nor the Seventh Day Adventists fully championed what today would be considered feminist issues. As with other Christian and Jewish groups, they were too committed to the biblical worldview and to middle-class conventions to be able to imagine a universe in which females were understood to be ontologically equal, if not superior, to males in terms of religious authority.

Metaphysical religion set biblical cosmology aside and imaginatively constructed new models of the universe that undercut the hierarchical world of Judaism and Christianity. Rather than understanding God as a male "power over" the universe, metaphysical religion recast God as an impersonal "power from within." Not only were females equal to males in their capacity to become inwardly receptive to this immanent spiritual power, but they were at least as likely to serve as healers, lecturers, and authors. The institutional forms of metaphysical religion were fluid, allowing women to demonstrate their natural leadership powers in ways that were not permitted in conventional churches or synagogues. Mesmerist, New Thought, and spiritualist theologies almost always displayed sensitivity to the dual-gendered nature of God. The metaphysical model of spirituality celebrated every person's potential for becoming receptive to the instreaming currents of divine spirit – unmediated by a male Savior or member of the clergy.

Darwin and the New Theological Climate

The last three decades of the nineteenth century witnessed a remarkable shift in Americans' understanding of themselves and their place in the wider universe. Science was rapidly altering the way that educated people thought about the forces affecting their lives. The Scientific Revolution of the eighteenth-century had long since taken hold among American intellectuals. The success of scientific inquiry reinforced practical common sense in rejecting ideas for which there was no empirical evidence. Scientific achievement gave rise to technological advances that gave nineteenth-century citizens confidence that humans could increasingly understand and take control of their world. By comparison, traditional religion appeared anemic. Belief in miracles or supernatural intervention seemed the stuff of ancient folklore.

Darwin's theory of biological evolution became the focal point of the cultural clash between science and religion. Although Darwin didn't publish *On the Origin of Species* until 1859, by 1880 virtually every important scientist in the United States had been converted to the new worldview. This new scientific view filtered into the educated public's awareness in a surprisingly brief period of time. The theory of evolution, after all, was understood by most Americans in ways that meshed perfectly with their progressive and forward-looking character. It seemed almost ideally suited to an optimistic people eager to learn that progress and development were intrinsic to the very laws of nature (the vision of evolution as morally blind, without direction, and driven largely by accident didn't fully emerge until the twentieth century). Yet the challenge that evolutionary science presented to religion was both blunt and unavoidable. If the evolutionary line leading to humans developed over millions of years, then there was no way of avoiding the fact that the Bible does not contain factual information. This discrepancy between two competing avenues to truth, science and biblical religion, caused a significant number of persons to experience an acute tension between head and heart, rationality and faith. Most had no choice but to choose what all their rational faculties showed them to be the most intellectually defensible: science. Many who in earlier eras would have chosen careers in the ministry instead opted for careers in science, philosophy, or the newly founded fields of psychology and sociology.

Evolutionary science did more than undermine belief in the literal truth of the Bible. It also eroded the entire foundation of evangelical Christianity: the view that God created humans to be perfect, but through willful disobedience humans fell into the condition of sin. The biblical worldview presupposes that humans are fallen due to perverse self-centeredness and therefore stand in need of redemption. Evolutionary science, however, provides a very different view of human nature. It shows humans to be an integral apart of the larger web of life on this planet and possessing a relatively large cerebral cortex that gives humanity potential for almost unlimited progress, growth, and development.

Science was not the only source of the new intellectual climate that emerged in the late nineteenth century. Americans were beginning to learn more about other cultures around the world, weakening confidence that any one society had a monopoly on "absolute truth." The Transcendentalist writer James Freeman Clarke published the *Ten Great Religions* in 1871, encouraging readers to find spiritual edification outside the Judeo-Christian tradition by examining Hinduism, Buddhism, and Confucianism. Clarke's volume found a receptive audience and eventually went through 21 editions. Walt Whitman furthered Americans' interest in nontraditional forms of religious thought in such works as *Leaves of Grass* and *Passage to India*. In 1892, the World's Parliament of Religions was held in Chicago in connection with the Columbian Exposition. The event attracted more than 150,000 visitors to exhibits and lectures offering sympathetic introductions to the teachings of the world's great religions. The event was also covered in almost every newspaper and popular magazine, introducing large audiences to alternative approaches to the subject of religion. Further weakening of confidence in the existence of fixed religious truths came from the field of modern biblical scholarship. While the most penetrating biblical scholarship would come a few decades into the twentieth century, academic scholars had already begun to use the techniques of scientific history and careful linguistic analysis to examine the origins of the Bible. Their sophisticated analyses established beyond scholarly dispute that the Bible was the work of numerous authors who collected, edited, and arranged their source materials according to their own conceptions of religious truth. Modern scholarship therefore made it difficult to view the Bible as a "delivered once and for all" revelation from God.

Protestant theology was challenged to respond to this changing intellectual climate or risk being deemed irrelevant. This response had its roots in the writings of Hartford, Connecticut, pastor Horace Bushnell who had in mid-century put a new, progressive spin on orthodox formulations. Bushnell's *Christian Nurture* (1847) and *Nature and the Supernatural* (1858) were two of the most influential books in the history of American religious thought. Bushnell's thought subtly turned Protestant theology away from the revivalist emphasis on sudden, dramatic conversions and instead to the wider natural and social contexts that progressively nurture spiritual growth. Bushnell argued that nature and supernature are consubstantial and interfused, together constituting "the one system of God." His belief in "a supernatural grace which inhabits the organic laws of nature and works its results in conformity with them" made it possible to pursue the scientific study of nature without giving up faith in God as the ultimate source of all natural processes.

The most prominent among those clergymen who developed a new, liberal theology was Reverend Henry Ward Beecher. Aware that the churches were in danger of being left behind by "the intelligent part of society," Beecher maintained that the church needed to adjust its theological system to take account of known facts about the universe. As he put it, "The providence of God is rolling forward in a spirit of investigation that Christian ministers must meet and join." Scientists were "that noble body of investigators who are deciphering the hieroglyphics of God inscribed upon this temple of earth," Beecher declared. In 1882, Beecher confidently described himself as "a Christian evolutionist" while affirming God's providential action at work stirring nature toward ever-higher levels of development.

Beecher's liberal accommodation to science was amplified in the final years of the century in such influential works as Lyman Abbott's *The Theology of an Evolutionist* (1897), John Bascom's *Evolution and Religion* (1897), and John Fiske's *Through Nature to God* (1899). Abbott exemplified liberal theology's tendency to invoke pantheistic categories when he described God as "the Infinite and Eternal Energy from which all things proceed." Fiske defined God as "the Power which is disclosed in every throb of the mighty rhythmic life of the universe." When Fiske proclaimed that "evolution is God's way of doing things," he was opening up new ways of understanding humanity's role in furthering divine providence. He and other theistic evolutionists believed that humans are inwardly linked with God's providential spirit. He declared that "the lesson of evolution is that … [the soul] has been rising to the recognition of its essential kinship with the ever-living God." Abbott amplified this important implication of religious liberalism when he declared the "foundation of spiritual faith is neither in the church nor in the Bible, but in the spiritual consciousness of man." Because anything that deepens humanity's "spiritual consciousness" could be affirmed as furthering the progressive evolution of the universe, liberal theology began looking well beyond the Bible for new sources of spiritual inspiration.

This new intellectual climate was an important factor in the gradual emergence of a theological spectrum. Denominations whose members were more likely to be exposed to modernizing forces (e.g., Unitarians, Congregationalists, Episcopalians, and Presbyterians) would become disinclined to charge their members to read the Bible literally and therefore drifted to moderate theological positions. This very trend inevitably mobilized other Americans to reaffirm the fundamentals of conservative faith, giving clear identity to denominations on the other end of the theological spectrum (e.g., Baptists, Lutherans, Latter-day Saints, Seventh-Day Adventists, and the many Holiness and Pentecostal groups that would emerge in the twentieth century). By the close of the Age of Empire, a person's religious identity had far less to do with specific denominational membership than where he or she (or the minister preaching from the pulpit) was located on the liberal–conservative theological spectrum.

The Closing of the Age of Empire: Tragedy and the Loss of Protestant Hegemony

The Age of Empire contained more than its share of tragedy. The cultural divide leading up to the Civil War (1861–65) saw American Protestantism splinter along lines of geography, culture, and theology. More importantly, the death of 620,000 soldiers and an undetermined number of civilian casualties ruptured American faith in divine providence and the nation's place in God's plan for the redemption of humanity. John Quincy Adams's confidence in the nation's manifest destiny had eroded substantially when the nation's sixteenth president, Abraham Lincoln, delivered his Second Inaugural Address in 1865. Lincoln could only conclude that "God has His own purposes" that may well have nothing to do with the nation's political or cultural ambitions. The nation that once thought of itself as performing an errand for God now realized it was capable of some of the most monstrously inhumane actions ever recorded in human history. True, the general public's headstrong determination to enter the Spanish-American War of 1898 expressed an expansionist sentiment driven by a persisting desire to fulfill the nation's manifest destiny. Yet the Civil War nonetheless left a festering wound in America's cultural psyche, making it far more difficult to envision the nation as the divinely appointed agent of the promised millennial kingdom.

American expansion came at a price. Extending the nation across the continent and subsuming all persons under one social contract produced countless victims. Those with cultural ties to either Spain or Mexico were among the first to realize that the nation's political mission, as viewed by white Anglo-Saxon Protestants as "destined by God and by nature," could be realized only by relegating them to the sidelines. It was, however, Native Americans who paid most dearly for the cause of national empire. From the moment Europeans first began to colonize North America, Native Americans were systematically exterminated or forced to relocate to ever-shrinking boundaries until almost all that was left to them was forced segregation onto bleak government reservations. And all the while the nation's most dominant forms of religion understood such genocidal treatment in the context of millennial aspiration. Native Americans were clearly outside the pale of those who considered themselves divinely chosen for God's errand into the wilderness. Biblically based understandings of America's manifest destiny even went so far as to suggest that Native Americans were agents of Satan or the Antichrist put on earth only to obstruct the efforts of those entrusted with establishing a nation pleasing to God.

The tragic destruction of Native American culture simultaneously inspired imaginative new belief systems. Handsome Lake's series of ecstatic visions beginning in 1799 was the first of several movements that appeared in the nineteenth century to provide innovative conceptions of how Native Americans might make adjustments to their new cultural surroundings without wholly sacrificing their cultural heritage. One of these movements was the so-called Ghost Dance phenomenon that first appeared in 1869. Central to the Ghost Dance movement was the prophet of peace Jack Wilson, often known as Wovoka, who had a vision in which God commissioned him to teach a new dance a millennial message. This millennial message initially taught there would be a peaceful end to white American expansion that could be hastened through clean living, moral earnestness, cross-cultural cooperation, and ritual dancing. Other prophet-dreamers made variations on Wilson's teachings and preached belief in the imminent return of the dead (from which the name "ghost" emerged) as well as supernatural and miraculous ousting of whites followed by the restoration of Indian lands and way of life. It was believed that this restoration could be accelerated by

performing the dances and songs revealed to the prophets as well as by strict observance of Christian morality. As Ghost Dance rituals gradually subsided (partially due
to their implication in the rise of the rebellion that ended in the massacre of nearly
four hundred Sioux at Wounded Knee when the "ghost shirts" failed to protect them
as Jack Wilson had prophesied), many of these same themes resurfaced in the rise of
the peyote rituals that spread across Native American reservations. Peyotism, like the
Ghost Dance, made innovative use of traditional shamanism and its belief in the ability of visions or trances to give persons access to spiritual power. And peyotism, too,
adapted such traditional beliefs to facilitate necessary accommodations to Christianity
and white culture.

It is also important to note that more than thirteen million new immigrants arrived
on American shores during the last three decades of the nineteenth century. Most of
these newcomers had languages, customs, and religious affiliations that differed sharply
from their Yankee "hosts." In 1850 only 5 percent of the total population was Roman
Catholic. But, beginning in 1870, continuing waves of Irish, German, and Italian
Catholic immigrants began to erode the hegemony formerly enjoyed by Anglo-Saxon
Protestants. These immigrants – much like the Spanish-speaking Roman Catholics
who had settled in regions of the Southwest and California that were gradually annexed
to the growing American empire – were slow both in creating an awareness of belonging
to a unified American Catholic church and in being assimilated into the Protestant-
dominated sources of cultural power. Yet, by 1898, one out of every three church
members in the country was Catholic. The new immigrants augmented the social base
of a church that already benefited from the intellectual leadership of bishops such as
John Hughes, Martin John Spalding, and John Carroll, as well as lay converts Orestes
Brownson and Isaac Hecker. Their writings adroitly addressed the relationship between
reason and faith, while providing theological and scriptural arguments in support of
the traditional Catholic emphasis on good works as a condition of salvation. In general, however, Catholicism wasn't sufficiently established in the United States to make
distinctive contributions to the worldviews animating the Age of Empire. It was, however, poised to become a major source of Americans' moral and religious orientations
in the twentieth century.

Although smaller in scale, the story of American Judaism followed a similar pattern.
In 1800 there were only about 2,000 Jews in the United States. Immigration enabled
the American Jewish population to grow to about 250,000 by 1880. Because Jews
were never forced to live in isolation as they often had to in Europe, they were free to
assimilate into American life and many were subsequently receptive to the Reform
movement that began in Germany in the 1840s. Most of the approximately 270
Jewish congregations that existed at the close of the Age of Empire were thus affiliated with Reform Judaism and were led by rabbis who were typically known in their
communities for intellectual accomplishment and civic leadership. Jewish religious
thought, of course, provided many of the principal themes that guided Americans in
the nineteenth century. The biblical story of Exodus whereby God decisively intervenes in world history to lead his people toward the creation of a divinely blessed
nation exerted a powerful influence on Americans' self-understanding as they steadily
pushed their empire across the continent. The rhetoric supporting American expansion drew heavily upon a host of distinctively Jewish religious conceptions such as
chosen people, the providential movement of history, a covenantal relationship with

God, and the anticipated realization of a New Zion or New Jerusalem. Yet, as with Roman Catholics, Jews lacked the social or cultural power to exert direct influence on nineteenth-century American life.

The growing presence of other faiths was a visible sign that Anglo-Saxon Protestantism was beginning to lose the hegemony over American culture it had enjoyed throughout the Age of Empire. And, as science continued to gain public prestige, the university soon replaced the church as the official source of Americans' knowledge about important matters. Yet the theological innovations that emerged during the Age of Empire had – despite the countervailing despair born of the Civil War – left an indelible mark on the "modern" outlook that launched America into the twentieth century. The modern outlook, rooted in the belief that the laws of nature (presumed to have been designed by God) are evolutionary or progressive in their purpose, suggested that discoveries or change of almost any kind would automatically lead the nation closer to its manifest destiny. Although such modernist faith in the predetermined harmony of life was destined to be called into question during the twentieth century, the Age of Empire laid the foundations for much of what continues to be characteristically "American" about American life and thought.

References and Further Reading

Ahlstrom, Sydney (1972) *A Religious History of the American People*, New Haven, CT: Yale University Press.

Albanese, Catherine (2007) *A Republic of Mind and Spirit*, New Haven, CT: Yale University Press.

Cross, Whitney (1950) *The Burned-over District: The Social and Intellectual History of Enthusiastic Religion in Western New York, 1800–1850*, Ithaca, NY: Cornell University Press.

Holifield, E. Brooks (2003) *Theology in America*, New Haven, CT: Yale University Press.

McLoughlin, William (1978) *Revivals, Awakening, and Reform*, Chicago: University of Chicago Press.

11

Community

Heather D. Curtis

Religious communities developed in new ways in nineteenth-century America in response to the establishment of the new American Republic, the expansion of American Empire, and demands for American "civilization." Galvanized by religious revivals and reform efforts of various kinds, many Americans committed themselves to building new religious communities, or to extending and improving existing ones. This expansive burst of religious organization coincided with territorial expansion and industrialization, and often linked religious communities to nationalism. Armed with interpretations of scripture linking biblical history with American destiny, more than a few community organizers aimed at the moral transformation of the nation and, from the nation, through the world. These efforts at community building triggered intense debates about slavery and segregation, gender norms and sexuality, immigration and the assimilation of newcomers with religious communities of their own. Whites fought over whether religious communities should include or exclude slave owners, while slaves and free blacks established numerous religious communities of their own. Women outnumbered men in religious communities, while male leaders often restricted their religious activities and challenged their influence. Catholics and Jews turned to religious communities for support in the process of becoming American, although they often met with hostility as foreigners who did not belong. Meanwhile, Native Americans struggling to survive on the margins of the new nation founded new religious communities, some of which promised an end to the American Empire and its Kingdom of God.

The era of "American Empire" (1803–98) was a time of remarkable innovation and change in American religious history. Religious people of all persuasions, and Protestant Christians in particular, began to address a host of political, cultural and social issues in ways that would have been relatively unfamiliar to their eighteenth-century forbearers. Following the separation of church and state, and the resulting "disestablishment" of Christianity, many religious groups founded benevolent societies, or voluntary associations – a new kind of community structure through which religious believers cooperated to influence American culture. Missionary societies were among the earliest voluntary organizations to form in the United States, but these evangelistic associations were soon joined by a host of groups committed to the establishment of Sunday Schools; the distribution of tracts and religious literature; the promotion of female purity through anti-prostitution campaigns; the observance of the Sabbath; the advancement of bodily health through temperance campaigns which advocated moderation in the use of alcohol, tobacco and diet, and sex; the sponsorship of women's rights; and the eradication of war, urban poverty, and, most controversially, slavery.

A variety of circumstances helps explain the emergence and growth of the nineteenth-century "benevolent crusade." The political climate of the new nation, and especially uncertainty about the success of the "democratic experiment," fueled a sense of urgency among many Americans to cultivate the kind of social and cultural institutions that would promote stability and nurture virtuous citizens. Urbanization, industrialization, and the rise of consumer capitalism prompted efforts to ensure the flourishing of the American economy amidst the rapid transformation of traditional structures of class, race, and gender that defined American communities. The Meriwether Lewis and William Clark Expedition (1803–06) stimulated westward migration and US territorial expansion, raising pressing questions about national identity and the status of Native Americans. The arrival of immigrants in massive numbers beginning in the 1840s and continuing throughout the century further intensified attempts to foster political, economic and social cohesion.

Within this context, religions and religiously-based organizations worked to guide the development of American political, social and economic life. Although religious voluntary societies sought to shape almost every facet of American culture during this period, controversies over race relations and gender roles were the focus of sustained and especially vigorous attention. The remainder of this chapter will explore how religion and religious associations influenced debates about race, gender and the structure of American society throughout the nineteenth century. The first two sections will examine the interplay between religion and race, focusing primarily on Christian approaches to Indian removal, racial segregation, and slavery. The final sections will highlight the diverse ways in which American Protestants, post-Protestants, Mormons, Catholics, and Jews interpreted, employed and revised ideas about womanhood, manhood, family life, and sexuality in order to strengthen community structures they deemed essential for religious life.

Religion and Race: Native and Anglo-American Encounters

On the morning of March 27, 1814, one thousand Native American warriors from the Muskogee (Creek) tribe prepared to defend the town of Tohopeka (located in modern Alabama) from an invading United States military force. Armed primarily with bows and arrows, clubs, spears and knives, the "Red Stick" warriors were confident that they would prevail against General Andrew Jackson's better-equipped army. As part of a wider revolt against Anglo-American territorial expansion, the Battle of Horseshoe Bend was, in the view of the Muskogee participants, a religious as well as military rebellion against impure American forces that threatened to destroy their communities. "Following shamanistic leaders and acting in accord with their religious visions," the Red Sticks fought to preserve their land and culture, and "claimed access to sacred power and believed enemy fire could not harm them" (Martin 1991: 1). By the end of the day, over eight hundred Muskogee warriors were dead.

Indians were not the only ones who linked religion with the strength, purity, and existence of their communities. Claiming "complete success" in quelling the Red Sticks' sacred revolt, US Army General Thomas Pinckney wrote that, "Almighty God" had "blessed the arms of the United States" and "severely chastised" the "insolent" Muskogee rebels (Martin 1991: 164). In August of 1814, the defeated Muskogees were forced to surrender fourteen million acres to the United States – territory that was quickly possessed by Anglo-American settlers eager to exploit the region's rich agricultural resources for the production of cotton and other lucrative crops. Over the next several decades, lust for land continued to crowd Muskogees out of their native region. In 1835–36, the remaining Muskogees were forcibly relocated to the western territories as part of President Andrew Jackson's Indian Removal policy.

The story of the Muskogee rebellion and its aftermath highlights the importance of religion in restructuring relations between Native and Anglo-Americans in the nineteenth century. United States governmental officials often described territorial expansion as a God-given mandate.

> The whole continent of North America appears to be destined by Divine Providence to be peopled by one *nation*, speaking one language, professing one general system of religious and political principles, and accustomed to one general tenor of social usages and customs, declared John Quincy Adams, president of the United States from 1825–1829. (McDougall 1997: 78)

The physical presence and cultural distinctiveness of Native Americans posed an obvious challenge to this vision. As the ideology of manifest destiny gained prominence over the course of the nineteenth century, dissolving Native community structures became an increasingly urgent political and religious imperative.

Christian missionary organizations played a central, if complicated, role in responding to this imperative. Missionaries had been interacting with Native tribes since the arrival of the first European immigrants on North American soil, and nineteenth-century proselytizers engaged in particularly vigorous efforts to convert and "civilize" the "Indians," especially in the relatively under-evangelized southern territories. After the Muskogee defeat in 1814, Protestant missionaries began to settle among Native communities in Georgia, Alabama, North Carolina and Tennessee. Linking the tasks of evangelization and "civilization," the American Board of Commissioners on Foreign Missions (ABCFM), along with other missionary societies, worked closely with governmental agencies to establish institutions for "the instruction of the rising generation in common school learning, in the useful arts of life, and in Christianity." Aiming to make "the whole tribe English in their language, civilized in their habits, and Christian in their religion" missionaries who participated in these endeavors argued that Natives could be assimilated into the new American nation through the process of "Christianization."

Some Native Americans responded positively to missionary offers of training and education, selectively embracing aspects of Christian faith and Anglo-American culture as a means of advancing their own political, social and spiritual agendas. For converts such as Elias Boudinot, editor of the first Cherokee newspaper in the United States, adopting Christianity was a strategy for tribal survival, and also a tactic for imagining a more racially integrated society: in 1826, Boudinet wed Harriet Gould, a white woman. The marriage provoked indignation and censure from many Anglo-Americans who felt that miscegenation was "an outrage" against their commitment to the separation of racial communities rather than a logical outcome of Christian assimilation.

Boudinet's initial confidence that converting to Christianity and espousing Anglo-American culture would preserve Native communities evaporated in the midst of increasingly aggressive encroachment on Cherokee lands in the early 1830s. Following the passage of the Indian Removal Act, signed into law by President Andrew Jackson in 1830, the state of Georgia began to redistribute Cherokee and Muskogee territory to white settlers by lottery. With the backing of several ABCFM missionaries, including Boudinet's close friend Samuel A. Worcester, Cherokee leaders resisted these imperialist invasions, pleading their case before the US Supreme Court in *Cherokee Nation v. Georgia* (1831) and *Worcester v. Georgia* (1832). Despite a favorable ruling in the second case, some Cherokees, including Boudinet, became convinced that westward migration was the only way to preserve Cherokee communities. In 1835, he joined a minority group of Cherokee leaders in supporting a "land exchange" treaty with the United States government. Those Cherokee who refused to comply with the terms of the treaty and emigrate voluntarily were rounded up by the United States army in 1838 and forcibly removed to "Indian territory."

Many Anglo-American religious leaders actively opposed Indian removal, arguing that territorial imperialism would undermine the cause of "civilizing and Christianizing" Native communities. Evangelical Protestants such as Jeremiah Evarts, an officer of the ABCFM from 1820 until his death in 1831, campaigned against the Indian Removal Act and lobbied on behalf of Native American rights. Missionaries Samuel Worcester and Elizur Butler engaged in acts of civil disobedience in challenge to government removal policies. Religious leaders from outside evangelical circles also objected to the forced migration of Native tribes. In 1838, transcendentalist Ralph Waldo Emerson wrote to President Martin Van Buren protesting "against the removal of the Cherokee Indians from the State of Georgia" and imploring him not to commit "so vast an outrage upon the Cherokee Nation." Such an "injustice," Emerson implied, would not only besmirch the piety and principles of the United States, but it would also negate efforts to civilize "the aboriginal population," many of which had met with success. "We have witnessed with sympathy the painful labors of these red men to redeem their own race from the doom of eternal inferiority, and to borrow and domesticate in the tribe the arts and customs of the Caucasian race," Emerson declared.

When the government pressed ahead with the policy of removal in the spring of 1838, a number of Christian missionaries joined the Cherokee and other native tribes on the "Trail of Tears" – the forced march westward that resulted in the deaths of approximately four thousand Cherokee. Baptists Evan and John B. Jones traveled to Oklahoma with the Cherokee, establishing a new mission station in order to continue their work among the Native community. ABCFM operative Samuel Worcester had relocated to Oklahoma in 1835, after he had concluded that forced migration of the Cherokee was inevitable. Once established in the West, Christian missions to Native Americans continued to reflect a dual emphasis on evangelizing and civilizing. Still hopeful that assimilation would protect Natives from extermination – a prospect that loomed large as Anglo-American settlers pushed further West in their quest for new lands to occupy – missionaries promoted Christian education and enculturation as the principal means of preparing tribal peoples for citizenship. As historian Michael McNally has argued, missionaries "touted the hymn as a particularly effective means for rooting out Indianness and for inculcating an Anglo-American, evangelical, agrarian way of life" (1999: 281).

For Native Americans struggling to preserve distinctive ways of life on increasingly diminishing tracts of land in the West, religion was a resource for adapting and accommodating to the harsh realities of reservation existence, as well as a source of innovative and improvisational resistance to cultural and territorial imperialism. Conversion to Christianity also enabled Native peoples to maintain religious communities and sustain crucial elements of their own religious traditions. Native converts found ways of integrating Christian beliefs and practices with older kinship structures that had long defined Native communities (McNally 1999: 282).

Not all Native Americans saw conversion as a strategy for safeguarding or transforming traditional religious values and community structures. Many Natives equated Christianity with violence, invasion, and oppression. From this perspective, Christianity and imperialism were inextricably entangled, conversion represented a betrayal of Native identity, and the survival of Native communities called for resistance, separation and secrecy. After the Battle of Horseshoe Bend, for example, many Natives in the Southeast "made special efforts to hide their own culture of the sacred from Christian scrutiny" and "tried to protect their ceremonies from white civilization" (Martin 1997: 163). Unlike the Cherokee, Creek tribes were stubbornly unresponsive to missionary efforts and continued to perform "rituals and dances that celebrated their identities as Indians" (Martin 1997: 164).

Later in the nineteenth century, Native religious movements such as the Ghost Dance emerged. A circle dance lasting hours that led to visions of ancestors living in a spirit world destined to replace the world Natives inhabited, the Ghost Dance was first performed among Nevada Paiute in 1889 and spread quickly among Native communities throughout the West. Inspired by the prophet Wovoka, the Ghost Dance promoted spiritual unity among diverse tribes, a new era of harmony among Native and Anglo-Americans, a cessation of white territorial expansion, and the rebuilding of Native communities. Although Wokova preached peace and cooperation with Anglo-Americans, the Lakota Sioux performed a version of the dance that incorporated apocalyptic prophecies about the removal of Anglo-Americans from Native lands. Frightened by the fervor that accompanied the Ghost Dance among the Sioux in 1890, and by the Ghost shirts that some of the Sioux believed would protect them from bullets, agents from the United States Bureau of Indian Affairs attempted to ban performances (Figure 11.1). In December of that year, federal troops fearful of being attacked by Ghost Dancers, killed at least one hundred and fifty Lakota Sioux, including women and children, camped at Wounded Knee in South Dakota.

The Ghost Dance reveals the role that religion played in Native communities, and their desperate effort to withstand American expansion. Throughout the nineteenth century, both Native and Anglo-Americans drew upon religious ideas and practices as they sought to uphold their communities, defend different visions of what it meant to live on the land, and interact with outsiders. In this conflicted context, religion served

Figure 11.1 Participants in the Ghost Dance of 1890 believed that shirts like this one rendered their wearers bulletproof.

as a justification for colonization, oppression, segregation and slaughter, but also as a resource for resisting imperialism and imagining community survival.

Religion and Race: Slavery and Segregation

Efforts to envision an America that made room for a multiplicity of religious communities and cultural identities during the nineteenth century were complicated not only by ambitions for the acquisition of new territory and anxieties about the flourishing of "Anglo-Saxon civilization," but also by the persistence and expansion of slavery. Although slavery was outlawed in most Northern states by the early nineteenth century, it remained legal in the South and in some western territories until 1865. As it developed in eighteenth-and early nineteenth-century America, slavery was increasingly defined in terms of race, with proponents arguing that Africans were an inferior class of humanity whose enslavement by whites was consonant with God's will. Religion was often at the center of controversies about whether or not slavery should endure as a facet of the United States' social and economic structure in the decades leading up to the Civil War, inspiring both indignation against the "peculiar institution" and impassioned defenses of its economic, social and spiritual benefits.

As a modern system of labor control that also enabled whites to enforce racial segregation and regulate the conduct (including the religious lives) of blacks, slavery, in the view of some supporters, seemed an ideal institution for promoting the economic welfare and social stability of the United States while also exposing enslaved Africans and their descendants to the blessings of Christian faith. In his *Exposition of the Views of the Baptists Relative to the Coloured Population* (1822), Baptist minister Richard Furman argued that slavery was both economically essential and morally justified.

A slave master, Furman contended, was to "be the guardian and even father of his slaves," providing for those who were weak, sick, aged or disabled, and offering "religious instruction ... from right sources.. where they will not be in danger of having their minds corrupted by sentiments unfriendly to the domestic and civil peace of the community." If masters complied with their paternalistic duties, Furman implied, slaves would receive the benefits of physical wellbeing and spiritual training, while the over-class would ensure the security of the state.

Presbyterian pastor George D. Armstrong articulated a similar position in *The Christian Doctrine of Slavery* (1858). Arguing that the Bible never condemned slavery, Armstrong claimed that Christians ought to embrace the practice as an opportunity to preach the "Gospel of God's grace" to "deeply degraded" slaves and to *protect* them against economic oppression. Emancipation, in his view, would have disastrous consequences for "the partially civilized slave race." Without a system of enforced segregation and labor control, he suggested, African Americans would face "inevitable destruction" because of their inability to interact appropriately with the "much more highly civilized" Anglo-Saxon people. Slavery, from this perspective, was a God-given blessing for African Americans because it required whites to provide for their basic needs and establish communal structures that enabled them to overcome "the debasing effects of generations of sin" through participation in "the Church of the Lord Jesus Christ."

Both Furman and Armstrong wrote their apologies for slavery in response to critiques of the system, many of which were also rooted in religious sensibilities. Many Protestants had been expressing opposition to slavery for decades, and a number of anti-slavery societies based on religious principles were established in the early nineteenth century. The American Colonization Society (ACS), founded by Presbyterian pastor Robert Finley in 1816, endeavored to purchase slaves from their masters and send them to Africa to establish a Christian colony. From the perspective of ACS supporters, colonization solved the problem of racial segregation by avoiding the need to imagine and construct a bi-racial society; it gave freed blacks an opportunity to return to their homeland and establish their own, independent state and culture; and promoted the goal of Christian mission: Liberia would be the base of operations for evangelizing the African continent.

By 1825, all of the major white Protestant denominations had officially endorsed the ACS. This unity proved short-lived, however, as the cotton industry based on slave labor expanded and several different groups grew disenchanted with colonization as a strategy for coping with slavery. White churches in the South began to withdraw their support from the ACS in the early 1830s, following slave rebellions that frightened many whites, especially in communities where blacks outnumbered them. Over the next several decades, bitter battles between pro- and anti-slavery factions took place among the Baptists, Methodists, and Presbyterians that resulted in schisms between the northern and southern branches of these denominations.

Abolitionists also grew impatient with the ACS in the 1830s. Although the Society had succeeded in gaining Congressional support for relocating blacks to Liberia, many of those who immigrated were free blacks, not redeemed slaves. In fact, the Colonization Society had purchased very few slaves – in the view of detractors, they were not making a dent. The strategy of gradual emancipation was too slow and too conservative. Abolitionists led by William Lloyd Garrison, Sojourner Truth, Theodore Dwight Weld, and Angelina and Sarah Grimke, all of whom had close connections with revivalist evangelicalism, began to agitate for "immediate emancipation" of all slaves, without compensation for slave holders. Slavery, they insisted, was not only inhumane, it was a sin. "Slavery is a crime against God and man," wrote Quaker abolitionist Angelina Grimke in her *Appeal to the Christian Women of the South* (1836). In the view of many abolitionists, Christian community and slavery were antithetical.

Abolition attracted a wide range of followers, but it also caused marked consternation among many Christians. Even those who condemned slavery as a moral evil often refrained from calling for immediate emancipation, and only a minority of white abolitionists considered blacks as equals. While some northern churches passed anti-slavery resolutions, not a single Protestant denomination took a public stand in favor of immediate emancipation. Many churches struggled with affirming even more moderate forms of resistance to slavery. Some white Protestants inherited a sense of responsibility for maintaining the political order and upholding the stability of society. Although Protestants participated in benevolent activities of many kinds – advocating on behalf of temperance and bodily purity, or engaging in the reform of common schools, or even promoting better treatment for the mentally ill – none of these campaigns posed challenges to existing social hierarchies or threatened the political security of the young nation.

But the liberation of enslaved Africans did promise to upset the economic, social, and political status quo. Indeed, some proponents of abolition, both black and white, embraced the cause precisely because they believed that immediate emancipation would usher in a more just, equitable and racially integrated social order. For some, such as the Grimke sisters, the Christian scriptures provided inspiration for imagining a society in which African Americans would be treated as equals. African Americans were also adept at emphasizing the egalitarian tendencies inherent in certain interpretations of the Bible. During the early nineteenth century, unprecedented numbers of African Americans living in the South converted to evangelical forms of Christianity, primarily through the efforts of Baptist and Methodist missionaries. Unlike the staid, hierarchical Anglicanism that had dominated southern religion throughout the eighteenth century, the ardent evangelicalism of the Baptists and Methodists resonated with traditional African spirituality and offered the possibility of a universal fellowship that subverted established notions of racial inferiority. The "slave religion" that flourished during this period enabled African Americans to shape a religious identity relevant to their situation as a subjugated people. By blending elements of evangelicalism with insights from their own spiritual and cultural traditions, slaves "made Christianity truly their own," celebrating in particular those portions of the biblical narrative that stressed spiritual equality and promised liberation from oppression. "In the midst of slavery," historian Al Raboteau has argued, "religion was for slaves a source of meaning, freedom and transcendence" (2004: 317).

For some African Americans, Christian faith was also a catalyst for rebellion. Inspired by the Exodus story in which God delivered the Israelites from bondage in Egypt, Denmark Vesey, a free black carpenter and leader within the African Methodist Episcopal Church in Charleston, South Carolina, preached that God would free enslaved Africans from their captivity on American plantations. His incendiary message infuriated white authorities. In 1822, Vesey and a group of his followers were accused of plotting a slave revolt and sentenced to death. After the executions, the Charleston AME church was destroyed. Several years later, Baptist slave preacher Nat Turner claimed that he had received a vision from God instructing him to mount an insurrection against his white oppressors. On August 21, 1831, Turner and his co-conspirators began liberating fellow slaves in Southampton County, Virginia, killing any whites with whom they came into contact. Although the rebellion was quickly crushed by a local militia, white authorities and angry mobs continued to hunt down and assassinate potential supporters – many of whom were entirely innocent – until Turner himself was captured and executed several months later.

While African Americans like Vesey and Turner interpreted Christianity as a force for freedom, others condemned American churches as utterly and irredeemably implicated in the perpetuation of oppression. In his *Narrative of the Life of an American Slave* (1845), abolitionist leader Frederick Douglass railed against the "corrupt, slaveholding, women-whipping, cradle-plundering, partial and hypocritical Christianity of this land." Rather than working to liberate the captives, Douglass declared, Christian churches, both north and south, provided slave masters with "religious sanction and support" for cruelty and barbarity. Although Douglass himself had become a licensed preacher in the African Methodist Episcopal Zion Church after his escape from slavery in 1838, he eventually denounced "colored churches" for helping to sustain segregation and, in so doing, upholding the ideology of racial inequality.

Other African Americans argued that black churches provided participants with opportunities for leadership and autonomy unavailable in predominantly white houses of worship. Free blacks in the North had begun organizing independent churches in the 1790s in opposition to discriminatory policies within the white denominations. After a conflict over segregated seating in St. George's Methodist Church (Philadelphia, PA), black preachers Richard Allen and Absalom Jones founded the Free African Society in 1787, a Christian community for African Americans. Jones established the first black Episcopal church in 1794, and Allen organized the first black denomination, the African Methodist Episcopal Church in 1816. Several years later, in 1821, a group of black worshippers in New York City formed another influential black denomination, the African Methodist Episcopal Zion Church.

In the first half of the nineteenth century, these religious communities played a crucial part in shaping African-American identity. After the Civil War, black churches became even more effective vehicles of political, social and spiritual formation. Emancipated slaves swelled the ranks of black Baptist and Methodist churches, finding opportunities in these institutions to exercise agency and independence without white oversight. Following the failure of Reconstruction to establish a multi-racial society, the church emerged as "the most powerful institution of racial self-help in the African American community" (Higginbotham 1993: 1). When the passage of discriminatory Jim Crow laws in the 1880s and 1890s reinforced racial segregation and restricted blacks from virtually all forms of political life, African-American religious organizations remained one of the few public arenas available for the expression and cultivation of black leadership and collective consciousness.

For some, such as Baptist leader Booker T. Washington, the black church served as an important forum for inculcating the Christian virtues of self-discipline, diligence and patience in the face of oppression–characteristics that would enable African Americans to work successfully within the system of a segregationist society. Others drew on Christian faith and church experiences in order to resist racism and to work toward an equitable political and social order. Leaders in the National Baptist Convention, USA, founded in 1895 as the largest African-American religious organization in the United States, actively opposed "the debilitating intent and effects of American racial exclusivism" (Higginbotham 1993: 6). Drawing upon the Bible, participants in this and other black religious associations argued that segregation and racial prejudice were unjust and fundamentally anti-Christian.

Disagreements within the African-American community about the implications of the Christian faith for coping with or countering discrimination illustrate the vital importance of religion in late-nineteenth-century disputes over the issue of race in American politics and society. During the era of American Empire, the question of how to structure relations between white and black Americans was often, if not always, religiously inflected. Those in favor of slavery and segregation found support for their position in the Christian scriptures. Racial inequality, in this view, was a divinely mandated social order. Some abolitionists and many African-American Christians reversed this reading of the Bible, insisting that freedom, justice, and equity for and among all human beings were the central themes of the Christian message. Although the United States Constitution outlawed slavery in 1865, proponents of a multi-racial America were a long way from achieving their goal at the turn of the twentieth century. In the ongoing battle to create an integrated society, religion would continue to play a critical, and often contested, part.

Religion and Gender: Protestants and "Domesticity"

The biblically-based arguments that abolitionists and African-American Christians offered in favor of freedom and equality inspired some reformers to address other disparities of power in nineteenth-century society. When sisters Angelina and Sarah Grimke challenged the institution of slavery on Christian grounds, for example, they simultaneously insisted that the Bible offered resources for rethinking prevailing ideologies of gender. In fulfilling their Christian duty to fight for the immediate emancipation of slaves, the Grimke sisters embarked on a speaking tour of the Northern states in 1836 that violated social conventions prohibiting women from publicly addressing mixed audiences.

This breach of propriety sparked one of the first public debates about women's rights in American history. Religion was a central theme in this disputation, as contestants on all sides of the issue invoked scriptural evidence in support of their conflicting positions. In July, 1837, the General Association of Congregational Ministers of Massachusetts issued a "Pastoral Letter" condemning the Grimke sisters' behavior as damaging to the structures of Christian community outlined in the Bible. "We invite your attention to the dangers which at present seem to threaten the female character with wide-spread and permanent injury," they wrote.

> The appropriate duties and influence of women are clearly stated in the New Testament. Those duties are unobtrusive and private, but the sources of *mighty power*. When the

mild, *dependent*, softening influence of woman upon the sternness of man's opinions is fully exercised, society feels the effects of it in a thousand ways.

The ministers' statement illumines several prominent assumptions about women and their relationship to American society that were extremely influential through-out the nineteenth century. Driven in part by the shift from an agricultural to an industrial economy in which men increasingly worked outside the home and women were charged with the education of children, the "doctrine of separate spheres" insisted that the public domain was the province of men, while the domestic sphere was woman's place. This division between the public world of affairs and the private realm of the home contained within it another important supposition: that a prop-erly ordered household served as a model of Christian community. The "cult of domesticity" upheld the home as the seat of religion, virtue and morality. Within this private, domestic arena, women were called to exercise their moral influence upon family members, servants and guests. Through their influence within the home, promoters of this ideology asserted, women had the power to transform individual character and even public culture. This conception of women's mission rested upon a third assumption about woman's nature. According to the "cult of true womanhood," woman's "natural" dependence and weakness were signs of her moral purity and spiritual superiority. Women, in this view, were inherently more attuned to the emotions, to the sentiments of the heart, and especially to religion. Because of their heightened sensitivity to affections and to spiritual realities, women were more capable of redeeming individuals and society through their virtuous example.

While these ideas were not entirely new, they took on a particular force in the early nineteenth century as they crystallized into a "domestic ideology" intended to be a powerful stabilizing force in the rapidly expanding American Empire. The domestic ideology also stipulated a corresponding collection of assumptions and prescriptions about manhood and proper male behavior. Where women were thought to be inher-ently dependent, submissive, passive, and self-sacrificing, men were supposed to be essentially autonomous, assertive, active and self-interested. Because of male partici-pation in the public domain, white middle-class masculinity, in particular, was associ-ated with ambition, competition and production, qualities a man needed to possess and exercise in order to succeed in the ruthless arenas of republican politics and entrepreneurial capitalism. Although early-nineteenth-century Protestants recog-nized the importance of "manly passions" for economic advancement and political achievement, they simultaneously condemned these characteristics as signs of a cor-rupt and sinful nature. Unless male aggression and avarice were appropriately chan-neled through the discipline of self-mastery, they might wreak havoc with the social order. In order to contain the potentially destructive possibilities of masculine pas-sions, the domestic ideology dictated that men's selfish impulses were subject to the chastening influence of female virtue within the home, and, as historian Anthony Rotundo has put it, "symbolically quarantined by the separation of spheres" (1993: 245). By segregating the public realm from the private, aspiring middle-class Protestants found a way to assuage the ambivalences associated with male passions and to achieve productivity without sacrificing social stability, pious morality, or reli-gious community.

Like all dominant cultural dogmas, the domestic ideology provoked several competing interpretations of Christian community. Opponents such as the Grimkes argued vehemently against the grounding assumptions that delineated male and female nature and isolated the aggressive public realm from the private religious sphere. In her response to the "Pastoral Letter," Sarah Grimke rejected the differentiation between "feminine" and "masculine" virtue, along with the idea that Christian community should not intrude into politics and public life. "Where does God say that he made any distinction between us, as moral and intelligent beings?" she demanded. Because men and women were created equal in "all respects" (except in the area of physical strength or "brute force"), they were endowed with the same inalienable natural rights and the same obligations to participate in public life. In fact, Grimke asserted, a woman who refrained from engaging in public reform efforts such as abolition abdicated her God-given responsibility and failed to fulfill "one of the important duties laid upon her as an accountable being."

For Angelina and Sarah Grimke, the domestic ideology was a fiercely repressive social philosophy that created a false, unbiblical distinction between women and men, and undermined women's agency by circumscribing them within the home. Others insisted that the tenets of the domestic ideology – and particularly its claims about woman's superior moral nature – provided a platform for asserting that the future of American society was dependent upon the influence of women. The greatest spokesperson for this interpretation of the domestic ideology was Catharine Beecher, the daughter of famous revivalist preacher Lyman Beecher, and novelist Harriet Beecher Stowe's older sister. In contrast to the Grimkes, Beecher asserted that the doctrine of separate spheres, the idea that the home is the ideal model for society, and the belief in the moral superiority of women offered women powerfully influential roles as agents of social and political change. She argued that it was precisely *because* women were restricted to the domestic arena that they could exercise a reforming influence on society. Against the corruption of the male-dominated political sphere, Beecher lifted up the home as a pure, moral realm – a place set apart that sheltered its inhabitants from the temptations of the world. Since women who remained in the private, domestic sphere avoided the pollutions of the public domain – the vices of democratic politics and the materialism of capitalist economic culture – they were "uniquely qualified" to serve as mirrors to corrupt society and as stabilizing forces for the young nation. By cultivating their unique and superior moral and spiritual sensibility within the domestic sphere, Beecher proclaimed, women would have a far-ranging influence beyond that arena.

Beecher was a strong proponent of female education. Because they were responsible for training young people to become virtuous citizens, women needed instruction in academic, not just "ornamental" subjects. In addition to studying music and French, Beecher argued, women should engage in intellectual pursuits customarily restricted to men, such as chemistry and moral philosophy. Mary Lyon, who founded Mount Holyoke seminary in 1837, also viewed women's education as a natural outgrowth of the domestic ideology. "Woman, elevated by the Christian religion, was designed by Providence as the principal educator of our race," Lyon declared. "From her entrance on womanhood to the end of her life, this is to be her great business." Like Beecher, Lyon believed that the collective efforts of a class of pure and pious teachers would gradually transform American culture. By creating a school of the highest intellectual order, Lyon aimed to equip women as missionaries to help esta-blish Christian communities all over the world.

Competing interpretations of the domestic ideology demonstrate the complex con-nections between Christian faith and gender politics in nineteenth-century America. Both advocates and opponents of domesticity defended their arguments about the nature, rights and responsibilities of women and men on biblical grounds. As the century progressed, new religious movements such as Spiritualism, Utopian Perfec-tionism, and Mormonism also engaged in efforts to revise prevailing assumptions about gender and religious community.

Religion and Gender: New Religious Movements, Immigrants and "Domesticity"

In March of 1848, Kate and Margaret Fox, two young women from upstate New York, claimed that they had developed a system for communicating with the dead. The Fox sisters inspired a host of women to become "spirit mediums," a role for which they were especially suited, proponents suggested, because of their "natural" piety and "superior" sensitivity to the spiritual realm. Unlike the Grimke sisters, who insisted that they had a right to address mixed audiences because they were equal with men, Spiritualist women claimed that their distinctly feminine characteristics qualified them to serve as public religious leaders. While their primary concern was religious, Spiritualist interpretations of the cult of true womanhood had radical social and politi-cal implications. In order to fully express their God-given capacities, Spiritualist argued, women needed to be liberated from all constraints that might impede their ability to communicate directly with the spirits. Because they insisted on the impor-tance of women's autonomy, Spiritualists became ardent supporters of women's rights, advocating for economic, political and social reforms that would emancipate women from unequal marriages, provide them better education and health care, and protect them from financial and sexual exploitation.

A number of other religious movements echoed Spiritualist critiques of conven-tional marriage and family life. In 1844, John Humphrey Noyes, a radical evangelical who was dismissed from Yale Divinity School in 1834 for declaring his belief in his own sinless perfection, established a community characterized by what he called "biblical communism" at Putney, Vermont. Participants in this utopian experiment, which moved to Oneida, New York, in 1847, adopted a series of practices designed to transform the existing social order by abolishing structures that caused discord; particularly private property, marriage, and gender roles rooted in the domestic ide-ology. Believing that they were charged with the task of establishing the kingdom of God on earth, Noyes and the Oneida Perfectionists turned to the New Testament Book of Acts as a model for their society. In addition to embracing communal owner-ship of material goods, Bible communists asserted that "the Community principle" they observed among the early Christians applied to persons as well as property. "Complex marriage," Noyes declared, abolished "exclusiveness in regard to women and children" by insisting that all adult members of the community were married to each other and could "express their unity" by engaging in sexual relations with multiple partners. In contrast to the "worldly social system" which promoted strife, jealousy, sexual frustration, social ills, and the oppression of women, complex marriage encouraged harmony, generosity, satisfaction, health and "a true union of the sexes."

Restoring "true relations" between men and women also involved revising prevailing gender norms. The Oneida community, like many other nineteenth-century socialist and utopian movements, challenged the doctrine of separate spheres, the cult of domesticity, and dominant ideals of "true" womanhood and manhood. Because all members of the community were expected to work collectively to make the venture a success, the division of labor into male and female domains broke down: both women and men engaged in "domestic" tasks as well as in manufacturing, farming, administration, and governance. Biblical communism and complex marriage also redefined home and family, stretching the boundaries of these institutions in ways that undermined conventional beliefs about the household as the model for and source of the good society. Finally, belief in the possibility of Christian perfection prompted Noyes and his followers to conceive of their community as a spiritual hierarchy in which individuals progressed through the ranks of "ascending fellowship." Ironically, then, Oneida preserved a system of inequality in the spiritual realm. Rather than erasing or leveling gender distinctions in this arena, Noyes actually asserted that men were spiritually superior to women and therefore naturally higher in the hierarchy.

Noyes was not the only nineteenth-century religious leader to reverse common assumptions about the spiritual superiority of women. Mormons, too, challenged the cult of true womanhood, arguing that the domestic ideology emasculated men, contradicted biblical conceptions of patriarchy and even threatened the stability of the social order. By asserting women's spiritual pre-eminence and dominion within the home, some Mormons asserted, conventional gender ideals inappropriately subjected men to female authority and subverted the "eternal laws of order, and of God" which gave men the right and responsibility to rule their families. The institution of marriage legalized this "ruinous, disorganizing, debasing principle" of female "power" and in so doing, poisoned society and proved destructive to the "whole nation." The solution to this problem, suggested Mormon writer Udney Jacob in *The Peace Maker, or, The Doctrines of the Millennium* (1842), was to reinstate the "divine pattern" of polygamy. Although he initially disavowed Jacob's text, Joseph Smith, Jr., the first prophet and founder of the Church of Jesus Christ of Latter Day Saints (1830), embraced the practice of "plural marriage" after receiving a revelation indicating that polygamy was a God-given law that must be obeyed. Although Smith never publicly defended plural marriage, his successor Brigham Young actively promoted the practice after leading the Mormon community to Utah, where the LDS church sought to reconfigure society on a theocratic, patriarchal model based on the Hebrew scriptures.

Opponents of both complex and plural marriage couched their criticisms in religious and political terms. The practices of "free love" and polygamy, detractors argued, contradicted Christian faith and threatened the character of American culture. Often, critics equated polygamy with slavery, characterizing both as "relics of barbarism" that besmirched "Christian civilization." Although polygamy was legally banned in all United States territories in 1862, the LDS church continued to defend the practice, arguing that plural marriage was a matter of religious freedom protected by the Constitution and an obligation of religious faith mandated by the Scriptures. In 1879, the Supreme Court upheld the constitutionality of anti-polygamy laws. That same year, John Humphrey Noyes fled the county to avoid arrest on charges of statutory rape. Several months later, he directed his followers to stop engaging in complex marriage. The LDS Church tried to resist governmental pressure to abandon polygamy for several more years, but finally renounced the practice in 1890 after the Supreme Court again upheld legislation outlawing plural marriage, disenfranchising polygamists, and allowing for the confiscation of church property. By declaring that he received a revelation from Jesus Christ commanding that the church "cease the practice and submit to the law," LDS president Wilford Woodruff paved the way for Mormons to assert their status as loyal American citizens and as faithful Christians – a project that they embraced wholeheartedly in the years to come.

Religious conflict over gender norms and sexual ethics during the nineteenth century was not confined to Protestants. Jews and Catholics who migrated to America over the course of the century carried with them a range of distinctive gender ideals and practices, some of which seemed to contradict prevailing Protestant assumptions about community order and proper relations between the sexes. Newcomers frequently encountered hostility from Anglo-American Protestants who saw these "foreigners" as a threat to national cohesiveness and stability. In this charged and often hostile environment, Jews and Catholics often stressed the continuities between their conceptions of gender and dominant Protestant notions, downplaying or changing those religious practices that appeared to clash with the cults of domesticity, true womanhood and virile masculinity.

The American Protestant was the organ of the American Protestant Association, formed in 1842 for the purpose of curtailing the growth of Catholicism in the United States. The APA, following the lead of anti-clericalists a half-century earlier, sought to discredit the Catholic Church by raising suspicions about the motives of its ecclesiastical leadership and especially by offering evidence that church leaders sought to frighten people into obedience to them. The magazine, in a commentary on a discovered "Letter from the Devil to the Venerable Sister Maria Crocefissa" stressed the seriousness of the European Catholic program of deception and its importation to America:

> The first thought of the reader as he glances at this letter, may be that it is published merely as a burlesque on the Roman Catholic Church. This is not the object. It is an authentic document. It illustrates the "pious frauds" of the Priests, by which they inspire their people with terror, not in the dark ages, but in the nineteenth century. Yes! At the present day ... ("Letter from the Devil," 1845: 153–154)

During the nineteenth century, Jewish communities multiplied as the number of Jews in the United States grew exponentially, from approximately 1,200 in 1780 to over one million by 1898. Many German Jews who migrated in these years were engaged in Reform Judaism, a movement that sought to revise Jewish worship and ritual in keeping with Enlightenment conceptions of reason. Reform rabbi Isaac Meyer Wise advocated a radical restructuring of Jewish religious practice, arguing that traditional modes of piety were archaic and untenable within a modern American context. Particularly problematic, from this point of view, was the exclusion of women from participation in public worship. Overturning centuries of Jewish tradition that segregated women from men in the synagogue, requiring them to sit silently behind a veil in the balcony so that they would not distract men from their prayers, reformers like Wise promoted mixed seating and also encouraged women to become more active in community life. These innovations helped allay concerns that Jews were at odds with dominant Protestant ideals of religious community that highlighted female piety. "In a society where women were celebrated for their spiritual influence and piety, it was difficult to defend practices that seemed to deny the fullness of female spirituality," historian Karla Goldman has written. For these nineteenth-century Jewish immigrants, she argues, "the reordering of gender was central to the process of Americanization" (Goldman 2000: 17, 9).

Not all American Jews supported the Reform agenda. Committed to the preservation of traditional forms of community life, other Jews emphasized the observance of dietary and Sabbath observances, the ritual bath following menstruation to preserve marital purity, and the separation of men and women in the synagogue. While Reform leaders seeking respectability within American society rejected these activities as embarrassing forms of superstition that ought to be abandoned, other Jews insisted that these rituals were essential to Jewish identity. Jewish immigrants from Russia and Eastern Europe who arrived in the United States during the 1880s and 1890s were especially alarmed by what they saw as excessive accommodation to American culture on the part of more assimilated Jews. Rosa Sonneschein, an emigrant from Hungary who founded the first English language publication for Jewish women in the United States, welcomed expanded opportunities for women associated with acculturation, but lamented the "destruction of belief in religious ceremonials ... of which women were the sacred keepers and safeguards from time immemorial" (quoted in Braude 1981: 171).

Catholic immigrants also confronted external pressure to conform to Protestant gender norms, and division arose among different ethnic communities over the limits and legitimacy of assimilating to American cultural expectations. During the middle decades of the nineteenth century, several million European Catholics migrated to the United States, most from Germany and Ireland. In order to allay the rampant fears of "nativist" Protestants, Irish Catholics, in particular, promoted integration into the dominant American culture on multiple levels. From the mid-nineteenth century on, for example, Irish Catholic priests, novelists, and educated lay people promoted a version of domesticity that celebrated the home as a hallowed sphere mirroring the divine, hierarchical order of heaven. Although men held ultimate authority in their households in keeping with the biblical, patriarchal model, women were charged with the sacred responsibility of nurturing pious children who would mature into good Catholics and virtuous citizens. A "Christian mother," according to one Catholic advice manual, made "maternity a priesthood" by pouring the "faith of Christ into the very veins of her child as she nurses him at her breast" (quoted in McDannell 1989: 61). By maintaining a clean, well-ordered home in which husbands could rest from their labor and children would learn the habits of discipline and self-control, women also contributed to the stability of society. According to proponents of Catholic domesticity, the family served as a "nursery of the nation" rather than a threat to American culture.

From this perspective, Protestant fears that allegiance to the Roman papacy and clerical hierarchy undercut a Catholic's loyalty to the United States and subverted his ability to participate in the democratic process were unfounded. Nor could stereotypes of Catholics as lazy, slovenly drunkards be justified. Thanks to their women, Catholic men could become reliable contributors to the economy and upstanding citizens of the United States. Although Protestants remained suspicious of the Catholic Church as an institution, and derided practices such as celibacy for clergy and women religious, the strong focus on the Catholic family helped mitigate these concerns and aided immigrant Catholics in their quest for acceptance within American society.

By the late nineteenth century, however, new communities of immigrant Catholics from Eastern and Southern Europe challenged the ideals of domesticity and assimilation that Irish Catholic leaders championed. Polish and Italian Catholics, for example, strongly resisted the push to abandon traditional worship and devotional practices that both American Protestants and "Americanized" Catholics scorned as retrograde and overly emotional. Rather than integrating into Anglo-American culture or embracing a more "modern" and universal form of Catholicism, many Eastern and Southern European immigrants isolated themselves into ethnic parishes and fought to retain distinctive and often profoundly gendered forms of piety that set them apart from both Protestants and their fellow Catholics. In Northeastern urban centers, for example, Italian Catholics expressed their religiosity through elaborate street processions and festivals celebrating the Virgin Mary and other beloved saints; a practice that the Catholic hierarchy consistently condemned.

Mexican Catholics who were incorporated into the United States through southwestern territorial expansion over the course of the nineteenth century also came into conflict with the Irish Catholic church leaders who advocated assimilation and Americanization. Because Mexican Catholics emphasized miracles, pilgrimages, festivals, saints, and home-centered piety, both Protestants and Catholic modernizers denounced their religious practice as a form of "medieval" superstition. In this view, Mexican Americans, like other inhabitants of the Southwest, were a threat to the cohesion of American culture and needed to be "civilized." During the second half of the nineteenth century, Irish Catholic priests participated actively in this project, encouraging Mexicans to adopt more "acceptable" forms of devotional piety and to reorient their religious life from home to parish. Mexican Catholics largely resisted these efforts, which continued well into the twentieth century despite a growing concern among Catholic leaders about the anti-Catholic bent of US imperialism during the Spanish-American War (1898).

Debates over gender and assimilation among immigrant communities expose the enduring centrality of religion in the process of imagining the meaning of America during the latter decades of the nineteenth century. Just as Native, African, and Anglo-Protestant Americans drew upon the resources of religious tradition and innovation in their efforts to endorse, challenge or simply survive customary social structures, so Catholic and Jewish newcomers to the United States saw religion as an essential means of adapting to, and sometimes resisting the influence of, the dominant culture of the American Empire. For all nineteenth-century Americans, the on-going project of envisioning, creating, and sustaining a new nation in an age of uncertainty and ambition, of social transformation and dissolution, involved complicated, contentious and creative interactions with religious communities, rituals, and ideas.

References and Further Reading

Andrew, John A., III (1992) *From Revivals to Removal: Jeremiah Evarts, the Cherokee Nation, and the Search for the Soul of America*, Athens, GA: University of Georgia Press.

Braude, Ann (1981) "The Jewish Woman's Encounter with American Culture," in Rosemary Radford Ruether and Rosemary Skinner (eds.) *Women and Religion in America*, vol. 1, *The Nineteenth Century*, San Francisco: Harper & Row, pp. 150–192.

Braude, Ann (2001) *Radical Spirits: Spiritualism and Women's Rights in Nineteenth-Century America*, 2nd edn, Bloomington, IN: Indiana University Press.

Bryant, Joan (1999) "Race and Religion in Nineteenth Century America," in Peter W. Williams (ed.) *Perspectives on American Religion and Culture*, Malden, MA: Blackwell, pp. 246–248.

DeRogatis, Amy (2004) "Gender," in Philip Goff and Paul Harvey (eds.) *Themes in Religion and American Culture*, Chapel Hill, NC: University of North Carolina Press, pp. 197–226.

Fessenden, Tracy (2004) "Race," in Philip Goff and Paul Harvey (eds.) *Themes in Religion and American Culture*, Chapel Hill, NC: University of North Carolina Press, pp. 129–161.

Foster, Lawrence (1984) *Religion and Sexuality: The Shakers, the Mormons and the Oneida Community*, Urbana, IL: University of Illinois Press.

Frey, Sylvia R. and Wood, Betty (1998) *Come Shouting to Zion: African American Protestantism in the American South and British Caribbean to 1830*, Chapel Hill, NC: University of North Carolina Press.

Goldman, Karla (2000) *Beyond the Synagogue Gallery: Finding a Place for Women in American Judaism*, Cambridge, MA: Harvard University Press.

Higginbotham, Evelyn Brooks (1993) *Righteous Discontent: The Women's Movement in the Black Baptist Church, 1880–1920*, Cambridge, MA: Harvard University Press.

Hyman, Paula (1995) *Gender and Assimilation in Modern Jewish History: The Roles and Representation of Women*, Seattle: Washington University Press.

Lerner, Gerda (2004) *The Grimke Sisters from South Carolina: Pioneers for Women's Rights and Abolition*, rev. and expanded, Chapel Hill, NC: University of North Carolina Press.

"Letter from the Devil to the Venerable Sister Maria Crocefissa, from a manuscript account of her life, exhibited by the Priests and Canons of the Cathedral of Girghenti," (1845) *The American Protestant* 1 (October, 1845): 154.

Lincoln, C. Eric and Mamiya, Lawrence H. (1990) *The Black Church and the African American Experience*, Durham, NC: University of North Carolina Press.

Martin, Joel W. (1991) *Sacred Revolt: The Muskogees' Struggle for a New World*, Boston: Beacon Press.

Martin, Joel W. (1997) "Indians, Contact, and Colonialism in the Deep South: Themes for a Postcolonial History of American Religion," in Thomas A. Tweed (ed.) *Retelling U.S. Religious History*, Berkeley, CA: University of California Press.

McDannell, Colleen (1989) "Catholic Domesticity, 1860–1960," in Karen Kennelly (ed.) *American Catholic Women: A Historical Exploration*, New York: Macmillan, pp. 48–80.

McDougall, Walter A. (1997) *Promised Land, Crusader State: The American Encounter with the World Since 1776*, New York: Houghton Mifflin.

McLoughlin, William G. (1984) "Champions of the Cherokees," in *Cherokees and Missionaries, 1789–1839*, Princeton, NJ: Princeton University Press.

McNally, Michael (1999) "Religion and Cultural Change in Native North America," in Peter W. Williams (ed.) *Perspectives on American Religion and Culture*, Malden, MA: Blackwell, pp. 270–286.

Prell, Riv-Ellen (1999) *Fighting to Become Americans: Jews, Gender, and the Anxiety of Assimilation*, Boston: Beacon Press.

Raboteau, Al (2004) *Slave Religion: The "Invisible Institution" in the Antebellum South*, updated edn, New York: Oxford University Press.

Rotundo, E. Anthony (1993) *American Manhood: Transformations in Masculinity from the Revolution to the Modern Era*, New York: Basic Books.

Sklar, Kathryn Kish (1973) *Catherine Beecher: A Study in American Domesticity*, New Haven, CT: Yale University Press.

Welter, Barbara (1966) "The Cult of True Womanhood, 1820–1860," *American Quarterly*, 18: 151–174.

12

Practice

Christopher White

As the embodiment of cosmology and forms of community, religious practice changed in many ways during the nineteenth century. New understandings of the body led to new bodily exercises in devotion, and as the scope of bodily perform- ances in worship was enlarged, the material culture of religion – the sounds of music and singing, the sight of holy art, the smells of things, and so forth – became more elaborate and sophisticated. Americans sometimes drew their inspiration for religious practice directly from their belief in the supernatural to direct their lives, while at other times they joined scientific ideas to established traditions to create new forms of practice. Euroamerican encounters with Native Americans, and the close associations between whites and African Americans in slave as well as free contexts provided the settings for important developments in the ways people lived their religions, and in some cases taught lessons to both sides about what was not beneficial. Gender had always been crucial in marking out the territory of reli- gious practice, but immigration underscored its importance. Catholic immigrants, often led by women, organized their very public devotional lives around trans- planted local devotions, Jewish women performed more private domestic rituals (among other things), and Protestant women became more involved in preaching and healing. As the country adopted more explicitly imperialistic leanings, reli- gious practice for dominant majorities, regionally and nationally, came to reflect a confidence in practical improvement, American power, and national destiny.

In nineteenth-century America, religious practices diversified and changed as immi- gration increased and as American Protestants moved west and south, encountering Native Americans, African Americans, Catholics and others. The first moment of dra- matic change, though, and the first section of this chapter, concerns remarkable changes within Protestantism, changes caused by Protestant revivals that swept the nation in the early decades of the century. This was a time of dramatic growth and diversification in American Christianity, a time that stimulated thinking about faith, ritual and ecstatic worship practices and ways of interpreting them. But after the revivals died down, there were other dramatic changes coming. The century began on a note of exploration and expansion, and it was not just Lewis and Clark's expedition (1803–06) in the West that turned attention to the untamed wilderness in the country's vast interior. At the same time, Protestants moved out onto two frontiers, the South and the West, and, in the crucible of encounter with non-evangelicals, they forged new, hybrid devotional styles that are examined in section two of this chapter. These encounters also stimulated new religious practices of resistance and revolt among those peoples evangelicals wanted to civilize or convert. In the third and final section, one last change, the rise of the city, is examined. New American cities promoted new thinking about religious practices and sacred spaces and created the conditions for a new consumer culture that reshaped holidays and other religious celebrations.

Body and Spirit in the Early Republic

Probably the most dramatic development in early nineteenth-century American religious history was the emergence of a culture of religious revival that fostered new ways of thinking about worship practices. Historians have pointed to different sources of these dramatic religious revivals – an egalitarianism abetted by Revolutionary discourses on freedom and liberty; a religious individualism that made colonial Calvinist regimes seem elitist and in other ways unappealing; and a religious experimentalism that emerged during frontier forays into the unchurched West, where daily piety was improvised and, inevitably, more free-wheeling. Surveying a vast landscape of visions, dreams and prophesies, Nathan Hatch and Ann Taves recently demonstrated that Americans in this period, eager to put behind them respectable churches and frowning clergymen, found in ecstatic revival experiences new forms of spiritual assurance. One of them, Henry Alline, discovered that the Calvinism of his youth had deprived his soul of God's love. Now free of old constraints, his soul was "ravished with a divine ecstasy beyond any doubts or fears, or thoughts of being then deceived." He and others blamed Calvinist clergymen for cramping their minds with ordered schemes of religious experience and rigid theological systems. For such believers, visions, dreams and other revival-inspired illuminations became normal channels of divine guidance. "I know the word of God is our infallible guide, and by it we are to try all our dreams and feelings," the Methodist believer Freeborn Garrettson conceded. "I also know," he added defiantly, that "things of a divine nature have been revealed to me" (Hatch 1989: 10). Ecstatic revival experiences revealed new things.

Many of the revived, like Freeborn Garrettson, were certain that the somatic performances accompanying revivals were signs that the spirit was acting in the self. The revivalist Barton Stone wrote:

> Many, very many fell down, as men slain in battle, and continued for hours together in an apparently breathless and motionless state – sometimes for a few moments reviving, and exhibiting symptoms of life by a deep groan, or piercing shriek, or by a prayer for mercy most fervently uttered. After lying thus for hours, they obtained deliverance. The gloomy cloud, which had covered their faces, seemed gradually and visibly to disappear, and hope in smiles brightened into joy – they would rise shouting deliverance.

Stone knew that only the power of the Holy Spirit could account for the ways believers were struck down in this way. He was not the only one to see theological meaning in these surprising bodily behaviors. Richard McNemar, a former Presbyterian revivalist and Shaker convert also writing about early nineteenth-century revivals, had noticed that ecstatic experiences often surprised sinners. Tepid revival participants, he noted, sometimes found themselves stricken by the spirit, forced into "demeaning and mortifying" postures that included "the jerks." "The exercise commonly began in the head which would fly backward and forward, and from side to side, with a quick jolt, which the person would naturally labor to suppress, but in vain; and the more any one labored to stay himself, and be sober, the more he staggered, and the more rapidly his twitches increased." Read in these ways, revival practices were divine ways of disciplining the self. But for some the jerks were merely a prelude to more intense fleshly mortifications. A select few were afflicted with "the *barks*," surely a humiliating chastisement, and obviously apparent in believers who suddenly would "take the position of a canine beast, move about on all fours, growl, snap the teeth, and bark" (Schmidt 2001: xxiv). God moved swiftly if he could convict sinners of their worthlessness or make them identify finally with the suffering Christ. He used bodily exercises to change people.

Of course, interpreting correctly God's signs in the body was never easy. Ecstatic experiences didn't seem always to produce enduring spiritual changes; and some observers hypothesized that they could be created merely by wishful thinking, vain imaginations or overly-agitated nervous systems. Though believers had different ways of discriminating true experiences from false ones, many turned to science, and scientific psychologies in particular, to understand with certainty how God operated in the self. Early in the century, many turned to sciences such as phrenology. Taking "the Bible for his chart in theology; Christ as his pattern in divinity; and Phrenology as his guide in Philosophy," the well-known Universalist writer George Weaver, for example, promoted phrenology because it linked body, mind and spirit. "There can be no doubt," Weaver insisted, "that every exertion of the intellect, every flight of the imagination, … every feeling of sympathy, every emotion of joy or pleasure, calls into action some portion of the physical organism." Was it possible, then, to see in the outer self certain signs of inner changes? Could, for example, the Holy Spirit's activity in the self change the head physically? A writer for the African-American *Christian Recorder* thought it quite logical that a change as dramatic as conversion might result in physical changes. "I cannot pretend to describe all that change, but I am of the opinion that this emotion rises higher and seems so sweet and new, not only because it is from God and inspired by such grand themes, but also because in its bursting forth it effects some physical change." It is a new growth, a new exercise of the brain's faculties, a truly new birth. This writer offered suggestive evidence. He said that "it is the testimony of all, that in conversion a perceptible change occurs, a change that can be felt." It was common for converts to say that "something seemed to come down and strike me right on the top of my head and run all over." Some said "a ball of fire seemed to strike me on the top of my head" or "the Spirit seemed to touch me on the top of the head." Might these sensations be caused by "the breaking away or releasing of these organs of the brain into joyful exercise?" The top of the head was, after all, the location of the self's spiritual faculties (Figure 12.1). Finally, this writer suggested that the permanence of the change might be explained by a physical change undergirding it (White 2008).

Figure 12.1 Phrenologists mapped out personality traits and dispositions on the human head.

While believers could debate whether Christians regenerated by the Holy Spirit were reshaped physically, many agreed that the outer body, and especially the head, somehow showed signs of saving inner states. Popular phrenologists honed their craft to see clearly signs of counterfeit experiences, deception, and hypocrisy. When lecturing in churches, for instance, some took opportunities to assess the religious merits of ministers and church officials. One phrenologist discovered an enormous organ of Acquisitiveness (greed) on a Methodist minister; he was a thief, and he later admitted as much. Others were surprised to find secret inner sins in outwardly pious preachers. In one shocking public examination of a deacon who handled the church's business affairs, a phrenologist found the man to be "grasping and selfish, but smooth and inclined to be tricky in his dealings." When confronted with this information, onlookers gasped – but they were persuaded when the deacon later disappeared with the church's treasury. On other occasions, itinerant phrenologists advised churchgoers and church officials about personality problems and helped sort sinners from saints (White 2008).

Triumphalist stories circulated about scientific ways of seeing clearly the inner self. Few of them match those of the outspoken former Baptist minister from Vermont, Josiah M. Graves. After lecturing in a Middletown, Connecticut, church sometime around midcentury, Graves had himself blindfolded and offered to perform physiognomic readings. He happened to have an uncle in the congregation, a temperance man and deacon of the church "regarded as a model in most things by every person in all that region." Someone thought it would be amusing to have Graves's uncle step forward, and the uncle obliged. The nephew, Josiah Graves, had a peculiar way of examining people that included rubbing vigorously different parts of the head and sampling resulting odors. He too was a temperance man and interested in particular in detecting the liquor habit, which he did "by rubbing the organ of Alimentiveness" (appetite) and smelling his fingers. He reproduced the procedure on his uncle, to titters of laughter, and announced, "This man drinks!" Shouts of laughter. "He drinks rum, brandy, something hot and alcoholic!" The audience laughed mostly at Graves's eccentricities, but his uncle, feeling the heat of the spotlight, became angry. How could his nephew accuse him of such things? "Now, uncle, I smell the odor of dead liquor when I rub your organ of Alimentiveness, and I believe you have taken liquor within forty-eight hours. On your honor now, in the presence of this painfully silent audience, tell me, have you not taken liquor within forty-eight hours?" After a moment, Graves's uncle admitted he "had a bad turn of colic night before last, and I got up at 12 o'clock and took some brandy and cayenne pepper to relieve it." The audience erupted. Skeptics hooted. Temperance advocates gasped. Everyone else laughed at the embarrassing and anomalous spectacle (White 2008).

But if the body could be an outer sign of inner, religious conditions, it also could be used as a way to stimulate those inner conditions. Fasting and abstemious living have a long history in Christianity, and in the intense revival atmosphere of nineteenth-century America, these practices were revived as additional ways of humbling the self and, some hoped, attracting God's blessings. Historians have long noted how pervasive this practice was especially in southern evangelicalism. Church leaders argued that fasting intensified prayer, humbled believers, and vivified the body. They were not above buttressing their notions with secular, scientific opinion. Fasting, the Princeton Theological Seminary professor Samuel Miller (1769–1850) wrote in 1831, "was founded in the clearest and soundest principles of physiology." Enlightened physicians agreed that fasting tends "to preserve us from the effects of habitual indulgence and repletion," and that it "cannot fail of contributing to the preservation and vigor of our bodily health, as well as preparing our minds for prompt and active application to the most important of all subjects." Reformers and revivalists alike believed that disciplining the body in certain ways, including fasting, enhanced spiritual emotions and dispositions (Griffith 2004: 33–35).

Though many Americans abandoned fasting as too austere by the middle of the nineteenth century, the practice was replaced by an astonishing variety of dietary and body reform movements that linked body control and personal holiness. Starting in the 1830s, Christian physiologists and reformers like William Alcott (1798–1859) and Sylvester Graham (1794–1851) promoted dietary and health reform as a part of a comprehensive plan for physical and spiritual regeneration. These programs of reforming body and spirit had different aspects, including general dietary restraint, the use of whole foods, a vegetarian diet, routine exercise and moderation in sexual relations. Graham, for one, drew on medical and neurological notions about the problems of over-stimulating the self, and he recommended abstaining from anything that would irritate the body and the nervous system, including meat, alcohol, tea, coffee and (of course) sex. Sex – "those LASCIVIOUS DAY-DREAMS, and *amorous reveries*" – a very tempting stimulant indeed, had to be carefully monitored; indulging once a month seemed acceptable. (Older couples could get by on less.) Excessive sex, animal products, spicy foods or stimulating drinks caused unnatural fevers and excitations, leading naturally to malaise or debility. Tight-laced dresses for women also were unnatural (they undoubtedly over-stimulated men as well).

Bodily conditions always had spiritual repercussions. In 1835 and 1836, Alcott, for instance, insisted that eating too much on the Sabbath led to sleepiness in church and obliviousness to the divine truths preached there (Griffith 2004: 45; Abzug 1994: 163-70). Even Christians who didn't consider themselves physiologists picked up these emphases. The great revivalist Charles Finney felt sorry for those who "indulge themselves in a stimulating diet, and in the use of those condiments that irritate and rasp the nervous system." In the end, he was sure, their bodies would become "so fierce and overpowering a source of temptation to the mind, as inevitably to lead it into sin." Many linked diet to salvation: In the 1830s and 1840s, temperance hotels and boarding houses emerged offering Graham's diet; colleges instituted dietary requirements; perfectionist communes with vegetarian menus were organized; new religions sprung up with strict rules about eating and drinking, including the Mormons and the Seventh-Day Adventists. Ellen Gould White (1827–1915), the prophetess of Seventh-Day Adventism, believed vegetarianism was a key way to overcome original sin and usher in the millennium (Gardella 2006: 312–316).

It was not so far from these reflections on diet to an emerging discourse on religion, health and healing, one that became important in the second half of the nineteenth century among both evangelicals and less traditional believers. On the less traditional side, an influential stream of mental-healing movements grouped together under the category "New Thought" insisted that spirit shaped matter, and that therefore sickness was the result of wrong ways of thinking or believing. New Thought practitioners spanned a range, from those who ignored the body because they believed it was epiphenomenal to those who recognized its power to shape in reciprocal ways the spiritual self. In the former category was the founder of Christian Science, Mary Baker Eddy (1821–1910), who thought that matter was an illusion best ignored. Hygienists, Grahamists and other body reformers, Eddy thought, were starting at the wrong end of the process. "If half the attention given to hygiene were given to the study of Christian Science and the spiritualization of thought, this alone would usher in the millennium," Eddy complained. But Eddy was more urgent in her denial of matter than most. Though many others agreed that spirit/thought determined bodily conditions, they also pointed to bodily practices that helped spiritual processes along, including diet restrictions similar to those advocated by earlier health reformers like Graham and Alcott. The body had at least a shadow reality – and what we did with it influenced the spiritual self within. For these reasons, many New Thought reformers were interested in what and how to eat, how to exercise, and, for some, how (and when) to have sex. Many recognized, for example, that while a robust, spiritual, inner self produced a strong, slim exterior, a strong exterior also helped "the mind and the soul in the realization of ever higher perceptions." Of course, in the twentieth century, slim, female bodies and strong male ones continued to be associated with vitality, intelligence, morality and even advanced spiritual states (Griffith 2004: 79, 99).

Spiritual healing was in the late nineteenth-century air, and evangelical Christians, perhaps challenged by the ubiquity of New Thought notions, recovered their own traditions of believing and healing. Their practices included meditation, prayer, the laying-on of hands and anointing and serving others, a set of practices that evangelists in the divine healing movement spread starting in the 1870s. When they enjoined fellow believers to ignore infirmity, these Christian healers sounded like New Thought practitioners: "I want you to pray believing and then act faith," one Christian counseled believers. "It makes no difference how you feel, but get right out of bed and begin to walk by faith." This was not so different from Eddy's idealism: The suffering body was unreal. Of course, performing this kind of selective attention was difficult; it required contemplative acts that could train attention on God's healing promises. Laying-on of hands and anointing helped, for physical contact reminded the afflicted of God's touch. Some were touched or anointed and felt intense warming, power or healing. Some felt an influx of divine energy that propelled them right out of bed.

Still, "acting faith" presented theological problems. What was the meaning of suffering? An unintended consequence of the divine healing movement was a move away from thinking about suffering as redemptive. By the late nineteenth century, suffering became less a sign of God's afflictive providence than a prelude to his restorative (and miraculous) beneficence. And divine healing posed still other challenges. How might Christians understand healing practices in a world hemmed in by God's sovereignty? Did Christian healers heal, or did God? For the most part, New Thoughters and other liberals avoided this problem, for their God pulsed immanently in nature and human nature. As a result, human actions, nature's ways, and God's will were constitutive of one another. Evangelical divine healers sometimes adopted this solution as well, pointing out that God's healing power was an "indwelling *life*" that enabled believers to "realize with wondering joy, that mystery which fleshly sense can never perceive, that 'we are members of His body, of His flesh and of His bones.'" God's healing forces were in you. At other times, however, evangelicals issued familiar cautions about human ability in a world governed by an omnipotent God. They advised believers not to trust in their own abilities to heal but in God's mercy and gifts. Healing with the former instead of the latter in mind led to failed healings. There was a certain passivity required, a resting in Christ and his will. Paradoxically, this passivity led to towering forms of vitality and power (Curtis 2006: 138–140, 149).

Exchange and Encounter on American Frontiers

Theologies and practices associated with the Christian body changed dramatically when American Christians moved south and west and encountered other kinds of believers. Though Christians began by trying to discipline and change others, often their encounters altered their own ways of thinking and worshipping and led to unexpected, hybrid religious practices.

In the South, a distinctive religious culture was shaped by the evangelical movement and the presence of large numbers of enslaved Africans. In the seventeenth and eighteenth centuries, an Anglican establishment failed to create an enduring religious system despite support from colonial legislatures and cultural elites. When they tried to instruct enslaved Africans – and more often than not, they did not try to do so – their systems of religious nurture required literacy and involved graduated lessons and memorization. Itinerant evangelicals of the eighteenth century brought a new religious mood to the South, however, one that emphasized personal religious experiences and the extraordinary bodily experiences that accompanied them. Enslaved Africans responded with alacrity to this type of Christianity, and during the First Great Awakening a significant number converted. Throughout the eighteenth century, revivalists, and especially Methodists and Baptists, conducted their meetings of prayer, exhortation and preaching, stirring up intense religious emotions among mixed-race audiences. By 1815 evangelical Christianity was a dominant influence among African-American and Afro-Atlantic peoples. But at about the same moment, earlier egalitarian impulses among revivalists were quashed by a white southern society that was moving toward evangelicalism as well. White evangelicals quickly shaped their own proslavery, patriarchal evangelicalism, one that buttressed efforts to keep the races separate and unequal. So while revival Christianity, especially in the earlier periods, held out egalitarian possibilities, it did not consistently lift out of bondage bodies that were black, or, for that matter, female (Frey and Wood 1998).

In any case, spirit-filled bodies, black and white, often followed their own unpredictable logic. Observers of one gathering in Virginia late in the eighteenth century noticed everyone "not only jump up, strike their hands together, and shout aloud" but also "embrace one another, and fall to the floor." Weeping, shouting, falling down, jumping up – these were bodily ways of knowing God's presence. Because both evangelicalism and African performance traditions pointed to these acts as signs of divine presences, somatic performances were particularly powerful in southern African American religion as it developed in the nineteenth century (Taves 1999: 86, 104). African American Christians depended on rhythm, music and dance more than white brethern, moving from song to praise and prayer. "In the blacks' quarter the coloured people get together, and sing for hours together, short scraps of disjointed affirmations, pledges, or prayers, lengthened out with long repetition choruses." Scriptural fragments would be attached to other refrains. "'Go shouting all your days,' in connection with 'glory, glory, glory,' in which go shouting is repeated six times in succession." The power of religious music stimulated new ecstatic practices, including the holy dance, or ring shout, which seems to have originated in clandestine gatherings or camp meetings and was being noticed by observers by 1810. The first motions of the ring shout were hand clapping, foot stomping, and jumping:

> With every song so sung, they have a sinking of one or other leg of the body alternately; producing an audible sound of the feet at every step, and as manifest as the steps of actual negro dancing in Virginia, etc. If some, in the meantime sit, they strike the sounds alternately on each thigh.

White observers noticed these unique practices with curiosity and revulsion. Observing a ritual dance in 1819, Benjamin Latrobe wrote about circles of dancers and drummers. "Most of the circles contained the same sort of dancers. One was larger, in which a ring of a dozen women walked, by way of dancing, round the music in the center." The songs struck him as too African. "A man sung an uncouth song to the dancing which I suppose was in some African language, for it was not french, and the Women screamed a detestable burthen on one single note." Thus, in the encounter between African and white evangelical styles, it was not just new religious practices that were born; it also was new ways of discriminating good ones from bad ones. Bad ones were excessive, irrational, primitive, pagan. White evangelicals often studied black evangelical practices in order to critique and debunk them (Frey and Wood 1998: 144–146).

But the South was not the only place of encounter and change. White evangelicals also were moving west, and on this frontier, too, they set out to conquer but often settled for compromise or alliance. Though many native peoples initially were open to Christian prayers and practices, they usually combined them with their own traditions, producing new, eclectic practices. Like enslaved Africans, they turned Christian tropes, stories and practices to their advantage, using them to critique white conquerors and missionaries. Protestant missionaries preaching to the Ojibwe, for instance, tried to use Christian hymns to instil Protestant values and ways of looking at God, the land and community. Lessons were simple and systematically taught, but Indians refused to absorb them completely. "I am deeply touched by their singing," an Episcopal bishop reported in 1881; "the *wild* Indian voice is harsh. Nothing could be more discordant than their wild yell and hideous war song. The religion of Christ softened this; their voices became plaintive, and as they sing from the heart their hymns are full of emotion." In this account and in native-Christian encounters more generally there is evidence of resistance and accommodation, even if missionaries reported the results of these encounters selectively to mission boards. In any case, at least with the Ojibwe, by the 1870s and 1880s Protestants could report some success. Concentrated on reservations and dependent on Christian missions for survival, Ojibwe people were learning to sing, keep the Sabbath, cut their hair and stop dancing and drumming in worship. They appeared finally to be adopting civilized ways. But in reality, the Ojibwe developed Christian practices into distinctive and even subversive religious styles. Ojibwe elders performed Protestant hymns in wigwams far from mission houses and used them to mark events they considered important (such as death). They also changed them. "Hymns were sung slowly, like laments, more the chanting of syllables really than the conveying of the discursive meanings of the texts themselves," one scholar has written. Thus Ojibwe "hymn societies became primary social networks through which age-old values of reciprocity, subsistence, and the seasonal round were negotiated within the demands of the new life on the reservation." They used hymns to affirm older values. It is no exaggeration to say that Ojibwe people borrowed Protestant hymns to help them preserve distinctively Native ways, values and traditions (McNally 2000: 841–842).

But sometimes even these forms of combination and accommodation were impossible, and native prophets warned their people to avoid Christians or destroy them. In 1751, a young Delaware woman had a vision that told her that conversion to Christianity was dangerous. According to the missionary who heard the story, her vision revealed that "God gave the white man a book, and told him that he must worship by that: but gave none to the indian or negro, and therefore it could not be right for them to have a book, or be any way concerned with that way of worship." In 1804, a Shawnee man named Lalawethika experienced a trance in which the creator warned him against missionaries, alcohol, and land cessions, among other things. He preached that whites were not created by God but by a lesser spiritual being, declared native allies of the whites "witches" and called for the violent expulsion of white people from Indian land (Martin 2001: 50). His brother, Tecumseh, took this message to the southeastern nations, where a civil war broke out among factions of Creek Indians in Alabama and Georgia. The US government intervened and slaughtered hundreds of native men, women and children. The nineteenth-century story of native–Christian encounter is often a story of the destruction of native peoples and ways of life.

There were other visions and prophecies of resistance. An apocryphal story circulated widely about an Indian convert whose visionary experience of the afterlife warned against Christian conversion. A missionary encountered this story and worried about its implications for the success of his work among the Ojibwe:

> One day an Indian … came to our house, and said that the chiefs had reported the case of a pious, or in their dialect, a praying Indian, who dies far away to the North. He had prayed a long time. On his death, he went to heaven, but was refused admittance on the ground that no praying Indians were admitted there. He then went to the place where

the white people go, but was not received. He next went to the place where the Indians go, but was there told he had been a praying Indian, and had forsaken the customs of his fathers, and they would not receive him, and ordered him away. After these repulses he came back again to this world, and assumed the body which he had before inhabited.

The moral of the story was not lost on other Native Americans: Stay away from Christians (McNally 2000: 840).

But if evangelical missions south to African Americans and west to Native Americans led to unexpected difficulties, there were other problems for the onward march of American Christians. Though framed on both sides as part of God's providential plan, the American Civil War proved over time to be a confounding existential and theological problem. How could brutal carnage on this vast scale be explained theologically? How could the merciful God of the Bible allow widespread crimes and atrocities and such massive casualties – and which side was the Christian God on? Unfortunately, for most of the war clergymen on both sides refused to consider the deeper complexities of these questions, and, certain of the truth of their own cause, encouraged young men to fight to preserve the divine order of things and usher in the millennium. The effect of framing the conflict as a millennial drama – the war was a baptism of blood, battlefields were altars, soldiers were holy warriors, the dead were martyrs – was to intensify passions on both sides and make bloodshed a genuinely religious practice. Northern believers were sure that a blood sacrifice was necessary to purify the nation of the sins of slavery, and their young men performed that sacrifice in spades; southern evangelicals were sure that their fight against northern aggression was authorized by a God who loved liberty and explicitly approved of slavery in his book (the New Testament). Both sides fought on with religious passion and seriousness. It was a non-evangelical, Lincoln, who, viewing the complexities and the carnage from a distance, knew that God's purposes in all of this were beyond the ken of ordinary men and women, northern or southern.

The war raised troubling questions but it did not stop evangelicals as they moved onto new frontiers, including the west, where other encounters awaited that, putting it optimistically, provided opportunities for Christian innovation and change. The obstacles that awaited Protestants there were Catholics, installed in their missions for many years in the western landscape, Mormons, whose surprising prosperity in the arid Utah desert confounded many eastern Protestants, and, not least, a liberal counter-culture that began in the middle of the nineteenth century and flourished in the frontier West. This liberal counter-culture emerged in eastern cities at the center of Protestant influence, but on the frontier it spread quickly, in part because of the lack of religious institutions and an ethos of independent thinking, religious iconoclasm and mobility. The result was a religious liberalism that found the divine in nature and in human nature, that appreciated and sometimes embraced religious truths in different world religions and that saw older, institutional forms, churches and doctrines as unseemly or overly "sectarian." The Unitarian minister Starr King developed this thinking in sermons at the First Unitarian Church of San Francisco, where he affirmed California's resistance to overly-organized religion and Protestant intolerance. God's grace, he said, did not move through prescribed doctrines and institutions, but fell naturally like the rains. "It falls on the mountain slopes; it collects in rills; it combines into streams and rivers; it hides underground and bubbles in fountains. Now it floods all its channels; now it leaves the old beds to cut new paths for its leaping music; and it will often burst up in fresh districts to gladden the ground with beauty." In general, King's nature mysticism – he saw the mind of God in Lake Tahoe – while indigenous to a liberal wing in his natal Protestantism, took on new forms in the nature writing of westerners like John Muir. Starr King, one historian has argued, "offered Californians a mystical cosmology that promised communion with God through nature and revealed correspondences between their own experience and Christian mythology." Liberal beliefs began appearing in a number of California congregations at about mid-century and in "metaphysical" traditions that were popular in the West: Christian Science, New Thought, Theosophy. The result was a California tradition more attuned to the inner life, healing traditions and especially inner/outer correspondences with nature.

Even prominent Protestants transplanted from New England, such as the Congregationalist minister Charles Reynolds Brown (1862–1950), became interested in metaphysical correspondences and spiritual healing. Brown was one of many liberal ministers, east and west, who wrote practical manuals for Christians who needed to develop right habits of thinking and will-power. Regular affirmations – biblical and psychological – might help. "We may educate the mind by suggestion to move in better channels and teach the heart to cherish more wholesome states of feeling, and in that way accomplish splendid results in securing health and developing character." This could be done by sitting quietly, letting the hands and legs relax, and repeating sets of suggestions with one's attention focused on them, such as this one to "banish fear":

> *I. To banish fear*
> Fear not – only believe.
> Fear not – it is your father's good pleasure to give you mastery.
> Perfect love casteth out fear.
> I will fear no evil, for Thou art with me.

Brown devised eight of these sets for all kinds of maladies and doubts, recommending one a day and two on Sunday. These were innovative religious practices (Frankiel 1988: 22, 24, 85).

California was not the only new spiritual frontier, however, nor was it the only place where believers fashioned new spiritualities. Even in old New England curious believers encountered new or foreign religions and assembled new religious practices, including especially meditative and affirmative worship styles not unlike Charles Brown's. Leigh Schmidt has examined these different styles and especially an eclectic renascence of meditation among late nineteenth-century liberals, including those associated with the ecumenical Greenacre conferences in Eliot, Maine. To cosmopolitan liberals, eastern meditative practices, New Thought forms of positive thinking and even older certainties about faith and faith healing reinforced a new piety of meditative concentration. "Thou hast to reach that fixity of mind in which no breeze, however strong, can waft an earthly thought within," the spiritualist and reformer Helena Blavatsky wrote. In its first "moment," at least, meditation produced emptiness. "Thus purified, the shrine must of all action, sound, or earthly light be void; e'en as the butterfly o'ertaken by the frost, fall lifeless at the threshold – so must all earthly thoughts fall dead." Another liberal, Annie Besant, a minister's wife who journeyed towards religious radicalism, also saw meditation at the heart of a universal quest for ultimate knowledge. She thought:

> Anyone who determines to lead a spiritual life, must daily devote some time to meditation ... Those who cannot spare half an hour a day during which the world may be shut out and the mind may receive from the spiritual planes a current of life cannot lead the spiritual life. Only to the mind concentrated, steady, shut out from the world, can the Divine reveal itself.

Obviously, Besant is concerned here not just with emptying the self; she also wants to fill it up with divine things. This could be done by concentrating on images of "the Beloved," real or imagined images of Christ, the Virgin Mary, the Buddha, Vishnu or Krishna – whatever. Besant learned meditative techniques from various Hindu gurus and missionaries, including Swami Vivekananda. Needless to say, such practices were a long way from earlier ways of thinking about religious progress, systems built on concepts such as sin, conversion, justification and regeneration (Schmidt 2005: 160–163).

Religious Practices in the City

One of the most dramatic changes in nineteenth-century life was the rise of the city. Suddenly, American believers had to reckon with the unceasing racket of industrial machines, a new commercial culture that competed for their attention and an unsettling influx of non-Protestant immigrants. All of these things changed how Americans at the end of the century thought about and practiced religion everyday.

The rise of industrial life was a traumatic development that seemed to threaten nervous and spiritual health. While at mid-century some celebrated machines as ways of spreading enlightenment, democracy and material wealth, by the end of the century Americans were ambivalent. As Alan Trachtenberg has noted, the machine was the prime cause both "of the abundance of new products changing the character of daily life" and of "newly visible poverty, slums, and an unexpected wretchedness of industrial conditions." Was the machine lifting up our society or tearing it down? A number of Americans also worried that industrial life was destroying both the muscular and the spiritual self. A physiological literature undergirded these new concerns, a literature that located the mind and spirit in the bodily self (Figure 12.2). Doctors and pastors diagnosed the effects of urbanization starting at mid-century: The mechanical rhythms and loud, unceasing noises of industrial life were producing indecisiveness, anxiety and nervous collapse (Trachtenberg 1982: 38).

Solutions to these nervous problems varied, but most believed that, for men at least, relief came by strengthening both the muscles and a related inner power that they called "the will." Athletic activities, organized sports, playground activities and other vigorous, outdoor contests – all of these things built muscular and moral capacities.

```
DIVINE LOVE

FILLS ME.
```

Figure 12.2 Henry Wood's affirmations for developing right habits for thinking and believing.

The Protestant churches, also worried about effete men and nervous enervation more generally, incorporated bodily activities into their piety. In the first issue of the cycling journal *The Wheelman*, for example, a journal published during a bicycling revival in the 1880s, all articles took up the issue of "Clergymen and the Bicycle," and all of them celebrated ministers who had stuck with bicycling despite occasional protests from more pedestrian believers. Bicycling could stir the spirit, mollify the mind and diminish dyspepsia. One clergyman writing anonymously confessed to seeing only "monotony" and ill health until he started cycling, when "as if by magic, away went the spirits that had tormented me so long, and as their cloven feet and writhing tails disappeared in the dark past I was met by the laughing, beautiful faces of the spirits of health and cheerfulness." Others, expressing mental and spiritual conditions in common physiological idioms, were convinced that "if bicycles were more generally used by American preachers, there would be fewer hollow chests, round shoulders, sensitive stomachs, and torpid livers." The general trend was characterized well by the liberal Congregationalist minister Theodore Munger, who showed that he had assimilated new psychological knowledge thoroughly when he announced that there could "be no health, no thought, no moral feeling, no sound judgment, no vigorous action, except in connection with a sound body." "Any religious experience connected with a weak or diseased body," he said further, "is to be regarded with suspicion." A sizable group of progressive thinkers and "body-as-temple" theologians insisted that the physical body was the "foundation which conditions the intellectual and spiritual superstructure." In this atmosphere it was hard to believe that the meek might inherit the earth. Watch out for "mollycoddles," the Rev. Frank Crane warned; "The road to hell is crowded with [them]" – "slouching, shuffling, blear-eyed, trembling morons" (Putney 2001: 45–59; White 2008).

There were other reasons to worry about American cities. Immigrants were flooding into urban areas, especially in the years after the 1880s, when large numbers of Jews and Catholics came from southern and eastern Europe. Protestant reformers saw these newcomers as another "frontier" to traverse and subdue, but the urban landscape they had to tame was complicated and internally diverse. Religious practice in the cities was eclectic and often improvised. Here many American faiths, new and old, were in motion.

Immigrant Catholics coming late in the century, for example, many of them from southern or eastern Europe, brought sensibilities and rituals that they adapted to America's urban landscape. An older, established Catholic Church existed, of course, dominated by an earlier generation of Irish immigrants; but newer immigrants had religious identities that were entirely their own. When Italian Catholic immigrants settled, they improvised religious rituals in apartments, rented rooms, tenement backyards and city streets. In 1881, for example, immigrants from Salerno brought devotion to their patron saint to East Harlem, kneeling before small printed pictures of the Madonna del Carmine that had traveled, as they had, from Italy to America. They said the rosary, prayed the Magnificat and ate together – and, when Italian priests were on hand, they celebrated mass. By the second half of the 1880s, devotion to the Madonna was so popular that it overflowed onto the city streets, where thousands of Italians, mostly women, processed with a Madonna statue adorned with precious stones and other tokens of gratitude. Italians and their Madonna wandered through new cityscapes together. Worship of the Madonna helped these Italians do several things. It collapsed time and distance, reminding these immigrants of older traditions and their homeland; it recapitulated their lost wanderings through American cities, full of doubt and hope; and finally it transformed the loud, threatening urban spaces they now occupied into new kinds of sacred enclosures, allowing them to be faithful to God and Italy while also becoming modern and American. Street-oriented devotion to the Madonna helped create a new Italian Catholic identity (Orsi 1985).

Devotion to the Madonna was primarily a woman's devotional practice, and it reminds us that gender always shaped how Americans thought about and improvised their religious lives. Worshipping the suffering Madonna was something Italian American women did to understand the proper Christian ways of enduring misfortune, sickness or the death of a child. How had the Madonna done it? The Madonna reminded women that the source of their power was a uniquely female set of capacities for religious sentiment, motherly compassion, and domesticity (though the worship itself, it should be emphasized, propelled women beyond these confining spaces and out into the public places of the street). In any case, Italian women were doing something that many other American women were doing: they were re-imagining religious practices in ways that gave them more power, more opportunities for leadership, more choices. So their worship of the Madonna reinforced the association between women and the home, a powerful certainty across the board in nineteenth-century America, but it also subverted that association, bringing women out on to the streets to organize, lead and worship publicly. Women, not male priests, organized and carried off this devotion. For this reason, these practices were critiqued by Catholic officials. For many Catholic men, including priests and intellectuals, it was primitive, superstitious, idolatrous.

In any case, the nineteenth century was full of women who used religious practices as ways of liberating themselves from sin and male authority figures at the same time. From evangelicals who felt so filled with the Holy Spirit that they prophesied against their husbands and ministers to others who claimed that feminine sensibilities made them better missionaries, prayer leaders or organizers, nineteenth-century women cleverly turned gender stereotypes to their advantage. The remarkable story of the African-American preacher Jarena Lee is a classic example. Converted by Richard Allen and coming to believe that the spirit called her to witness and exhort, Lee went to Allen to ask his permission. Allen repeatedly warned Lee against moving outside of her place, telling her that her inner impressions must be mistaken. The result was an intense inner conflict for Lee, who could not understand why the spirit said one thing and Allen another. When the spirit moved Lee on another powerful occasion, she rose (in Allen's church) and exhorted the congregation powerfully, and this time Allen relented. Perhaps the spirit had inspired her, Allen thought, perhaps it did authorize her to speak out. This was a common experience for nineteenth-century women who got the spirit at a revival, prayer meeting or mass. They had received the spirit, so why couldn't they be equals in Christ? Men pondering this problem, men who led their religious communities but were outnumbered many times over by women in the pews, usually refused to give up authority to those who asked for it. This would change in the twentieth century.

How did immigrant Jews adjust to life in new American cities? One fundamental change in their perspectives involved redefining Jewishness less in terms of the Jewish community and more in terms of being "Jewish at heart" – and Jewish at home. The emphasis on domestic piety was not particular to American Jews, of course; and certainly Jews had always had a piety of the home. But because modernity and citizenship moved Jews out of homogenous European ghettos and into diverse, secular states, Jews were no longer obligated to move in tandem with the rhythms of the traditional Jewish calendar, and Jewish religious and cultural life became anchored in the family and the life cycle: birth, puberty, marriage, death. Jewish holy days, of course, were not ignored, but transformed, as one analyst has put it, into "exercises in domestic felicity" that were "heavy on sentiment and light on ritual." On Passover, the *Hebrew Standard* instructed in 1915, "every nook and corner in the Jewish house bespeaks festivity, and every member of the household, in festive garb and festal humor is doing his or her level best to give Passover a right royal welcome." The biggest burdens fell, though, to the Jewish housewife, who did so much spring-cleaning, stocking up on motzoh and polishing stemware that the pre-Passover period was pronounced by newspapers as the "Jewish matrons' week of trial." Fortunately, by the turn of the twentieth century, these trials were mitigated by American Jewish etiquette manuals that instructed women on everything from how to entertain the extended family to how to make a Seder. On other matters, too, immigrant Jews would be helped by America's emerging consumer culture. What were the rules for Jewish participation in modern inventions such as romantic love and dating? What should an American Jewish wedding look like? How should Jews interact with Christians? What happened when the unthinkable occurred and the Jewish home was threatened by that other modern invention, religious intermarriage? These really were twentieth-century concerns, but even late in the nineteenth century Jews were turning to Yiddish advice manuals, marriage consultants, and matchmakers. Sanctifying daily life in the modern city was a new thing altogether (Joselit 1994: 294, 221).

The consumer culture that helped Jews fashion new forms of piety also was transforming the religious lives of other Americans. Religion and consumer culture have combined in surprising ways ever since the beginning of the nineteenth century. Modern American Easter celebrations, for example, were created out of different impulses in mid-nineteenth-century America – a revival of gothic church architecture, a rising appreciation among urban believers for decoration and especially floral decoration, and a new "display aesthetic" of variety, originality and experimentation. Increasingly, church altars lost their austerity and incorporated lilies, roses and tropical plants in astonishing variety. All were attempts to communicate the promise of new life in Christ, a "form of popular piety," one historian has written, "that evoked the ancient coalescence of the rebirth of spring and the resurrection of Christ." Church decoration of this kind provided a model for holiday displays in department store windows, a development clearly in evidence by the 1880s. Easter display windows at department stores borrowed staples of church decoration – crosses, lilies, angels, ecclesiastical vestments, religious banners and (open) heavenly gates. These sacred decorations were used quite clearly to sell things; and yet it is hasty to dismiss them as wholly secular. For there is no question that store owners, like the department store titan John Wanamaker, thought of these displays as ways of marking his store's Christian identity. These were ways of consecrating commerce, ways of making culture Christian. This sentiment emerged quite powerfully among liberal Protestants in particular, those who had a cultural faith that insisted all things – matter and spirit, Christ and culture – were a part of a single world, the Kingdom of God. But traditionalists worried about these changes. Wasn't this new gospel of prosperity, consumption and fulfillment obliterating earlier emphases on restraint and self-abnegation? Had the city and its busy entrepreneurs merely used Christian symbols to sell products? These questions puzzled many Protestants (Schmidt 1995: 253).

Nevertheless, for the most part, piety and commerce bumped and jostled amicably in American urban cultures. The late nineteenth-century combination of Easter services and Easter fashions in New York illuminate this trend. The New York Easter parade developed out of the new, adorned style of Easter services in the city. New clothes for Easter is an old tradition, but in New York the high concentration of fashionable churches meant that before and after services men and women could display and observe style and beauty. By the 1880s, the post-worship "fashionable promenade" on Fifth Avenue became the "great fashion show of the year"; and in the 1890s it became the Easter parade. New York merchants quickly discerned the link between Easter and fashion; and they developed elaborate displays especially to attract women. But calculating merchants and everyday believers in the pews did not necessarily see commerce and Christ as enemies. The diary entry of New Yorker Elizabeth Orr suggests how fashion, display and piety often were jumbled together:

> Easter Sunday came in bright and beautiful[,] ... Every one seemed to be influenced by the weather, bright happy faces. Most every one out in their holiday clothes gotten up for the occasion. Dr. Eddy gave us one of his good discourses on the rserection [*sic*] of Christ and his followers. Oh that I may be one of that number! Am I his or Am I not! should be a question with us. I know and feel my sinfulness, and he came to save just such a sinner. I repent every day, and trust I am forgiven.

Easter clothes and the deeper mysteries of sin and repentance – for many people, these activities did not exist in tension. Believers saw useful things in both the spectacle of Easter parades and the rituals and preaching involved in Christ's resurrection (Schmidt 1995: 259–261).

In the end, then, American Protestants moving into twentieth-century cities, like Protestants moving onto other frontiers, developed unexpected alliances and compromises that changed American religious practices definitively. Easter practices that incorporated the newest fashions were merely a beginning. Businessmen's revivals, store-front churches, Christian radio and television programs – all of these innovations pointed to American religious resilience and creativity. Though some believers resisted change, most were innovative in reworking practices to satisfy new converts, the demands of urban spaces, and the pleas, which were always insistent, of younger generations wanting to work out salvation in more modern ways.

Nineteenth-century America was a place of astonishing religious exchanges, combinations and encounters. These encounters produced new hybrid forms of religiousness, such as African American evangelicalism and different Native American Christianities. Evangelicalism, too, with its powerful missionary impulse, was also changed in the process. But it should not be overlooked that all of the groups participating in this great, nineteenth-century ferment were not equal. When evangelicals moved west and south on new frontiers, when in cities and towns they attempted to "civilize" and uplift Catholics and Native Americans, they did so with enormous human and financial resources. In many of these encounters they controlled the outcome or dictated the terms of resulting compromises and agreements. They also brought with them a complicated set of motivations, from genuine compassion to arrogance and imperiousness, and this same mix of attitudes continued to inform America's sense of mission and chosenness in the twentieth century. As that century began, and as the western frontier no longer appeared so wild and uncivilized, Americans turned to other frontiers in other places, hoping to bring their mission and lifestyle to other peoples. When the Spanish-American War broke out in 1898, the same mix of American mission, charitableness and imperiousness animated it. Across the oceans lay another frontier to traverse, other wildernesses in which American believers might fulfill their errand of spreading – forcibly, sometimes – all of the divine gifts that God had so bountifully bestowed upon them.

References and Further Reading

Abzug Robert (1994) *Cosmos Crumbling: American Reform and the Religious Imagination*, Oxford: Oxford University Press.

Curtis, Heather (2006) "Acting Faith": Practices of Religious Healing in Late-nineteenth-century Protestantism," in Laurie Maffly-Kipp et al. (eds.) *Practicing Protestants: Histories of Christian Life in America, 1630–1965*, Baltimore, MD: Johns Hopkins University Press, pp. 137–158.

Frankiel, Sandra Sizer (1988) *California's Spiritual Frontiers: Religious Alternatives in Anglo-Protestantism, 1850–1910*, Berkeley, CA: University of California Press.

Frey, Sylvia and Wood, Betty (1998) *Come Shouting to Zion: African American Protestantism in the American South and British Caribbean to 1830*, Chapel Hill, NC: University of North Carolina Press.

Gardella, Peter (2006) "Christian Physiology and Diet Reform," in Colleen McDannell (ed.) *Religions of the United States in Practice*, vol. 1, Princeton, NJ: Princeton University Press, pp. 310–319.

Goldman, Karla (2001) *Beyond the Synagogue Gallery: Finding a Place for Women in American Judaism*, Cambridge, MA: Harvard University Press.

Griffith, Marie (2004) *Born Again Bodies: Flesh and Spirit in American Christianity*, Berkeley, CA: University of California Press.

Hatch, Nathan (1989) *The Democratization of American Christianity*, New Haven, CT: Yale University Press.

Joselit, Jenna W. (1994) *The Wonders of America: Reinventing Jewish Culture, 1880–1950*, New York: Henry Holt.

Martin, Joel (2001) *The Land Looks After Us: A History of Native American Religion*, Oxford: Oxford University Press.

McDannell, Colleen (1995) *Material Christianity: Religion and Popular Culture in America*, New Haven, CT: Yale University Press.

McNally, Michael (2000) "The Practice of Native American Christianity," *Church History*, 69(4): 834–859.

Orsi, Robert (1985) *The Madonna of 115th Street: Faith and Community in Italian Harlem, 1880–1950*, New Haven, CT: Yale University Press.

Putney, Clifford (2001) *Muscular Christianity: Manhood and Sports in Protestant America, 1880–1920*, Cambridge, MA: Harvard University Press.

Raboteau, Albert (2001) *Canaan Land: A Religious History of African-Americans*, Oxford: Oxford University Press.

Schmidt, Leigh (1995) "The Easter Parade: Piety, Fashion, and Display," in David Hackett (ed.) *Religion and American Culture*, London: Routledge, pp. 247–269.

Schmidt, Leigh (2001) *Holy Fairs: Scotland and the Making of American Evangelicalism*, Grand Rapids, MI: Eerdmans.

Schmidt, Leigh (2005) *Restless Souls: The Making of American Spirituality*, San Francisco: Harper San Francisco.

Taves, Ann (1999) *Fits, Trances and Visions: Experiencing Religion and Explaining Experience from Wesley to James*, Princeton, NJ: Princeton University Press.

Trachtenberg, Alan (1982) *The Incorporation of America: Culture and Society in the Gilded Age*, New York: Hill and Wang.

White, Christopher (2008) *Unsettled Minds: Psychology and the American Search for Spiritual Assurance, 1830–1940*, Berkeley, CA: University of California Press.

IV
Global Reach (1898–Present)

13

Politics

Charles H. Lippy

In the era of globalization, long-standing linkages between religion and politics became both more pluralistic and more tenuous. The growing number, and growing visibility, of different religions in the United States meant that the political implications of religious freedom were expanding to incorporate respect for the contributions that different religious groups made to the rich fabric of American culture. But enthusiasm for religious pluralism challenged older, more conservative views of America as a biblically constructed Protestant Nation and stimulated reactionary efforts to reassert traditional religious values in American political life. Thus, while some Americans celebrated religious diversity as a great democratic achievement, others expressed concern about the erosion of religious values and their loosening hold on national life. Throughout this process of cultural transformation and debate, religion continued to operate as a medium for political expression, as it had since the era of exploration and encounter. At the same time, however, connections between religion and politics became more self-conscious over the course the twentieth century than ever before and thereby more vulnerable to challenge, criticism, and need for defense.

When William McKinley took the oath of office as president of the United States in March 1897, what many have dubbed the "Methodist century" in American history was drawing to a close. Barely one hundred years later, when all groups were combined together, Christians still accounted for the largest cluster of religious Americans, but Protestants were for the first time likely a minority of the population, non-Christian groups were flourishing, and politicians who drew on religious rhetoric to add a transcendent imprimatur to their programs and policies were facing increasing challenges in finding a vocabulary that reflected anything like a national consensus on moral and religious values.

It was not so in the age of Methodist William McKinley. Looking ahead to religion and public life in the twentieth century, the leading Protestant journal called itself the *Christian Century*. After leading the nation into a brief war with Spain in

1898, the Methodist McKinley confessed that he frequently sought divine guidance as he pondered whether there was justification for a war to wrest control of Cuba and the Philippines from Spain, noting that finally one night he received a revelation that "[t]here was nothing left for us to do but to take them all and to educate the Filipinos and uplift and civilize and Christianize them and by God's grace to do the very best we could by them, as our fellow men for whom Christ also died" (Olcott 1916, vol. 2: 110–111). It mattered not that most Cubans and Filipinos by then were Roman Catholic. As Josiah Strong had warned in his *Our Country* published just over a decade earlier, Roman Catholicism was among the religious forces whose global growth and increasing presence in the United States (thanks to immigration) threatened to undermine American democracy and demolish the American way of life. Further, racial bias played into the popular views promoted by McKinley, whether wittingly or unwittingly, for Filipinos were often portrayed as "brown" and therefore as a people racially inferior to, and thus in need of rescuing by, Anglo-Saxon white Protestants.

Relationships between religion and public life, faith and politics, and church and state have taken new directions in the age of globalization. This chapter takes each of these relationships in turn. First the chapter will examine shifts in religious images of the nation that have nudged national understanding away from the kind of evangelical Protestant notion that shaped McKinley's consciousness to an increasingly pluralistic and more highly nuanced one. Then, the ways in which organized religious bodies – from individual groups and denominations to special interest associations and cooperative enterprises – have sought to influence political policy and public life will come under scrutiny. Finally, court cases, particularly at the level of the US Supreme Court, that have dealt with religious issues will receive attention in order to give concrete illustration of the transformations that have occurred. The chapter will conclude with some comments about forces that challenge any simplistic understanding of the links between religion and the common life of the American people in the early years of the twenty-first century.

Religious Images of the Nation: The United States as a Christian Country?

Between 2000 and 2003, William Hutchison, Diana Eck, and I all published books tracking aspects of the idea of religious pluralism in the US. Hutchison provided a history of pluralism from the colonial epoch to the dawn of the twenty-first century, my study centered on the twentieth century as a time when pluralism came into its own, and Eck zeroed in on the "new" pluralism that came after changes in the immigration laws in 1965. All three reflected an increasing awareness that the story of pluralism lifted up something vital, not only about American religious culture, but about the nature of the national enterprise. None would have framed the issues as they did had not the twentieth century brought the US more centrally into a global enterprise. Yet the idea of a radical pluralism would have struck someone like William McKinley a century earlier as odd, if not preposterous. McKinley's use of the language of evangelical Protestant conversion to talk about the American effort in a war with Spain presumed a different nation and a different world, even if

McKinley did appear in public with Roman Catholic James Cardinal Gibbons at a prayer service marking the close of the war.

For much of the twentieth century, polls indicated that roughly the same proportion of the American population claimed a religious affiliation – the majority as Christian of one sort or another. Yet in the last third of the century, the numbers of those without any affiliation slowly but steadily began to increase. By the dawn of the twenty-first century, the figure hovered around 40 percent. Some of that reflected yet another continuous strand in American religious life, a stark rationalism that rejected any form of theism, often combined with a humanism that looked solely to this world for meaning in life. The idealism of religious humanism gained some ground early in the twentieth century when many expected that science and technology, both regarded as manifestations of the best in human reason, would transform society into a utopian ideal. Later in the century, popular forms of spirituality engaged individuals in personal quests for meaning that drew on multiple sources, only some of which were overtly religious.

A hundred years ago, despite the presence of literally hundreds of different Protestant bodies, representatives of every strand of Judaism, a burgeoning Roman Catholicism, a growing Eastern Orthodoxy, and an undercurrent of skepticism, the popular public perception of the United States was that the country was indeed a "Christian" nation, meaning a land where a broadly evangelical style of Protestantism was both dominant and normative. In 1908, when the Federal Council of Churches organized to facilitate cooperation on political and social welfare matters among mainline Protestants, the idea that the US was a Protestant nation barely muted an anti-Catholicism in the council, and its spokesmen drew on the language of evangelical Protestant Christianity to define the nation as a political entity. At the launching the council in 1908, speakers proclaimed that the policies of the federal government were essentially "Christian in spirit" and that the nation itself represented the "truest development of the church" (1986: 277).

With the outbreak of World War I less than a decade later, the council, along with other religious groups, plunged into patriotic activities, often ignoring fellow Protestants who sought conscientious objector status. American Catholics cemented their loyalties to the nation as the National Catholic War Council mustered grass-roots support for the war and promoted ancillary activities to support the military endeavor. These Catholic patriotic endeavors era helped not only to integrate Roman Catholicism more firmly into American religious culture, but also to begin to dispel some of the anti-Catholicism that evangelical Protestants harbored. But the anti-Catholicism that was just beneath the surface came to life again in 1928 when the Democratic candidate for the presidency, Gov. Al Smith of New York, was the first Roman Catholic to receive the nomination of a major party for the nation's highest office.

Of course, World War I also moved the nation into the center of global life. Led by a president, Woodrow Wilson, a devout Presbyterian, the American people unconsciously imposed religious images onto the war effort. Wilson's rhetoric, especially in wartime, drew from the emphasis on preaching from the Bible, a form of sermonic proclamation from his Calvinist heritage that Wilson absorbed almost by osmosis as the son of an ordained Presbyterian seminary professor. The war to make the world safe for democracy was in Wilson's mind a sacred crusade, with the American nation anointed to bring regeneration to a lost world. In other words, the political task of the American state in the war was essentially a religious task, a Protestant Christian one. As another religious spokesman for America put it, the American effort in World War I was nothing less than an attempt to "Christianize every phase of a righteous war" in order to save democracy itself (Stewart and Wright 1918: 13).

Even if political leaders of the 1920s attempted to take the US back into a cocoon of normalcy, developments in Europe, especially the solidification of Communist control of Russia, kept alive a sense of righteous superiority and religious calling. The Red Scare of the 1920s paralleled controversies within American Protestantism pitting emerging fundamentalists against modernist liberals. The resulting fundamentalist subculture thrived on a premillennial dispensationalist reading of history that always seemed to place the present as the last days before God's final intervention in time. Both the Red Scare and fundamentalist premillennial dispensationalism sustained a sense that the US was somehow different from other nations and that this difference had to do with a morality grounded in Protestant Christianity.

That profound sense of religious nationhood came into even sharper relief in the years after World War II. In part because the Soviet Union was an American ally during the war, politicians and religious leaders downplayed the contrast between the religious democracy of America and the Soviet's atheistic regime. But as the cold war replaced the struggle against Hitler, the contrast became a major talking point. When World War II military hero Dwight D. Eisenhower took the oath of office as president of the United States in 1953, he paused to lead the nation in prayer before delivering his inaugural address, the first prayer to be offered at this civic rite. His simple prayer stood as a profound symbol of the nation's religious identity, in implicit contrast to "godless communism." The following year, Congress added the now controversial phrase "under God" to the Pledge of Allegiance and ordered the words "in God we trust" placed on all US coins and currency, reinforcing the image of the nation as a religious entity. When in 1955 sociologist Will Herberg published his analysis of American religious culture and national identity, *Protestant, Catholic, Jew*, he could argue that a "religion of the American way of life" rooted in democratic ideals, free enterprise, and material consumption had grown to envelop particular faiths and that most Americans respected the three religious families named in the title as equally legitimate means of molding good citizens. Popular evangelist Billy Graham, coming onto the world scene in the 1950s, repeatedly contrasted the godlessness of communism with the potential for righteousness in the American nation if its people remained true to the God that had inspired those of earlier generations such as McKinley's and Wilson's.

The collapse of the Soviet empire in the last decades of the twentieth century made it harder to contrast the US as a religious nation threatened with a godless foe. However, following the terrorist attacks of September 11, 2001, religious rhetoric again came to the fore. This time the contrast was not with a single political entity whose government and economic system seemed at odds with that of the US. Rather, the mantle of evil was transferred to another religious tradition, a radical expression of Islam, that had pockets of support in many nations. It mattered not that Islam was among the fastest growing religions in the US, thanks both to immigration and conversion. Rather, popular thinking pounced on a misconstrued notion of *jihad* or holy war to paint a portrait of Islam as a religion of violence intent on the destruction of all that was civilized and humane. Building on negative religious images of the Taliban regime in Afghanistan, where US forces remained mired in a seemingly endless struggle to install a stable government whose policies would reflect American democratic ideals, the war on terror again lifted up the US as a paragon of all that was right and moral, thanks to its religious underpinnings (however diverse they might be), and Islam as the exemplar of all that was demonic and deleterious to human welfare. The truth of American goodness remained constant, but the falsehood of its enemy had shifted from godless communism to heinous terrorism.

Over the course of the twentieth century there were also challenges to the simplistic notion of a righteous America rooted in an ethos where a religious style associated with evangelical Protestantism held sway. Just as the struggle with godless communism reached a fever pitch in the mid-1950s the civil rights movement began to transform American life. Drawing heavily on biblical language – especially that of the Hebrew prophets, in rally speeches that were in reality sermons, the Rev. Martin Luther King, Jr. reminded the world that there was a stunning inconsistency at the heart of America's self-image. Patterns of segregation based on the "separate but equal" principle endorsed by the Supreme Court in *Plessy v. Ferguson* (1896) gave the lie to the ideals of liberty, justice, and equality central to the American self-image. As the civil rights movement gained momentum with the Birmingham, Alabama, bus boycott that began in December 1955, other voices soon identified additional arenas where, to use a religious term, hypocrisy prevailed. Second-wave feminists lifted up gender inequity, calling for an Equal Rights Amendment to the Constitution; Native Americans began to sue for reclamation of sacred lands and burial grounds seized long before in the name of "Manifest Destiny": gay and lesbian Americans added to the chorus the issues of sexual orientation and identity following the Stonewall riot in New York City's Greenwich Village in 1969. In the midst of all these efforts to identify flaws in the American character and correct them came the rising protests of those who found in US policy in Southeast Asia, particularly the military engagement in Vietnam, a blatant contradiction of national purpose and wellbeing. If the Communist menace had provided an overarching sense of common purpose, then the burgeoning liberation and anti-war movements seemed destined to rip apart the bonds that united Americans together as one people.

To be sure, there were efforts to recapture a sense of common purpose, to endow the nation with a religious quality once again. The most notable came in 1967 when sociologist Robert Bellah published his now classic essay, "Civil Religion in America." Looking to the nation's past, particular times of war and struggle, Bellah argued that there existed alongside the more obvious religious institutions and traditions a civil religion that provided a mystical bond giving all Americans a sense of common purpose and identity. Looking at religious language in presidential inaugural addresses, sacred texts such as the Declaration of Independence and the Constitution, pilgrimage sites such as the Gettysburg battlefield, and even a nationalistic hymnody with anthems such as "America the Beautiful" and "The Battle Hymn of the Republic" at its heart, this civil religion should, Bellah insisted, provide a social glue that bound all Americans together and set them apart as a nation among nations. Of course, in one sense, what made Bellah's cause urgent was the disunity that seemed to come in an age of protest and liberation movements. It mattered little, for example, that the civil religion really reflected only the lived history of middle- to upper-class white Protestant males. What seemed lacking was a single worldview, a religious *raison d'être*, that Bellah presumed had once been there in a nation that existed "under God" and whose people were reminded in every financial exchange that "in God we trust."

At the same time, it was becoming harder to affirm the uniqueness of the American political enterprise as American culture itself became more entwined with other cultures, peoples, and different religions. Some of that transformation had direct links to changes in immigration laws in 1965, right at the time when Bellah and others were struggling to find a common core of values that knit the American people into one body politic. Although Congress had imposed restrictions on immigration from Asia as early as the 1880s, the National Origins Act of 1924 that was part of the return to presumed normalcy after the conflagration of World War I placed severe quotas on immigration, using figures of foreign stock from the 1890 census to fix them. The intent clearly was to perpetuate the broad Anglo-Saxon evangelical Protestant domination of American culture, since the lowest quotas went to areas in southern, central, and eastern Europe that brought millions of Roman Catholics, Jews, and Eastern Orthodox Christians to American shores. World War I proved to have brought only a temporary hiatus to some of the anti-Semitism unleashed in the lynching of Leo Frank in Georgia in 1915 for a murder committed by a witness against him, along with anti-Catholicism and anti-immigrant sentiment more generally as some Protestant leaders spoke forcefully in favor of the legislation to restrict immigration on the grounds that it would keep America an Anglo-Saxon Protestant culture. Nearly a generation later, the basic principles of that law received reinforcement with some minor modification in the McCarran–Walter Act of 1952, passed in the wake of the communist menace. The latter did at least make it possible for some refugees from the emerging communist-based People's Republic of China to enter the country. It thus undid the 1924 provisions that had barred Asians in general from seeking naturalization, in part because of ethnic prejudice but also in part because of a veiled antagonism to the religious traditions indigenous to Asia. The 1952 law also provided some accommodation for the "war brides" married to American military personnel serving in Asia during World War II and the Korean conflict.

A major overhaul of the law in 1965 made it possible for ever larger numbers of immigrants to make their way to the US from Latin America, Asia, and Africa. Although the change in the law was not designed to alter the religious landscape, transformation in the religious sector became one of its more stunning consequences. Political ramifications are also legion. Immigrants from Asia, for example, have swelled the ranks of America's Hindu, Buddhist, and Sikh populations, bringing Hindu temples and scores of Buddhist centers – many often serving a specific ethnic population – to every major city across the nation. Immigration from Africa, Asia, and other parts of the Near East has added significantly to the nation's Muslim population, although precise figures are hard to come by. Muslims, especially in the wake of anti-Islamic sentiment following the terrorist episode of September 11, 2001, have retreated from most active proselytizing, although the religion is one that by nature seeks converts. The largest immigration, that from Central and South America, is predominantly Roman Catholic, with a robust Protestant Pentecostal minority. Regardless of whether Latina/o immigrants are Protestant or Catholic, they have a vibrant charismatic dimension to their religious expression and a decidedly conservative posture on many theological and social issues. Politicians have been quick to court voters among the newer immigrant populations as millions have become naturalized citizens, but 40 years after the immigration law changed, no enduring patterns of political affiliation have emerged. By the middle of the first decade of the twenty-first century, Latina/o Americans had surpassed African Americans as the largest ethnic minority in the US, and their numbers were bringing increasing pressure on Congress to pursue even more immigration reform, especially as concern mounted about the ever larger number of "illegal" or undocumented immigrants from Mexico and lands further south.

The presence of these newer immigrant populations has important ramifications for the religious image of the nation as a political entity and for the American civil religion in whatever form it takes. For newer immigrants, as for those whose ancestry was rooted in African slavery, the mythic reconstruction of the American past into a tale of Divine Providence's guiding the nation towards its sacred destiny has little, if any meaning. From American independence through Manifest Destiny to the struggle against godless communism, the majestic story – usually construed through the theologies of an Anglo-Saxon evangelical Protestantism – of a nation led by God to achieve ever greater liberty, justice, and equality for all humanity rings hollow. These formative events are not part of the collective subconscious of newer immigrants. So the new pluralism has had a profound impact on the way in which religious language and religious images can hope to capture the aspirations and political ideals of the people, and the increasingly apocalyptic metaphors that marked political discourse after the American invasion of Iraq, for example, are more likely to conjure fear rather than inspire pride.

Religious images of American nationhood represent only one way religion has interacted with politics in the US since 1898, even as that interaction became more complex as Americans experienced an ever more global context for national events and concerns. Efforts to construe the nation in religious terms, to erect a civil religion that would provide an overarching framework of meaning for the common life, the political life, of all Americans encountered struggles as the nation became more pluralistic. At the same time organized religious groups, from denominations to cooperative associations and special interest groups, sought to impress on political life programs and policies that reflected their own sense of what was right and just.

Organized Religious Efforts to Influence the Political Sphere

The ideal of separation of church and state, as the provisions prohibiting a religious establishment are popularly known, has never meant that the realm of religion has refrained from having vast influence on the political sector. From provisions in colonial legal codes to blue laws outlawing government and business work on Sundays finally dismantled at the close of the twentieth century, religion has permeated public life. In the nineteenth century, as public school systems emerged, curricula and instructional materials readily presumed common consent to a broadly conceived evangelical Protestant way of thinking and acting, even as non-Protestant immigrants experienced extraordinary numerical growth. Since the end of the nineteenth century, however, more direct efforts to press for legislation, programs, and policies thought consonant with particular religious worldviews have been a constant of American common life.

The progressive Federal Council of Churches (FCC) founded in 1908 – and its subsequent reorganization as the National Council of Churches in 1950 – provided a cooperative institutional voice for mainline Protestants that not only often masked an anti-Catholic and anti-Semitic posture but also sought to influence enactment of federal legislation designed to reflect the social, moral, and religious values of its constituent bodies. The council emerged as the Social Gospel movement was reaching its peak. A leading exponent of that movement, Baptist theologian Walter Rauschenbusch published his classic *Christianity and the Social Crisis* in 1907 in response to the rapid industrialization and urbanization after the Civil War that was fueled by a surge in immigration. The Social Gospel leaders of the FCC called for legislation to improve working conditions in the nation's factories, higher wages, a shorter work week, and restrictions on women and children in the industrial workforce. Several denominations followed the lead of the Methodist Episcopal Church, an FCC member, in promulgating "social creeds" or statements of an economic and political bent. American Catholics, who were the mainstay of the emerging industrial labor force, found a voice in Fr. John A. Ryan, who developed a strong argument in favor of better working conditions in his book, *A Living Wage*. Concomitantly, much of the leadership of the developing labor union movement came from clusters of Jews, motivated not only by a sense of justice but also by an opportunity for political and social activism that had often been impossible in Europe.

At the same time, many religious bodies were devoted to the cause of Prohibition, making the case for a national ban on the manufacture and sale of alcoholic beverages not just on religious or moral grounds, but as well on claims that alcohol consumption was deleterious to family life and to industrial productivity. Many of the concerns relating to labor and industry fused with the political movement known as Progressivism and lost their overt religious aura. World War I interrupted all such efforts, but following the war, with added support from groups such as the Anti-Saloon League and the Women's Christian Temperance Union, the Prohibition movement saw its goal achieved when a constitutional amendment and enabling legislation made the manufacture and sale of alcoholic beverages illegal, a policy not rescinded until the 1930s. Much of the grass-roots leadership for Prohibition came from those now called first-wave feminists, who added to their concerns the matter of granting women the right to vote. For some women, calling for the ordination of women to professional ministry was a cognate issue. As previously noted, Protestant leaders also by and large supported the restrictive legislation curtailing immigration that came in the 1920s, believing that the quotas and limitations imposed would help assure that a broad, generic evangelical Protestantism would continue to set the religious tone for the entire culture and its political life. Some saw immigrants as those most likely to abuse alcohol. So the Prohibition forces sometimes joined with those seeking to limit immigration since both could be cast as ways to preserve Anglo-Saxon Protestant domination of the larger culture. As well, in the 1920s, those religious leaders who called for further regulation of business and industry to protect American workers and their families were counterbalanced by those who saw free enterprise as divinely ordained. The darker side of this broad engagement of religion with social and political forces came with the rebirth of the Ku Klux Klan in a venomous form that was not only blatantly racist, but also anti-Catholic, anti-Semitic, and anti-immigrant. This incarnation of the Klan garnered much of its support among white Protestants who feared that the world they had known was vanishing with the rise of urban, industrial America and its movement onto the global scene.

The global economic depression signaled by the stock market crash of 1929 and the response in the US called the New Deal had enduring consequences for the role of religion in American political life. Prior to the New Deal, launched by President Franklin Roosevelt when he first took office in 1933, there had been little federal interest in social welfare programs or in direct public assistance to those Americans most in need. By and large, most social welfare programs then operated under the aegis of denominations or individual congregations. With the New Deal creating government-sponsored agencies and programs, such as the Social Security benefit program for retired workers, religious institutions began to cede to the government many such responsibilities. Of course, during the Depression, religious institutions were themselves strapped for resources and could not have been nearly as effective as government agencies. Yet the shift had enduring consequences, for Americans and their religious leaders began to assume that providing care for the needy, however defined, was a political issue, not a matter of living out one's religious faith. Government agencies were reluctant to work with or through religious-based social welfare programs, lest the boundary between church and state vanish. Not until the opening decade of the twenty-first century, when during the presidency of George W. Bush the government began to channel funds to "faith-based" groups that offered a range of social services, presumably without religious strings attached, did the gap begin to close. But that initiative, as we shall see, raised fresh questions about the proper relationship of institutional religion and the political sector.

As the nation moved from economic depression into World War II, political and international events eclipsed matters of how religion and politics should relate to each other. In one sense, however, it was the era of the Cold War that saw perhaps the peak of religious influence, albeit often subtle and indirect, in political affairs. Legislative moves such as adding "under God" to the Pledge of Allegiance may be the most obvious. Yet in the years after the war, most mainline denominations and some inter-denominational or ecumenical cooperative groups established a presence in the nation's capital, perhaps having the headquarters for a social concerns agency there. For example, the Baptist Joint Committee on Public Affairs, formerly the Baptist Joint Committee on Religious Liberty, opened its Washington office in 1946. Issuing position papers and filing "friend of the court" briefs in Supreme Court cases, groups kept before politicians perspectives and positions that echoed resolutions and such bypassed denominational and ecumenical legislative bodies. The results of this indirect impact have received relatively little attention and analysis. For the most part, religious leaders were content to operate behind the scenes, lest their advocacy of particular laws and programs (or opposition to them) appear intrusions that breached the constitutional separation of church and state and threatened the tax-exempt status of religious groups that, as charitable organizations, were prohibited from direct lobbying or endorsing candidates for public office.

In time, however, religious leaders addressed matters of political import. Roman Catholic bishops, for example, have consistently criticized *Roe v. Wade*, the 1973 Supreme Court decision allowing women greater access to abortion, since church teaching condemned almost all abortion. But the bishops also spoke out collectively on matters such as capital punishment and economic injustice. Similarly, in 1986 the United Methodist Council of Bishops released a document that all congregations were urged to study; it raised serious moral and religious objections to the nuclear arms race. From the 1970s on, many religious bodies and leaders lent their support to environmental and ecological movements, seeing them as consonant with a theological understanding of creation and stewardship. But the most strident voices have come from conservative Christians, primarily Protestants but sometimes in concert with Roman Catholics depending on the issue at stake. Particularly troubling were Supreme Court decisions such as those in the 1960s on prayer and Bible reading in the schools and especially the 1973 abortion decision that conservative Protestants believed had stripped the nation of its presumed religious grounding. The Moral Majority, started by independent Baptist pastor Jerry Falwell in 1979 (and formally, but by no means informally, dismantled a decade later) and the Christian Coalition, set up by religious media mogul and Pentecostally-oriented preacher Pat Robertson in 1989, are the two best-known examples of special interest groups grounded in a decidedly conservative Protestant religious belief system that worked directly to change the course of national politics. Sometimes soliciting members to run for local school boards to restrict the teaching of evolution in public schools, more often calling for support for Republican Party candidates, and always laboring to overturn the abortion and school prayer decisions as well as restrict pornography and otherwise enhance "family values," groups of the "new religious political right" have remained a fixture on the national scene since the 1980s. Although pundits debate just how much influence such groups have actually wielded, the publicity they garner and the image they promote of an America restored to a mythic purity more basic than the calls for a civil religion keeps alive among conservative Christians especially a sense that political action is necessary to save the soul of the nation. Not all evangelicals concur with the shrill tone or even with the specific policy goals of the religious right; Jim Wallis of the Washington-based Sojourners Fellowship, for example, in his best-selling *God's Politics* sought to offer an evangelical program of social justice as an alternative to both the religious right and the less conservative mainline.

The engagement of religious groups with issues in the public sector represents one way to see the interplay of religion and politics in modern America. Just as powerful are cases that have come before the nation's courts, especially the US Supreme Court. Such cases in very concrete ways reveal the difficulty of responding to increasing religious diversity while still retaining a sense of common national identity.

The Courts and Religion: From Free Exercise to Avoiding the Appearance of Establishment

Legal cases dealing with religion are legion, even if few tangle with thorny issues such as determining what actually constitutes religion or religious belief. Most have come before lower courts, where they often provided the basis for precedent cited by higher courts. Because those resolved by the US Supreme Court are better known, they will illustrate here how judicial concerns in the era of globalization have shifted from guaranteeing the free exercise of religion guaranteed by the First Amendment to the Constitution to assuring that government and government-supported public entities, when challenged, avoid the appearance of endorsing or favoring a particular form of religion. The constitutional provision undergirding the latter also derives from the

First Amendment in its declaration that Congress shall make no law respecting an establishment of religion. Some controversies, of course, involve both free exercise and perceived establishment issues.

Cases concerning conscientious objection to participating in military combat, examples that fuse free exercise and establishment matters, came before the courts with some frequency for much of the twentieth century. Historically, when the federal government enacted legislation requiring citizens to serve in the military through the draft or selective service, provisions exempted those who were members of religious groups opposed to all war, although they might be compelled to perform alternate, non-combative service. Indeed, the first conscription law in the twentieth century, enacted in 1917 at the beginning of American participation in World War I, limited exemption to members of the historic peace churches and groups such as Quakers and Mennonites. However, exemption did not include those who were in the process of becoming naturalized citizens, and Supreme Court cases in the late 1920s and early 1930s endorsed the position that those seeking citizenship but who refused to bear arms on whatever grounds should be denied citizenship, a position not rejected until 1946. So, too, the court saw no problem with a University of California requirement that all male students, regardless of religious belief, participate in an R.O.T.C. program.

Looming in the background, however, were more difficult issues. Some religious groups supported members whose personal beliefs prohibited bearing arms, even though they did not call for all members to refrain from such activity. By mid-century, cases were emerging in which individuals who were not members of any particular group, but whose personal moral and religious views opposed war, were seeking exemption. In the era of the Vietnam War, cases moved even further, when issues such as whether insisting that objection to military service stem from religious beliefs represented an unofficial establishment of religion, not just a matter of free exercise, and whether such objection, if rooted in a philosophical and ethical worldview that was not even necessarily theistic, was also protected. As well, some raised questions about "selective" conscientious objection; that is, might one have moral or religious objections to a specific war or combat situation, but not necessarily in theory to all. As the century proceeded, the courts moved to drop formal religious affiliation as condition for conscientious objection, but did not embrace the idea of selective conscientious objection.

Cases having to do with military combat service were not the only ones that raised issues of conflict between persons of faith and the state during wartime. Others mixed free exercise concerns with subtle ways common practice seemed to promote religion and thus hint at a religious establishment. During the ear of World War II, the group known as Jehovah's Witnesses became a symbol for this web of considerations. From their beginnings in the later nineteenth century, the Jehovah's Witnesses had regarded all human government as a tool of Satan at worst, a necessary evil at best. Regardless, no Witness would as a matter of faith pledge loyalty to any government in a way that would seem to defy one's absolute loyalty to God. When what became the Pledge of Allegiance to the American flag first appeared in a youth magazine in 1892, it lacked both the phrase "under God" and the imprimatur of the government. As World War II loomed, however, Congress enacted legislation mandating the population to salute the flag, and school districts across the nation began requiring all children to begin the school day with patriotic exercises that included recitation of the pledge to the flag. Although many objected on religious grounds, the Jehovah's Witnesses gained national attention in the mid-1930s when more than 100 children were expelled from schools in Pennsylvania for refusing on religious grounds to salute the flag. By 1938, lower courts generally affirmed the right of these children to refrain from saluting the flag on religious grounds, but in 1940 the US Supreme Court ruled against them, noting in the majority opinion that the flag was a symbol of national unity, a secular matter rather than a religious one, and those who failed to salute it represented a dangerous threat to the nation. Much controversy ensued since those who disagreed with the decision believed the Court transformed a matter of religious belief and practice into a political weapon and thus denied Witnesses and others the right to free exercise of their faith. Three years later, however, in a similar case, the Court affirmed the right of citizens to refrain from saluting the flag should religious convictions prohibit them from doing so. In retrospect, the earlier cases were as much about promoting a sense of national unity and common identity as the Nazi menace loomed on the horizon; by the later decision in 1943, the tide was turning in World War II, and it was clear that groups like the Witnesses and others who had religious reservations about taking political oaths of any kind were really no threat to national security at all. One could be a good American and not salute the flag if that action contradicted one's ultimate allegiance to God alone.

Seldom reaching the Supreme Court were cases involving "blue laws" or restrictions placed by local and state governments on activities permitted on Sundays, Christianity's day of worship. Nor did many cases where the issue was a refusal to seek or accept certain forms of medical treatment on religious grounds often move beyond state and local court. Yet both illuminate matters of free exercise and even of religious establishment. Laws that prohibited some forms of activity, including many business operations, on Sundays because that was a sacred day within the Christian tradition seemed to Orthodox Jews and Seventh-Day Adventists, for example, to favor or establish Christianity as well as to place undue constraints on the free exercise of persons for whom another day was sacred and Sunday a day for work. Curiously, the court in two 1961 cases upheld blue laws using an "argument from history" and the claim that restricting activity on one day out of seven in a week, albeit a day sacred to Christians, promoted the general welfare of all the people by mandating a day of rest. Unwittingly, however, those cases spurred many state and local governments to begin the process of dismantling blue laws.

Medical treatment cases tended to center on Jehovah's Witnesses and Christian Scientists, both of whose beliefs either prohibit use of scientific medical protocols or of specific procedures, such as blood transfusions. The most controversial have involved parents who refused medical treatment for minor children. Generally, courts have affirmed the right of adults of legal age to refuse treatment, but have often intervened when the health of children was at stake on the grounds that the duty of government to promote the general welfare superseded the right of parents. By the early decades of the twenty-first century, other ethical dilemmas, from physician-assisted suicide to halting medical treatment for persons considered "brain dead" or unable to make decisions for themselves, suggested that issues of free exercise and the intertwining of religious beliefs with other aspects of life had become increasingly nuanced and problematic. So, too, certain religious practices, such as handling serpents or ingesting poisonous liquids as acts of worship, have prompted debates over the limits of free exercise sometimes resulting in court action. The trend over the course of the twentieth century, with some exceptions, was to extend the parameters of free exercise for mentally competent adults.

Greater awareness of religious diversity, one of the consequences of the globalization of American society during the twentieth century, has posed different dilemmas regarding free exercise. As with court cases that more directly involve religious establishment, several of these emerge from a growing appreciation of the presence of religious minorities in a culture once dominated by various strands of the Christian tradition. Some fuse free exercise issues with other constitutional rights such as free speech. For example, did free speech mean that one could proselytize on public property? A 1981 case involving the International Society of Krishna Consciousness (Hare Krishna) brought this matter to the fore, with free speech, if confined to a specific area, trumping any potential infringement on the rights of others using public space. Immigrants who brought from the Caribbean their adherence to *Santeria* ran afoul of laws in some communities when they slaughtered chickens as part of ritual practice, but the Supreme Court affirmed their right to do so.

More complicated were state and then federal court cases that dealt with the practice in a ritual context of ingesting peyote, a controlled substance, by members of the Native American Church. Initial federal legislation in the early 1990s sought to prohibit the use of peyote, but amendments to the Native American Religious Freedom Act in 1994 for the moment secured the practice. In one sense, the legal issues surrounding the Native American Church represented simply another chapter in a long story of Euro-American misunderstanding of the contours of Native American tribal religious expression and a failure to recognize how aspects of tribal life had absorbed and adapted some ideas and practices received from Christian missionaries from a variety of denominational backgrounds. From the forced relocation of many Southeastern tribes to reservations in Oklahoma in the middle-third of the nineteenth century to the efforts to snuff out a Native American apocalypticism that echoed Christian millennial expectation at Wounded Knee in 1890, Euro-Americans had denied the integrity of the internal dynamics of Native American religious life. In the wake of the civil rights movement, many different minority groups sought not only to reclaim a sense of pride in their own identities and heritage, but also to assure that the larger culture and the state affirmed the integrity of their corporate being. In this context, the legal cases surrounding the use of a controlled substance became a symbol of Native American assertion of the validity of a tribal practice, albeit one that fused tradition with some Christian elements. Other less volatile cases often concerned restoration of land, particularly ancient burial grounds, to tribal control.

Alongside conversation about free exercise, the matter of religious establishment received greater attention as American society became more diverse and pluralistic during the twentieth century. Many matters of debate concerned public schools whose curricula had, during the nineteenth century, reflected the evangelical Protestantism that dominated the country. In the first half of the twentieth century, several court cases focused on whether religious instruction could take place on public school property, even outside normal school hours, and whether tax money collected for education and other assistance could be dispersed to parochial or religious schools as well as to public schools. Some addressed whether, on religious grounds, students could refuse to recite the Pledge of Allegiance, a matter that moved again into the public eye after Congress added the phrase "under God" to the pledge in 1954. But the two Supreme Court cases that continue to eclipse all others came nearly half a century ago. In *Engel v. Vitale* (1962), the Supreme Court held that requiring public school students to recite a prayer, even if presumably non-sectarian in content, amounted to an unacceptable establishment of religion. The following year, in *Abington v. Schempp*, the Court banned mandatory devotional Bible reading in the public schools on similar grounds. In neither did the Court prohibit the academic study of religion, and in time courts tended to allow student religious groups to use school property outside of instructional hours on the same terms granted to other special-interest groups. Those who applauded these moves claimed they not only protected the rights of students for whom such activities were not part of their personal lives or practice, but also refrained from endorsing any form of religion, in theory keeping the schools neutral and therefore devoid of any hint of religious establishment. Americans were simply of too many different minds when it came to such matters as to agree on any prayer or generic religious activity. Critics, however, insisted that the decisions infringed on the rights of the majority to engage in exercises integral to their own identity and beliefs.

Courts at every level have had to address whether placing on public property symbols associated with one religion at the time of a holiday also represents an unconstitutional, even if indirect, endorsement/establishment of religion. By the close of the twentieth century, that debate had expanded to include posting the Ten Commandments in courtrooms, classrooms, and other public venues and even the language in some state mottoes. If the courts demonstrated a passion to protect religious minorities and assure strict neutrality, opponents argued that they had overstepped their constitutional responsibility and had instead become aggressively anti-religious.

Schools provided the locus for other controversies about the place religion or religious views should or should not have in public life. Many of those concerned teaching theories of evolution and alternatives such as creation science and intelligent design. Such controversies stretched back to the early decades of the twentieth century. The Tennessee legislature, for example, had prohibited teaching evolutionary theory in the state's public schools, leading to the famed Scopes Trial of 1925 that became a symbol of that age's struggle between religious liberals and fundamentalists to set the tone for the larger culture. Later, when courts ruled that creation science was not really science but religious belief in disguise, those who demanded that science curricula include an alternative to evolution reformulated their thinking under the rubric of intelligent design. In late 2005, a lower federal court in Pennsylvania decreed intelligent design theory to be more faith than science and therefore inappropriate subject matter for public school instruction. The national debate continues, for Americans are not of a single mind when it comes to talking about the origins and/or meaning of life.

Perhaps more than disagreements over what should or should not be taught in the public schools and more volatile even than the continuing controversy over the school prayer and devotional Bible reading decisions of the 1960s is the national acrimony that followed on a decision that does not even directly deal with religion per se, namely *Roe v. Wade*. That decision in 1973, striking down many of the state and local ordinances that restricted access to abortion in the early stages of pregnancy, initially seemed more directly tied to second-wave feminism and the right of a woman to determine whether she wished to bear a child. In time, however, a religious furor that still stirs national debate developed, for opponents of the decision injected a religious component into the argument in their insistence that life begins at conception. That position virtually equated abortion with murder, at least according to bumper stickers on automobiles. But the question of when life does begin was indeed a religious and theological matter, not just a medical one. Beyond the ongoing contention over abortion, similar questions plagued the national conversation over euthanasia, for it was no easier to reach consensus about when life ended than it was about when it began. By the beginning of the twenty-first century, cognate arguments informed discussion about stem-cell research.

Among the challenges that remain is how to acknowledge the signal importance of religion, with its attendant beliefs and practices, for millions of Americans in an era marked by diversity and pluralism. When persons of faith disagree over matters with enduring political consequences, whose position should prevail? Even efforts to speak in generic terms about religion are fraught with difficulty, for different traditions understand the nature of religion differently, and the term itself defies consensus. Such difficulty marks contemporary efforts of the government to give financial assistance to certain social welfare programs and community activities run under religious auspices, but that seek to address social problems and needs. As "faith-based initiatives," such enterprises on the surface promote the general welfare and presumably take the burden off governmental agencies and programs to meet all social welfare needs. But critics contend that the religious groups sponsoring them could too readily coerce allegiance or impose religious tests as a condition of receiving help, while some groups refuse to accept financial assistance from the government because they fear that doing so would lead to efforts to control religious belief and practice. Yet behind all the debates is a recognition that religion remains integral to American common life.

Even as diversity and pluralism have mushroomed since 1898, religious institutions continue to flourish – even if those once dominant have dwindled in size and others have assumed greater influence. The United States remains by any measurable standard among the most religious of nations. That consideration alone may suggest why issues of free exercise are so prominent; religion is important to Americans although it assumes many forms. It may also help explain why, along with the tradition of trying to keep the sphere of religion and the sphere of government separate and distinct, so many court cases and controversies dot the historical record. In an age of ever increasing globalization, religious groups themselves have sought new ways to assure that what they believe to be right and true informs American public life, for the common ground that someone like William McKinley presumed many years ago has eroded. So, too, efforts to have a single vision of the nation, an image of America that resonates with all Americans, becomes more challenging when placed in the context of globalization.

American international engagement has other ramifications for the tapestry that weaves together religion and politics in the US. After World War II, the US became the first nation officially to recognize Israel as an independent nation-state. As a historic "homeland" for Jews of scores of national backgrounds, Israel itself has struggled with ways to affirm being a Jewish state with the expectations of democratic freedom. Yet the virtually unswerving US governmental support for Israel, particularly when armed conflict has rocked the Middle East, seems to some a breach of that fine division between religion and government and more of an endorsement of Judaism in Israel that denigrated Palestinian and other Muslim religious identities. So, too, after the debacle of September 11, 2001, on a global level it was easy to collapse the American struggle against terrorism with an inherent anti-Muslim prejudice, in this case overlaying religious prejudice on public policy. The convoluted nature of this enterprise complicated calls from government leaders for other nations to cease persecuting persons based on religion and to affirm basic religious liberty for all. That dilemma came to light especially as the US repeatedly sought to convince the People's Republic of China to institute policies less hostile to religion and more open to human rights.

Nevertheless, despite the legal separation of church and state at home and the complicated meshing of elements of religion with political concerns in international affairs, religion and politics remain intertwined in how Americans actually operate as a collective people. If greater diversity and disparity prevail now than when McKinley fell to his knees in the White House on the brink of the Spanish-American War in 1898, it is because the nation itself has become more diverse and pluralistic. Recognition of that diversity underscored many of the court cases that struggled – never without anguish – to protect the free exercise of religion and avoid even the appearance of a religious establishment. Much of it echoes through the efforts to construct a religious vision of the nation as a political entity, whether through advocacy of a civil religion or through using religious language to capture the hopes and aspirations of the people. Yet such endeavors face frustration, for there simply is no longer any common core of religious beliefs and values, despite differences in denomination or tradition, to support them. As the US has become more ethically and religiously diverse and pluralistic, the difficulty in articulating a single vision of the nation that would embrace all who see themselves as genuinely American has intensified. At the same time, religious voices continue to offer commentary on political matters, particularly those that have obvious moral and ethical dimensions, and religious leaders engage in activities designed to sway public opinion and encourage political leaders to enact legislation and financially support programs that reflect their particular beliefs and ideals, With every such activity, the web holding religion and politics together becomes more intricate and fragile.

References and Further Reading

Bellah, R.N. (1967) "Civil Religion in America," *Daedalus*, 96: 1–21.

Eck, D.L. (2001) *A New Religious America: How a "Christian Country" Became the World's Most Religiously Diverse Nation*, San Francisco: Harper San Francisco.

Engstrom, D.W. and Piedra, L.M. (eds.) (2006) *Our Diverse Society: Race and Ethnicity– Implications for American Society*, Washington, DC: NASW Press.

Everett, W.J. (1988) *God's Federal Republic: Reconstructing Our Governing Symbol*, New York: Paulist Press.

Herberg, W. (1960; orig. 1955) *Protestant, Catholic, Jew: An Essay in American Religious Sociology*, Garden City, NY: Doubleday.

Hutchison, W.R. (2003) *Religious Pluralism in America: The Contentious History of a Founding Ideal*, New Haven, CT: Yale University Press.

Lippy, C.H. (2000) *Pluralism Comes of Age: American Religious Culture in the Twentieth Century*, Armonk, NY: M.E. Sharpe.

Lippy, C.H. (ed.) (2006) *Faith in America: Changes, Challenges, New Directions*, 3 vols, Westport, CT: Praeger.

Martin, W. (1996) *With God on Our Side: The Rise of the Religious Right in America*, New York: Broadway Books.

Marty, M.E. (1986) *Modern American Religion*, vol. 1: *The Irony of It All, 1893–1919*, Chicago: University of Chicago Press.

Marty, M.E. (1991) *Modern American Religion*, vol. 2: *The Noise of Conflict, 1919–1941*, Chicago: University of Chicago Press.

Marty, M.E. (1996) *Modern American Religion*, vol. 3: *Under God, Indivisible, 1941–1960*, Chicago: University of Chicago Press.

Miller, W.L. (1985) *The First Liberty: Religion and the American Republic*, New York: Paragon House.

Olcott, C.S. (1916) *The Life of William McKinley*, 2 vols, Boston: Houghton Mifflin.

Rauschenbusch, W. (1964; orig. 1907) *Christianizing and the Social Crisis*, New York: Harper.

Ryan, J.A. (1971; orig. 1906) *A Living Wage: Its Ethical and Economic Aspects*, New York: Arno.

Stewart, G., Jr., and Wright, H.B. (1918) *The Practice of Friendship*, New York: Association Press.

Strong, J. (1963; orig. 1886) *Our Country: Its Possible Future and Its Present Crisis*, Cambridge, MA: Belknap Press of Harvard University Press.

Toulouse, M.G. (2006) *God in Public: Four Ways American Christianity and Public Life Relate*, Louisville, KY: Westminster John Knox Press.

Vinz, W.L. (1997) *Pulpit Politics: Faces of American Protestant Nationalism in the Twentieth Century*, Albany, NY: State University of New York Press.

Wallis, J. (2005) *God's Politics: Why the Right Gets It Wrong and the Left Doesn't Get It*, San Francisco: Harper San Francisco.

Wuthnow, R. (2005) *America and the Challenges of Religious Diversity*, Princeton, NJ: Princeton University Press.

14

Cosmology

Kathryn Lofton

With the westward rush coming to an end and the accelerated pace of Americans relocating from hither to yon and back again, religiously grounded notions of place were in flux as the nation moved decisively onto the global stage. New cosmologies were present in abundance as Asian religious ideas mingled with religio-philosophical thinking, increasingly more articulate African-American versions of cosmic order, and views of the world that had sprung up out of the experience of commerce, technology, and improved communications and travel. World Wars and the threat of nuclear annihilation prompted rethinking of time and place, and identity as well, leading some to envision the end, and others to recast their sense of their situatedness in a tenuous global framework. The mood of the nation was aptly expressed in the pride of place accorded the individual, and especially as that ideal was manifest in suburban life. Religion at the same time broached possibilities for inclusion, in cosmologies that were less tailored to defining difference and more attuned to structuring collaborations, in open-ended ways, to search for purpose, setting approximate goals along the way.

Two Pictures

In 1911, a postcard was sent and a painting was begun. The postcard was from a woman named Stella visiting Ohio, and it was mailed to her friend Emeline. "Dear Emeline," it began, "Am in the city shopping. Was to hear Billy Sunday." The image on the postcard was a domestic portrait, a photograph of the popular evangelist Billy Sunday with his wife and four children on the steps of their Winona Lake, Indiana, home (Figure 14.1)

We see Sunday's family posed on the stairs: Billy hiding at the upper left, his son George Marquis turned slightly away at the upper right. His wife, Nell, and his eldest daughter, Helen, sit along the left side. William Ashley and Paul Thompson, the two youngest, sit in the foreground, possibly plotting mischief. Attendants at revivals knew

Figure 14.1 Billy Sunday with his wife and four children.

all about Sunday's family; he used them as anecdotal referents in his vivid sermonic rambles. Such an image was a popular keepsake, sold in large quantities on Sunday's tours. We have to imagine Stella selecting this postcard among a variety of trademark Sunday images, such as those with Sunday in an athletic pose or those memorializing city-specific tabernacle tents. Perhaps Stella selected it on a whim; or maybe it was chosen with great intention, echoing an inside joke she and Emeline had about the world-renowned Billy Sunday. Or maybe it was one of the 15 postcards Stella sent that day, particular only because it was the one at her fingertips when she decided to write to Emeline.

The same year that Stella wrote Emeline, Marcel Duchamp began a new canvas in his Paris studio. Struggling to define his style, Duchamp labored over a first draft of a figure, fractured into several profiles, ostensibly descending a staircase. After attempting an initial draft, Duchamp completed a second, more substantive version of this painting, *Nude Descending a Staircase, No. 2* in 1912 (Figure 14.2).

Less than a year after the completion of the second draft, Duchamp's masterpiece became the scandal of the 1913 Armory Show in New York, symbolizing for many the incomprehensibility of modern art. The Armory Show, also known as the International Exhibition of Modern Art, was exhibited from February to March 1913 at New York's 69th Regiment Armory. Although it included more than 1,200 paintings, sculptures, and decorative works by over 300 European and American artists, Duchamp's painting was the show's centerpiece, hanging in the first room of the Armory. Crowds were reportedly so large in that gallery that visitors could barely get a glimpse at it. This notoriety was premised as much on its opacity as its aesthetic value; few observers claimed to understand the image. For men and women weaned on nineteenth-century landscape paintings and family portraits, *Nude Descending a Staircase, No. 2* conveyed an unrecognizable context and an incommensurable subject. The title suggested clarity not immediately apparent in the fractured cubist clatter scattered on the large oil canvas. In one image, all suppositions about the relationship between

Figure 14.2 Duchamp's *Nude Descending a Staircase, No. 2.*

pictorial content and artistic form were demolished. Although Duchamp would continue to contribute to multiple artistic movements (and avoid acknowledging allegiance to any), this painting remains his most stunning contribution to twentieth-century painting.

If Virginia Woolf was correct that "on or about December 1910, human character changed," then what character do these two images relate (Woolf 1984: 194)? What history do these portraits document? Seen together, one could argue that the Sunday postcard represents the close of a century, and that the Duchamp signaled the inauguration of another. Historians have frequently situated Billy Sunday as the triumphant last stand of "old-time" American religion. With his gymnastic onstage stunts and elaborate tabernacle touring, Sunday's evangelistic work was part vaudeville, and part revival. His waning popularity in the 1920s indicated not only a decline in his own popularity, but also an overall shift in the religious tastes of a nation. When Sunday died in 1935, so did the sawdust trail and its noble hero, the frontier itinerant minister. This postcard, framing a sweetly dressed and cohesive family unit, is the last gasp of a bygone era, where father was tough and mother wore lace. This little postcard thus becomes not merely a note from Stella to Emeline, but also a telegram from one century to the next, a reminder of a world no longer.

Duchamp's painting is easily elevated to equally dramatic historical heights. Histories of American twentieth-century art place *Nude Descending a Staircase, No. 2* at the epicenter of artistic modernism. Duchamp's painting wasn't merely a paradigmatic example of Cubism or a highlight of a 1913 exhibition; for many critics it signaled a monumental transition from classically inspired to modern art, from the cloying vestiges of French academic painting to the emergence of an expressionistic, bohemian avant-garde. Duchamp's painting single-handedly conferred intellectual consequence on an entire iconoclastic century, paving the way for Dada, Surrealism, and Abstract Expressionism. *Nude Descending a Staircase, No. 2* was therefore not just a fractured painting of a woman; it was a metaphor for art itself, the descent of figuration from academic classrooms to Parisian garrets, from the rarefied to the idiosyncratic. The nude was the modern artist, shifting and dissimulating into the cacophonous aesthetic of the twentieth century. This century would be Duchamp's: one in which order was lost, chaos reigned, and every man was a disassembled, descending body.

Or maybe not. Seen from another light, perhaps these images bookend different epochs. Perhaps it was Stella and Sunday who presaged the twentieth century, not Duchamp. Recall Stella's pairing of activities: she was in the city for shopping, and also stopped by the Billy Sunday revival show. Shopping and religion as correlate endeavors, punctuated on a postcard as equal sharers, not contradictions. To worship was to consume a product, a product that was, in the case of Sunday, a carefully plotted performance. Moreover, as a precursor to twentieth-century evangelical kingpins Billy Graham and Jerry Falwell, Sunday and his ideological ilk persisted well into the twenty-first century. His dogmatic theology and conservative domestic recommendations would reappear, again and again, as evangelicals pursued politics and conversion with equal force. In the twenty-first century, the Christian Coalition and Focus on the Family reproduce the Sunday family portrait through their rhetoric and their activism, continually reaffirming the prescience of Sunday's "old-time" axioms. Sitting on their steps at the dawn of the twentieth century, Sunday and his family stare into a future that they will dominate, if not in literal memory, then in their represented meanings. Their Winona Lake world will be an American ambition for a century to come.

Similarly, perhaps Duchamp didn't open an epoch. Maybe he concluded one. After all, *Nude Descending a Staircase* was Duchamp's last genuinely figurative work. Following this painting, he moved to his conceptual and sculptural stage, one that included such found objects as *Bicycle* (1913) and *Fountain* (1917), with Duchamp transferring street rubbish to a gallery and entitling it "art." Although these objects would also be heralded as masterpieces, Duchamp's abandonment of the figure, and of painting, is suggestive. The world of art in the twentieth century saw an increasing turn towards the conceptual and away from studied artistic craft. *Nude Descending a Staircase, No. 2* can be read, then, as an end to over two thousand years of painting, of noble attempts by the artist at mimesis. Metaphorically, then, it seems Duchamp's fractured nude predated a century too abundant, too complicated, to be captured by realist figures or clean lines. The craft of the painter was, like all old-time homespun skills, lost to automation and surplus. Now, the nude descended from the civilized (near divine) heights of the nineteenth century to the skeptical morass of the twentieth.

It is tempting to read these images with such ease, to imagine that they cleanly bookend some canonical epoch. But such chronological cleanliness is rarely found in history. Who would determine the century to come, and how? The truth probably lies somewhere between inauguration and conclusion, somewhere between the birth of the modern and the death of the old. Perhaps the most revealing thing about setting these pictures side-by-side (Figure 14.3 and Figure 14.4) is not their divergence, but their simultaneity. For whatever these images are, and however they embody the spirit of an age, what is certain is that any explanation of their age must incorporate them both. For theirs was a shared epoch. If we are to understand their moment, we must understand it as an era for both Duchamp and Stella, for both the shifting nude and the stoic Sundays.

Constellations of the Modern

The turn from the nineteenth to twentieth century is consistently identified as one of the most fractious and transforming eras in American history. Turn-of-the-century writers claimed that theirs was a time of rapid, widespread, and significant change in almost all areas of social life. Historians have concurred with this dramatic summation, pointing to the late-nineteenth century as a peak moment in the industrialization of the nation, the translation of a Victorian landscape into the purportedly "modern" world. The reverberations of this revolution were seemingly infinite. During the sixty years bridging the two centuries, there was a 50 percent rise in the national population, in part, the result of the largest influx of immigrants in the country's history. Progressive political movements flourished alongside conservative domestic programs. The close of the frontier occurred at the same time as the furious growth of extended cities. Massive migratory movements from east to west, and south to north, led to dramatic shifts in the ethnic composition and class apportionment of America. In the arts, machinery, mass taste, and scientific theory led to manipulations of color, sound, and material in ways that revolutionized ancient traditions of art. Included within this epoch was also the invention of the safety bicycle, the automobile, the airplane, the nationalization of electricity and the local incorporation of water systems. As systems were extended at home, so were they abroad, as America expanded its holdings in Central America and the Pacific. With the conclusion of the Spanish-American War in December 1898, Spain ceded control of its overseas empire, leaving the United States as the dominant political and economic force in the Western Hemisphere. But national incorporation and nascent overseas imperialism only hint at the more intimate shifts in American culture. In US households, there was increase of 1500 percent in the number of telephones and 1000 percent in the number of commercial ice plants. The safety razor with disposable blades was introduced in the same year as the teddy bear, the creation of federal police power, and the release of the first feature film, *The Great Train Robbery* (1903). Modern advertising and anti-trust legislation, the isolation of radium and the first flight at Kitty Hawk; this was an age of exuberant innovation and unending abundance.

Alongside the affirmations of modernization, social tensions simmered and finances fluctuated. Increasing industrialization and cyclical industrial depression resulted in the most violent labor unrest in American history (and the eventual establishment of national labor unions). The quadrupling of the number of married women in the workforce fueled gender optimism and anxiety, as women found new vistas of opportunity and men discovered new plateaus of inadequacy. The urgency expressed in social reform movements and the dearth of utopian writings in the 1890s reflected the country's unsettled condition. Adding to the worries of the times were the innumerable scientific

Figure 14.3 Billy Sunday with his wife and four children.

Figure 14.4 Duchamp's *Nude Descending a Staircase, No. 2*.

and historical discoveries of the moment, discoveries that unmoored theological certitude and motivated bouts of neurasthenia. All of which, claims historian Robert Rydell, "gave American Victorians an intense desire to organize experience" (1984: 4).

Religious institutions and ideas frequently provided this desired organization. Just as industries incorporated and inventions provoked social change, so did denominations order, charismatic prophesy, and individuals antagonize the known theological paradigms. "In the crisis of the loss of a coherent framework for what we know or what we can know," wrote historian Bryan Appleyard, "the modern world was created" (1992: 53). Despite frequent jeremiads about the secularizing effects of modern life, religious innovation abounded in this modern world. After all, it was the 1888 founding of the Student Volunteer Movement (SVM) which inaugurated the "Golden Age" of American missions; the number of American foreign missionaries, which stood at 934 in 1890, reached nearly 5,000 a decade later and over 9,000 in 1915. Groups originated and consolidated, like the Theosophical Society, the Jewish Theological Society, and the Polish National Catholic Church, which formed its own Scranton "Polonia" in 1897. The first prayer house of Sweet Daddy Grace's Peace Mission movement opened in 1921, welcoming a decade that would also include the first Moorish Science temple and Nation of Islam mosque. On January 1, 1889, a Paiute rancher named Wovoka dreamed of a new and glorious world for native peoples; in that same year, Jodo Shinshu missionaries arrived in Hawaii. In 1901, a student in Topeka, Kansas, spoke in tongues, thus launching modern Pentecostalism. The adaptation of the "Pittsburgh Platform" in 1885 provided some coherence for American Reform Jews; the establishment of the United Synagogue of America in 1913 provided similar respite for Conservative Jews. In 1913, George Hensley introduced snake handling to the ritual cue of southern evangelicals; a year later, Jehovah's Witnesses were sure the world would end. This was an age for both the liberal Baptist William Newton Clarke and Reuben Torrey, editor of "The Fundamentals"; for Catholic "Americanist" Archbishop John Ireland and girl evangelist Uldine Utley; for touring Buddhist Anagarika Dharmapala and African-American missionary William H. Sheppard. It was also the age of Edward Bellamy's Christian socialism, Sinclair Lewis' religious cynicism, and Robert G. Ingersoll's atheism. It was, indeed, an age of marvels and expectations, tribulations and evolutions. The world of religious belief swirled as quickly as the new wheels gracing Model T's, opening new landscapes of ritual and adventure.

It would be easy to leave it at that, to stop the story there, in the midst of all that enthusiasm and creativity. Yet, for many historians, this religious abundance signals the existential crisis of the age. Martin E. Marty has termed the turn from the nineteenth to the twentieth century as a "Crisis in the Protestant Empire" (Marty 1984). For Marty, the exuberant expansion of American evangelicalism during this era was an obvious disciplinary mechanism. He describes prominent preachers (like Billy Sunday) as "keepers" of a "Protestant empire," men who defended a prescriptive morality against the "alternative" religious styles practiced by the new immigrants swarming in urban areas. In *The Spiritual Crisis of the Gilded Age* (1971), Paul A. Carter defined a similar "crisis," provoked by unruly industrialization and devastating discoveries in science. These factors, Carter argues, prompted a confrontation between doubt and faith, a "crisis of inner morale" (Carter 1971: 16). A 1908 editorial from the Baptist *Watchman* extends the economic description of the crisis:

> On the one side ... the people are becoming the serfs of large employers, and on the other the subjects of labor unions. In either case, freedom, independence, and the chance for the formation of the highest character is lost; and the people are being reduced to a state of feudalism with two classes of overlords instead of one ... The combinations of capital seek to reduce him to the position of a working serf and the combinations of labor would reduce him to a simple member of a labor union.

In his biography *Billy Sunday Was His Real Name* (1955), William McLoughlin combined the economic interpretations of the *Watchman* with the questions of faith posed by Martin Marty and Paul Carter:

> All was not going well with the American system of free enterprise and laissez faire capitalism. The rugged individualism and self-reliant optimism of the early nineteenth century suffered more frequent shocks and disappointments. The farmer found himself caught in the meshes of monopolistic railroads and unscrupulous price speculators who seemed to be robbing him of the just fruits of his labor. The farmer's children who went to the city found themselves either without jobs or without any chance of working their way up from the drudgery of factory or clerical employment into the longed-for financial success and independence ... The country as a whole seemed at the mercy of unpredictable and uncontrollable panics and depressions. In short, America was in the throes of a gigantic transformation from a primarily agrarian to an industrial economy, and no one knew how to manage the transfer without causing great suffering to millions of hardworking and honest men and women. Though the old optimism did not give way to despair, many Americans were sorely troubled. (McLoughlin 1955: 120)

"Sorely troubled" Americans, economically worried and theologically confused, seem at the center of the crisis perceived by Marty and Carter. Note how disenchantment litters their descriptions. Farmers, faithful to the frontier which promised them prosperity, are overrun by railroads and gauging speculators. Migrants from those rural estates moved to cities in the promise of industry's fortune, finding instead low-paying labor and slum housing. Unseen forces created economic depressions even as men worked their fingers to the bone. Such mythic debunking could produce cynicism and despair, or new cosmologies of possibility. The century to come would offer both in abundance.

Religious Creativity and Cosmological Order

Throughout the twentieth century, Americans imagined religious worlds to ease and explain their troubled occupations. Against the backdrop of two World Wars, bombings in Hiroshima, Nagasaki, and Baghdad, and body bags returned from Korea, Vietnam, and Nicaragua, US citizens imagined a cosmos over which they had increasingly violent control. Extreme global antagonism defined this century; as such, explicating (or evading) the consequences of that violence enjoined much cosmological work. A signifying feature of this violence was its distance: with the critical exceptions of Pearl Harbor and the terrorist attacks of 9/11, Americans were separated from their battlegrounds. To be sure, violence on the home front could be found, from the anti-Semitic lynching of Leo Frank in 1915 to the 1993 federal assault on the Branch Davidian compound. Ignorance about religious practice and belief has fostered localized incidents of prejudicial aggression. Yet if the twentieth century saw the perfection of mass destruction, then it was also a century that did so while averting American soil. The experience of warfare was through photographs and veterans, documentary film and press release. Theology would then offer an approximation and examination of suffering seen from afar.

Such suffering occurred during the ascent of the United States as the dominating global power: it was, by the mid-twentieth century, the wealthiest nation on earth, including a massive market economy, educated citizenry, and media networks sustained through the most sophisticated technologies available. Billy Sunday's domestic prosperity hummed alongside geopolitical mayhem, a contrast of stolidity and chaos, figuration and abstraction. Systematic theologies and doctrines mirrored the duality of Duchamp and Sunday, combining fierce ambitions for unity with discordant multiplicity; homogeneity with heterogeneity; faith in tradition alongside avid innovation. To summarize such a cosmos would be impossible. It is tempting to suggest that over the course of one hundred years, dramatic shifts transpired. That theology was replaced by ritual practice. That denomination was replaced by corporation. And that individual optimism was increasingly paired with social pessimism. Yet such summations might be countered with any number of particular cases, biographies, or religious movements.

In the space remaining, then, we will not extend conclusive theses about cosmological shifts in the twentieth century. Rather, we will focus on consistent tropes. This chapter offers four motifs as the cultural points of origin for American cosmology during the last century: (1) the social acceptance of scientific reasoning; (2) the plurality created through immigration; (3) the potential for mass destruction through technological warfare; and (4) social resettlement in non-urban communities. From these topical points of departure, the chapter will engage with two or three examples demonstrating the theological and epistemic consequences of science, diversity, war, and suburbanization.

Scientific Reasoning and Theological Logic

The eighteenth-century founding of the United Stated coincided with a scientific revolution, in which the natural world came increasingly under intellectual scrutiny and classification. By the start of the twentieth century, scientific logic permeated the culture. Industrialization supplied goods to calibrate each home towards progress. Electricity, plumbing, and telephones connected individual homes to corporate grids offering assimilation, cleanliness, and efficiency to processes that were once atomized and labored domestic exercises. Just as these processed goods received accolades for their salvific role in modernity, the natural world was under harsh scrutiny for its uncivilized form. "Nature" was increasingly interpreted as primitive and dangerous, rather than a metaphor for the perfect architecture of God. Religion, too, was sometimes associated with more "primitive" forms, as scholars of religion experimented with developmental schemas positing that science would, eventually, replace religion. Outside the academic world, religious groups found ways to assimilate new knowledge about nature into their belief systems. Mary Baker Eddy's Christian Science, for example, offered a theology which described each human as a deistic body, fully capable of self-control and regulation. Ideas of mechanistic science combined with a mystical faith in the human spirit, which Christian Scientists believed could resolve any medical ailments of the body.

But evolutionary theory, not individual healing, provided the grounds for the greatest cosmological contest of the twentieth century. The 1920s forged two camps in American Protestantism. On the one side stood the World's Christian Fundamentals Association and those self-described Bible believers called "the fundamentalists." On the other were proponents of evolution, the American Civil Liberties Union, and liberal theology. These "modernists" combated attempts by "fundamentalists" to insert creationist narratives in high school curricula. The fundamentalists take their name from *The Fundamentals* (1910–15), a 12-volume series of books published to codify the conservative position.

Conceived in 1909, *The Fundamentals* was the brainchild of Lyman Stewart, founder of the Union Oil Company of California. Stewart designed *The Fundamentals* as a series of 90 articles by 64 authors re-inscribing "the fundamentals of the Christian faith." Moderate in tone, the articles avoided political topics entirely, focusing on a grounded defense of the scriptures. Approximately a third of the essays guarded the Bible against the new criticism, arguing that the Old and New Testaments were without inconsistency. Another third of the essays discussed foundational theological questions, such as the meaning of the Trinity and the role of sin. The remaining pamphlets were a diverse smattering, addressing everything from the modern "heresies" (such as Christian Science, Roman Catholicism in the US, and Mormonism) to missionary ambitions. The authors of these essays deployed modern scientific research to serve scriptural logic and argue their creationist archaeologies. Any definition of "fundamentalism" which relies on *The Fundamentals* would overwhelmingly emphasize the scholastic bent of the movement, a scrupulous scholarly effort to reconcile Christianity with new data.

The Tennessee trial of John Scopes for teaching evolution offered a national advertisement for fundamentalist anti-intellectualism rather than a showcase for the scholarly prowess exhibited in *The Fundamentals*. Despite the immediate legal condemnation of Scopes, journalists like H.L. Mencken were so successful in their skewering of fundamentalist attitudes that the movement went underground. Mencken's profile of fundamentalism was lopsided, however, posing creationism as an anti-science when, in fact, it was a scientific argument for God's centrality in human development. The twentieth century would present several renditions of this fundamentalist argument. In 1963, ten creationist scientists founded the Creation Research Society, declaring in their statement of belief that "the Bible is the written Word of God, and because it is inspired throughout, all its assertions are historically and scientifically true in the original autographs." Creationists argued that creation science and evolution science should be taught concurrently in the public school, since both offered versions of scientific truth.

In the media, the modernist-scientist is still pitted against the fundamentalist-creationist, with one (the modernist) believing science leads the way to progress as the other (the fundamentalist) sits certain that science seduces men to a materialist view which contributes to fascisms and decay, not uplift and newness. Such a duality fails to recognize how deeply entrenched each party is with academic science. For those unfamiliar with the writings of creationists, it seems impossible to imagine creation science as any sort of "science," since "science" is supposed to supply a natural explanation for the world while religions solely pursue supernatural descriptions. Yet the vast majority of believers and practitioners (creationists and not) fall in between this divide, knitting scientific ideas into religious readings, and religious ideation into scientific predictions. Philosophers and scientists have expended serious effort attempting to fuse a faith in science with a faith in God. John Dewey authored *A Common Faith* (1934) to advocate for a scientific humanism that centered rigorous scientism as the common outlook for moral democratic citizens. Over forty years later, astronaut Edgar Mitchell founded the Institute of Nortic Sciences in 1972 to connect great mystical traditions with quantum mechanics and subatomic physics. Likewise, physicist Fritjof Capra authored *The Tao of Physics* (1983), writing, "The further we penetrate into the submicroscopic world, the more we shall realize how the modern physicist, like the Eastern mystic, has come to see the world as a system of inseparable, interacting and ever-moving components with the observer being an integral part of this system" (Harvey and Goff 2005: 130). Science toyed with religion to express the grandeur found through telescopes and microscopes.

Systems of spirituality, too, arose that utilized scientific discourse. "We now experience that we live not in a material universe, but in a universe of dynamic energy," wrote James Redfield in his bestselling *Celestine Prophecy* (1994); "Everything extant is a field of sacred energy that we can sense and intuit" (Harvey and Goff 2005: 501). Although many individual texts have explored the spiritual consequences of science, none have been more successful than L. Ron Hubbard's *Dianetics: The Modern Science of Mental Health* (1950). In that book, Hubbard offered a series of self-improvement techniques that launched a global new religious movement, the Church of Scientology. The premises of his techniques were a fusion of Aleister Crowley's theories of the occult, the Vedic scriptures, the *Tao Te Ching* and Freudian depth psychology. Each individual, according to Hubbard's descriptions, is an immortal spiritual being (termed a thetan) that has lived through many past lives and will continue to live through many more. Through "auditing," individuals can free themselves of previous traumas and ethical transgressions, recovering the original spiritual abilities of the individual. People are basically good, Hubbard wrote, they had simply been made aberrant by unconsciousness in life. While much of this is derived from Eastern traditions, Hubbard's commitment was to scientific proofs. The tenets of Scientology were expected to be tested by practitioners to prove their merit. Research into time travel, space exploration, and new polygraph mechanisms contributed to Hubbard's cosmo-logical creativity.

While Scientology adamantly argued for the end of war and violence, other new religious movements offered a more complicated embodiment of scientific aspiration. Begun in the 1970s, Heaven's Gate was a religious group founded by Marshall Applewhite and Bonnie Nettles. Convinced that their bodies were only vehicles on a longer spiritual journey, 38 followers committed suicide in 1997. They believed their souls would be conveyed to a spaceship hiding behind the Hale-Bopp comet. Riding on that spaceship were Nettles, who had died previously, and Jesus, who the followers would join just as the Earth was wiped clean and recycled. Heaven's Gate combined millennialism and astronomy to fatal effect.

The twentieth century began with the trumpeted promise of science and concluded on a far more ambivalent note. Nonetheless, to understand American religious culture now is to understand the mechanistic premises of the culture at large. Some religious groups continue to seek a time before technology, before incorporation and machines. But the vast majority of believers struggle to reconcile the utility of tradition against the forward momentum of knowledge. Historian Grant Wacker has observed this combination in Pentecostalism, which he believes has successfully combined primitiv-ist and pragmatic impulses. If the primitivist urge "represented a powerfully destruc-tive urge to smash all human-made traditions in order to return to a first century world where the Holy Spirit alone reigned," then the pragmatic reflected acquies-cence to "technological achievements and governing social arrangements of the postindustrial West" (Hackett 1995: 441). Science had infiltrated even the most primitive church paradigms, and their world would never be known in quite the same way again.

The End of the Cosmos

World War I made it impossible for Americans to continue their stalwart faith in the positive progress of science. The 1919 publication of Karl Barth's *Commentary on Romans* inaugurated several decades of reappraisal by theologians of the cosmologies which fed European and American culture prior to the war. The uncritical support of WWI by German intellectuals and churches concerned subsequent religious thinkers. How could modernism have been such a failure? Late nineteenth-century liberal the-ology argued that education and religious experience would counteract forces of evil and ego. Yet despite the pervasive optimism of these liberal ideas, World War I occurred without loud condemnation from theological circles. Following Barth's dra-matic restatement of theology, many stateside observers joined what would be referred to as Protestant neo-orthodoxy. Included in this argumentative sphere was Reinhold Niebuhr, whose *Moral Man and Immoral Society* (1932) indicted liberal assumptions about progress. He and his neo-orthodox compatriots argued for a return to the Bible, to Reformation-era descriptions of sin, and to a theology of the cross. Sin was ingrained in human nature, neo-orthodox theologians suggested. All human responses were conditioned by this taint, requiring serious individual battle to compel these sinful selves to social service.

Neo-orthodoxy made some sense of the homicidal evil that overtook Europe during World War II. Mass organization, totalitarian political strategies, and technological might combined to counter the progressive potency of modernity. Individual men were unable to relinquish their solipsism for the sake of a better good. Yet what did it say about God's existence that an event as horrible as the Holocaust could occur? For Jews, the theological labor needed to be done after the Holocaust seemed insurmountable. Richard Rubenstein even argued, in his *After Auschwitz* (1962), that Jews must now enter an age without God, since the Holocaust had decimated the viability of Jewish theism. "The paradigm evil event to which virtually all theodicists now refer," observed Christian philosopher Stephen Davis in 1981, "is the Holocaust, i.e., the murder of six million Jews and millions of others by the Nazis during World War II" (Heinze 2004: 344). To some extent, Zionism emerged as a replenishing ideology in this grieving nihilism, offering to some Jews the hope that God would supply a new nation to focus their religious renewal.

Meanwhile, however, the European theater was divided by an "iron curtain." The cold war prodded an arms race between two titular nations – the United States and the USSR. This race had grand cosmological consequences, as the rampant development of weaponry offered humans the deified threat of global destruction. "The content of this society will so develop as to destroy itself," preached Harold John Ockenga, pastor of Park Street Church in Boston and first President of the National Association of Evangelicals. "The Holocaust which will destroy western civilization may begin at any moment. We are now living in the economic and political stage of World War III" (Harvey and Goff 2005: 13). Long-range munitions made possible devastating warfare controlled from a computer console. To specify the enemy, cold war discourse elaborated the communist threat; in this effort, federal officials were assisted by evangelical activists. Evangelicals had a long history with socialism, believing in the early twentieth century that socialism was a form of experimental Darwinism.

Now, nuclear gains on the USSR were framed as in the best interest of the nation, pressing many religious groups to debate internally their loyalties. For some, it seemed hypocritical to endorse the potential massacre of life; for others, the arms race was figured into a broad cosmology of American destiny. "No previously conceived moral position escapes the fundamental confrontation posed by contemporary nuclear strategy," wrote the National Conference of Catholic Bishops in 1983, "The task before us is not simply to repeat what we have said before; it is first to consider anew whether and how our religious-moral tradition can assess, direct, contain, and, we hope, help to eliminate the threat posed to the human family by the nuclear arsenals of the world" (Harvey and Goff 2005: 61). No matter their response, religious groups had to acknowledge that Americans possessed an increasing amount of agency and global direction that had preciously been the sole purview of God.

Plural Inclusion

Although immigration had its origins at the outset of the American experience, the twentieth century witnessed the arrival of a truly post-Protestant culture in which no single denomination or group compromised a statistical majority. The impact of such a plural culture had cosmological consequences, as Protestants struggled with their own majority loss. Will Herberg, Drew University professor, wrote in his *Protestant, Catholic, Jew* (1955):

> What seems to be really disturbing many American Protestants is the realization that Protestantism is no longer identical with America, that Protestantism has, in fact, become merely one of three communions (or communities) with equal Status and equal legitimacy in the American scheme of things in the American scheme of things. This sudden realization, shocking enough when one considers the historical origins of American life and culture, appears to have driven Protestantism into an essentially defensive posture, in which it feels itself a mere minority threatened with Catholic domination.

For Herberg, Protestantism's greatest enemy was Catholicism; by the middle of the subsequent decade, many more groups would enter the national landscape, contesting their marketplace share. From war-torn East and South Asia, the Middle East, the Caribbean, and Latin America, immigrants poured into the United States, creating a panoply of practices and congregations, a pluralism that was simultaneously touted and feared. Pluralism has always been a signifier against which a posited majority reacted.

Foreign traditions blended with cultures to form pastiche imaginaries. The Beat poets used Buddhist imagery to articulate their discontent with the material world; black radicals borrowed from Islam an ascetic discipline; and Hare Krishnas sang and danced their way across a landscape. The Hare Krishnas were members of the International Society for Krishna Consciousness (ISKON). Founded in New York City in 1966 by Abhay Charanaravinda Bhaktivedanta Swami Prabhupada, the Hare Krishnas surrendered all material goods, practiced sexual denial and vegetarianism. Their practices encapsulated a sense that the universe had grown too chaotic, decadent, and selfish. Within the maelstrom of countercultural excess, they invented local communities in the hopes that these utopian localities could model global reformation. Groups like the Hare Krishna embodied the sorts of amalgamations that would become patterns in US religious belief, as immigrant groups build worship communities in once-upon-a-time Protestant church spaces. What was once called a "melting pot" is now better imagined as a multicultural bricolage in which groups are compelled less to assimilation than plural articulation, blending the varieties of intellectual, theological, and international materials available to represent their cosmopolitan selves in the pews.

Just as new ethnicities and global traditions found footing in the US, so did revolutionary ideas about social identity shift the emphases of theologies across the spectrum. Mary Daly's *The Church and the Second Sex* (1968) and James Cone's *A Black Theology of Liberation* (1970) argued that critical voices had been excluded from the theological witness of Christianity. Women and African Americans may have been allowed in the churches, but they were not reflected in the creedal claims and intellectual project of Christian belief. As Beverly Harrison, Professor of Christian Ethics at Union Theological Seminary in New York remarked:

> Let us note and celebrate the fact that 'woman-spirit rising' is a *global* phenomenon in our time. Everywhere women are on the move. Coming into view now, for the first time, on a worldwide scale, is the incredible *collective* power of women so that anyone who has eyes to see can glimpse the power and strength of women's full humanity. (Harvey and Goff 2005: 213)

Denominational committees subsequently altered hymns, language in liturgies, and pronouns that used biblical translations to conform to nonsexist principles. Central to feminist theology was displacing androcentrism (male-centeredness) and core doctrines in Christianity that centuries of patriarchy and misogyny had obscured.

Black theologians argued for the liberation of black people from the oppressive arm of Christianity. As with feminist theologians, the primary labor of black theology was at first the deconstruction of historic racism in Christendom. Blacks were argued into a particularly Christian platform, unique in their suffering and equally unique in their recovery of freedom for all people. African-American women resisted both feminist and black theologies, innovating further through womanist theology. "Black men who have an investment in the patriarchal structure of White America and who intend to do Christian theology have yet to realize that if Jesus is liberator of the oppressed, all of the oppressed must be liberated," wrote Jacquelyn Grant in 1980 (Harvey and Goff 2005: 185). Included in the revision ranks during this period were also gay believers. Gay theology reinterpreted scriptural passages (Jewish and Christian, Muslim and New Age) with the same hermeneutic of suspicion that feminist, black, and womanist theologians applied. Theology was not merely a force of social explanation, but individual self-identification.

As pluralism pervaded American religion, so did individual congregations seek to revive their attendees. Every parish sought the revitalization of charismatic faith, from spirit-filled Christian worship to mystical Jewish midrash. Latino commentator Andrés Tapia refers to this as the difference between *la iglesia fría* (the frigid church) and *la iglesia caliente* (the hot and spicy church). Made manifest at the level of practice, the presumption of such rejuvenation is that worship should be designed to energize and entertain the parishioner. Plural populations not only disassembled the Protestant presumption which had defined America from the outset, but also shifted religious authority even further from the pulpit. Disestablishment (literal and statistical) goaded religious institutions to compete for the best ritual and cosmological buffet, one which inevitably culled from as many traditions as were available to the organizing ecclesiology. The idea of diversity formed a postulated opposition for American believers, new and old, immigrant and mainline. This opposition was both deeply desired and deeply feared.

Strip Mall Exodus

Rampant pluralism accompanied population migrations. By the twenty-first century, cities were not the weight-bearing geographic centers; rather, new suburban growth pressed believers into an expansive sprawl. The national prosperity which funded this exodus was not shared equally; however, with particularly dramatic demographic change in the South and West, many who before were at the edges of urbanity now found themselves at the centers of strip mall suburbia. Consumption and access were the organizing principles of these communities, with ontological consequences for their inhabitants. "The freedom to treat the whole of life as one protracted shopping spree means casting the world as a warehouse overflowing with consumer commodities," described sociologist Zygmunt Bauman (2000: 89). Late-twentieth-century American religious practice thus took on a corporate sheen, as mosques, synagogues, temples, and mega-churches were opened in rapid-growth regions like Orlando, Dallas, San Diego, and Charlotte.

This increased mobility reflected something similar shifting in the cosmological strategies of the nation. As early as 1949, Bishop Fulton J. Sheen, a popular Catholic radio preacher, remarked, "One of the favorite psychological descriptions of modern man is to say that he has an anxiety complex" (Sheen 1949: 12). Anxieties over money, over God, over the panoply of modern possibilities – anxiety simmers in the founding documents of twentieth-century new religious movements and their resultant cosmological innovations. Although anxieties may matriculate through social bodies, talk of anxiety indicates the pervasive success of psychoanalytic discourse in the broader culture. One of the premises of nearly every new cosmology was an intrigue and devotion to the exploration of human personality. If psychological observers were correct that the individual person was the primary site of conscience formation, then the moral nurturing of that individuality should be the focus of familial and religious labor. "From the hottest and most sophisticated forms of theology to the most basic forms of pastoral care and counseling, the deliberate, self-conscious concern expressed for the individual personality and its needs was unprecedented," observed Amanda Porterfield (2001: 96). Such calls to the individual conscience would inspire many to grand heights of social service, such as the followers of the civil rights movement; however, this personalism would also contribute to the dramatic privatization of religious life in the latter twentieth century. Religion retreated from the streets to the suburbs, from chambers of commerce to faith-based nonprofit organizations. Religion, like corporations, were simultaneously widening their berth and downsizing their bureaucracies.

The Beat generation and subsequent counterculture stood in adamant opposition to this suburbanization which made commodity of spiritual endeavor, producing in its outrage an array of dissents against the Protestant establishment. For some, like the founders of the American Atheists in 1963, divinity had no place in modern culture. Some seminarians agreed, albeit through the construction of complex radical theologies, the formation of which goaded *Time* magazine cover to ask in 1966, "IS GOD DEAD?" Such antagonistic positions were always a minority feature of American discourse, however, as the percentage of atheists in America may never have surpassed the single digits. Rather than a total dismissal of God's possibility, a wide swath of the counterculture encouraged a more expansive interpretation of spiritual life. In a 1966 *Paris Review* interview, Allen Ginsberg described the tumult of his countercultural epoch: "Knowing how to feel human and holy and not like a madman in a world which is rigid and materialistic and all caught up in the immediate necessities. Like if it's time to cook supper and you're busy communing, the world says there must be something wrong with you" (Harvey and Goff 2005: 81).

New Age spiritualities as descendants of and (in part) produced by the iconoclasm of Ginsberg and his artistic brethren fill bookstores, afternoon television talk shows, and yoga studios. In addition to the Eastern inflections of this New Age, much of it relied upon images from Native American history and culture. Books like John Neihardt's *Black Elk Speaks* (1932) and Carlos Castaneda's *The Teachings of Don Juan* (1968) offered views of alternative cosmologies that many found to be compelling alternatives to the monotheism of the Abrahamic traditions. For Amerindians, this is no easy exchange. "Today an entire industry has sprung up in which Indigenous spirituality is appropriated, distorted, used, and sold without respect or permission, *even while* physical assaults on Native people, lands, and ways of life, continue," explains Christopher Ronwanièn:te Jocks (1996: 416). To be sure, New Age writers and practitioners borrowed often without consciousness of context, treating a variety of religions (Sioux and Hindu, Tantric and kabbalistic) as components of a buffet. Yet the intention of this usage was not hegemonic but liberationist. From the revival of medieval kabbalah to the self-help assignments of talk show host Oprah Winfrey, Americans focused increasingly on their spiritual self-cultivation as implicit and explicit forms of resistance to dogmas, existent church structures, and social control. The supposition of these New Agers is that the individual – not God, not the congregation, and not scripture – forms the centerpiece of the cosmos. Melding that individuality with universal energy fields and communing with multifarious spiritual beyonds is the goal of such expansive, pluralist religious practice.

The expansion of corporate Christianity in the suburbs is not distinct from the cultural cache of spirituality discourse. Although New Age spirituality and the revival of evangelicalism are often placed in different outlets of the religious bazaar, their success has been correlate and contingent. An example of this confluence is the Vineyard Movement. Calling themselves "Empowered Evangelicals," members of this church-building, ecumenical Christianity argue that they occupy the radical middle between evangelicalism and Pentecostalism, offering rigorous confessional standards and charismatic worship. Begun in the early 1980s, the Vineyard Movement emphasizes connection through home-group worship and one-on-one ministry. In many ways, Vineyard is typical of contemporary evangelicalism, including elaborate use of web-based educational mechanisms, popular music in worship services, and the sale of multiple embossed products to coordinate a Vineyard lifestyle, including Vineyard hats, duffel bags, fleece shirts, and a $35 "Lady's Computer Bag." Although Vineyard contains the predictable emphases on Christ and Bible study, there is also a passionate commitment to the presence of a spiritual landscape individuals may access through prayer and meditation. Vineyard has designed a particular insignia and color scheme that lean upon existent palettes and iconography of environmental spiritualities. They even go so far as to suggest theirs is a spiritual, and not religious, endeavor. "So we do not become religious, but stay quite earthy, expressed plainly by the earth-tone colors," explains their website. Vineyard sermons and social events encourage radical egalitarianism and individual self-improvement, aspects which resonate within evangelical history but also the emergent history of New Age spiritualities. Practices here suggest overlap that ceases at the basic level of theology, since Vineyard is committed to Christ's return in ways no New Age aspirant could concur. But their joint responses to contemporary sprawl and individual anxiety commingle an existential angst with a pragmatic staging for American revelation.

Imaging American Cosmology

Let us end as we began: with an image. As the twenty-first century began, Americans were pummeled with a stunning iconic contrast. On the one hand, images of 9/11 and the War on Terror clogged media montages. At the same time, celebrity spectacle hit an all-time high, with magazines filling supermarket check-out racks with divorce, pregnancies, and romantic traumas of an elite, glamorous few. Within this pantheon of stars, no one glowed more brightly than Brad Pitt, actor, humanitarian, and persistent star of publicized marital melodramas. In an age where celebrity quips were the stuff of newspaper headlines, Pitt's every word and movement were recorded by the paparazzi. Not until a 2007 interview, however, did he offer a picture of his theological outlook. In that moment, Pitt offered a stock portrait of contemporary cosmology; he described a faith accountable solely to himself: "What's important to me is that I've defined my beliefs and lived according to them and not betrayed them" (Silverman 2007). Raised Southern Baptist in Missouri, Pitt turned from his doctrinal roots in his teenage years. "I'd go to Christian revivals and be moved by the Holy Spirit, and I'd go to rock concerts and feel the same fervor," he explains, "Then I'd be told, 'That's the Devil's music! Don't partake in that!' I wanted to experience things religion said not to experience." Despite this iconoclastic impulse, Pitt describes himself as pro-faith: "Religion works. I know there's comfort there, a crash pad. It's something to explain the world and tell you there is something bigger than you, and it is going to be all right in the end."

In these few short statements, Pitt captures the cosmological presumptions of contemporary belief. Belief should be experiential, it shouldn't be bossy, and it should include purchasing power. It's a safe haven, a mechanism of individual (and national) self-explication. Religion is comfort against a darkening cosmos, not a revision of cosmos. To be sure, exceptions to his duvet theology exist. Ritual dogma and social discipline continue to thrive amidst a wide variety of religious contexts in the US. But the driving ontology of Pitt's self-description has succeeded in toppling many ecclesiastical structures. The American religious imagination is one now dependent on the postulated agency of the self. This is an economic and psychological agency as much as it is a theological one; Pitt wants to enjoy what he wants to enjoy, and he will hold himself accountable only to his consistencies of practice within that personal arbitration.

Yet media reports suggest a raucous divide in American culture, with secular liberals pitted against hard core conservatives. This is, of course, a continuation of the modernist–fundamentalist controversies of the early twentieth century, a controversy that was premised on opposing aspirations for the track of mankind. "Liberals abhor the smugness, the self-righteousness, the absolute certainty, the judgmentalism, and the lovelessness of a narrow, dogmatic faith," explained an official from the National Council of Churches in 1984, "[Conservatives] scorn the fuzziness, the marshmallow convictions, the inclusiveness that makes membership meaningless – the 'anything goes' attitude that views even Scripture as relative. Both often caricature the worst in one another and fail to perceive the best" (Hackett 1995: 371). Pitching these invented opposites makes for fine copy, but limited theological truth. As demonstrated in this chapter, few Americans fall cleanly into easy dichotomous opposites.

What is profoundly resonant about this perceived battle is not the participants, but its suggested teleology. At the core of any modernist controversy is the question of how we function with modernity, how best a citizenry may apply individual piety to social purpose. The question of America's role in the divine cosmos drives political rhetoric and results in profound human cost. "For lack of appreciation of how truly powerful it is, the nation begins to lose wisdom and perspective and, with them, the strength and understanding that it takes to be magnanimous to smaller and weaker nations," wrote Arkansas Senator J. William Fulbright in 1966. "Gradually but unmistakably America is showing signs of that arrogance of power which has afflicted, weakened, and in some cases destroyed great nations in the past. In so doing we are not living up to our capacity and promise as a civilized example for the world." In 2004, new data profiling the North American Protestant missionary community showed a net increase of personnel serving full-time as missionaries (Coote 2005: 13). Even as the Golden Age of missions is long past, groups like the Southern Baptist Convention International Mission Board and the Wycliffe Bible Translators continue to press American Christians to unconverted fields in an attempt to compel the world to their ideas of an ideal life. Evangelical political lobbies encourage international relief efforts that couple moral reformations with civic improvements, demonstrating the Protestantism of American foreign relations. Yet this new evangelical internationalism no longer refers solely to a Western incursion of non-Western peoples. To be sure, the US remains the single largest producer of missionaries in the world, but South Korea is second, with the nations of Africa and Latin America close on their heels. Produced in large part by satellite churches of American denominations, the Christendom of this global missionary south constructs a different relationship between evangelizer and evangelized, nation and colony. On the other side of the American century, just how religious citizens will determine the cosmological positioning of their nation remains an open inquiry. For now, it seems the Sundays continue to stare at us from the past, marveling at our shifting forms, at our ease with distant violence and corporate habit.

References and Further Reading

Allitt, Patrick (2003) *Religion in America Since 1945: A History*, New York: Columbia University Press.

Appleyard, Bryan (1992) *Understanding the Present: Science and the Soul of Modern Man*, London: Picador.

Bauman, Zygmunt (2000) *Liquid Modernity*, Cambridge: Polity Press.

Brown, Richard D. (1976) *Modernization: The Transformation of American Life, 1600–1865*, New York: Hill and Wang.

Buskirk, Martha (1994) "Thoroughly Modern Marcel," *October*, 70: 113–125.

Carter, Paul A. (1971) *The Spiritual Crisis of the Gilded Age*, Dekalb, IL: Northern Illinois Press.

Coote, Robert T. (2005) "Protestant Full-time Missionary Community," *International Bulletin of Missionary Research*, 29: 12–13.

Goff, Philip and Harvey, Paul (eds.) (2004) *Themes in Religion and American Culture*, Chapel Hill, NC: University of North Carolina Press.

Hackett, David G. (ed.) (1995) *Religion and American Culture: A Reader*, New York: Routledge.

Handy, Robert T. (1971) *A Christian America, Protestant Hopes and Historical Realities*, New York: Oxford University Press.

Harvey, Paul and Goff, Philip (eds.) (2005) *The Columbia Documentary History of Religion in America Since 1945*, New York: Columbia University Press.

Heinze, Andrew R. (2004) *Jews and the American Soul: Human Nature in the Twentieth Century*, Princeton, NJ: Princeton University Press.

Herberg, W. (1955) *Protestant, Catholic, Jew: An Essay in American Religious Sociology*, Garden City, NY: Doubleday.

Lalich, Janja (2004) *Bounded Choice: True Believers and Charismatic Cults*, Berkeley. CA: University of California Press.

Lutz, Tom (1991) *American Nervousness 1903: An Anecdotal History*, Ithaca, NY: Cornell University Press.

Mancini, JoAnne Marie (1999) "'One Term is as Fatuous as Another': Responses to the Armory Show Reconsidered," *American Quarterly*, 51: 833–870.

Marty, Martin E. (1984) *Pilgrims in Their Own Land*, Boston: Little, Brown and Co.

Marty, Martin E. (1986) *The Irony of It All, 1893–1919*, vol. 1, *Modern American Religion*, Chicago: University of Chicago Press.

May, Henry F. (1963) *Protestant Churches and Industrial America*, New York: Octagon Books.

McLoughlin, William (1955) *Billy Sunday Was His Real Name*, Chicago: University of Chicago Press.

Orvell, Miles (1989) *The Real Thing: Imitation and Authenticity in American Culture, 1880–1940*, Chapel Hill, NC: University of North Carolina Press.

Porterfield, Amanda (2001) *The Transformation of American Religion: The Story of a Late-Twentieth-Century Awakening*, New York: Oxford University Press.

Ronwanièn:te Jocks, Christopher (1996) "Spirituality for Sale: Sacred Knowledge in the Consumer Age," *American Indian Quarterly*, 20: 415–431.

Rydell, Robert (1984) *All the World's a Fair: Visions of Empire at American International Expositions, 1876–1916*, Chicago: The University of Chicago Press.

Sheen, Fulton J. (1949) *Peace of Soul*, New York: McGraw-Hill Book Company.

Silverman, Stephen (2007) "Brad Opens up about his Faith," *People.com*, http://www.people.com/people/article/0,,20111821,00.html

Szasz, Ferenc Morton (1982) *The Divided Mind of Protestant America, 1880–1930*, University, AL: University of Alabama Press.

Wiebe, Robert H. (1980) *The Search for Order, 1877–1920*, Westport, CT: Greenwood Press.

Woolf, Virginia (1984) "Mr. Bennett and Mrs. Brown," in *The Virginia Woolf Reader*, ed. Mitchell A. Leaska, New York: Harcourt.

15

Community

Peter W. Williams

The peoples of North America have organized themselves in religious communities since prehistoric times. While religion's important role in creating social order and group identity has persisted, modern social forces have also transformed religious communities and their place in people's lives. During the last century, religious communities in America changed dramatically as a result of their interaction with one another as well as a result of new technologies, political and economic challenges, and secular opportunities. Increasing interaction led religious communities to borrow from and react to one another, often becoming more similar to each other, even when they disagreed. New technologies such as air travel, radio, television, and computers changed the way religious communities presented themselves to the world and communicated internally. Political and economic challenges led many religious communities to take stands against injustice, and to organize themselves in reaction to problems they confronted through powerful forces of global change. Secular opportunities such as those associated with private enterprise, individual freedom, and new forms of media allowed religious communities in America to expand their outreach and led them to translate traditional beliefs and practices into forms of expression that were more spiritual than religious, and often removed from church buildings and other religious institutions.

Religious Life in the Twentieth- and Twenty-first-century United States

The "splendid little war" with Spain in 1898 was emblematic of some of the major changes in American society that would affect – and be affected by – religion during the century to come. The nation's willingness to go to war with a European power – decrepit as it may have been – in the putative interest of extending liberty but in the more serious enterprise of acquiring a miniature empire was a sign that the battle for internal consolidation had come to an end. As historian Frederick Jackson Turner had announced a few years prior to the turn of the century, the frontier – defined as space which had not yet been settled by Euro-Americans – was now closed. Although Turner's argument that the frontier had been the most single determinative factor in American history is no longer widely held, two truths remain. First, agricultural expansion had come to a virtual end, and family farming as a way of life began to decline. Second, the native peoples who had, from the Euro-American perspective, been the primary human obstacle to westward expansion, were no longer significant players in the struggle for social, economic, and political influence. Reduced to a bleak life on a reservation system created with nearly complete disregard for their traditional ways of life, they became relegated to the periphery of the American story and had to find innovative ways to perpetuate their cultures while living in a very different world from that of their forebears. Having rendered the Indians invisible and impotent, Euro-Americans were free to seek new outlets for their expansionist impulses abroad.

The war with Spain was also a reaffirmation of what had been for decades, if not centuries, a self-evident truth for many Americans. At the beginning of the twentieth century, there was little question in the minds of most Americans that the United States was, if not a Protestant nation, at least a nation in which Protestantism enjoyed a place of prestige, if not outright hegemony. Roman Catholics had long since become the single largest religious group, but could not compare in numbers or social influence with the combined ranks of the Protestant denominations. To be sure, African American Protestants did not enjoy the same deference as did their white counterparts, but the vast majority of African American church-goers nevertheless self-identified as Protestants. Taking up what Rudyard Kipling had deemed "the white man's burden" in the acquisition of Hawaii, the Philippines, and other areas of Roman Catholic or pagan benightedness was a reaffirmation of the Protestant sense of mission that had been part of American ideology since the time of John Winthrop, and the war was enthusiastically supported by Protestants of all stripes. The attempt to impose the American version of Protestant Christianity on far-flung peoples that followed the war with Spain was part of a longer trajectory of the missionary imperative with roots in the Second Great Awakening, which manifested itself in the early twentieth century in the Student Volunteer Movement and its campaign to "evangelize the world in this generation."

By the end of the new century's third decade, this Protestant hegemony began to come under critical scrutiny not only from excluded Catholics and Jews, but from within the Protestant community itself. In 1929, H. Richard Niebuhr startled the American Protestant world with the publication of his *The Social Sources of Denominationalism*. Americans had for many decades lived with the notion that denominationalism was the natural configuration of American Protestantism as a result of the First Amendment and the pluralistic patterns of settlement that had characterized the new nation. Further, most believed that the issues that separated Protestants were primarily matters of belief, worship, and polity. (One popular guide to American religions from mid-century was entitled *What Americans Believe and How They Worship*.) Niebuhr instead subjected the notion of denominationalism to sociological analysis – a rather daring move at the time – and found that the divide between, say, Presbyterians and Baptists had as much to do with race, region, ethnicity, and social class as it had to do with infant vs. adult baptism or presbyterian vs. congregational polity.

First, Protestant denominationalism was in considerable measure a *regional* phenomenon. Congregationalists and Unitarians were the institutional descendants of the Puritans of colonial times. Both groups were still firmly based in New England, though their meeting-houses had followed the trail of New England settlement that ran through upstate New York and the upper Midwest to the Pacific Northwest and northern California. Presbyterians, their Calvinist cousins, were strong throughout much of the rest of the nation, including the South. Methodists were also a national church, although their greatest concentration was in the region described as "the south of the North and the north of the South," and they remained divided on regional lines until 1939. (Northern and southern Presbyterians united in 1983.) Baptists were also national in outreach, but their natural tendency towards fragmentation, exacerbated by the slavery issue in the previous century, had divided them into the Northern (later American) Baptist Churches and the Southern Baptist Convention, as well as an almost uncountable number of smaller groups based on racial and theological differences. Episcopalians were strongest in the areas of earliest English settlement along the east coast from Massachusetts to Virginia, though they had become a significant presence in most of the newer cities of the Midwest and West as well. Lutherans were concentrated in areas of ethnic settlement, especially Pennsylvania (from the eighteenth century) and then throughout much of the upper Midwest. The Campbellite (Restorationist) movement, poised on the brink of *de facto* division at the turn of the century, was strongest in Indiana and parts of the Old Southwest (Missouri, Arkansas, Texas.) Pentecostal and Holiness groups, the newest presences in the Protestant spectrum, proliferated in the South, Indiana (culturally as much southern as Midwestern), and California.

Region, however, was only one marker of denomination difference. *Ethnicity*, though not as clearly correlated as in the days of first settlement, nevertheless remained strong. Episcopalians, Congregationalists, and Unitarians tended to be of old stock English descent, while Scotland remained emblematic of Presbyterian origins and values. White Methodists and Baptists tended to be of British background, although open in the Midwest to German, Swedish, and other ethnic replenishment. Lutherans were overwhelmingly German and Scandinavian in origin, which was reflected in the multiplicity of denominational divisions that existed early in the century along ethnic as well as regional and confessional lines. Similarly, the persistence of Dutch, German, and Hungarian Reformed churches mirrored the rapidity of assimilation in those bodies, with the Dutch continuing to exist into the twenty-first century in the form of the (now English-speaking) Christian Reformed Church and Reformed Church in America. Holiness and Pentecostal groups began in a variety of mixed racial and ethnic contexts, but usually shook down into new configurations that followed the "color line."

Race inevitably played a major role in denominational identity. Although most major denominations had African American constituents, individual churches were usually formally or *de facto* segregated. Many cities had African American Episcopal parishes whose members were usually more sophisticated urbanites or recent immigrants from the West Indies, in much of which the Church of England had been the established religion. The United Methodist Church maintained a separate jurisdiction for blacks until 1969. Most African Americans, however, affiliated with one of three predominantly black traditions: Methodist, divided into African Methodist Episcopal (AME); AME Zion (AMEZ); and Colored (later Christian) Methodist Church (CMC). Three major Baptist denominations took shape, the names of which were variants on the phrase "National Baptist." Holiness and Pentecostal churches (collectively known as "Sanctified" churches) ranged in size from isolated urban store-fronts and rural independent congregations to the large-scale Church of God in Christ (COGIC) based in Memphis.

Finally, social class played a role as a marker of denominational culture and identity. By most measures, Episcopalians and Presbyterians held their place throughout the century as the wealthiest, best educated, and most influential of the traditional Protestant communities. (Jews and Christian Scientists, both predominantly urban, also ranked high.) Methodists were as much in the center socially as they were geographically. Lutherans were more identifiable regionally and ethnically, although most tended to be farmers or middle-class residents of the towns and cities of the Midwest. Congregationalists and Unitarians, strongest in New England, had historically been well represented in the upper reaches of regional society, although their position had been challenged by the early twentieth century by newly-fashionable Episcopalians. (The same dynamic obtained in Quaker Philadelphia.) Baptists and Holiness-Pentecostals tended to cluster in the lower reaches of the social spectrum, although recent research has demonstrated that Niebuhr's characterization of Pentecostals as "churches of the disinherited" overlooked their strength in the working and middle classes. Among African Americans, a similar hierarchy existed, with the various Methodist denominations enjoying the most prestige (where a black Episcopal parish was unavailable, such as St. Philip's in Harlem), followed by the Baptists and, in the lowest strata, "Sanctified" churches.

Denominationalism, however, was not the only factor that divided Protestants one from another. Controversies over the related issues of Darwinian evolution and the interpretation of scripture had begun in the previous century and had, by the turn of the twentieth, begun to arouse serious discord and internal battles for control within the northern wings of the Baptists and Presbyterians in particular. The Scopes Trial of 1925 was a highly visible turning-point in the playing out of these controversies before a national audience reachable in "real time" by the new medium of radio as well as more traditional print journalism. The small-town Tennessee setting of this contest also pointed up the regional character of the divide, since the Protestant religious communities of the South were nearly unanimous in their rejection of these various forms of "Modernist" thought, including evolutionary biology and historical criticism of the Bible. In the North, progressives espousing Modernist thought emerged victorious from their intradenominational battles. Various split-offs, such as the Orthodox Presbyterian Church, resulted, making even more complex the denominational spectrum of the day.

Prohibition was another major battle that had united many Protestants for some time but ultimately proved disastrous as a strategy for retaining Protestant control of American social life. Prohibition was a direct descendant of the temperance movement of the previous century, but twentieth-century reformers substituted legal coercion for voluntary abstinence as a means of weaning the nation from its fondness for beer, wine, hard cider and "booze" of various sorts. The failure of the 18th Amendment (1918) to put an end to the liquor trade, and the widespread disregard for the law that it fostered, helped undermine the claims of evangelical Protestants to national moral leadership. (Even the term "evangelical" was subject to dispute as a result of the dominant status of theological liberalism, which downplayed the need for cathartic experiences of conversion in many northern seminaries and pulpits.) Shortly after Franklin Roosevelt's election in 1932, the 18th Amendment was repealed and the new administration began to be populated with the same Jews and Catholics who had been largely shunned in previous regimes. (Roosevelt, an Episcopalian, belonged to a denomination that historically had been identified with a social elite that utilized alcohol both sacramentally and recreationally.)

Many scholars point to this period in American religious history as constituting a "second disestablishment" of religion. The first had taken place with the adoption of the First Amendment to the US Constitution, which had prohibited the federal government from favoring one religious group over another. This second and more informal turning point was characterized by a rapid erosion of the prestige and influence that evangelical Protestants had collectively though unofficially enjoyed during the nineteenth century. A popular sociological study, Will Herberg's *Protestant, Catholic, Jew* of 1955, argued that membership in American community had evolved into a "triple melting pot" based on religious identification. To be fully accepted as Americans, individuals were expected to be religiously affiliated. As part of this religious melting pot, Catholics and Jews as well as Protestants had now gained entry into the broader society since they had shed much of their ethnic baggage and become culturally recognizable as Americans. (Herberg's argument has been attacked for, among other things, failing to recognize the distinctive situation of African Americans; however, his basic take on assimilation still rings reasonably true.)

The major "others" in the religio-cultural tensions at work in pre-World War II United States were the Eastern Orthodox, Jews, and Roman Catholics whose arrival in the heyday of the "New Immigration" prior to World War I had dramatically altered the demographic balance of the nation's cities. First the "Great War" and then a series of Acts of Congress during the 1920s had brought this immigration to a virtual standstill, and the children and grandchildren of the newcomers were being raised primarily as English-speaking Americans. Prejudice against Jews and Catholics certainly persisted in Protestant circles, but these feelings began to erode as the bearers of these faiths became less visibly "foreign" over the decades. During the early decades of the century, however, the Ku Klux Klan, which had originated in the Reconstruction-era South as a backlash against the empowerment of blacks, reemerged with a strong nativist component, targeting Catholics, Jews, and immigrants in general as well as African Americans for social restriction and, on occasion, actual violence. The 1915 lynching of Leo Frank, a Jewish businessman in Marietta, Georgia, on dubious charges was a dramatic example of the lengths to which proponents of white Protestant community in America would go.

The members of the various Eastern Orthodox churches were the least visible of nonProtestant newcomers, because of their relatively low numbers, their decentralized polity, and their propensity for religio-ethnic self-segregation. The largest of these communities were the Greeks and Russians, who were usually the first to establish parishes in new areas of immigrant settlement. Interestingly, the two groups began on different ends of the continent. The earliest Russian Orthodox presence was in Alaska and then in the San Francisco Bay area, although later immigrants arrived on the east coast. Greeks followed the more traditional route, establishing presences in urban areas in the northeast and in the Great Lakes states. Other Slavic groups, each with its own onion-domed churches, settled in the manufacturing and mining areas of the northeast, especially Pennsylvania and Ohio, as well. (Chicago and Cleveland became notable centers for Orthodox churches of all backgrounds.) They often coexisted with the Uniate churches (named for their history of willingness to enter into union with Rome) who followed similar Eastern European and Middle Eastern liturgical traditions but remained in communion with the Roman Catholic Church. When clergy of these churches learned upon arrival in the US that the bishops in the new land would not respect their custom of having a married clergy, many of the latter joined the ranks of the Orthodox (and kept their wives).

The Jewish presence in the United States dated from colonial times, but was vastly enhanced numerically by the New Immigrants, who came mostly from the outlying regions of the old Russian Empire. Earlier waves of Jews from Iberia and the German states were often educated and highly skilled, so that they assimilated easily, if imperfectly, into American society. The newcomers, however, were largely Yiddish-speaking artisans whose languages and customs were nearly as perplexing – not to say offensive – to their fellow Jews as to the gentile majority. Whereas many German (Ashkenazic) Jews had migrated to the cities of the Midwest and far West after establishing a presence in New York City, these poorer and less mobile newcomers tended to remain in the latter metropolis, their port of entry and home to tens of thousands of compatriots. The Lower East Side became the core settlement for the first generation, and soon boasted a profusion of synagogues, theaters, and tea houses where Yiddish- and Russian-language culture briefly flourished. Subsequent generations frequently took advantage of the free education offered by New York's City College (now CCNY), and left the old neighborhood for professional lives in more desirable parts of Manhattan, the Outer Boroughs, and New Jersey. Eventually, the descendants of these "Russian" Jews found their way to urban centers throughout the nation and lost much of the distinctive culture that had set their forebears apart from their coreligionists in earlier decades.

By the early twentieth century, American Jews now had several formal options for congregational affiliation, as well as the choice of no affiliation at all. Orthodox Jews and the newly-founded Conservative movement both emulated Reform in constructing denominational apparatus for communication, common endeavors, and the promotion of a distinctive sort of religious identity. Many Orthodox congregations, consisting of close-knit communities of first- and second-generation Jews of common geographical origin, remained aloof from (or simply oblivious to) these new options as they attempted to perpetuate Old World ways in New World urban enclaves, primarily in greater New York City. Reform and Conservative Jews, who attempted to steer a middle way between tradition and modernity, were more oriented towards assimilation; their temples or synagogues soon began to mark the urban, and then suburban, communities in which they settled – partly through choice and partly through "steering" by realtors with a vested interested in keeping them out of gentile neighborhoods. Following WWII, many Hasidic Jews who had survived the Holocaust created enclaves in and around New York City that constituted virtually independent societies, maintaining their old educational and social institutions and opposing, sometimes fiercely, Hasidim from other traditions.

American Catholicism also grew by waves of immigration. The Irish and Germans who arrived in the middle decades of the previous century had increased Catholic numbers vastly, rapidly overshadowing the English and French who had staffed and worshipped at the earliest churches along the Atlantic coast. By the time of the arrival of New Immigration Catholics from Italy, Poland, Hungary, Lithuania, Slovakia,

Slovenia, Croatia, and other areas of southern and central Europe, the Irish-born and-descended Americans controlled the Catholic Church in the US and its increasingly centralized ecclesiastical apparatus. Resistance, however, came in the cities of the Great Lakes especially from Germans, Poles, and other ethnic Catholics who began to organize to assert what they saw as their right to equitable representation in the ranks of the clergy and hierarchy. Success came only gradually, and in a time when the passing of generations had eroded the issues of ethnic distinctiveness that had prompted the protests at the beginning.

By the end of WWI, the American Catholic hierarchy was well on its way to creating a material and social infrastructure that helped American Catholics of whatever ethnic origin develop a uniform religious identity and spend their entire lives within cultural communities of uniformly English-speaking American Catholics. The prime vehicle for this socialization was a comprehensive educational network that began with universal parochial schools and expanded to include secondary schools, colleges and universities, seminaries, and religious instruction for children outside the system. Social service institutions such as hospitals, orphanages, youth hostels, and cemeteries staffed by men and, primarily, women members of religious orders also contributed to the strength of American Catholic communities. The community structures of American Catholic life played powerful roles in many cities; the alliance of church offices with union hiring halls and urban machine politics was a potent one for several generations in cities like Boston, Chicago, New York and Philadelphia. The ultimate goal of the entire apparatus was to insure that American Catholics – most of whom were of ethnic, working-class, urban background – were equipped with sufficient education to prosper materially and participate politically in the American context, while remaining protected from Protestant proselytizing and secular temptations.

Although many American Catholics and Jews – as well as Eastern Orthodox – may have been assimilated into Herberg's "triple melting pot" by mid-century, millions of Americans of non-European origin remained outside the boundaries of social acceptability, political influence, and economic enfranchisement. Prior to 1965, Asian immigrants and their descendants were excluded by punitive immigration laws, and did not yet constitute a sufficient presence, save for some West Coast enclaves, to register visibly on the national ethno-religious radar screen. Native Americans had from the end of the previous century definitively lost their battle for autonomy, which may be said to have expired with the end of the Ghost Dance and the Wounded Knee massacre in South Dakota in 1890. Those who remained in their traditional environment were now legally forced into resettlement on reservations no longer conducive to the semi-nomadic styles in which many had lived for countless generations. The main features of religious life for them were in the versions of Christianity offered by missionaries, Catholic and Protestant, as well as in the Peyote religion that spread across the continent as a new cultural form that combined aspects of traditional native and Euro-American religiosity in a new, highly decentralized and eclectic religious hybrid. Many other native peoples drifted off to urban areas where they often led marginalized existences cut off from traditional sources of cultural and religious identity.

The largest single group of Americans of non-European origin was, of course, those millions who claimed African descent. As a result of the labor shortage caused by the military draft of white men in WWI, African Americans began the trek from the cotton fields and hamlets of the South into the cities of the Northeast, the Great Lakes, and eventually the Pacific coast in search of freer and more prosperous lives. Christianity in its Methodist, Baptist, and "Sanctified" versions was one of the principal cultural properties of these in-migrants, and began to manifest itself in increasingly visible forms in New York's Harlem, Detroit's Paradise Valley, and numerous other urban black enclaves. The clergy was one of the few professions open to African Americans, especially those who lacked formal educational credentials, and the role of clergy as community leaders and spokesmen highlighted the centrality of the black church in American religious life. Black clerical leadership sometimes manifested itself in dynastic form, as in the careers of Adam Clayton Powell, Sr., and Jr., at Harlem's Abyssinian Baptist Church, and Martin Luther King, Sr., and Jr., at Atlanta's Ebenezer Baptist. It was in this social context that the Civil Rights movement of the 1950s and 1960s had much of its genesis.

African American religious life, however, was not entirely confined to such visible and influential urban Baptist and Methodist churches with predominantly middle-class clienteles. Many recent poor in-migrants found their places in urban store-front churches, usually of the "Sanctified" persuasion, in which women and men both exercised charismatic leadership while holding down day-jobs in the secular world. (In the middle-class churches, women – especially the older, established, hat-wearing "mothers" of the church – seldom served as pastors or preachers but exerted substantial influence in community life.) Other Depression-era blacks joined the followers of urban prophets such as Father Divine and "Sweet Daddy" Grace, who provided charismatic leadership, innovative interpretations of the gospel, and the provision of food and shelter to those in desperate need.

The end of WWII brought with it massive social transformations on what had been the home front as countless GIs returned, eager to resume life not only where it had left off but now with new opportunities for educational and vocational advancement through the GI Bill of Rights, one of the most revolutionary measures ever passed by Congress. These aspirants to the middle class, and their newly begun families, rapidly abandoned their traditional neighborhoods for the new belt of suburbs, such as Long Island's Levittown, that became synonymous with both social and geographical mobility during the late 1940s and the 1950s. Although this movement was of little help to African Americans, who had served during the war in segregated circumstances and returned to a similar social status, these new "burbs" did to a large extent embody the values of Herberg's "triple melting pot," and a building boom not only in single-family homes but in houses of worship ensued as well. This suburban "churchscape" of Catholic and Protestant churches and Jewish temples and synagogues was characterized by a blend of contemporary design and a revival of the colonial American architecture that had become an icon of the "traditional American values" which the suburbs represented for many of their new residents.

Although the 1950s are often looked upon as a time of social stability, they were also an era in which the movement for civil rights for African Americans began to take on a new urgency. Although leadership of the movement had had from its WWI-era beginnings both white and secular components, the new phase that began with the Montgomery, Alabama, bus boycott of 1955 focused on black churchmen such as Martin Luther King, Jr., as its most visible public representatives. Members of predominantly white Christian and Jewish communities joined in as well, while southern white churches mostly united in caution or active resistance. The moral capital rapidly acquired by the movement's strategy of active but non-violent resistance challenged

Figure 15.1 Martin Luther King, Jr. and Malcolm X represented two divergent attitudes on how best to realize civil rights for African-Americans.

racist interpretations of southern identity and religious community, and culminated with Lyndon Johnson's signing of the epoch-making Civil Rights Acts of 1964–65.

Even as these victories rolled up, the movement's leadership began to move on to other causes that were not as readily winnable. King began to lead protests not in exotic (to northern eyes) Alabama and Mississippi but in the blue-collar suburbs of Chicago, where he encountered resistance just as determined as further south. King also became an active protestor against the rapidly accelerating American engagement in Southeast Asia before his assassination in Memphis in 1968. This loss of focus within the older civil rights leadership coincided with the emergence of newer, more militant movements such as the Nation of Islam, of whom Malcolm X became the iconic emblem, and the Marxist-inspired Black Panthers (Figure 15.1). The Vietnam War – and the military draft disrupting the lives of young people of all sorts – soon replaced civil rights as the issue of the day, and liberal churchmen such as Yale's chaplain William Sloan Coffin and the Berrigan brothers, both Catholic priests, served as markers of a polarization that was rapidly developing in American society. The ensuing social chaos, abetted by the countercultural expressions of many of these same young people, launched long-lasting changes in the dynamics of American religious communities.

By the late 1960s, two political leaders who helped foment this backlash emerged on the national scene. George Wallace, the governor of Alabama who had "stood in the schoolhouse door" to resist desegregation of that state's flagship university by federal order, launched an independent presidential campaign in 1968. Richard Nixon gained the presidency in 1968 by following a "southern strategy" designed to take advantage of white discontent, especially in the South, over what was widely perceived as unsettling social turmoil.

This populist mobilization began as a social and political movement, but by the mid-1970s had begun to acquire a religious dimension. Although traditionalist

Protestants hailed the election of Southern Baptist Jimmy Carter, former governor of Georgia, to the presidency in 1976, disillusionment with his moderate social views helped launch the Religious Right as a new conservative movement aimed at harnessing the energies of previously apolitical white evangelicals and fundamentalists to an explicitly political agenda. Its leadership, which included Virginia televangelists Pat Robertson and Jerry Falwell, utilized up-to-the-minute communications technology as well as traditional pulpit oratory to recruit many Americans – including some conservative Catholics and Jews – into a campaign for national moral reform with the newly "southernized" Republican Party as its major vehicle. Energized by religious conservatives, the reborn Republican Party proclaimed its commitment to restoring America's moral strength as a national community.

The success – by no means unlimited – of the Religious Right was predicated on underlying demographic changes which had profound implications for other aspects of religious life as well. By the 1970s, the economic infrastructure that had made the northeastern quadrant of the nation its population center began to collapse, as witnessed most dramatically in the overtaking of Detroit's iconic auto industry by Asian competitors. Simultaneously, economic opportunity for the rising young or the middle-aged whose traditional employment was now in jeopardy rapidly swung from the "Rust Belt" – the Great Lakes regional economic complex – to the "Sunbelt" that stretched from Florida to California. The popularity of this Sunbelt, whose culture had displaced that of the older rural South, was built in part on a social tradition that had never been hospitable to the organized labor that had dominated Rustbelt economic life. The growing regional economy helped create a new middle class that was poised between traditional southern religious and social conservatism and a newer economic conservatism.

This new Sunbelt class, a mix of regional natives and newcomers, was highly mobile, prosperous but insecure, and educated to the point of competency but not cosmopolitanism. It was thus a ready-made audience for the newly revivified evangelicalism that had provided the institutional infrastructure for the Religious Right. The televangelism that had attracted much public attention in the 1970s began to lose credibility with the "Preachergate" scandals of the late 1980s, and the mega-church movement rapidly emerged as emblematic of this new version of the "old-time" religion. The mega-church was an institutional descendant of the urban institutional church of the late nineteenth century, accommodating a large congregation in a theater-style auditorium oriented towards musical and hortatory performance, and also providing facilities for a wide variety of non-worship social and educational programming. Mega-churches, which were defined by membership in the 2000–18,000 range, flourished especially in the new "exurbs" – suburbs or satellite cities built beyond the ring of the post-WWII suburban explosion. Founding and leadership were often entrepreneurial rather than traditionally clerical in character, and successful preachers frequently had a background in business or communications rather than seminary training. Although many such churches were affiliated with the Southern Baptist, Assemblies of God, or other established evangelical or Pentecostal-Holiness denominations, many others were independent, and the most recent have often been affiliated with such post-evangelical California-based "franchises" such as Saddleback or Vineyard. By the early twenty-first century, a new generation of mega-church leaders such as Rick Warren had drawn back from the "old-time religion" of Falwell and Robertson and substituted instead a self-actualization and success orientation more in line with the aspirations of a new middle class that was becoming more "at ease in Zion."

As the fortunes of the new evangelicalism were rising in the latter decades of the twentieth century, those of what are now generally known as the "mainline Protestant" persuasion were moving in the opposite direction. Many of the seven mainline denominations – American Baptist, Disciples of Christ, Episcopal, Evangelical Lutheran (ELCA), Presbyterian (PCUSA), United Church of Christ, and United Methodist – were the results of various twentieth-century mergers that had helped unify groups of similar tradition that had previously been separated by ethnicity, region, doctrinal differences, or other factors that had ceased to be operative by mid-century. In the 1950s, these mainline groups stood as emblematic of a unified Protestant community, with evangelical-fundamentalist and Holiness-Pentecostal groups relegated to obscurity by virtue of regional and class identity. All were – and still largely are – based on an inclusive strategy that shunned doctrinal rigor and welcomed all who felt at home in their increasingly suburban ambience.

By the late 1960s to mid-1970s, however, the fortunes of the mainline had been compromised by the resurgence of evangelical churches, which now courted a national middle-class constituency, as well as by the progressive stances on social issues, such as civil rights, opposition to the Vietnam War, and the emerging second wave of feminism, often called the women's liberation movement, which challenged the patriarchal structures of American religious, economic, and family life. The Episcopal Church, for example, was plagued by division not only over civil rights and Vietnam but also by its move in the 1970s to ordain women to its priesthood and to modify elements perceived as sexist in its traditional forms of public worship. A dramatic increase in both the age and gender of seminarians – older and more female – in mainline denominations contributed to an ethos that traditionalists found distasteful. Growing secularism among the more highly educated young and diminished support for campus ministries in favor of social change projects resulted in a falling-off of younger members as congregations became conspicuously grayer. All of the mainline groups lost roughly one-quarter to one-third of their membership in the last quarter of the twentieth century, and the smallest, the Disciples of Christ, dipped well below the million mark. The largest, the United Methodist Church, which had at one time been second in membership only to the Roman Catholic Church, began to decline and was overtaken by the conservative Southern Baptist Convention.

By the late twentieth century, American Protestant communities stood divided into two camps: the mainline and the evangelical. These camps were not entirely mutually exclusive, since the mainline denominations included a considerable number of clergy and laity who self-identified as evangelical and who in a number of cases formed intradenominational caucuses to work against the legitimization of abortion rights, gay ordination and marriage, and other conservative issues. On the other hand, a similar movement had begun within evangelical circles to break away from a narrow focus on divisive issues and focus instead on more broadly-based causes such as environmentalism and global warming, relief of hunger, and the like. This movement benefited from the more moderate and non-partisan policies of evangelical leaders such as Rick Warren and Joel Hunter, associated with the new, post-denominational wave of mega-churches, as well as the Democratic turn in the 2006 congressional elections.

The second half of the twentieth century also witnessed a dramatic transformation in the nation's Roman Catholic community. Vatican II, the worldwide ecumenical council convened by the charismatic Pope John XXIII in 1961, brought about a wide-scale program of *aggiornamento* – modernization – within Catholic practice, most dramatically illustrated in the change from Latin to vernacular languages in the celebration of the Mass and other sacramental rituals. Vatican II also brought about a major shift in Catholic attitudes towards the broader world and other religious traditions. Where American Catholic clergy had previously been forbidden to play any role that implied official recognition of the legitimacy of other (mainly Protestant) religious groups, the new watchword was *ecumenism*: active dialogue with Protestants, Jews, Buddhists, and others based on the mutual recognition of each other's good faith and intrinsic worth. The insular worlds of American Catholic communities began to disappear.

The impact of Vatican II on American Catholicism coincided with a complementary long-term change in the social status of American Catholics. The GI Bill benefited untold numbers of Catholic young men who had entered the military from working-class families and ethnic neighborhoods. These now enjoyed the prospect of a college education, a middle-class occupation, and a home in the suburbs surrounded by similar young families from a variety of religious and ethnic backgrounds. This prospect of advanced education and secure employment also diminished the lure of the priesthood as an avenue to social advancement – but one with the high cost of mandatory celibacy. Similarly, the opening up of a wide variety of attractive careers to young women that began in the 1960s undercut the appeal of a call to life in the convent. The immediate exodus of professional religious – priests and sisters – that followed Vatican II's upgrading of the status of the laity was thus reinforced by this longer-range trend of young Catholics pursuing worldly rather than ecclesiastical vocations. The attempts of long-reigning Pope John Paul II to reverse this trend towards secularity met with only limited success among the laity, who rapidly adopted a "cafeteria" approach of personal judgment on moral issues such as artificial contraception.

Catholic education also underwent major changes during in the post-Vatican II era. With the erosion of the old "ghetto" attitude of Catholic wariness towards the non-Catholic social world, and the evaporation of the minimally-compensated institutional workforce of clergy and sisters, many Catholic children and young people found themselves attending public or private secular schools from kindergarten through university. As a result, Catholic students became an improbable plurality at colleges such as Southern Methodist University, while working-class oriented Catholic institutions such as Boston College, Georgetown, and Notre Dame now became nationally-known schools with considerable numbers of non-Catholics competing for admission. The old Catholic folk culture that focused on the rigor of authoritarian teaching sisters – a mixture of European traditional piety and American working-class social attitudes – now slipped into the realm of bittersweet nostalgia, to be replaced by an attractive middle-class educational environment appealing to ambitious non-Catholic minorities because of superior discipline and academic achievement among students.

That American Catholics had now achieved full membership in Herberg's "triple melting pot" was symbolized by the election of John F. Kennedy as president in 1960. Kennedy exemplified a new American Catholic style in his mixed background of

Boston Irish machine politics and the academic world of his alma mater, Harvard, only recently a bastion of anti-Catholic sentiment. Although no other Roman Catholic has as yet been elected to the presidency, Catholic religious identity has subsequently been largely a non-issue in the political realm, as the majority of Catholics on the Roberts Supreme Court illustrated. Ironically, Senator John Kerry, the unsuccessful Democratic nominee for president in 2004, was opposed by many Catholic bishops and organizations on the grounds of his excessively liberal stand on a variety of social issues.

The American Jewish community underwent many of the same changes as its Catholic counterpart during the second half of the twentieth century in terms of ascent in social status and general acceptance. The candidacy of Connecticut Senator Joseph Lieberman as Democratic nominee for Vice President in 2000, though unsuccessful, was remarkable in its demonstration of the attenuated role that historic anti-Semitism now played in the public arena. Although anti-Catholicism had been a significant force in pre-Kennedy America, it was not based on such enduring prejudice as had bedeviled Jews for centuries (in part through traditional Catholic teaching and folk belief). American Jews had also found themselves in a different social and economic situation from Catholics. Colonial and nineteenth-century Jews had come to the United States in small numbers but with considerable cultural capital, and many succeeded rapidly in carving a niche for themselves in the expansive American economy. The massive waves of Eastern European "New Immigration" Jews, however, brought a less assimilable multitude into America's clogged cities. Some ultra-Orthodox Jews preferred to withdraw into isolated cultural enclaves where they could pursue a lifestyle based on religious tradition (much like the rural Amish). Many, however, instead sought secular success through educational attainment and entrepreneurship, both in traditional Jewish professions such as the garment industry and new areas free from discrimination such as film-making. Educational ambition met with resistance in the infamous "quota" system adopted in the 1920s by many prestigious colleges, while newer institutions such as country clubs and suburban housing developments overtly limited membership to white Protestants. The wave of national revulsion that accompanied unfolding knowledge of the Holocaust following WWII, together with the increasingly middle-class cultural attitudes of many American Jews, led to the dissolving of older discriminatory behavior.

By the 1960s, American Jews reflected a spectrum of attitudes towards the perennial issue of what it meant to live as a Jew in a society where Jews had always been and always would be a numerical minority. At one extreme, Jews could leave the US and resettle in Israel – *aliyah*. Hasidic Jews in the US often self-segregate into geographically isolated communities, enabling them to follow practices and maintain traditions strictly. Other religious Jews – about half of the American Jewish population – have the option of joining a temple or synagogue affiliated with Orthodox, Conservative, Reform, Reconstructionist, or some smaller denominations, on the Protestant model, each reflecting a different attitude towards the accommodation of traditional religious practice to modern secular culture. Still others incorporate elements of Jewish tradition – e.g., Kabala – eclectically with practices from other traditions in a latter-day personal "spirituality." The vogue for Asian religions such as Tibetan and Zen forms of Buddhism has been particularly strong among the Jewish educational elite. Meanwhile, many American Jews self-describe as JNR ("Jewish, non-religious") while maintaining a loose sense of cultural or ethnic identity. Still others drift gradually, often through intermarriage, into the broader secular culture, causing dismay among Jewish leaders concerned with attrition of the American Jewish community through these forces combined with the low birth rate characteristic of groups high in educational and economic attainment.

Some sociologists have argued that by the 1960s a "third disestablishment" had taken place in American society in which religious affiliation of any sort was no longer a prerequisite for acceptance and success. This may have been somewhat premature, given the subsequent impact of the Religious Right on the political scene, and polls in the mid-2000s reveal that many Americans would not vote for an atheist for high office. Although self-avowed atheists have always been few in number, if occasionally highly vocal, in American society, the "culture of disbelief," in Stephen Carter's phrase, nevertheless asserted itself as a part of the American scene. The Pacific Northwest, for example, has been dubbed by sociologists as the "None Zone," that is, the region in which those surveyed by pollsters are most likely to select "none" as most descriptive of their religious affiliation. The loosened hold of familial tradition resulting from higher levels of education, intermarriage, and social and geographical mobility has resulted in what sociologist Robert Bellah and his associates have dubbed "Sheilaism," that is, an eclectic religious individualism that draws upon various sources and traditions to mold a distinctively personal religious identity.

More organized skepticism of traditional religiosity has found an institutional home in the Unitarian Universalist Association, a 1961 merger of the two liberal groups named in this new denominational label. More positively, UUs' self-identify as seekers of religious and ethical truth, which many believe can be found in a variety of traditional and non-traditional sources. Many UUs and Euro-American Buddhists come from Jewish backgrounds, seeking to retain that tradition's emphasis on social justice while abandoning its traditional religious and cultural trappings. The vilification of "secular humanism," whether manifested in the UU movement or in advocacy groups such as the American Civil Liberties Union, became a staple of the rhetoric of the Religious Right during its early years until new bugbears emerged or were created.

On the theme of enhanced tolerance for religious pluralism, the unsuccessful candidacy of Mitt Romney, an active Mormon, for the 2008 Republican presidential nomination provoked doubt among many evangelicals as to the suitability of members of the Church of Jesus Christ of Latter-day Saints for that office. Ironically, the Mormons themselves had experienced a major transformation in social identity. After being pressured by the federal government into forsaking polygamy early in the century, the community utilized its cohesiveness and work ethic to attain a high level of economic success while maintaining conservative social postures very similar to those of their evangelical antagonists. In their zeal for missionary work, moreover, the LDS became a genuinely international community, with large numbers of converts in dozens of nations. In this achievement they not only successfully emulated but outdid earlier efforts by American Protestants to spread their faith through aggressive spiritual colonialism.

The international character of American religion also received a major boost from the Hart-Cellar Act of 1965. This epoch-making law repealed tight restrictions on immigration from nations outside northwestern Europe that had been adopted by

Congress in the 1920s. Instead of being aimed at the "huddled masses yearning to breathe free," however, it favored those with professional skills valuable to the American economy. These included many Asians – especially South Asians from India and Pakistan – who brought with them their traditional Buddhism, Hinduism, and Islam. The high economic status of many of these newcomers meant that they could avoid the traditional route of assimilation, beginning in the inner city, and start instead with homes in the suburbs, leadership roles in religious community, and visible places in the social system.

Also visible were their houses of worship, with central suburban locations near interstate highways. These American Hindu temples and Islamic Centers reflected distinctively American circumstances. Temples in India, for example, were dedicated only to one deity rather than the panoply that American circumstances necessitated, since each New World temple served Hindus from many regions of the old country. Similarly, the Islamic Center – in contrast with the mosque that makes up part of each such institution – is a distinctively American creation, since the Arabic language and Islamic religion are taken for granted in many countries from which these immigrants arrived. Islamic centers have also served as refuges in which American Muslims, vilified indiscriminately by some for the role played by militant Islam in the 9/11 attacks in 2001, have been able to sustain religious communities while under cultural and occasionally even physical assault. (Hindus and other Asians have also been assaulted on occasion by those incapable of perceiving the differences between them and Muslims.)

The theme of international cross-fertilization and its importance in building religious communities that stretch across the globe can be illustrated with many other examples. The American Muslim community, for example, is made up primarily of recent immigrants and their families together with substantial numbers of African American converts, only a small number of whom belong to Louis Farrakhan's hybrid Nation of Islam. Hindus are easily able to visit their native India through inexpensive airfares, and import priests from the old country to staff their new American temples. There are now more Presbyterians in Korea than in the US, a statistic that would surprise the American missionaries who planted that faith in Asia. Evangelical Protestantism, especially in its Pentecostal form, was originally exported from the US to Latin America, where it thrives, and is being brought back to the US by immigrants so that some 20 percent of Latinos have left their traditional Catholicism for an evangelical alternative. American Jews may hold dual citizenship with Israel, and their advocacy of American support for the Israeli government has become a staple of American foreign policy deliberations. And so continues the list of international give-and-take among American religious groups – which is hardly new, given the perennially international character of Roman Catholicism and the Anglo-American network of evangelical Protestant connections in previous years.

By the beginning of the twenty-first century, religion in the United States was clearly part of a global network – much like its economy and broader culture. On the one hand, America was an importer of religion at a variety of levels. Among the educated elites, Zen Buddhism, Transcendental Meditation, Sufi mysticism, and other "exotic" imports provided alternatives to traditional Christianity and Judaism. Among African Americans, Islam in its traditional form similarly began to rival black

Christianity, and the home-grown "Nation of Islam" faded after the death of Elijah Muhammad. A wide variety of religious traditions also began to change the American religious landscape with the onslaught of new immigrants from Asia and the Middle East, including Islam, Hinduism, and Buddhism.

But American religion was also an export commodity. Mormons continue to be indefatigable in seeking converts and building temples on a global scale, although the rates of long-term retention of LDS converts are in some dispute. Mainline denominations have largely abandoned the optimism represented in the earlier Student Volunteer Movement about evangelizing the world, and have instead turned to medical and social aid and advocacy, as have their evangelical counterparts to a considerable extent as well. The earlier American campaign to export its native-born brand of evangelicalism – Pentecostalism – was so successful that it had become one of the most rapidly growing religious movements in Africa and Latin America by the late twentieth century, and was making serious incursions into Roman Catholic hegemony in the latter continent.

One of the most ironic developments is that the Worldwide Anglican Communion, with the Archbishop of Canterbury as its spiritual leader, was being riven in the early twenty-first century by an escalating quarrel between the Episcopal Church in the US – the first non-British Anglican church to attain independent status – and its third-world counterparts, led by Nigerian Archbishop Peter Akinola and other bishops in more recently independent areas of the old British Empire. Among the most vexing issues behind this family feud were the leadership of the American church by a female – Presiding Bishop Katherine Jefferts Schori, elected in 2006 – and the inclusion in the American episcopate of an openly gay bishop, Gene Robinson of New Hampshire, in 2003. Deeper causes were lingering resentments over the legacy of colonialism, the threat of Islam to African Christianity, and the attempts of American conservatives to train third-world Anglicans in the techniques of political manipulation to further what the former perceived to be a common cause of resistance to modernity. The secession from the Episcopal Church of a number of parishes and even entire dioceses, who subsequently sought to align themselves with bishops in Africa and Latin America, not only brought anguish and confusion to the Anglican community but also illustrated the complexity of the interplay between the "import" and "export" dimensions on what had traditionally been the most elite and Anglophiliac of American denominations.

The Roman Catholic Church similarly represents this complicated interplay of "import" and "export." As its name suggests, the Catholic Church has always conceived of itself as a universal organization, so that American Catholicism has always existed in a relationship – at times a tense one – with the central authority in Rome, recently embodied in popes of Polish and German birth. American Catholics had for some time sponsored foreign missions, and sponsoring "pagan" babies was part of the lore of parochial schools of the pre-Vatican II era. By the early twentieth century, American Catholic life had been deeply affected by the shortage of native-born clergy that had resulted from the decline in prestige of the priestly vocation, as well as from an influx of new immigrants – largely from Mexico and other Spanish-speaking nations – for whom priests able to relate to them linguistically and culturally were in even shorter supply. The result has been a dramatic success among Pentecostals and other evangelicals in creating Latino congregations, as well as the importation of foreign clergy to serve English-speaking parishes.

By the early twenty-first century, the American religious scene had not only become more pluralistic than ever, but was also increasingly implicated in an international network of cultural exchange. African American Muslims, Jewish Buddhists, Chicano Pentecostals, and Vietnamese Catholics all illustrate that the distinctive character of American religion lies in its always being in process – importing, exporting, combining, conflicting, and cooperating – but never attaining a point of stability or stasis. As such, it continues to reflect and engage in the broader patterns of American – and international – society.

16

Practice

Candy Gunther Brown

As in past eras, what people do reveals as much about their religion as what people say they believe. Also as in the past, repeated, disciplined performance of particular actions informs belief, enabling people to inhabit their beliefs, finding the meaning of their beliefs in bodily exercises, diet, dress, and interactions with others, and displaying their beliefs in ways that define identity and convey it to others. As in past eras, some ways of practicing religion reflect the regulatory efforts of religious specialists who authorize certain behaviors and instruct followers in how to enact and perfect them. Other ways of practicing religion are ambiguously sanctioned or even practiced in opposition to official religious doctrine. Most religious practices are layered with religious and cultural implications: meaning more than one thing at the same time, even to the same individuals. In the course of the twentieth century, these perennial aspects of religious practice changed as ways of doing religion diversified and intermingled in the context of modern globalization. Americans had more different kinds of religious practice to choose from than ever before and these expansive options stimulated experimentation and exchange. New forms of pilgrimage and healing attracted religious consumers, and innovations in music and sexuality in popular culture inspired religious responses. While the authority of religious specialists by no means disappeared, their power to control practice required increasing accommodation to religious diversification, intermingling, and globalization.

Over the past century, Americans practiced religion in a modernizing world kept in motion by immigration, urbanization, commercialization, and globalization. Religious practices offered a sense of continuity with tradition, even while, often seamlessly, changing form or meaning in response to modernity. Today, as in earlier eras, many Americans pursue a relationship with God or other spiritual powers through devotional activities, such as prayer, worship, and pilgrimage, which demonstrate their love and commitment. Religious practice is not simply about holding beliefs, but also about embodying beliefs through actions that involve the human body. Actions related to sexuality, dress, diet, exercise, and healing are all ways of acting out, and sometimes transforming, religious beliefs. This chapter is organized around these three over-lapping themes: (1) peoples and practices in motion; (2) devotional activities; and (3) bodily disciplines.

Peoples and Practices in Motion

At the beginning of the twentieth century, most Americans were Protestants, Catholics, or Jews whose religious practices were deeply rooted in long-established traditions. Today, the religious landscape is strikingly more pluralistic. In part, religious change reflects the modernizing processes of immigration, urbanization, commercialization, and globalization. Not only do more Americans adhere to tradi-tions outside the Judeo-Christian mainstream, but even among the majority of Americans who self-identify as Christians or Jews, religious practices have become more varied.

By the end of the nineteenth century, a generation of American men who had grown up in the shadow of the Civil War (1861–65) and who felt their manhood threatened by the rise of more independent "New Women," even as their religious moorings were being challenged by the rise of post-Darwinian theological liberalism, looked beyond the geographic boundaries of the United States to reassert their mas-culinity and orthodoxy through "Muscular Christianity." In 1898, white Protestant American men found an opportunity to demonstrate their avowed manliness – as well as their presumed racial and religious superiority – by reversing a national tradition of neutrality in foreign affairs to rally for the US entrance into the Spanish-American War. The legacy of this war was a new era of US involvement in the internal affairs of overseas territories, including Spanish-Catholic-influenced Cuba, Puerto Rico, Guam, and the Philippines – whose peoples American emissaries sought to "civilize" and "Christianize," justifying the use of violent means by citing apparently lofty cultural and religious ideals.

Even as the US became increasingly involved in foreign affairs, successive waves of immigration from overseas and migration from rural to urban areas within the US have made America a predominantly urban nation since the 1920s. Early twentieth-century cities were filled with pockets of recent Catholic and Jewish immigrants who retained or accentuated religious traditions to preserve a sense of connection with homelands in Southern and Eastern Europe and to find a sense of home within diso-rienting new urban landscapes. As children and grandchildren moved from inner-city ethnic neighborhoods to suburbs by mid-century, religious practices became less tied to traditions established within church or synagogue-centered ethnic communities.

After the passage of the Immigration Reform Act in 1965, immigration from Latin America and the Caribbean, Asia, and Africa increased dramatically. Most new arrivals were Christians who frequently shared churches with established ethnic groups, re-infusing older communities with new ways of calling upon the Spirit of Christ, or venerating Mary and the saints. Significant minorities practiced Islam, Buddhism, Hinduism, Santería, or Vodou. As immigrants built mosques and temples and practiced religion in offices and on street corners, the dense population of metropolitan areas made visible diverse values and practices.

The Civil Rights and counterculture movements of the 1960s encouraged cross-fertilization among cultures, lifestyles, and worldviews. As sociologists Robert Wuthnow and Robert Bellah have explained, many twentieth-century Americans redefined freedom of conscience, an individual's ability to choose right over wrong without external restraint, as freedom of choice, an individual's right to pick and choose from among moral options. As American culture commercialized, religion itself became something that individuals could "shop" for within a competitive marketplace – not only picking the religious institution that best met individual needs, but also drawing spiritual insight from popular books, counseling professionals, and television shows. The entertainment, advertising, educational and therapeutic industries, all of which blossomed in the second half of the twentieth century, shaped a culture that tended, ironically, toward uniformity in its celebration of religious individualism. More and more Americans, even if they attended services at a church or synagogue, practiced an eclectic, seeker spirituality, sampling religious practices from various sources.

The New Age and holistic healthcare movements of the 1970s reflected the quest of many Americans of European ancestry to appropriate spiritual resources from Native American, Asian, and metaphysical religious traditions. Practices such as meditating, reading horoscopes, channeling departed spirits, talking to angels, exercising using yoga or martial arts, or seeking healing through reiki or acupuncture became increasingly commonplace in middle-class, suburban America. Some Asians and Native Americans ignored criticisms from traditionalist members of their communities about the dangers of white cultural imperialism and offered to teach New Age seekers how to borrow traditional practices. For instance, in 1966, the Chippewa teacher Sun Bear founded the Bear Tribe Medicine Society for non-natives who wanted to learn about such practices as sweat-lodge and pipe ceremonies, pilgrimages to Indian sacred sites, or the uses of rattles, drums, feathers, beads and gemstones in shamanism. By the 1990s, health and life-style magazines and other genres of self-help literature made it even easier for Americans to experiment with metaphysical religions by downplaying religious meanings and emphasizing the "scientific" health benefits of selected techniques, such as dietary procedures, exercises, and relaxation methods. Reflecting the utilitarian strain of American culture, few people paused to ask why particular techniques were used or worried about whether it was fully possible to extricate specific practices from the larger belief systems that make them meaningful.

In a technologically connected global society, even ideas embraced by relatively few people diffuse rapidly, lending credibility to practices that most Americans once regarded as fringe or threatening. During the 1970s, *Star Wars* popularized the idea of a universal spiritual Force, similar to the Eastern ideas of *prana* or *qi* (chi), which individuals can tap into to gain empowerment. Late twentieth-century television programming, such as *Touched by an Angel* (1994–2003) and *Buffy the Vampire Slayer* (1997–2003), like the phenomenally successful *Harry Potter* (1997–) series of novels and movies about the training of a young wizard, reflected and encouraged interest in the activity of supernatural agents and magic in the modern world. By the 1990s, a wide variety of spiritual options, including wicca, the modern-day practice of witchcraft, had become culturally respectable.

Devotional Activities

Practicing religion is centrally concerned with relationships: with divine or transcendent powers, and with one's self, family, community, and environment. People cultivate relationships by exhibiting devotion through activities such as prayer, worship, and pilgrimage.

Prayer

Despite the Supreme Court's ban on schoolroom prayer in 1962, recent public opinion polls report that 88% of Americans pray and 60% consider prayer very important, although only 42% ask God to meet material needs (Poloma and Gallup 1991). Prayer, conducted individually or with others, can involve the recitation of written or memorized scripts, such as the Lord's Prayer, or improvisational conversations that include listening as well as speaking. People may ask God for something for themselves (petitions) or on behalf of others (intercession), or may seek to become attuned to the presence of God or some higher reality (meditation).

Participants in the Azusa Street revivals of 1906 that marked the birth of Pentecostalism expected prayer to result in supernatural interventions in the natural world, such as miraculous healings or an ability to speak in unknown languages (*glossolalia*). In the Charismatic and third-wave (referring to waves of the Holy Spirit) renewals of the 1960s and 1980s, members of mainstream evangelical churches similarly expected an increase in supernatural activity as a byproduct of cultivating fellowship with the person of the Holy Spirit. Today, Pentecostal and Charismatic Christians envision prayer both as soaking in God's presence, and also as a form of spiritual warfare through which they battle demonic forces. Influenced by the Argentine revivals of the 1980s, Americans sometimes draw spiritual maps of their communities, pinpointing regions that merit special prayer. Devotional imagery is simultaneously feminine, envisioning the church as the bride of Christ, and masculine, portraying Christians as an army engaged in a battle between the Kingdom of Heaven and the Kingdom of Darkness.

By contrast, liberal Protestants since the 1920s have, alongside a relatively small, but growing stream of religious skeptics, considered it unreasonable to expect supernatural intervention in response to prayer, given what scientists have discovered about the regularity of natural laws. Typically, William Adams Brown, in *The Life of Prayer in a World of Science* (1927), argues that prayer requests should be restricted to spiritual and moral concerns, and not include pleas for changes in the natural order.

As historian Gregory Johnson has noted, evangelical Protestants, many of whom shared liberal, rationalist doubts about the ongoing availability of biblical miracles, promoted the "quiet time" as an antidote to both the busyness of modern life and the seeming presumptuousness of Pentecostal petitions for supernatural aid. The InterVarsity Press tract *Quiet Time*, continuously in print since its publication in 1945, urges readers to spend an hour every morning in solitude reading the Bible and listening to God. Protestant devotional guides, such as the Lutheran Church-Missouri Synod's *Little Visits with God* (1957), encourage families to pray together. Since the 1980s, millions of Protestants have met in homes to study the Bible and pray with Christians beyond their immediate families.

Catholic prayer practices are meaningful within the broader framework of Catholic sacramentalism: using words, objects, and physical gestures as external signs and instruments of the internal communication of God's grace (or gifts) to the human soul. In the Eucharist (or communion), the central sacrament of Catholic worship, the bread and wine become the body and blood of Christ when consecrated by the priest at Mass. Catholics genuflect, or kneel, to honor the presence of Christ (the Eucharistic bread) in the tabernacle; make the sign of the cross to recall the death of Jesus; and say the rosary to meditate on scenes and stories from the life, death, and resurrection of Christ. During the first half of the twentieth century, Catholics used a wide array of material artifacts to aid their prayers to God and their requests for the intercessions of the Virgin Mary and the saints. For example, a nationwide devotional culture developed around Saint Jude, patron saint of hopeless causes, after his statue was installed in a Chicago church in 1929. Jude's devout, many of them women who felt abandoned by the men in their lives and disoriented by social change, wrote to the shrine voicing needs and expressing gratitude for favors granted. As scholar Robert Orsi has argued, devotion to Jude intensified as petitioners asked for holy oil to be mailed, exchanged prayer cards picturing Jude with friends at times of crisis, and talked intimately with duplicate statues on their nightstands.

The liturgical reforms of the Second Vatican Council in Rome (1962–65) emphasized the celebration of the Eucharist and relegated much of devotional Catholicism to a secondary position. Reformers divided the Mass into a "liturgy of the Word," focusing Catholic attention on the Bible, and the "liturgy of the Eucharist," which was the celebration of a community meal rather than a representation of the sacrifice of the cross. Many churches moved or eliminated statues and votive candles, and the altar was turned around so that the priest celebrant faced the congregation and spoke in Latin rather than the vernacular. The congregation participated in the Mass by responding to particular invocations by the priest; for instance, "The Lord be with you" was answered by the congregation with "And also with you." The Catholic Charismatic movement that began in Pittsburgh in the 1960s, and spread throughout the country, was the Catholic version of the Pentecost experience. In Charismatic prayer groups, Catholics read Scripture, improvised prayers, and experienced spiritual gifts like glossolalia and healing.

Even after Vatican II, Catholic devotional practices continued to take a variety of forms. Catholics today hang medallions or carry glow-in-the-dark figurines of Mary in automobiles, fishing boats, or farming equipment, believing these images to embody spiritual power that protects the vehicles' occupants. Marian devotions revived in the 1980s through the influence of recent immigrants from Latin America. Haitian immigrants who practice both Catholicism and Vodou in cities like Brooklyn, or Cuban immigrants who combine Catholicism with Santería in cities such as Miami, revere Catholic saints as representations of African deities, endowing images and holy water obtained from Catholic shrines with Afro-Caribbean religious meanings. Botánicas, or specialty stores, across the US sell images of Catholic saints alongside herbs and ritual implements used to invoke African spirits by drumming, lighting candles, or dancing.

Whereas Haitian and Cuban immigration had expanded dramatically after 1965, European Jews had formed sizable communities, especially in New York City, since the early twentieth century. Many Jewish prayer practices continue to be centered on the synagogue. Orthodox Jews live in walking distance from the synagogue, since cars may not be driven on the weekly day of rest, or Sabbath (*Shabbat*). In Orthodox Jewry, a quorum of ten men is required for a full prayer service, which is conducted in Hebrew. Jews traditionally recite formal prayers three times daily, adding a fourth prayer on the Sabbath and holidays, as well as briefer prayers upon waking and before and after meals. Some Orthodox men wear a prayer shawl (*tallit*) all day, moving it from inside to outside their shirts during prayer services. Orthodox women are excused from many synagogue prayers in order to attend to domestic responsibilities; when attending, they sit in a screened off balcony and remain silent during prayers and songs in order to avoid distracting the men. Women, however, preside over domestic devotions by lighting Sabbath candles, setting apart a sacred portion of bread (*challah*) before the Sabbath meal, and observing laws of family purity (periods of abstinence from sexual practice) and ritual bathing. Reform and Conservative Jews object to many of the gender distinctions that Orthodox Jews observe and often place greater emphasis on their responsibility for contributing to social justice in the world.

As in Judaism, the formal recitation of daily prayers is one of the Five Pillars of Islam required of all Muslims. Sunni Muslims, who represent a major branch of Islam, pray five times daily in Arabic, while bowing toward Mecca. Shi'a Isma'ili Muslims assemble daily before sunrise, at sunset, and later in the evening to recite prayers in Arabic, having first bathed and dressed formally to maintain ritual purity. Some American mosques discourage women's attendance; others seat men and women separately, and still others practice mixed seating.

In contrast to the formal prayers of Judaism and Islam, Buddhists, whether recent Asian immigrants or European converts, practice meditation or mindfulness. Right Mindfulness is the seventh element of the Noble Eightfold Path of Buddhism. Through visualization, chanting, and assumption of bodily postures, the goal is to achieve emptiness, a spiritual state of non-acquisitive openness necessary for Enlightenment. In some forms of Mindfulness practice, the repetition of a syllable or phrase infuses the practitioner with the wisdom of a Buddha, or fully realized being. The Mindfulness-Based Stress Reduction (MBSR) program, developed in 1979 by Dr. John Kabat-Zinn of the University of Massachusetts Center for Mindfulness in Medicine, Health Care, and Society, introduced Buddhist meditation and yoga to the medical and business mainstreams. Mindfulness promoters attracted non-Buddhist practitioners at retreats sponsored by secular companies and hospitals and gained entrance into public school curricula by deemphasizing religious meanings, at least for beginners, and highlighting the benefits of stress reduction, pain management, and enhanced productivity.

Just as Buddhist meditation can be done anywhere, many forms of prayer are practiced in offices, malls, and especially homes, across America. Supplied by a multi-billion dollar market in religious artifacts, American homes display religious objects and images, such as statues and scripture mottoes, as reminders to pray amidst daily routines. Warner Sallman's *Head of Christ* (1941), reproduced more than five hundred million times, invites prayer as intimate conversation with Jesus. Catholic, Buddhist, and Hindu shrines occupy kitchens, bedrooms, and backyards in many Mexican, Italian, Portuguese, Irish, and Asian homes. Prayer rugs and wall plaques in Muslim homes set apart a special place for prayer and indicate the direction of Mecca.

Worship

Alongside prayer, many religious communities worship, or honor, God or supplicate deities through music, song, and dance. Singing about religious beliefs, whether individually or in the company of others, socializes the young into religious traditions, reinforces beliefs among older generations, and communicates religious messages to outsiders. Even as songs preserve religious traditions through doctrinal content that changes relatively little over time, musical styles are adaptable to shifting cultural norms. At the turn of the twentieth century, many Protestants combined the singing of older hymns with newly popular gospel songs, written in the vernacular styles of African-American camp-meeting traditions. Ira Sankey and Philip Bliss's *Gospel Hymns and Sacred Songs* (1875) had sold over fifty million copies by the early twentieth century. The gospel songs employed everyday language, repetition and direct address, and catchy melodies that singers could easily remember and hum amidst daily activities.

Like the gospel-song revivals of the early twentieth century, the Jesus People movement that began among Christian hippies during the 1960s and 1970s influenced many Protestant and Catholic churches to exchange hymns performed by choirs with organ accompaniment for new choruses sung by everyone to the tunes of guitars and drums as the words are projected overhead. John Wimber (1934–97), who founded the Association of Vineyard churches in the 1970s, was a former jazz musician and the keyboardist and manager for a secular rock band, the Righteous Brothers. Vineyard music blended European and African styles, including rock and roll, jazz, reggae, and rap. Contemporary Christian music companies such as Marantha!, founded in 1974, popularized the new musical genres. Maranatha! lyrics are sung in churches of nearly every denomination and stream over car CD players, iPods, and radio and television stations throughout the week, creating a common Christian musical culture that crosses social and national boundaries. The new music is especially embraced by "seeker-sensitive" congregations that make church more accessible to spiritual seekers by dispensing with traditions that seem disconnected from modern culture. For megachurches like Willow Creek Community Church, founded in a Chicago suburb in the 1980s and now home to 25,000 members, dispensing with traditional hymns goes along with removal of stained glass, crosses, and pews that are perceived as "religious" in a negative sense of the term, constituting inessential barriers rather than aids to worship. Reflecting the multi-directional diffusion of cultural influences in an era of globalization, American churches also borrow songs written outside the US, in languages other than English. For instance, the Brazilian musical group Casa de Davi (House of David) sells Portuguese-language worship CDs to Americans who believe that the anointing of the Holy Spirit transcends language to impart a sanctifying influence to English-speaking worshippers.

For African-American youth who feel that churches and mosques have failed to address the poverty, racism, and violence of urban America, rap music offers an alternative source of theological insight. Drawing on Christian symbols such as the crucifix in videos and CD art, rap reinterprets Christian theology to make God seem more accessible from the streets, without formal religion. Christian rap artists, such as members of the Holy Hip Hop Ministry, founded in 1997, preach a traditional Christian message using rap musical styles and lyrics that speak to the struggles of inner-city life. Similarly adapting traditional religious teachings to changing cultural norms, Native

Deen is an Islamic rap group formed in 2000 by three African-American Muslims. Believing that Muhammad forbade the use of wind or string instruments, Native Deen uses only traditional drums in live performances, although including a wider variety of percussion instruments in their CDs, videos, and internet broadcasts. Explaining that Deen means religion or way of life in Arabic, the group presents its music as a distinctively American adaptation that offers Muslims religiously orthodox music in English that sounds "hip," or culturally relevant.

Music can preserve distinctive traditions rather than facilitating cultural adaptation. In the 1980s, Ojibwe Indians in Minnesota revived the use of hymns introduced by Protestant missionaries in the nineteenth century, redefining the hymns as emblematic of Ojibwe ethnic and spiritual identity. Chanted by groups of elders in the Ojibwe language, which few people speak fluently today, hymns function, as scholar Michael McNally has noted, as a reminder of past communal traditions and as a resource for survival in an uncertain future. Traditionalists resist the hymns as disrespectful of the drum, although chants are accompanied by traditional burning of sage incense and pipe ceremonies; Christian Ojibwes reject hymn-singing as contaminated by traditional practices.

Similarly concerned with contamination, many conservative Protestants forbid dance inside or outside church services. For Charismatic and Pentecostal Christians influenced by African-American traditions, dancing or waving flags is a vital expression of worship. Members of the Mevlevi Order of Sufi Islam, who emigrated from Turkey after 1965, are known popularly as the whirling dervishes (or ascetics) because of their characteristic religious dance (*sema*). In the Mevlevi Order of America, both men and women may participate in the formal ritual, first donning long robes and tall, cylindrical hats. With musical accompaniment, the participants extend their arms, right palms up and left palms down, and repeatedly turn counterclockwise, pivoting on the left foot; they understand each turn as a form of prayer and worship.

Pilgrimage

Although many prayer and worship practices are conducted close to home, pilgrimage is an act of religious devotion in which individuals or groups undertake round-trip journeys, today often using automobiles and airplanes, to sites they consider sacred or religiously transformative.

In some traditions, pilgrimage is a religious duty to be performed by all adherents. According to the Five Pillars of Islam, every able Muslim should undertake a pilgrimage (*hajj*) to Mecca at least once. One of the best-known Muslim pilgrims, Malcolm X (1925–65), withdrew from the Nation of Islam to become a Sunni Muslim (considered more orthodox by many Muslims) as a result of his pilgrimage in 1964. Much more controversially, the terrorist attacks of 11 September 2001 can be viewed as a one-way pilgrimage – although such an interpretation, as scholar Robert Orsi has commented, brings into sharp relief the problem of defining authentic or "good" religious practices. The handful of Muslim men who flew hijacked airplanes into the World Trade Center and the Pentagon buildings understood themselves to be using a technologically sophisticated strategy to perform a sacred, transformative religious journey. The men envisioned themselves as martyrs zealously pursuing Allah's holy war (*jihad*) to punish American oppressors. Many American Muslims were understandably quick to distinguish their interpretations of Islam from the terrorists'. Denunciations of the terrorists went a step further, denying that their actions should be considered authentically "religious" in any sense; instead, the attacks represented an immoral exploitation of religion for political purposes.

Critiques of religious authenticity sometimes focus not on the social and political consequences of particular practices, but their purported triviality. For Catholics, pilgrimage is often motivated by a need for help with problems related to health, finances, or relationships, or performed after a petition has been granted to express gratitude or fulfill a vow. Throughout the twentieth century, American Catholics have undertaken pilgrimages to well-known shrines such as the Lourdes grotto in France, established in 1858. More controversially, reproductions of the Lourdes shrine, which similarly attract steady streams of pilgrims, can be found in cities across America. The Bronx Lourdes is a replica constructed in 1939 that today attracts pilgrims of European, Caribbean, and African descent, not all of whom are Catholic. Pilgrims drink the holy water – drawn from the city reservoir – or pour it into their car transmissions in order to convey protection. For the devout, the shrine shares in the sacred meanings associated with the original shrine in France. But to detractors, as Robert Orsi has noted, the clearly non-miraculous source of the water and the seemingly superstitious uses to which it is put invalidate the authenticity of pilgrimage to the shrine.

Although Protestants have sometimes accused all Catholic pilgrims of behaving superstitiously, twentieth-century Protestants often undertake religious travel that can usefully be described as pilgrimage. Following reports of Latin American revivals in the 1980s and 1990s, nightly services dubbed the "Toronto Blessing" began at a small Ontario church in 1994. During the following decade, an estimated three million people from around the world, representing nearly every stream of the Christian church, undertook pilgrimages to Toronto searching for physical healing or spiritual renewal, and many claimed that when they returned home they brought the revival fires with them. Heidi Baker was one such pilgrim – a self-described "burned-out" American missionary to Mozambique. After visiting Toronto in 1996, Baker reported that her ministry grew from two churches and an orphanage to more than 7,000 churches and homes for 10,000 orphaned children. Envisioning Toronto as a place with particularly sacred associations, Baker periodically retraced her steps there, especially at crisis moments when she felt the need for healing and retooling for her work in Mozambique.

In 2008, Lakeland, Florida, became a popular destination for Protestant pilgrims from across the US and dozens of other countries. The "Florida Outpouring" began with the visit of an unconventional Canadian healing evangelist to a moderately sized Pentecostal church in Lakeland. The evangelist, Todd Bentley, is avowedly a former drug addict with a criminal record and an eighth-grade education who is still covered with tattoos, and rides Harley Davidson motorcycles. As reports of miraculous healings spread worldwide over nightly broadcasts via the internet and the satellite station GOD TV, upwards of ten thousand people turned up nightly for months – causing the meeting organizers to seek a series of new venues – including an 8,000-seat convention center, a baseball stadium, and a 10,000-seat tent erected on the grounds of a local airport cum campground. As discount airlines offered affordable fares to the neighboring cities of Tampa and Orlando, many visitors reported learning about the revivals by internet one day and hopping on a plane the next day to, in Bentley's words, "come get some" of the presumably transferable, tangible anointing of the Holy Spirit present in Lakeland. Upon returning home, pilgrims held "impartation" services to pray for others to receive the anointing. However, unlike Toronto, which continued to attract visitors for years – in part because pilgrims were traveling to a church and a place rather than following a specific evangelist – trans-local interest in Lakeland waned once Bentley was no longer regularly featured, particularly when Bentley soon thereafter took a leave from public ministry and divorced and remarried.

Bodily Disciplines

As the example of pilgrimage suggests, many religious practices fully involve the human body. Bodily disciplines related to sexuality, dress, diet, exercise, and healing provide means for religious adherents to involve their whole bodies in practicing their faith and to set apart their communities as uncontaminated by the world.

Sexuality and dress

Sexual relationships outside of marriage are prohibited by most Jewish, Christian, and Muslim communities. The Catholic Church restricts entrance into religious orders to celibate men and women, many of whom wear distinctive clothing as outward signs of their vocations. The Catholic Church also forbids artificial contraception among married couples, although many Catholics have departed from church teachings on birth control since the development of oral contraceptives in 1961.

Some religious communities use dress codes to repudiate fashions, especially women's fashions, that presumably encourage sexual immorality. Certain Pentecostal denominations, such as the African American Church of God in Christ, require conservative clothing and hairstyles and prohibit the use of makeup or jewelry. Such practices prevent sexual connotations from being associated with exuberant worship, and symbolize the community's separation from the world. Similarly, many Muslim women wear veils as a sign of modesty and religious submission.

Other religious communities use distinctive patterns of dress to indicate their more complete rejection of modernity. The black hats and long robes worn by Hasidic Jews can be traced back to pre-modern Europe (Figure 16.1). Traditional Amish clothing and hairstyles resemble those worn in eighteenth-century rural Germany. For the Amish, clothing symbolizes a broader rejection of modern technologies, such as automobiles and telephones, which interfere with the rhythm of life established by God's law.

For participants in modern American culture, religious objects worn next to the body remind wearers of beliefs while they are engaged in daily activities, or protect them from harm while living in the modern world. Pre-Vatican II Catholics wore scapulas, small pieces of cloth blessed by a priest and placed on the shoulders under clothing, to attain spiritual merit and secure protection from danger. Today, some Catholics pin medals of saints to their underwear when reporting for radiation therapy. Similarly, Protestants in need of healing might wear blessed prayer cloths, or secretly sew them into the clothing of non-Christian family members.

Figure 16.1 Hasidic Jewish men.

Clothing can also communicate religious meanings to outsiders or to members of one's own community. Christian bookstores market t-shirts and baseball caps that play off of seculars mottos, for instance, replacing Coca-Cola advertisements with "Jesus is the Real Thing." In the 1980s, many Christians sported WWJD ("What Would Jesus Do?") bracelets – drawing inspiration from Charles Sheldon's long-running bestseller *In His Steps* (1896), which introduced the phrase. Mormon men and women, prior to going on mission or marrying, begin to wear a special undergarment consecrated during a temple ceremony and embroidered with sacred signs. The garment, which has become progressively shorter during the twentieth century, is usually not visible to outsiders, but, as historian Colleen McDannell has observed, is a sign of communal identity to other Mormons. More visible to outsiders are the dark suits, starched white shirts, and ties that, even during summer weather, herald the approach of pairs of young Mormon missionaries.

Diet and exercise

Like patterns of dress, food practices solidify religious identity, foster relationships with God or other spiritual forces, and promote harmony with the environment.

Feasting plays a role in celebratory worship for many religious communities. The African American Father Divine's International Peace Mission attracted thousands of followers during the 1930s by providing sumptuous feasts, which Divine termed Holy Communion banquets and presented as tangible signs of God's love. Thousands of Catholics from Italian, Haitian, and other ethnic communities in New York City celebrate the annual festa of Our Lady of Mount Carmel. The event begins with eating a large meal, followed by dancing and parading through the city streets behind an image of the Madonna. German Lutherans participate in church suppers that represent the community's religious and ethnic identity. Mid-century African-American church cookbooks prominently featured pork as soul food, a symbol of black pride during the Civil Rights era.

Dietary restrictions, in contrast to feasting, marked the distinctiveness of some religious communities. Denouncing the eating habits of most African Americans, Nation of Islam leader Elijah Muhammad (1897–75) insisted that pork should be avoided as a sign of rejecting the filthy, health-destroying influence of white people. Similarly, for twentieth-century Jews, dietary restrictions solidify communal identity and separation from the world. Orthodox, and to lesser degrees Conservative and Reformed, Jews, continue to follow traditional dietary laws for keeping kosher, or ritually pure. Only certain types of meat may be eaten, and only when slaughtered properly and kept separate from milk products. The week of Passover is a time of both dietary restriction and feasting; all leavening must be avoided throughout the season, which begins with the Passover Seder, an elaborate meal for family and friends celebrating the exodus of ancient Israelites from bondage in Egypt. (Eating unleavened bread throughout Passover Week helps practitioners identify with the Israelites who did not have time to bake leavened bread before their flight from Egypt.)

Many religious communities promote dietary restrictions on the grounds that certain foods are both physically and spiritually contaminating. Religious campaigns to ban the manufacture and sale of alcohol because of its harmful and immoral effects resulted in nationwide Prohibition from 1920 until 1933. Early Pentecostals rejected not just alcohol, but cigarettes, and even chewing gum as spiritually as well as physically polluting. Today, Mormons and Seventh Day Adventists prohibit the use of alcohol, cigarettes, and coffee. Some Seventh Day Adventists practice vegetarianism as an aid to worshipping God by promoting health. Many Buddhists embrace vegetarianism as a means of showing compassion to other living creatures.

Periodic fasting from all food is an aspect of worship for many religious Americans. According to Nation of Islam teachings, the traditional Muslim requirement of fasting from food and water sun-up to sun-down during the month of Ramadan, does not go far enough. Elijah Muhammad urged his followers to eat just one meal a day and to fast monthly for three, nine, or 27 days, in order to cleanse the body from accumulated toxins. Twentieth-century Jews continue to observe Yom Kippur, or the Day of Atonement, a day of fasting in repentance of sins. Prior to Vatican II, Catholics abstained from eating meat on Fridays and fasted from all food and water on any day they planned to eat the Eucharist.

Some religious communities promoted fasting, not only as a sign of repentance and humility, but also as a route to spiritual empowerment. Franklin Hall's widely read *Atomic Power with God Through Prayer and Fasting* (1946) urged Protestants to renew their attention to fasting, even for periods of as long as 40 days, in emulation of Jesus, as a means of heightening the effectiveness of prayer. Similarly, Mahesh Chavda's *The Hidden Power of Prayer and Fasting* (1988) represents the recent concern of Charismatic and Pentecostal Christians to fast as a weapon of spiritual warfare against sin, sickness, and demonic oppression.

Rather than envisioning fasting as a route to spiritual power, some Protestants, as scholar Marie Griffith has observed, promote dieting and exercising for weight loss as a physical counterpart to spiritual purity. Popular Christian diet books, like Patricia Banta Kreml's *Slim for Him: Biblical Devotions on Diet* (1978) and Gwen Shamblin's *Rise Above: God Can Set You Free from Your Weight Problems Forever* (2000), associate fat with sin, and slimness with purity. Since the 1980s, Christian exercise programs like Praise Aerobics, Believercise, and Cross Training have attracted tens of thousands of Americans by promoting physical fitness as a means of worshipping God and strengthening one's Christian witness to outsiders.

Exercising the body is for many Americans also a means of exercising the spirit. Since the 1970s, yoga and martial arts classes, often sponsored by community centers and secular universities – and sometimes even by Christian churches – have introduced many Americans to Eastern religious practices. Developed in India, the Sanskrit word yoga means to yoke or unite the mind with the Universal Mind or Life Force (*prana*), the vital energy that Hindus believe created and permeates everything. The most popular yoga form in the US, hatha yoga (from the Sanskrit *ha*-sun and *tha*-moon) is the practice of balancing the male and female energy principles through a combination of bodily postures (*asanas*), breathing techniques (*pranayama*), and meditation. The goal of yoga practice is the realization of Absolute Truth, also known as Enlightenment or Self-Realization. Controlled breathing, which is envisioned as linking body and mind, takes in and regulates the flow of vital energy through the power centers (*chakras*) of the body's subtle energy system. While breathing deeply and holding postures, practitioners use meditation, sometimes assisted by repetition of a prayer or sacred word (*mantra*), to withdraw the senses from the everyday world and focus the mind on the Infinite. Similarly, pilates, developed by Joseph Pilates in the 1920s and popularized in the 1990s, combines practices based in yoga, Zen Buddhist meditation, and martial arts.

One of the most popular martial arts forms in America at the end of the twentieth century, Tai Chi, is rooted in Chinese Taoism and I Ching. T'ai Chi Ch'uan is literally translated as Supreme Ultimate Boxing. Tao is envisioned as the power that brought the world forth from chaos and generated the opposing forces of yin and yang, or male and female, energy. The goal of Tai Chi is to balance yin and yang, thereby circulating the life force energy (*qi*) that is believed to animate the human body and permeate the universe. The controlled use of force, in such movements as hitting, lifting, and throwing, balances yin and yang and opens the flow of energy. Movement is combined with meditation, often aided by guided imagery and nature-infused visualizations. The thirteen basic postures of Tai Chi also correlate with the eight I Ching trigrams (mystical sequences of three symbols) and five elements of Chinese alchemy used in divination.

Healing

Just as religious meanings and physical health are closely connected in various dietary and exercise regimens, many healing practices are envisioned as simultaneously promoting the health of body, mind, and spirit.

Despite modern advances in biomedicine, many Americans have combined or replaced medical treatments with alternatives that are laden with religious meanings. Surveys conducted in 1924 and 1990 each reported that 34 percent of Americans used alternative medicine (Whorton 2002). When people desperately need healing, they tend to worry less about why a particular technique is thought to work than whether it is effective. Thus, Americans often experiment with healing practices from religious traditions other than their own. Because what people do inevitably shapes how they think, healing, as historian Robert Fuller has argued (Fuller 1989), may be one of the most powerful engines for reshaping religious beliefs in the pluralistic society of modern America.

Rejecting conventional medicine's exclusive focus on human bodies as biological organisms, the holistic healthcare movement became widely popular in the 1970s by emphasizing the interconnectedness of physical, mental, and spiritual health. Holistic healing presumes the existence of a life-force or vital energy that flows through the universe and permeates the human body. Blockages or imbalances in the flow of energy are believed to cause illness. Healing practices, such as acupuncture, shiatsu massage, and reiki, involve opening blockages and restoring equilibrium in the flow of energy (*qi*) through the body's energy channels (*chakras* and *nadis/meridians*). In Therapeutic Touch, developed by nursing professor Dolores Krieger in 1972, the practitioner, with hands positioned several inches away from the patient, feels around the sick person's energy field (*aura*) for evidence of congestion in the flow of universal life-force energy (*prana*) and mentally concentrates on the patient with intent to heal. Similarly in chiropractic, developed by Daniel David Palmer in 1895 and popularized in the 1970s, the adjustment of displaced spinal vertebrae is envisioned as unblocking the free flow of a universal life force (*Innate Intelligence*) and restoring harmony between the human body and the cosmos. Studies indicate that as many as 80 percent of chiropractors today embrace metaphysical views in line with Palmer's, while as many as 88 percent self-identify as evangelical Christians, an indication that chiropractic appeals to patients who similarly want the best of both worlds when healing is at stake (Moore 1993).

Like healing systems in which practitioners physically manipulate energy with their hands or by using instruments such as needles, other practices involve the ingestion or external application of substances thought to restore a proper energy balance. Indeed, holistic healing has become a major industry in the US that draws on exotic plants and healing practices from around the world to serve American consumers. Despite a growing number of studies documenting the ineffectiveness of many alternative medicines, and the dangers of ingesting substances whose effects are poorly understood, the market for alternative remedies continues to grow as part of America's sprawling healthcare economy. Some nutritional therapists classify cancers as yin or yang, and prescribe eating the opposite kind of food in order to attack the cancer. In homeopathy, invented by Samuel Hahnemann in the early 1800s and revived in the 1980s, the procedures of grinding, shaking, and diluting herbs and other plant substances are believed to unleash the vital force of the plants. In aromatherapy, a term coined in the 1920s and mass marketed in the early 2000s, plant oils are envisioned as the essence or spirit of the plants; inhaling or absorbing appropriate oils through the skin is thought to restore the body's subtle energy system.

Some healing practices combine the manipulation of impersonal energy fields with the invocation of aid from personal deities or spirits. Mexican American folk healers (*curanderos*) perform purification rituals (*limpias*), in which they pass objects, such as herbs, over the body in order to absorb negative vibrational energy. Folk healers, like other herbalists, believe that the efficacy of remedies depends upon establishing a spiritual relationship with the plants from which herbs are harvested. This procedure may involve asking the plant's permission, drawing spiritual energy from the sun or moon by gathering herbs at a particular time of day or month, and invoking the help of saints or deceased spirits. Recitation of the Lord's Prayer and the use of ritual objects appropriated from Catholicism, such as crucifixes, pictures of saints, holy water, burning candles, incense, or oils, are believed to emit vibrations and fragrances pleasing to the spiritual world. Native American communities similarly combine herbs with direct appeals to spiritual beings for healing. Navajo families hire specialist singers to perform chants that invoke the aid of divine powers. Apaches envision the coming-of-age ceremony for young girls as an occasion on which the initiate temporarily becomes a powerful Apache deity who possesses supernatural healing power.

In contrast to healing approaches that manipulate immanent spiritual energy or invoke spiritual beings to transform material bodies, in other traditions practitioners believe that all reality is spiritual. New Thought groups, such as Christian Science, Jewish Science, and the Unity School of Christianity, assert that illness is error, which can be corrected by truthful thinking and speaking (mind cure) – such as daily affirmations of good health and denials of the reality of disease. Because illness is not caused by material factors, many New Thought practitioners avoid conventional medicine.

For different reasons, namely a conviction that blood is sacred and must not be consumed, Jehovah's Witnesses refuse blood transfusions, although many will accept blood substitutes made possible by late twentieth-century science. Most Americans do affirm the reality of material existence and make full use of modern medicine, even if they combine it with religious alternatives. Many Christians and Jews have enthusiastically supported medical science, founding hospitals and pursuing medical careers out of a sense of religious calling to love those in need.

There is in the Judeo-Christian tradition a history of ambivalence about the meanings of sickness and the nature of the human body. Although affirming that the body is good because created in God's image, early twentieth-century Christians worried that a healthy body might prove an obstacle to the progress of the soul. Sickness was typically envisioned as something that should be accepted as having been sent by God in chastisement for sin or as an opportunity for spiritual growth. The Second Vatican Council's decision to change the sacrament of Extreme Unction to the Anointing of the Sick symbolized a shift in Catholic teaching: placing greater emphasis on God's willingness to heal diseases, through supernatural as well as natural means. By the late twentieth century, the Pentecostal and Charismatic movements had likewise spurred many Protestants to redefine sickness as something that should be resisted as having been sent by the devil, and to expect that God is both able and willing to provide divine healing for the body as well as the soul. Recent public opinion polls indicate that nearly 80 percent of Americans believe that God supernaturally heals people in answer to prayer (Lindberg and Numbers 2003).

Despite media caricatures of "faith healing," the vast majority of divine healing practices (the term preferred by believers) bear little resemblance to the glitzy, fraudulent exploits of the healing evangelist portrayed in the movie *Leap of Faith* (1992) or common stereotypes of snake-handling Pentecostals. There are small communities of Pentecostals living in rural Appalachia who do pick up poisonous snakes or drink strychnine-laced water during church services, and who rely solely upon supernatural, rather than medical healing. These communities base their practices upon a particular Bible verse, Mark 16:18: "They shall take up serpents; and if they drink any deadly thing, it shall not hurt them; they shall lay hands on the sick, and they shall recover." By engaging in practices that could prove deadly if this verse is not to be read prescriptively, certain communities demonstrate their belief in the Bible's relevance to life in the modern world. Critics, among them many Pentecostals, cite another verse of the Bible, Matthew 4:5–7: "You shall not put the Lord your God to the test," to deny that intentionally engaging in dangerous practices is an authentic expression of faith.

For most Christians, divine healing does not preclude the use of modern medicine, but offers hope when medicine has reached its limits. Unlike healing approaches that seek to unblock the flow of universal life-force energy or rally the forces of mind over matter, divine healing presumes the existence of a personal God who intervenes in nature on behalf of individuals. Christians often point to Isaiah 53:5: "and with his stripes we are healed" as indicating that Jesus' atoning death provided not only for the forgiveness of sins, but also for the healing of physical diseases. Using modern communication technologies to circulate their testimonials, Americans have claimed divine healing of nearly every form of disease or disability – headaches, depression, AIDS, Down syndrome, cancers, blindness, deafness, restoration of missing body parts, even resurrections from the dead.

Citing specific Biblical passages as precedents for many of their actions, Christians pray for divine healing in a variety of ways: confessing sins and forgiving others; eating communion; laying hands on the sick and anointing them with oil; applying blessed cloths to diseased parts of the body; commanding sicknesses and demons to depart in Jesus' name; petitioning God for gifts of healings and miracles. Often healing practices are mediated by modern technology: reading printed testimonies, placing one's hands on radios and televisions during broadcasts of prayers for healing, emailing prayer requests, faxing prayer cloths, or praying for healing by cell phone. Some practices occur in large healing services, but others take place while a sick individual is at home alone, surrounded by two or three others in a hospital room, or amidst the daily commotion of a business office or shopping mall.

Reports of miraculous healing first attracted many participants to the Azusa Street revivals of 1906. After World War II, scores of healing evangelists set up tents that seated upwards of 10,000 people, distributed prayer cards for the afflicted to identify their needs, or claimed to know conditions without being told through a "word of knowledge" (believed to be one of the nine gifts of the Holy Spirit, alongside healings and miracles, described in I Corinthians 12). Evangelists such as Oral Roberts (1918–) spent untold hours laying their hands on the sick as they waited in healing lines, or praying *en masse* for all the sick present to be healed while they placed their own hands on their diseased body parts. During the Charismatic revivals of the 1960s, evangelists like Kathryn Kuhlman (1907–76) rarely prayed for the sick individually, instead cultivating an atmosphere of worship that presumably made the Holy Spirit feel welcome to come and heal people where they sat – even when the sick individuals failed to express sufficient "faith." In the 1990s, advocates of divine healing further deemphasized the role of the gifted evangelist or the necessity of extraordinary personal faith on the part of the sick, recruiting teams of "ordinary" Christians to pray for healing.

Reflecting a similar emphasis on the prayers of ordinary Christians, hundreds of store-front "healing rooms" opened in medical and business office parks in the early 2000s. Modeled after efforts by the Pentecostal John G. Lake in Spokane, WA from 1914–20, today's healing rooms look more like doctors' offices than churches (Figure 16.2). Teams of two or three lay Christians, representing various Protestant and Catholic churches, pray for the healing of sick visitors, free of charge. Shortly after "re-opening" Lake's Spokane healing rooms in 1999, retired California real-estate

Figure 16.2   Healing room.

Figure 16.3   Healing room testimonials.

developer, Cal Pierce, established an International Association of Healing Rooms (IAHR), which had, within a decade, networked more than six hundred healing rooms in almost every state and more than 40 countries.

Exportation Abroad

The global reach of the Spokane-based IAHR is typical of the outreach orientation of many religious movements at the turn of the twenty-first century. Jehovah's Witnesses and Mormon missionaries have succeeded in attracting significant followings not only in the US, but also abroad. American Protestants have actively sent missionaries overseas since the nineteenth century. In 1900, the total number of Christian foreign missionaries from all countries combined was estimated at 5,000. By the 1920s, Americans constituted 40 percent of a total of 30,000 Christian missionaries worldwide, 60 percent of whom were women – reflecting the greater leadership opportunities afforded to women as missionaries than within American church life. The Student Volunteer Movement for Foreign Missions, founded in 1886, enhanced the missionary ranks by recruiting college and university students. Since 1946, the campus ministry group InterVarsity Christian Fellowship has sponsored national Urbana Missions Conferences that have attracted a total of more than 200,000 participants. At the turn of the twenty-first century, many Protestant missionaries are more attentive than their predecessors to criticisms of cultural insensitivity, arrogance, and complicity with American imperialism and exploitation. American missionaries increasingly recognize their need to learn, as well as teach, Christians in the "global South," where Christianity is expanding more rapidly than in North America.

In the wake of the Toronto Blessing of the 1990s, the visiting American pastor whose sermons ignited the revivals, Randy Clark, formed a missionary organization, Global Awakening (GA), which reflects the new missionary ethos. Self-consciously borrowing practices from Argentine revivalists of the 1980s and 1990s – for instance, casting out demons and asking God to send healing angels – Clark developed an extensive travel circuit that regularly took him and hundreds of volunteers influenced by Toronto to conduct religious conferences in 36 countries. As GA volunteers preached and prayed for the sick, they attracted crowds numbering as many as 100,000 people at a time. By Clark's account, his teams imparted the spiritual anointing (or presence of the Holy Spirit) that had characterized Toronto to people in the places they visited through the laying on of hands and prayer. Yet, increasingly, North American volunteers expected to receive as much as they gave away – by visiting sites and interacting with churches that seemed uncontaminated by North American skepticism of the supernatural. Groups such as GA developed partnerships with largely indigenous ministries, such as Casa de Davi in Brazil and Iris Ministries in Mozambique. In a triangular relationship, GA regularly sends short-term missionary teams to Brazil and Mozambique, in both of which countries Portuguese is the national language. Brazil, as well as 16 other countries, sends long-term missionaries to Mozambique where they work alongside Mozambican leaders. Simultaneously, missionaries from Brazil, Mozambique, and other countries, notably Korea, send missionaries to the United States, Canada, and Europe, which many Southern Christians envision as hotbeds of rationalist skepticism and immorality. In the period of global reach, cultural influences are multi-directional, and the US is a great importer as well as an exporter in a diverse world market of religious practices.

References and Further Reading

Bellah, Robert N. (1998) "Is There a Common American Culture?" *Journal of the American Academy of Religion*, 66(3): 613–625.

Curtis, Edward E. IV (ed.) (forthcoming) *Looking for Islam: Sourcebook of Muslims in the United States*, New York: Columbia University Press.

Fuller, Robert C. (1989) *Alternative Medicine and American Religious Life*, New York: Oxford University Press.

Griffith, R. Marie (2004) *Born Again Bodies: Flesh and Spirit in American Christianity*, Berkeley, CA: University of California Press.

Hall, David D. (ed.) (1997) *Lived Religion in America: Toward a History of Practice*, Princeton, NJ: Princeton University Press.

Johnson, Gregory O. (2007) "From Morning Watch to Quiet Time: The Historical and Theological Development of Private Prayer in Anglo-American Protestant Instruction, 1870–1950," Ph.D. diss., Saint Louis University.

Lindberg, David C. and Numbers, Ronald L. (eds.) (2003) *When Science and Christianity Meet*, Chicago: University of Chicago Press.

Maffly-Kipp, Laurie F., Schmidt, Leigh Eric and Valeri, Mark R. (eds.) (2006) *Practicing Protestants: Histories of Christian Life in America, 1630–1965*, Baltimore, MD: Johns Hopkins University Press.

McDannell, Colleen (ed.) (1995) *Material Christianity: Religion and Popular Culture in America*, New Haven, CT: Yale University Press.

McDannell, Colleen (2002) *Religions of the United States in Practice*, vol. 2, Princeton, NJ: Princeton University Press.

McGuire, Meredith B. and Kantor, Debra (1988) *Ritual Healing in Suburban America*, New Brunswick, NJ: Rutgers University Press.

McNally, Michael David (2000) *Ojibwe Singers: Hymns, Grief, and a Native Culture in Motion*, New York: Oxford University Press.

Moore, Dinty W. (1997) *The Accidental Buddhist: Mindfulness, Enlightenment, and Sitting Still*, Chapel Hill, NC: Algonquin Books.

Moore, J. Stuart (1993) *Chiropractic in America: The History of a Medical Alternative*, Baltimore, MD: Johns Hopkins University Press.

Orsi, Robert A. (1996) *Thank You, St. Jude: Women's Devotion to the Patron Saint of Hopeless Causes*, New Haven, CT: Yale University Press.

Orsi, Robert A. (2002) *The Madonna of 115th Street: Faith and Community in Italian Harlem, 1880–1950*, New Haven, CT: Yale University Press.

Orsi, Robert A. (2005) *Between Heaven and Earth: The Religious Worlds People Make and the Scholars Who Study Them*, Princeton, NJ: Princeton University Press.

Ostrander, Richard (2000) *The Life of Prayer in a World of Science: Protestants, Prayer, and American Culture, 1870–1930*, New York: Oxford University Press.

Pinn, Anthony B. (ed.) (2003) *Noise and Spirit: The Religious and Spiritual Sensibilities of Rap Music*, New York: New York University Press.

Poloma, Margaret M. (2003) *Main Street Mystics: The Toronto Blessing and Reviving Pentecostalism*, Walnut Creek, CA: AltaMira Press.

Poloma, Margaret M. and Gallup, George (1991) *Varieties of Prayer: A Survey Report*, Philadelphia, PA: Trinity Press International.

Tweed, Thomas A. (1997) *Our Lady of the Exile: Diasporic Religion at a Cuban Catholic Shrine in Miami*, New York: Oxford University Press.

Wacker, Grant (2001) *Heaven Below: Early Pentecostals and American Culture*, Cambridge, MA: Harvard University Press.

Whorton, James C. (2002) *Nature Cures: The History of Alternative Medicine in America*, New York: Oxford University Press.

Wuthnow, Robert (1998) *After Heaven: Spirituality in America since the 1950s*. Berkeley, CA: University of California Press.

Acknowledgments

The editors and publisher gratefully acknowledge the permission granted to reproduce the copyright material in this book. Every effort had been made to trace copyright holders and to obtain their permission for the use of copyright material. The editors and publisher apologize for any errors or omissions in the credit lines and would be grateful if notified of any corrections that should be incorporated in future reprints or editions of this book.

1.2 *William Penn's Treaty with the Indians When He Founded the Province of Pennsylvania in North America, 1681*. Painting by Benjamin West. Public domain image courtesy of the Library of Congress

2.1 Christopher Columbus (1451–1506) receiving gifts from the cacique, Guacanagari, in Hispaniola (Haiti) from "Americae Tertia Pars IV," 1594 (engraving) (b/w photo) (see also 111006) by Bry, Theodore de (1528–98) Bibliothèque Nationale, Paris, France/Giraudon/The Bridgeman Art Library Nationality /copyright status: Flemish /out of copyright

4.1 John Vanderlyn's *Columbus Landing in the Bahamas*, 1847. Vanderlyn's Indians cower at the fringes of the piece, witnessing to the perception that Columbus' landing was a protrusion of European civilization into an otherwise uncivilized wilderness. Courtesy of the United States Capitol

7.1 A New Orleans slave market. In the relatively relaxed environment of New Orleans, slaves developed relationships at markets which could open doors to new work prospects. Image courtesy of the New York Public Library (ID#807844)

8.2 *George Washington as a Master Mason*, 1856, by Emanuel Gottlieb Leutze, American, oil on canvas. Source: Courtesy of the 32nd Degree Masons, Valley of Detroit, Michigan

11.1 "Ghost dance" dress, Arapaho Tribe (buckskin) by American School Private Collection/Peter Newark Western Americana/The Bridgeman Art Library Nationality/copyright status: copyright unknown

12.2   Taken from *Ideal Suggestion Through Mental Photography: A Restorative System for Home and Private Use*, Henry Wood (Boston: Lee and Shepard, 1902).

14.2 & 14.4   *Nude Descending a Staircase, No. 2*, 1912. 1950-134-59 Duchamp, Marcel. Philadelphia Museum of Art: The Louise and Walter Arensberg Collection, 1950. © Succession Marcel Duchamp/ADAGP, Paris and DACS, London 2009

15.1   Martin Luther King, Jr. and Malcolm X represented two divergent attitudes on how best to realize civil rights for African-Americans. Public domain image courtesy of the Library of Congress

16.1   Hasidic Jewish Men. Picture courtesy of Ted Levin, Brooklyn, NY

Index